GW00362281

The Corn Economy of Indonesia

The Corn Economy of Indonesia

EDITED BY
C. Peter Timmer

CORNELL UNIVERSITY PRESS
Ithaca and London

First published 1987 by Cornell University Press.

International Standard Book Number 0-8014-1961-1
Library of Congress Catalog Card Number 86-23939
Printed in the United States of America
Librarians: Library of Congress cataloging information appears on the last page of the book.

The paper in this book is acid-free and meets the guidelines for permanence and durability of the Committee on Production Guidelines for Book Longevity of the Council on Library Resources.

Contents

PART FIVE Policy Perspective

Foreword

Sukriya Atmaja

Vice-Chairman, Badan Urusan Logistik (BULOG)

In his foreword to *The Cassava Economy of Java,* Minister Saleh Afiff noted the slow progress of research on non-rice cropping systems: "Indeed, there is now a critical need for a series of commodity volumes to complement the classic studies by Leon Mears on rice published in 1959 and 1981 and the current volume on cassava." This study of Indonesia's corn system is a direct response to that plea. Minister Afiff arranged the funding for the corn study from a World Bank technical assistance grant, and the National Food Logistics Agency (BULOG) offered to serve as implementing agency. Although BULOG had played a similar role informally during the cassava study, the agency's mandate to stabilize corn prices by using import controls and domestic procurement in defense of a floor price meant that there was an operational interest in the study as well as an intellectual interest in the methodology and results. In particular, the senior management of BULOG hoped to learn something about the effectiveness of its corn policies because the team of researchers was known to be sympathetic to the basic objectives of Indonesian food policy, knew the country well from long involvement, and had been requested to provide a critical evaluation of government policies and performance.

We have not been disappointed. The corn study has already made important contributions to Indonesian food policy in at least three areas. Methodologically, the corn study has further developed the three-dimensional approach used in the cassava study: the commodity system approach, which traces the technical and market links from input supplier to producer, processor, and consumer; the macro-trade approach, which analyzes the role of the commodity in generating domestic value-added and foreign exchange; and the food policy approach, which analyzes the efficiency of commodity systems and the distribution of their benefits in order to evaluate potential public investments and policy interventions. This study sets new standards for the rigor with which each individual component is carried out. At the same time, all three components are integrated into a coherent and understandable story accessible to nonspecialists and policymakers.

The substantive results have provided several surprises. The reason for choosing corn as the commodity to study at this time was a growing concern among Indonesian policymakers that corn imports would have to expand rapidly to provide adequate supplies for the domestic livestock feed industry, a pattern Indonesia had already observed in South Korea, Taiwan, and Malaysia. On the basis of extensive field surveys of village-level farming systems, the corn study discovered significant dynamism in several corn systems. In addition, the productivity of the new hybrid corn seeds began to be apparent during the study. Farmers with favorable growing conditions who have adopted hybrid seeds have doubled their yields. The study concludes that with conducive policies Indonesia can become a modest exporter of corn.

There were surprises on the consumption and marketing side as well. Most government attention had been focused on the rapid increase in use of corn by the modern livestock feed industry, primarily for the egg and broiler industry. But the traditional livestock economy uses as much corn as the modern sector; with slower economic growth forecast for the rest of the 1980s, the traditional livestock sector will remain very important. The largest end use for corn, however, remains consumption within rural households. Unexpectedly, this source of demand has grown rapidly since 1970, despite a tendency for consumers to substitute rice for corn whenever their incomes increased. Part of this surprising pattern seems to be explained by a tendency for members of corn-farming households to consume a significant portion of any increase in corn production; part also may be due to higher inventories and on-farm storage losses. Neither of these factors is likely to contribute significantly to increased on-farm utilization in the future, and most production increases will be marketed either to the local feed industry or for exports.

The study concludes that exports on a regular basis will be feasible only if marketing costs can be lowered. Marketing channels between major surplus areas in East Java and the Jakarta wholesale market are remarkably efficient, but whenever corn must move through a port or be stored for significant periods of time, the efficiency breaks down. The implications of these findings are already being incorporated into government deliberations over new corn policies. As a result of this study, BULOG hopes to coordinate the design of a consistent set of policies for the long-run development of Indonesia's corn system.

The joint effort to produce this book by Stanford's Food Research Institute and BULOG, with extensive cooperation from several other Indonesian agencies, provides a model for generating high-quality scholarly research that is also directly relevant to the day-to-day concerns of policymakers and implementing agencies. We at BULOG hope this example will serve to stimulate our colleagues in other countries to search for similar arrangements. When these relationships work successfully, as they have during this study, food producers and consumers benefit in the short run because of better government policies and investments. At the same time, the research contributes to better understanding of the appropriate role for public policy and how it can help develop an effective private sector. This learning process, which is the only long-run hope for eliminating poverty and hunger in our society, justifies the time, energy, and resources that have been invested in this study.

Preface

The Corn Economy of Indonesia has been many years in the making. It is the latest in a series of studies on the Indonesian food economy conducted primarily through the Food Research Institute of Stanford University, although other organizations and individual scholars have also made notable contributions over the years. The original parent of all these studies is no doubt *The Rice Economy of Monsoon Asia* by Vernon Wickizer and Merrill Bennett, published by the Food Research Institute in 1941. This volume established for the first time the economic framework to be used in analyzing a commodity system. Its purpose was to organize the agronomic, social, cultural, and political factors that affect a commodity and to place them within the matrix of economic decisions that ultimately link inputs, production, marketing, and consumption by rural and urban households.

This volume on corn follows directly in that tradition, but it is part of a newer tradition as well. The goal is not merely to increase understanding of a commodity system but to use that knowledge to improve the functioning of the system. Most improvements come through investments by the private sector, but these investments are strongly conditioned by public infrastructure and by the economic policy environment. Designing public policy so that it is conducive to the growth of individual commodity systems while it reflects broader macroeconomic constraints and objectives is a complicated task. This corn study is the first to be completed within a formal macro food policy framework that specifically seeks to reconcile these two tasks. Each field survey was sensitive not only to the production constraints but also to household decision making for consumption and marketing, to employment issues and choice of technique, and to the extent of integration of the village economy into the broader macro economy. Each chapter in this book pursues the same integrated themes: how the specific topic fits into the wider perspective of the corn system, and what the opportunities are to improve public investment or economic policy on behalf of an efficient corn economy in Indonesia. Within chapters, each topic has its own unique technical and institutional details which need to be treated independently. It is only in Chapter 10 that the entire policy integration can be pulled together.

By that time a fascinating story has emerged. Indonesia seems to be different from other oil exporters in its potential to supply a rapidly growing demand for livestock feed from domestic corn production. Indonesia's success with rice production is already widely known, but the corn story has attracted less attention. Indeed, the study team was prepared to determine how rapidly corn imports would grow along a path similar to that of Mexico, Nigeria, and Malaysia. But new technology, productive farmers, and conducive policy have set the stage for a different journey. This volume analyzes the potential for corn exports and the need for government investments and policies on behalf of the corn economy that are outward rather than inward looking.

This new orientation is the result of three years of work in Indonesia and the United States by a team of researchers from Stanford University, Harvard University, and several Indonesian institutions. The diverse backgrounds of the collaborators reflect to some extent the diverse audience for which this book is intended. The authors hope to reach students, who will see in this research an example of how to pursue their own commodity studies, as well as their teachers and fellow academics, who can evaluate the framework used here with others that have been used over the years to study commodity systems. Policymakers in Indonesia and elsewhere can use the framework and results of the study to judge the efficacy of planned investments and policy interventions designed to develop agricultural commodity systems.

No set of acknowledgments is ever complete, and the listing that follows cannot include all the Indonesian producers, consumers, traders, processors, and government officials who helped the research team. The study was instigated by Dr. Saleh Afiff in June 1983, while he was Senior Deputy at BAPPENAS, the National Planning Agency. Now Minister for Administrative Reform and Professor at the University of Indonesia, Minister Afiff arranged funding for the project from the World Bank/IDA credit to the government of Indonesia. Minister Bustanil Arifin, Chairman of the National Food Logistics Agency (BULOG) and Minister of Cooperatives, agreed that BULOG would serve as the executing agency.

Staff members of BULOG were true collaborators throughout the study. Gen. Sukriya Atmaja, Vice-Chairman of BULOG, offered wise counsel on a wide range of administrative and substantive issues. He also arranged for a Project Advisory Committee chaired by Chrisman Silitonga of BULOG. Other members of the committee included Ratna Djuwita (National Planning Agency), Faisal Kasryno (Agriculture), Sutedja (Trade), Tomasoa (Finance), Suwandi (Central Bureau of Statistics), Anas Rachman (BULOG), James Mullin and Laurie Effron (World Bank), and

Leon Mears (representing his usual cantankerous self and BULOG). The Advisory Committee met four times during the project, usually in conjunction with policy seminars presented by the team at BULOG.

Considerable assistance was also received from the International Center for the Improvement of Maize and Wheat (CIMMYT), headquartered in Mexico. Staff members visited the project twice, and the study benefited greatly from the technical advice and comments on drafts offered by Larry Harrington, Kenneth Fischer, Richard Wedderburn, and A. F. E. Palmer. Representatives from the private sector, especially from P. T. Cargill and P. T. Pokphand, also cooperated warmly with the team.

The project produced sixteen working papers, which included seven production surveys. These papers formed the basis of a report to the government of Indonesia in June 1985. Many details of local environments and specific sectors are contained in the working papers and the report; these are not included in this volume. Authors of those field studies note with special appreciation the work of Anton Mart Irianto, Marak Ali, and Moehar Daniel, who were collaborators on two of the analyses. The field surveys would not have been possible without the assistance of numerous regional staff of the national food logistics agency, Department of Agriculture, and of Fred Roche, the Agricultural Development Council representative in Malang. At Stanford, Susan Maher, Deborah Prentice, Ellen Barker, and Nell Villars assisted with the working papers and with the many administrative details associated with a project of this scope and duration. At Harvard, Diane Shapiro was invaluable in the final stages of the preparation of the manuscript.

The individual chapters of this book are signed by their authors, who took primary responsibility for drafting, although they uniformly insist that the editor exercised a very heavy hand and is thus partly to blame for any remaining problems or ambiguities. The same might be said of Stephen Mink, who has contributed visibly to this book as an author or coauthor of six of the ten chapters. But Stephen's role extends well beyond that. He has served as a critical sounding board throughout the writing and editing process, and his cheerful willingness to play this role is fully appreciated. With all the special acknowledgments, however, the project required a genuinely collaborative effort and could not have been completed without the full cooperation and enthusiasm of all those involved. For that cooperation and enthusiasm, the editor expresses heartfelt thanks. Lastly, the invisible hand of Carol Timmer is felt on every page of this book. If each sentence that she fixed were deleted, the volume would be blank. Carol's capacity to juggle minute detail, Indonesian terms, general analytical themes, and stylistic clarity literally holds this book together. Without her involvement, this book simply would not exist in anything like its present form, and the Timmers' electronic cottage would not have had the same intensive hum over the past two years.

C. PETER TIMMER
John D. Black Professor At-Large, Harvard University

WALTER P. FALCON
Director, Food Research Institute, Stanford University

PART ONE

Overview

1. Introduction to the Corn Economy of Indonesia

Paul A. Dorosh, Walter P. Falcon, Stephen D. Mink, Douglas H. Perry, and C. Peter Timmer

Corn is the staple foodstuff in Indonesia for more than 18 million people and is grown by more than 10 million farm households. In an average-sized country these figures would indicate that corn is the primary staple in the food system, and for these particular Indonesians it is. But in a country as large as Indonesia, with its 160 million people, corn as a starchy staple is a distant second in a food system heavily dominated by rice. More than one-half the average Indonesian's daily calories comes from rice, and only about 10 percent is supplied by corn. These averages hide much diversity, of course, and within that diversity corn plays important roles indeed, particularly for the 18 million people for whom it is the primary source of calories.

The averages explain why rice has received so much analytical and policy attention and corn has received so little. Rice has been studied in good times and bad. When weather, pests, and poor incentives led to stagnant production in the mid-1970s and when aggressive research on new rice varieties and better prices for farmers stimulated output to surplus levels by the mid-1980s, Indonesia's rice economy was the focus of major analytical studies and of high-level policy attention.

A surprising result of the rice studies done in each of these production environments was that they emphasized the importance of secondary food crops in Indonesia's multi-staple food system. When it appeared that rice production could not keep up with growth in domestic demand and Indonesia would be forced to rely heavily on a thin and unstable world rice market to meet its consumption needs, expanded production of corn and cassava seemed to be a potential route toward reduced dependency on rice imports. When it appeared that rice surpluses would need to be exported at a budgetary loss, diversification into exports of corn and cassava seemed desirable because of Indonesia's cost advantage in world markets in these commodities. Events over the last decade have thrown the potential role of *palawija* commodities into prominence.[1]

Unfortunately, this newly found prominence was not matched by the

[1]The Indonesian term *palawija* can be roughly translated "non-rice," but technically *palawija* applies only to non-rice food staples—corn, cassava, peanuts, and legumes such as soybeans and mung beans. It normally does not include fruits and vegetables.

level of understanding available for rice. By the late 1970s the knowledge gap was quite obvious, and a sequence of commodity studies was begun jointly between Indonesia's government agencies that deal with food and agriculture and the Food Research Institute at Stanford University. Using earlier work on the rice economy as a base and partial model, researchers began to analyze the cassava economy in 1979 and the corn economy in 1983.[2]

Two analytical themes served to organize each of these studies. The first treated the commodity in its economic, technological, and institutional setting, an approach that required integrated analysis of the decision makers in all key sectors of the system—input suppliers, farmers, traders and processors, consumers, and government policymakers. The analysis had to treat a commodity system and recognize the important trade-offs that might exist between short-run gains for individual parts of the system and the long-run health of the overall system itself. This theme is central to this study of the corn economy.

The second theme emphasized that the analysis of a commodity system itself, whether corn or cassava, be undertaken as part of the country's overall food policy. Such analysis of a country's food policy aggregates individual commodity systems into an overall food system and then shows its connection to macroeconomic and trade policy. This "food policy analysis" is sometimes described as economic development policy from a food system perspective, but the key point for analysis of individual commodity systems is the context in which analysts must operate. Research on a commodity system is useful to policymakers only when it answers important questions about how policy-induced changes in the commodity system can foster better results for economic development. The government may want to see results in a variety of areas: more rapid economic growth; improved distribution of income; a more reliable nutritional floor for low-income groups; and increased food security for the country.

In carrying out this kind of analysis, there are important trade-offs among these objectives—sometimes characterized as growth versus equity, short run versus long run, or public control versus private initiative.

[2]By mid-1985, a substantial amount of research on the Indonesian rice economy and on cassava was available. Although early studies of the rice economy date to the Dutch colonization, the first modern work is that of Mears (1959). Early reviews of policies after 1968 are in Timmer (1975) and Afiff and Timmer (1971), and the recent volume by Mears (1981) and the monograph by Timmer (1985a) bring the story up to date. Attempts to identify linkages across commodity systems are in Timmer (1972) and in Afiff, Falcon, and Timmer (1980), which also presents a food policy research agenda based on the difficult rice situation seen in 1978. Cassava was the first of the secondary food crops to receive detailed attention on the basis of this agenda; the results were published in Falcon, et al. (1984). The current volume on corn is the second effort in this sequence. Oilseeds, especially soybeans and peanuts, are obvious candidates for a next round. The integrating framework used to link commodity studies to development policy is in Timmer, Falcon, and Pearson (1983).

Each commodity system reflects these general trade-offs and issues within a particular country's circumstances. The goal of a commodity study is to provide a sound empirical base for analyzing the specific trade-offs and set them in the context of the general issues and overall objectives.

How can a commodity study that meets all of these goals be carried out? At one level, it must be realized that a commodity system functions in a general equilibrium setting. At another level, the focus must be on the decision-making environment of individual farmers, traders, and consumers. This tension between macro and micro elements can be healthy and provide research direction for identifying key links. But it can be immobilizing. Where does one begin when everything depends on everything else?

Even if the concern that motivated the study turns out to be unfounded, as it was in this study of the corn system, the concern provides a starting point. After that point, good research, flexibility and integrity on the part of the researchers, and the connections within the system itself will set the story straight. Knowing what kinds of questions must be asked helps identify the connections. Most of the following questions are likely to need answers at some stage of the commodity study.

What are the domestic components of the commodity system? Farming systems that incorporate the commodity in their cropping patterns are usually the primary source of supply and the major basis of income generation. Understanding these farming systems was the first priority of the corn study. After that, marketing and end uses require attention because these components tie the system together.

What are the links between the domestic commodity system and the international market for that commodity? These links can vary enormously for different commodities. In Indonesia the wheat system relies totally on imports, most rubber is exported, and corn has been both imported and exported since the mid-1960s. The relationship between world prices and domestic price formation organizes the answer to this question.

How do various domestic commodity systems relate to each other? The multi-staple food system of Indonesia is particularly complicated and intertwined. The success of the rice intensification program in the mid-1980s, coupled with the rapid growth in the economy since the mid-1960s, has strengthened these links, primarily through the rapid emergence of a significant industry producing livestock feed. The corn system is at the center of this trend, and the Corn Project spent much of its time understanding the livestock sector, the alternative feedstuffs, and the role of corn. Direct consumption of corn by humans is also subject to substantial substitution from other starchy staples, especially rice and cassava. Substitution in end uses and in production systems is driven by technology and prices and is one of the primary forces that link different commodity systems.

What are the major policy interventions into the commodity system and what impact do they have? Given the country's objectives for its food policy, actual results need to be compared to the intent of policies. No technical analysis suffices here; a political economy analysis that incorporates objectives and constraints into an understanding of policy formation is needed. Good policy analysis often succeeds by clarifying constraints and identifying ways to loosen their bind on what policymakers can accomplish. The same is true for policy analysis of individual commodity systems. Finding important constraints on development of the system and determining the appropriate policy interventions are underlying goals of the analysis of each component of the system. Policies for other commodities and macroeconomic policies further enlarge the scope, and it is in this sense that the food policy framework serves to integrate a commodity study into a general policy setting.

Answering these basic questions provides the direction for a commodity study. The analytical tasks are broken down into domestic components, international connections, cross-commodity links, and major policy issues. Most commodity studies are only as good as their understanding of domestic production systems. These systems usually provide the basis for a large share of the value-added to an economy by the overall commodity system; a lack of potential competitiveness for domestic producers means the system will depend on imports or require continuing subsidies. From this point of view, the Indonesian corn system surprised the research team because one major justification for conducting the study was to see how quickly demand for corn imports would grow under the impetus of rising consumption of livestock products. But almost a year of field observation of how farmers grew corn revealed a diversity and dynamism not reflected in the baseline statistics available at the start of the study and gave the surveys of farming systems a prominence not entirely anticipated at the beginning.

The Corn Study's Findings

From this initial conception of the Corn Project, the research team focused its attention on the key linkages that integrate the various sectors of the corn system. The production surveys established a data base for analysis of changes at the farm level that could be expected if seed technology, prices of corn and other commodities, or marketing options available to farmers changed. The field surveys reflected the enormous diversity among different corn production systems, both regionally and from one season to another. Documenting this diversity was the first task of the project, followed by observation and analysis of local consumption, market sales, and potential for expanding output of corn. Chapters 2, 3, and 4 integrate the local studies into a comparative farming systems framework and produce evidence of considerable dynamism in several important corn-producing systems, especially in East Java, North and West Sumatra, and South Sulawesi.

The outlook for future corn production depends significantly on the development, multiplication, and distribution of new corn seeds that incorporate higher genetic yield capacity. Both open-pollinated and hybrid varieties have great potential; the C-1 hybrid produced by Cargill generated the most excitement in the mid-1980s. Demand for this seed exceeded the capacity to produce it, although the Department of Agriculture and Cargill officials were working closely to break this bottleneck. A second season of full-scale field trials and farmer use confirm a minimum yield potential of 6 tons per hectare in areas where open-pollinated varieties are yielding only 3 tons.

The production potential led the project team to assess the outlook for domestic end uses at the expected trend level f.o.b. export price of $120 per metric ton. The prospect that Indonesia might become a significant importer of corn in the 1980s has receded in response to the new production potential for corn and the government's determination to keep the foreign exchange rate at levels that make agricultural exports competitive. This latter factor will become increasingly important if oil prices continue to be weak. Offsetting the positive production outlook is the likely gradual removal of the fertilizer subsidy and the implied slow decline necessary in real corn prices to farmers for Indonesia's exports to remain competitive.

Within the domestic economy, corn has multiple end uses. Its primary use on a worldwide basis is as a high-quality livestock feed for intensive beef, dairy, poultry, and swine operations, but in Indonesia its main use remains as food for direct consumption by humans, especially, as Chapter 5 shows, among rural low-income groups. The fastest-growing component of corn use in Indonesia, however, is for the livestock feed industry, and Chapter 6 presents two alternative methods of projecting future demand for corn from this sector. Both reach similar conclusions: the rate of growth for the rest of the 1980s is likely to be roughly one-half the rate of the previous decade. Only minor volumes of corn are used industrially, such as in cornstarch production or food processing. No high-fructose sweeteners are yet produced from corn in Indonesia. Current sugar policy and domestic corn prices are conducive to the private profitability of operating a fructose plant, but Chapter 7 calculates that the social profitability of such a plant is seriously in doubt.

Because corn marketed from the farm can to a large extent be used interchangeably among various end uses—problems of color and moisture level aside—all consumers must compete in the same market. On the consumption side, corn serves as an important integrating force in Indonesia's food system since each end use for corn has its own competitors: rice and cassava for household consumption; wheat pollards or rice bran for livestock feed; and sugar for sweeteners. On the production side, acreage substitutions also serve to integrate economic forces across other commodities.

For corn to play this important integrative role, the price signals received by farmers and consumers must accurately reflect the demand from various end users and the resource costs of consumption, especially the opportunity costs of other crops forgone. For this to happen, the corn marketing system must work efficiently; the project team gathered evidence, presented in Chapter 8, that price integration is excellent between the Jakarta wholesale market for corn, primarily for livestock feed, and major producers of marketed corn supplies in East and Central Java. Field evidence and statistical analysis also confirmed, however, that several locations with small marketings, yellow varieties instead of locally preferred white, or corn with very high moisture content after the harvest were not well integrated into this national market. The record showed a positive role for cooperatives (KUD), expecially in South Sulawesi, in guaranteeing a market for innovative farmers who wanted to grow yellow corn for the market.[3] As volumes grow, the private trade soon learns to undertake this activity profitably.

The major problem in corn marketing has been the extremely wide price spreads from harvest to preharvest, which seem to be caused by the high cost of storing corn. Because moisture levels after sun drying are as high as 16 to 18 percent even in the dry season, spoilage and aflatoxin contamination cause high losses. The extreme seasonal price movements and storage losses cause equally strong seasonal patterns in household consumption. As long as other starchy staples, such as rice or cassava, are available in seasons of high corn prices, there is little problem for human welfare. But the growing livestock feed industry will require regular monthly supplies, from either storage or continual harvests in different provinces.

Users of corn for livestock feed have had little incentive to build storage facilities since government price policy has made corn available from world markets at stable and uniform prices. Investment in storage and drying facilities will be made only if there is a sufficient spread between the f.o.b. export price during the harvest season and the BULOG dis-

[3]The KUD, *Koperasi Unit Desa*, is a village unit of the national cooperatives organization whose functions range from crop procurement to input distribution.

tribution price, which is available year-round but relevant only during preharvest months, and if the feed industry is assured of profitable returns on average to its investment.[4] Consequently, corn pricing policy will be a key influence on the corn system for the foreseeable future.

Pricing policy will affect all three levels of policies that influence the corn system in Indonesia: macroeconomic, agricultural sector, and commodity-specific policies and programs for corn. As Chapter 9 demonstrates, the key macro policy variable is undoubtedly the foreign exchange rate. The project team documented the impact of an overvalued rupiah and subsequent devaluations on corn exports and imports since the mid-1970s. Continued efforts to maintain the competitiveness of agricultural exports will be essential for corn production to grow rapidly. Domestic demand for corn is not expected to keep pace with this potential. Exports of corn will thus be required, and a competitive exchange rate is needed to translate the relatively low expected f.o.b. dollar price of corn back to farmers at a remunerative rupiah level. In addition to the exchange rate, an export-oriented trade strategy is required, particularly in minimizing regulations on corn exports and perhaps in creating a free-trade zone for South Sulawesi to develop corn export potential.

Chapter 10 focuses on government policies and the ministries and agencies that implement them. Several sectoral policies have important ramifications on corn production or domestic end use. Perhaps the most important in the short run is the possible phasing out of the fertilizer subsidy if rice remains in surplus supply at prices prevailing in the mid-1980s. A rough calculation shows that Indonesia would be a corn importer rather than an exporter by 1990 if domestic fertilizer prices were at world levels.

Pricing strategies are likely to be the key to the successful takeoff of Indonesia's corn system if the production potential continues to develop. Keeping Indonesia's corn competitive in export markets so that the f.o.b. price sets an effective floor at the farm gate is an important objective. However, there is much that recommends a stabilization role for BULOG in this pricing strategy, with price support levels announced well in advance but moving up and down with world corn prices from year to year. There is little reason to subsidize either corn producers or consumers in the long run, and the high degree of substitution across production and end uses for corn points to the ineffectiveness of a corn subsidy program. The important conclusion is that the potential of Indonesia to be a low-cost producer of corn is consistent with a pricing policy that balances the interests of both producers and consumers.

[4]Badan Urusan Logistik (BULOG) is the national food logistics agency, which has broad responsibilities for food policies and price stabilization for rice and other food commodities.

FIGURE 1.1. *Major corn-producing provinces of Indonesia with survey sites by* kabupaten

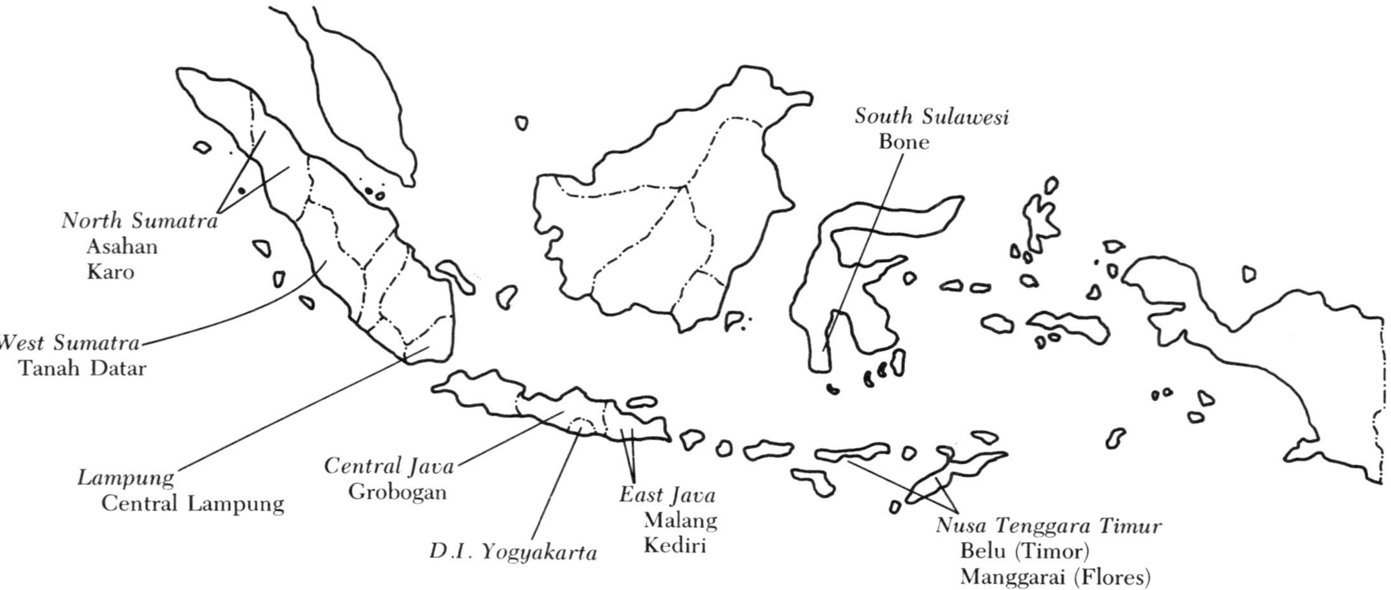

FIGURE 1.2. *Average weekly household consumption of corn grain*

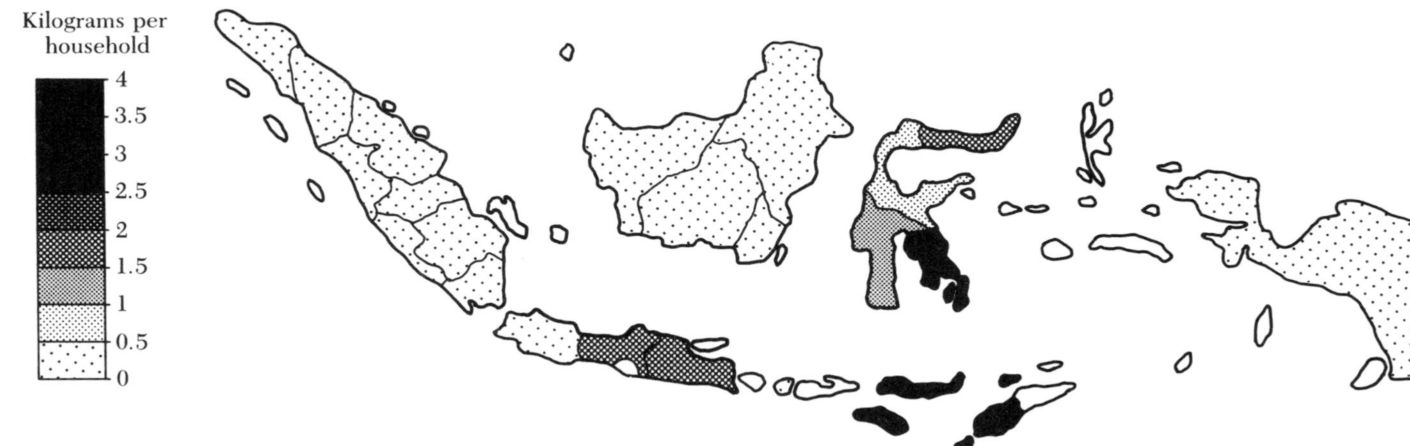

SOURCE: Data from Indonesia, Central Bureau of Statistics, National Socio-Economic Survey (SUSENAS), for 1978.

Surveys of Farming Systems

The sites for the field-based production surveys were chosen to provide a reasonable cross section of Indonesia's corn production systems. At each location, thirty to forty farmers were interviewed, and additional background information was gathered from extension agents, government offices, and corn traders. Details of each survey can be found in the individual working papers by Dorosh (1984a, 1984b, 1984c), Mink (1984a, 1984b), and Perry (1984a); the basis for choosing sites and the variety of physical environments are described here to establish a base from which to judge the further analysis.

Figures 1.1 and 1.2 show the survey site locations and levels of corn consumption throughout Indonesia. The survey sites are spread widely across the archipelago in seven provinces, with a total of ten sites investigated in varying detail. Two themes help explain the choices of particular locations and provide guidance in understanding the sharp diversity from site to site. First, each corn-producing area occupies a place along a rough continuum from highly commercial, where farmers sell virtually all of their corn, to highly subsistence-oriented, where only a little corn is sold occasionally to meet important expenses but most corn is eaten directly within the producing household. This theme provides the order for the later discussion of the physical characteristics of each major site, which are summarized in Table 1.1. The most highly commercialized corn farms are found in North and West Sumatra, followed by Malang and Kediri farms in East Java, then by farms in Lampung and Central Java. Farms in South Sulawesi are much less commercialized, and those in Nusa Tenggara Timur are the most subsistence-oriented.

Along this continuum, a second set of characteristics of corn-producing areas can be mapped. These characteristics do not match identically the extent of commercialization but in combination help explain it. For instance, whether farm households in a locality prefer white or yellow corn is a key factor in determining commercialization; in the mid-1980s higher yields were available from the yellow varieties of corn, which are preferred by the livestock feed industry, a major source of market demand. The nature of soils on which corn is grown strongly conditions yields; volcanic soils are capable of producing much larger yields than the limestone-based or highly acidic soils found in many corn-producing regions. Higher incomes per capita in an area also contribute directly to commercialization, both by providing farm families—even if they grow corn—the opportunity to eat rice instead of corn and by creating demand for livestock products, especially poultry, which in turn creates a market demand for corn.

Perhaps the most important result from organizing the discussion of

TABLE 1.1. *Summary of characteristics of survey sites*

Province and survey site	Land type	Market orientation of corn production	Other characteristics
West Sumatra			
Rambatan	highland, fertile	commercial crop (Rambatan, Karo, Asahan)	advanced technology (Rambatan, Karo, Asahan)
North Sumatra			
Karo	highland, fertile		
Asahan	lowland, fertile		
East Java			
Malang	rain-fed land, fertile	commercial crop and household food staple	advanced technology
Kediri	irrigated *sawah*,[a] fertile		
Lampung			
Central Lampung	poor, acidic soils	commercial crop	
Central Java			
Grobogan	rain-fed *sawah*, floodplain	household food staple and commercial crop	white corn
D.I. Yogyakarta[b]			
Gunung Kidul[c]	poor, eroded limestone soils	household food staple	
South Sulawesi			
Bone	poor, acidic upland soils	household food staple	white corn
Nusa Tenggara Timur	low rainfall uplands	household food staple	

[a] *Sawah* is level, bunded rice land.

[b] D.I. Yogyakarta is a special administrative district, which in this book is treated as a province.

[c] Gunung Kidul *kabupaten* was not among the project team's survey sites, but the results of the survey carried out by Roche (1983) have been included in the comparison of production systems in Chapter 3.

survey sites along a commercialization axis is the clarity with which the connection can be seen between an area's integration into the market economy and its residents' household income and standard of living. Corn marketing is only a small part of this general tendency, of course, but the pattern for corn simply reinforces the goal of the study to set the analysis of the corn system into a broader agricultural and macroeconomic context.

A reasonably complete and representative picture of corn production systems must be available to do this. The field studies, which observed and documented these characteristics, were carried out over an eleven-month period. Not all the survey sites were representative of the province in which they were located, however, nor were all corn-producing provinces surveyed. North Sulawesi is the main gap in this regard, and time and distance prevented a field survey in that province. Although the surveys do not provide the in-depth knowledge of village society of an extended anthropological village study, they nevertheless achieve a rich and sophisticated understanding of the workings of local corn systems and sources of dynamism—and barriers to it. What has been achieved with the field surveys is a clear sense of the variance in the system; sites were chosen to reflect dynamics and potential rather than current averages. Since the averages are available from existing data, this sense of where various corn production systems are headed and what might influence their speed and direction of change are the main lessons to take away from the analysis of production systems.

West Sumatra and North Sumatra

The corn survey sites in northern and western Sumatra were chosen to represent two major corn areas: the older highland farm areas and the relatively new lowland locations. The highland farm areas contain the best soils on the island, and farming is ideally suited to high-value vegetables, fruit, and corn. Gravity irrigation is common, with wet-rice cropping near the homestead and one or two upland plots on the adjacent mountain slopes. Rambatan in Tanah Datar *kabupaten* of West Sumatra is typical of this highland farm system, and corn and rice are the two major crops.[5] Rambatan serves as a production center for West Sumatra, and its corn is marketed west to Padang for animal feed and east to the fresh market in Pekan Baru.

In North Sumatra the Karo highland corn system near the provincial capital, Medan, features a unique cropping pattern and represents an advanced, market-oriented food system. At altitudes below 600 meters, farmers plant one rice crop each year and follow it with corn. Above 600 meters, corn is followed by either corn or vegetables such as cabbage,

[5]A *kabupaten* is an administrative unit roughly equivalent to a county.

tomatoes, potatoes, or hot red peppers.[6] Cooler temperatures at high altitudes slow the maturation of the corn variety Metro grown in the area, and farmers grow only two corn crops a year. But yields are the highest on the island; estimates made from the survey indicated an average of 3 tons per hectare each season, which compares to an average of 2.5 tons per hectare for the province as a whole. Extensive use of custom plowing and machine shelling has reduced labor constraints and turnaround times, and corn can be planted very quickly after rice or vegetables. The older corn systems supply major amounts of corn to urban consumers in Sumatra as well as corn for export either to other islands or to Singapore.

The other survey site in North Sumatra was Asahan *kabupaten*, which represents a highly successful expansion of corn farming to lowland locations. Upland areas in the province are reaching maximum economic output, but nearby lowland sites show marked potential for lowland corn. Residents of Asahan are largely spontaneous transmigrants from Java, who since the mid-1970s have removed old rubber hectarage and replanted it with rice and corn.[7] Asahan has doubled its corn hectarage since the late 1970s, and most farmers in the survey triple crop the new higher-yielding Arjuna variety of corn. The combination of mechanical tillage and Arjuna corn has meant an intensive land-use system, which appears ready to spread corn production out from its traditional highland areas. Much cultivable land is available for farm sites for new transmigrants—about 200,000 hectares.

Corn plays a major role in the Sumatran economy. Farmers are sensitive to the market opportunities that corn presents. As urban incomes rose since the mid-1970s, demand for meat, especially chicken, rapidly increased in major urban centers. Established highland agricultural areas responded by producing corn for animal feed. With good transport and a cool, dry climate, these areas moved to three crops a year in some places. The older areas have now reached economic limits of corn production and await new corn varieties. Export markets established in the late 1960s, particularly Singapore, and developing transport and communications have improved the integration of the corn market between Padang, Medan, and Jakarta.

East Java

East Java is Indonesia's leading province in terms of corn production and average yields. It accounts for 45 percent of area planted with corn and has average yields 33 percent higher than the national average. In the

[6]The Indonesian term for hot red peppers is *cabe merah*.

[7]Official transmigrants are resettled from Java under the Department of Transmigration's auspices. Provided with farm site, house, and production and consumption credits, these settlers live in areas under official sponsorship. Spontaneous transmigrants have made private decisions to resettle from Java or other islands, and they use their own resources.

Kediri and Malang survey sites, corn yields of about 3 tons per hectare are among the highest in East Java; yields are only about 1 ton per hectare on the island of Madura and in parts of the eastern uplands of East Java. Although both the Kediri and Malang samples are typical of general cropping patterns, there is wide variability in levels of fertilizer use, soil fertility, and marketings among regions. The corn systems studied in Kediri and Malang represent dynamic areas where new technology and high levels of purchased inputs are widely used.

In terms of area planted, Malang ranks as the fourth largest corn-producing *kabupaten* (county) in East Java. Farm households sell most of the corn they grow in this region, which is an important source of corn for the market in the provincial capital, Malang. The area is bordered on the south by the erosion-prone, limestone-based soils in the uplands that extend along the southern coast of Java. Corn is frequently intercropped with cassava on these poor soils. This corn-cassava intercrop is also found in the more fertile uplands of the Kediri area.

Kediri *kabupaten* has the largest amount of corn grown on irrigated land in East Java, which accounts for about 60 percent of the corn area in the *kabupaten*. Farmers often do not plow the soil after the rice crop and plant soybeans on irrigated land in a rice-soybeans-corn rotation. The village of Kepung, in the *kecamatan* of the same name, was chosen as the survey site, and it is the leading *kecamatan* in Kediri in total corn area planted.[8] Most of the irrigated land gets sufficient water for only one rice crop each year, so two crops of corn follow the harvest of the rainy season rice crop. But corn-producing households in Kediri do not consume much of their own production because they strongly prefer rice. Estimates obtained from interviews with large corn merchants indicate that about 80 percent of Kediri's corn is shipped to other parts of Java, mostly for animal feed. Kepung's corn farmers market over 80 percent of production; corn's role in the farm household is mainly as a source of cash income.

Lampung

Unlike East Java, the province of Lampung in southern Sumatra is plagued by poor, acidic soils. But in the mid-1980s, with fertilizer use increasing, the province is one of the most commercial of corn-producing areas, along with other parts of Sumatra and East Java. Farm households consume little of their own production and grow corn primarily for cash income. From the mid-1960s to the mid-1970s, Lampung had been a major corn-exporting province, second only to East Java. In 1972 about 44,000 tons of corn were exported to foreign markets from Lampung, which represented 56 percent of all of Indonesia's corn exports in that

[8]A *kecamatan* is an administrative subdivision of the *kabupaten*, and usually consists of fewer than a dozen village units, the *desa*.

year. The Lampung average was approximately 28 percent of Indonesia's corn exports from 1969 through 1973. But an outbreak of the plant disease downy mildew in 1974–1975 reduced corn hectarage from over 70,000 hectares to under 20,000 hectares in one year. No corn was shipped from the province again until 1977; Lampung exported about 4,000 tons in that year and averaged 2,816 tons for the three-year period 1977–1979. Corn production and hectarage have been rising ever since the devastation, but only recently has output reached the pre-1974 levels.

Partly as a result of disease problems with corn, farmers shifted to cassava production and invested fewer resources in corn. By the mid-1980s, most corn was intercropped, but this may be changing with increasing marketings. The Lampung livestock feed industry increased rapidly in the early 1980s and is based to a large degree on local corn purchases. This feed, primarily for poultry, is used by local poultry firms or shipped to the Jakarta feed market. A comparison of marketed corn between 1972 and 1984 shows the dramatic rise of this local market: in 1972, 41 percent of the corn produced was marketed; in 1984, 85 percent was marketed.[9]

At the same time, farmers have dramatically increased their use of fertilizer, from virtually none in 1972 to levels estimated from the survey to be about 250 kilograms of fertilizer per hectare on corn in monocropping and other systems. These two changes—the expanding local feed industry and the increased use of fertilizer for corn—have increasingly commercialized corn production in Lampung, which in the mid-1980s had about 50,000 hectares under corn, with strong demand from Jakarta. Concomitant improvements in shipping facilities between Lampung and Jakarta, secondary roads, and communications also have contributed to this trend; corn's importance in the regional economy is increasing.

Central Java

The province of Central Java produces mostly white corn, which is a basic staple, in addition to rice, for farm households. Because of this consumer preference, farmers are reluctant to shift to yellow varieties, which the government has attempted to promote through corn intensification programs. Taste appears to be one factor, but white corn is also considered to process into a higher proportion of flour—the main form in which corn was consumed—than yellow corn. More recently, growth in incomes has led farmers in this region increasingly to sell their corn to buy rice for home consumption.

Programs promoting longer-maturing yellow varieties with higher yields have met with spotty success. As a consequence of varietal mixing,

[9]Although the earlier sample is a much larger, more widely dispersed group of farmers, the difference in the surplus of corn marketed is quite large.

these areas produce mixed-color lots of corn, which receive a price discount since most market demand is for single-color lots—white for local household consumption and the noodle industry and yellow for the poultry feed industry. By the mid-1980s, use of yellow varieties by farmers appeared limited also by lack of an appropriate improved seed.

A major production area in Central Java stretches along the northern coast of Java from Grobogan *kabupaten* in Central Java to Lamongan *kabupaten* in East Java. Lack of controlled irrigation on this region's otherwise fertile soils limits rice to one crop a year, although rainfall the rest of the year is sufficient to grow two non-rice crops. With two corn harvests a year quite common, this is a major production area for Central Java. Since the late 1950s, average annual corn area planted in Grobogan has risen by 70 percent, and this expansion exceeds that of any other *kabupaten* in Central Java. Grobogan produces on average 20 percent of Central Java's annual corn output, although the *kabupaten* has only 5 percent of the province's arable land.

Farm households in Grobogan on average produce 1.7 tons a year of dry corn grain equivalent. Milled rice production is roughly equal, but other field-crop output is much less. The typical farm household consumes about 50 percent of its corn production. Corn is the largest component of the diet and plays a significant role as a basic staple. Corn is an important source of income to farmers of Grobogan, second only to rice among agricultural sources of income. But reflecting their importance in household consumption, neither corn nor rice is marketed to the extent of other crops, and only 35 and 43 percent of output, respectively, are sold. Corn thus accounts for 17.7 percent of gross farm income but only 8.2 percent of cash income. By contrast, the entire crop of soybeans is sold, which accounts on average for 20.8 percent of cash income and generates the cash to buy inputs for the next rice crop.

In this region, farmers are shifting important quantities of corn land to *padi gogo rancah* production in the first rainy season. In this special rice-growing technique, rice is directly seeded, and although it does not tolerate flooding in the early stages of growth, it does well with late season flooding. Such flooding would cause severe damage to other crops such as corn and soybeans, and by growing rice in this way, farmers have greatly reduced the risk of crop loss for this season of the year. This shift began in 1979 when the potential for further extension of short-duration, high-yielding rice varieties on non-irrigated land began to be explored. *Padi gogo rancah* area in Grobogan rose from virtually nil in 1979 to more than 4,500 hectares in 1983. New government plans since 1983 to promote further extension in areas with appropriate soil and rainfall characteristics will encourage even further shifts from the corn-bean intercrop that is currently planted. More than half of Grobogan's corn land is potentially involved.

South Sulawesi

South Sulawesi has long been a leading corn producer among the outer island provinces of Indonesia. The province ranks third in corn production, after East and Central Java, and much of this corn is consumed by farm households themselves. Like Central Java, the population of South Sulawesi strongly prefers white corn. But local use of corn is growing slowly, and future surpluses will have to be marketed off the island. Infrastructure—transport, mechanical driers, warehouse space, and port capacity—is probably adequate for handling expanded trade. But the province's supply of almost entirely white corn faces thinner market demand off the island than yellow corn. Adoption of higher-yielding, yellow varieties of corn has been slow because farmers have difficulty finding buyers in existing marketing channels. There has been no significant growth in corn area or yields since 1970.

Corn production and consumption in South Sulawesi are highly concentrated in the corn crescent, which curves from Soppeng *kabupaten* in the central plain, down the east coast, and back along the narrow, southern coastal plain toward the provincial capital Ujung Pandang. In this area, corn hectarage makes up from 25 to 35 percent of total food crop hectarage, which indicates the importance of corn in the local economy. Corn surpluses are transported west to urban port markets for use in the poultry industry or for inter-island trade and export.

Despite corn's tolerance of relatively acid soils, high levels of soil acidity are a problem in much of the corn crescent and are part of the reason for South Sulawesi's low average corn yields. Corn is grown on land that is often quite hilly and rocky and requires rough terracing, of quite narrow widths. Rocky soils present particular difficulties for corn cultivation: plowing is impossible, hand hoeing works the soil only to a shallow depth, and regular plant spacing becomes nonsensical. In the words of one farmer, the seed is placed "between the rocks." Crops that require more fertile soil, such as tobacco and cotton, do well on newly opened fields but yield less in following years. Several factors—poor soils, low fertilizer use, a preference for white corn, and trade channels that will expand more rapidly for yellow corn—characterize corn production in South Sulawesi.

Nusa Tenggara Timur

The province of Nusa Tenggara Timur lies to the east of Java and Bali.[10] It consists of three main islands—Flores, Sumba, and the western half of Timor—and over one hundred smaller ones. The region is characterized

[10]The island group, Nusa Tenggara, has two provinces: Nusa Tenggara Timur (NTT) in the eastern part and Nusa Tenggara Barat (NTB) in the western part. Together with the province of Timor Timur (East Timor), these islands were formerly known as the Lesser Sunda Islands.

generally by long dry seasons, mountainous or hilly terrain, and low levels of economic development. Corn is a major food source for much of the rural population, which has the highest consumption of corn per capita in all of Indonesia. Corn is widely grown throughout the province. Overall, Nusa Tenggara Timur accounts for 6 percent of Indonesia's corn production and 8 percent of area planted to corn, but only 1.9 percent of the population.

The 1981 income per capita in the province was the lowest of all Indonesian provinces—only about one-half the national average of $530 per capita. Low levels of agricultural productivity, few natural resources, and a small industrial sector (less than 4 percent of GDP) help explain the low incomes. Of the three major islands, Flores and Timor each produces 43 percent of the province's corn, while Sumba accounts for 9 percent. The remaining 5 percent is produced on the island of Alor. Yields stagnated at about 0.8 tons per hectare throughout the 1970s, a time when average yields in Indonesia increased by over 50 percent. About 85 percent of corn in the province is planted on rain-fed, upland soils, and serious erosion problems have resulted when farmers failed to plant trees or shrubs to help hold and replenish the soil on steeply sloped hillsides.

In general, corn farmers in the province use only simple tools to cultivate their land, typically using either hoes to till newly cleared land or large, pointed sticks about two meters long to turn the soil. About 90 to 100 workdays are required to till 1 hectare of upland soil by the latter method. The crash intensification program, Operation Fertile Islands (Operasi Nusa Makmur), which began in 1981, was designed to increase agricultural production rapidly through new seeds, fertilizer, and improved planting techniques. For corn, the introduction of new seed (Arjuna) and fertilizer distribution were the key ingredients of a BIMAS package that included production credits.[11] The program was at least partially successful in increasing yields through the introduction of Arjuna seed and the use of chemical fertilizers. But the package proved better suited to Java, where many farmers sell a significant percentage of their corn and where storage requirements are much less stringent. Storage is perhaps the key constraint in the province's corn system. Corn is a major food staple, but since rainfall patterns allow only one corn crop each year, corn is stored much longer than elsewhere in Indonesia. The intensification program was undermined by storage losses due to insect attack, which began while the corn was still in the field. Several other factors probably also accounted for the program's limited success: late arrival of

[11]BIMAS, *Bimbingan Masal* or "Mass Guidance," is the government's crop intensification program. It was started in the late 1960s to increase rice production with use of subsidized inputs and credit. It was broadened in the 1970s to include *palawija* crops as well.

fertilizer, marketing difficulties during the wet season on poor roads, and, interestingly, failure of farmers to understand that the loan-improvement package had to be repaid. Nusa Tenggara Timur is Indonesia's least market-oriented province. Farm households grow corn as a major staple foodstuff for their own consumption, and amounts of marketed corn are small. Even at the height of the crash intensification program, government purchasing agents procured less than 2 percent of total corn production in the province.

PART TWO

Corn Production

Analysis of commodity production systems will naturally concentrate on the unique features of the commodity and the diversity among regions where it is grown. Corn in Indonesia provides rich material for this story, but underlying this uniqueness are several general issues that ground such analysis in a broader economic setting.

The most important task is to understand the environment in which farmers make decisions. The question is not how farmers *should* use their opportunities, but how they actually *do* see the world around them. Farmers may adopt new technology hesitatingly if they have no access to credit, limited household food reserves, a highly variable pattern of rainfall, or crops likely to be infested with pests. On the other hand, individual farmers may discover new cropping patterns or strategies for reducing risk of input use that are not apparent in central research stations.

This decision-making environment connects production systems for individual commodities to other commodities and the rest of the economy. A farm household's decisions on use of inputs—especially fertilizer, hired and family labor, and purchased seed—and its decisions to market crops in the face of varying output prices affect choices of technique in production as well as patterns of home consumption. Understanding the basis on which farmers make these decisions is one of the essential elements needed in an analysis of a farming system.

A second important element is the nature of opportunity costs of growing alternative crops. An increase or decrease in output for a commodity is not the net economic effect. Increased corn production may come at the expense of rice or cassava output and is likely to use inputs, especially labor, that could be used in other economic activities. Consequently, decision making with respect to corn cannot be understood in isolation from technology and prices for competitive crops or from the market opportunities for all the inputs used to grow corn. Farmers see private opportunity costs—those actually reflected in markets—but the task is also one of evaluating any large differences between these private costs and social opportunity costs. No plea for sophisticated programming models that calculate optimal shadow prices is implied here. The analysis should simply identify any wide divergence between private and social costs where policy interventions might alter decision making to good effect. A clear example is seen in Chapter 7, which analyzes the potential use of corn to produce fructose sweeteners.

Finally, an analysis of a country's production system can reveal a sense of its dynamic comparative advantage. Simply listing production costs converted at the current exchange rate relative to c.i.f. quotations for the commodity is useful. But by this criterion, Indonesia's corn production would not be competitive with a half dozen other crops in the farming system and would be even less so with imports. What needs to be understood are the dynamic elements of crop competition, such as technology, timing of rotations, and risk, that are not captured directly by simple comparisons of cost structure. This understanding comes only from looking at farmer behavior in the context of local and regional variations in farming practices.

Chapters 2, 3, and 4 address each of these issues. They integrate the survey information into an economic framework for evaluating costs and returns to alternative farming systems and production techniques. The potential opportunities and roadblocks for change that are identified are a function of the physical environment, the available technology, and prices for corn and other commodities. Agricultural technology and commodity prices are primary vehicles for government interventions, and the focus on farm decision making highlights potential policy initiatives.

2. An Overview of Corn Production

Stephen D. Mink and Paul A. Dorosh

Corn is Indonesia's second most important food crop. Harvested area, which fluctuated around 3 million hectares in the 1970s, is roughly one-third of the area devoted to rice and twice that of cassava. Production remains almost entirely a smallholder activity and provides income and a staple food for over 10 million farm households, which rarely operate more than 2 hectares of land.

Prior to the mid-1970s, corn production techniques were very rudimentary, scarcely influenced by the dramatic changes that swept over other crops and countries with the spread of improved plant varieties and fertilizer. Farmers used simple hand tools and animal-drawn implements, and high labor intensity compensated for very low use of capital inputs. Fertilizer application was uncommon and low where it did occur. Farmers used mostly local, low-yielding corn varieties and produced less than 1 ton per hectare.

The potential for raising production from this base was recognized, although there were many obstacles. Fertilizer was difficult to obtain in rural areas because of overall shortages and inefficient distribution channels. Farmers had little experience using fertilizer, and in most cases its use was still experimental. "Improved" corn varieties were susceptible to the disease downy mildew and slow to be adopted by farmers.

By the mid-1980s many of the barriers had been greatly reduced. In part these improvements in corn cultivation were side effects of the tremendous investment in rice intensification in the 1970s. Farmers have had over a decade of experience using a variety of fertilizers and substantial quantities. Having experimented with rice varieties, they have seen the potential for yield improvements and disease resistance. In most corn-producing areas, fertilizer channels are now well established, deliveries are timely, and prices are low by world standards. Corn breeders have made advances in developing several higher-yielding varieties of medium to long duration until maturation. Crop losses to downy mildew have been reduced with the use of these new resistant seeds, fungicide seed treatment, and more timely planting.

The response of farmers to these developments in inputs has. in places, been impressive. Average fertilizer use on corn rose to 115 kilograms per hectare in 1981, accompanied by increases in corn yields of 50 percent over those of 1970. Improved open-pollinated varieties are now commonplace in some areas, and the demand for seed often exceeds the capacity for multiplication and distribution. Farmers' growing sophistication in corn production is demonstrated by their adjustments of corn variety and fertilizer amounts according to growing season and land type. Although corn production has benefited from farmers' experience with rice, serious difficulties remain. In some areas low yields persist as a result of the great environmental diversity of corn-growing areas. This diversity precludes general recommendations for seeds and agronomic practices and requires a decentralized approach to adaptive research and extension activities. Sizable areas have yet to accept seed and fertilizer recommendations, and production remains at mid-1970 levels. Temperature, moisture availability, and soil fertility vary tremendously over corn-producing areas. These elements are largely uncontrollable, and production techniques thus need to take into account these local influences. Breeding new corn varieties is highly complex since there is a need for a spectrum of corn varieties from short to long duration to fit widely varying corn-producing systems, which range from high-density monoculture on fertile, moist soils to intercropped corn systems on poorer, drier soils. A substantial part of corn hectarage is planted as an intercrop, and short-stature varieties are sought to reduce shading. In some areas farm households prefer white corn, and over 35 percent of Indonesia's corn area is planted in white varieties. But breeding programs lag behind in developing higher-yielding white corn.

In the following chapters, this diversity of agronomic and economic environments is a recurring theme. Chapter 2 highlights recent trends in area and yields and describes the seasonality and geographic distribution of corn production. These general features are followed by more specific assessments of agronomic factors—the role of rainfall, soils, temperature and altitude, pests and diseases, and varietal use—and the consequences of each on future corn production. Chapter 3 presents a typology of corn production systems in Indonesia, classified by a combination of variables—land base, current yields, and constraints to future increases in productivity. Costs and returns are calculated for two *tegalan* (rain-fed) and two *sawah* (floodable rice land) systems.[1] Chapter 4 presents an economic assessment of alternative levels of input use in these corn systems.

[1]Chapter 3 clarifies the distinction between the two land types, *tegalan* and *sawah*. Land that is dependent on rainfall (*tegalan*) is distinguished from level, bunded rice land (*sawah*). Corn is grown in certain growing seasons on both types, but most of Indonesia's corn is grown on *tegalan*. This book uses "rain-fed land" as the equivalent to *tegalan* but retains the Indonesian term *sawah* for "floodable rice land." When *sawah* does not have permanent irrigation infrastructure, the term *rain-fed sawah* is used.

Major Factors in Corn Production

Corn production has gone through three distinct periods in Indonesia since the 1920s. Table 2.1 shows that from the 1920s to early 1960s, average production increased from about 2 million to 3 million tons per

TABLE 2.1. *Indonesian corn production*

Year	Area (hectares)	Production (metric tons)	Yields[a] (tons per hectare)
1916–19	1,540,000	1,275,000	0.95
1924–29	1,810,000	1,847,000	0.91
1930–34	2,000,000	1,933,000	0.97
1935–38	2,048,000	1,978,000	0.86
1939	2,030,000	1,985,000	0.98
1940	1,983,000	1,900,000	0.96
1948–50	2,031,000	1,571,000	1.10
1952	2,232,000	1,657,000	0.74
1953	1,919,000	1,560,000	0.81
1954	2,500,000	2,668,000	1.07
1955	2,042,000	1,971,000	0.96
1956	2,232,000	1,965,000	0.88
1957	2,086,000	1,860,145	0.89
1958	2,702,000	2,634,151	0.97
1959	2,307,000	2,092,013	0.91
1960	2,639,671	2,460,117	0.93
1961	2,462,485	2,283,124	0.93
1962	3,175,116	3,242,940	1.02
1963	2,559,166	2,357,759	0.92
1964	3,646,048	3,768,629	1.03
1965	2,507,871	2,364,517	0.94
1966	3,778,251	3,717,438	0.98
1967	2,547,148	2,369,101	0.93
1968	3,220,012	3,166,046	0.98
1969	2,434,823	2,292,876	0.94
1970	2,938,311	2,825,215	0.96
1971	2,651,793	2,606,494	0.98
1972	2,160,053	2,254,382	1.04
1973	3,433,166	3,692,802	1.08
1974	2,666,868	3,010,781	1.13
1975	2,444,866	2,902,887	1.19
1976	2,095,054	2,572,139	1.23
1977	2,566,509	3,142,654	1.23
1978	3,024,611	4,029,201	1.33
1979	2,593,621	3,605,535	1.39
1980	2,734,940	3,993,771	1.46
1981	2,955,039	4,509,302	1.53
1982	2,061,299	3,234,825	1.57
1983[b]	3,017,746	5,094,645	1.69
1988[c]	3,310,000	6,656,000	2.01

SOURCES: For 1916–19 to 1959: FAO Production Yearbooks cited in Berger (1962). For 1960–present: Indonesia, Central Bureau of Statistics, *Statistical Pocketbook of Indonesia,* various years.

[a]Multi-year average yields were calculated separately and do not exactly equal production divided by area.

[b]Estimated.

[c]Projected in the Fourth Development Plan.

year, almost entirely through area expansion. In the next decade, production was static because further area expansion proved difficult. Since the start of the 1970s, an increase in yields of about 4 percent per year has provided the base for new increases in total output. By 1983, average yields were approximately 1.7 tons per hectare. Government targets indicate the expansion of both yield and area through the end of the Fourth Development Plan in 1988. Planned area is to increase by 150,000 hectares, primarily outside Java and particularly in new transmigration areas. Yields are projected to increase to 2 tons per hectare by 1988.

Factors Affecting Area

The major positive influence in expanding corn area has been the government's program to relocate people from Java to sparsely settled regions of other islands. Corn is often an integral part of agricultural plans for these transmigration areas, particularly in the first years after settlement. Corn serves as a subsistence crop before cash-earning perennials reach maturity. Isolated by distance and poor roads, farmers in these areas face difficulties moving any surplus corn to markets. However, the crop tolerates a wide variety of soils with varying fertility in the outer islands and, along with cassava, is often a major staple grown by settlers.

Although there are large swings from year to year in the amount of area planted in corn on Java, average corn area has changed very little since the mid-1970s. New irrigation systems and rehabilitation tended to be negative forces on corn area because they permitted substitution of irrigated rice for rain-fed crops. An estimated 75,000 to 100,000 hectares of new or rehabilitated irrigated land was completed in the period from 1970 to 1978. (For the progress of irrigation development in Indonesia, see Nyberg and Prabowo 1979; Booth 1977.) In some cases, however, this expansion *added* to the potential for growing with some irrigation a dry-season corn crop, where previously production was of a risky, low-yielding rain-fed crop. Irrigation projects continue in the 1980s, but the future impact of this infrastructural investment on corn area is expected to be minimal.

The Central Bureau of Statistics' data, available through the annual "Agricultural Surveys" and reproduced in Figure 2.1, show that changes in relative net return between corn and other *palawija* (non-rice) crops have not been major factors influencing corn production in the 1970s. Although net returns from corn improved over the decade in relation to upland rice on Java, they just managed to hold their own in competition with cassava, peanuts, and soybeans. Reductions in per unit costs of corn production through yield increases have helped corn maintain its position, despite a general decline in relative output prices.

A more dramatic point made in Figure 2.1 is the consistently inferior

FIGURE 2.1. *Net returns to corn per hectare, 1971–1981 (ratios to other crops)*

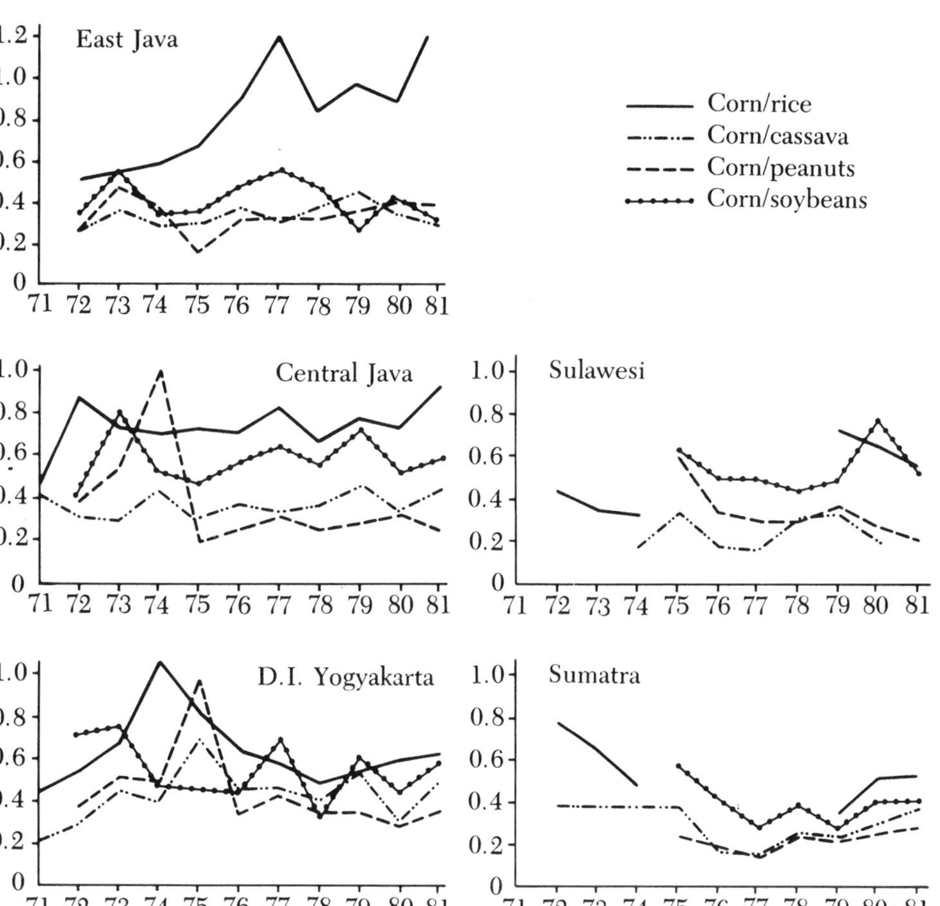

SOURCE: Indonesia, Central Bureau of Statistics, "Agricultural Survey," various years.

returns for growing corn, often less than half the returns achievable with other *palawija* crops. These low returns have not led to a decline in aggregate corn area for several reasons which differ by crop. Higher cassava returns are offset by the long period that cassava occupies land, from 9 to 12 months or over three times as long as the normal corn season. For peanuts and soybeans, high average net returns do not reflect the risks associated with these crops and the frequency of crop losses, which tend not to be calculated in the "Agricultural Survey's" net returns.

Furthermore, these and other legume crops tend to do poorly on inferior acid soils where low but stable corn yields can nevertheless be expected. Hence, low relative net returns for corn have not been a powerful force in reducing corn area.

Farmers are nonetheless sensitive to crop options and switch to alternatives that provide an assured market or easy credit arrangements. Some farmers change crop mixes in response to crop promotions. Competing *palawija* crops may fall into these categories in various regions of the country, as do other field and perennial crops. Cotton, with a guaranteed price, is an alternative in the dry season in South Sulawesi. Fruit crops such as citrus (in Jeneponto *kabupaten* in South Sulawesi) and papaya (in Malang) have rapidly expanded on rain-fed land where transport links to urban markets have been established. At higher altitudes vegetables are generally much more profitable to grow than corn, so long as risks associated with marketing and pests can be reduced. Sugarcane—not only as part of the government's credit program but also as an independent farmer venture—competes with corn rotations on both *sawah* and rain-fed land, especially in East Java.[2] This competition occurs despite many uncertainties regarding cane yields, crushing yields, factory acceptance of cane deliveries, and credit administration. In short, shifting economic opportunities in competing crops, whether *palawija*, vegetable, fruit, or industrial, are continually redefining areas where corn production is profitable. In specific regions, losses in corn area to these alternative crops can be dramatic. In the aggregate, however, a general decline in corn area is not noticeable.

Factors Affecting Yield

Rapid increases in fertilizer use, the spread of higher-yielding varieties, and possibly a shift from intercrop to monoculture corn help explain the rise in corn yields evident from the early 1970s. Although the increase in corn yields of about 4 percent per year is not disputed, the actual yield level reported in official statistics needs cautious interpretation. Comparisons of regional and seasonal yields are difficult to make since in official statistics yields from predominantly monoculture areas cannot be distinguished from those of intercrop systems. Hence low yields from an area may result only from low corn densities in an intercrop system, rather than from low fertility or management skills. Yield statistics are officially collected from an intercrop as long as the spacing is no greater than three times the "normal" spacing, which also varies by region. As a consequence, published data on yields compile results across a wide range of corn densities and provide no means for distinguishing among

[2]The credit program for sugarcane is *Tebu Rekyat Indonesia* (TRI).

these variations. Moreover, yield statistics published by the Central Bureau of Statistics are often significantly higher than those compiled in statistical yearbooks (*Laporan Tahunan*) released by provincial Departments of Agriculture. Table 2.2 shows the extent of these differences and the consequences for national production if an adjustment is made for only three major producing provinces. The jump in yields between provincial and national statistics has no clear explanation. But from survey results and field observations, the provincial figures appear more reliable.

A tripling of the use of inorganic fertilizer on corn in Indonesia during the 1970s was an important part of increasing yields. Average figures hide a great deal of regional and seasonal variance. Rates of fertilizer application are highest in East and Central Java, where *sawah* corn farmers often apply from 400 to 600 kilograms of combined urea and TSP (triple superphosphate) per hectare. In production centers on South Sulawesi and Nusa Tenggara Timur, however, rates are still very low. Farmers often have less than five years of experience applying fertilizer on corn, despite much longer use on rice. Furthermore, dry-season, upland corn receives less fertilizer in almost all regions, as fewer inputs are used on this more risky crop.

The release and spread of new, improved corn varieties since 1978 have also contributed to growth in yields, as shown in Table 2.3. The release of Harapan-6 in that year, followed by Arjuna in 1980 and the hybrid C-1 in 1983, has enabled farmers to shift to higher-yielding varieties that are resistant to downy mildew. Distribution of improved seeds is still inadequate, and they do not reach many areas on a regular basis. Even with open-pollinated, improved corn varieties, regular renewal of seeds is important since cross-pollination in fields adjacent to those planted in local varieties is unavoidable and results in declining yields and a mixing of plant characteristics if farmers save and replant the seed. Yield increases from currently available seed technology have only begun to be exploited and will be realized at a rate largely dependent on improvements in multiplication and distribution of seeds. Finally, there is tentative evidence that corn yields have increased because of greater densities associated with a general shift from intercrop to monoculture plantings. Survey results from East Java and Sumatra show that the principal corn crop and sometimes the secondary planting are monoculture stands. According to the 1973 census figures shown in Table 2.4, over 50 percent of corn in these two areas was intercropped. Since then, this percentage seems to have declined substantially. In some areas, corn intercropping remains a dominant and stable system, but survey results and field observations suggest that as farmers intensify corn production through use of improved varieties and more fertilizer, they shift to monoculture production.

TABLE 2.2. *Official and adjusted production and yield statistics*

Year	Area harvested (000 hectares)	Production (000 tons)		Yields (tons per hectare): Central Bureau of Statistics				Yields (tons per hectare): Department of Agriculture, provinces			
		Official	Adjusted[a]	East Java	South Sulawesi	Central Java	Total	East Java	South Sulawesi	Central Java	Total
1970	2,939	2,825	2,224	0.90	0.86	1.15	0.96	0.66	0.75	0.75	0.76
1971	2,651	2,606	2,105	0.91	0.74	1.22	0.99	0.70	0.74	0.72	0.79
1972	2,160	2,255	1,753	1.01	0.70	1.27	1.04	0.70	0.70	0.78	0.81
1973	3,433	3,693	2,951	1.04	0.82	1.28	1.08	0.78	0.82	0.81	0.86
1974	2,667	3,011	2,296	1.05	1.13	1.18	1.13	0.75	0.63	0.87	0.86
1975	2,445	2,903	2,315	1.19	0.98	1.30	1.19	0.83	0.65	1.04	0.95
1976	2,095	2,572	2,430	1.28	1.19	1.27	1.23	0.95	0.67	1.42	1.16
1977	2,567	3,143	2,573	1.29	1.03	1.32	1.22	1.01	0.72	1.28	1.00
1978	3,025	4,029	3,393	1.34	1.26	1.48	1.33	1.04	0.78	1.30	1.12
1979	2,594	3,606	2,853	1.48	1.25	1.53	1.39	1.05	0.70	1.21	1.10
1980	2,735	3,994	3,419	1.53	1.30	1.62	1.46	1.18	0.84	1.55	1.25
1981	2,955	4,509	3,858	1.60	1.35	1.79	1.53	1.18	0.73	—	1.31

SOURCES: Indonesia, Central Bureau of Statistics, *Statistical Pocketbook of Indonesia*, various years.
[a]Obtained by substituting provincial data for East Java, South Sulawesi, and Central Java.

TABLE 2.3. *Seed varieties*

Name	Duration (days to harvest)		Yields (tons per hectare)		Color	Downy mildew resistance	Origin	Year of release
	Low altitude	High altitude	Farmer[a]	Experimental plot				
National releases								
Nakula	85	100	—	3.6	yellow	yes	Suwan 1 × Penjalinan	1983
Sadawa	86	100	—	3.7	yellow	no	Suwan 1 × Genjah Kretek	1983
Hibrida C-1	95–100	110–115	5.5	5.8	yellow	yes		1983
Abimanyu	75–80	90–105	—	3.0	yellow	yes	Randu × Arjuna	1983
Parikesit	100–105	115–120	—	4.5	yellow	yes	H-DMR	1981
Arjuna	90	105	3.3	4.2	yellow	yes	Thai Composite #1 Early DMR (Suwan 2)	1980
Bromo	90	105	—	3.4	white	yes	Philippines DMR Comp. 2	1980
Harapan-6	105	120	3.0	3.5	yellow	yes	Harapan × Phil. DMR 5	1978
Bogor Composite 2	105	120	—	—	yellow	no	—	1969
Metro	110	125	3.0	—	red-yellow	no	Tequisate Golden Yellow	1956
Harapan	105	120	3.0	—	yellow	no	—	1956
Local varieties (sample)								
Genjah Kretek	85–90	—	2.5	2.7	yellow	—	—	—
Penjalinan	80–85	—	—	2.5	yellow	—	—	—
Genjah Kertas	75–80	—	—	2.9	yellow	—	—	—
Genjah Tongkol	90	—	1.9	—	yellow	—	—	—
Genjah Tengahan	75	—	1.5	—	white	—	—	—
Papelo	—	—	—	—	white	—	—	—

SOURCES: Survey data; Indonesia, Department of Agriculture, "Improved Varieties of Corn" (1981); Subandi, et al. (1979).
[a]Farmer yields are best average yields from survey sites.

TABLE 2.4. *Corn area harvested from intercropped stands, 1973*

Farm size (hectares)	Indonesia	Java/Madura	Sulawesi	Sumatra	Other[a]
0.1–0.29	51.8%	51.1%	36.5%	51.9%	73.7%
0.3–0.49	51.1	51.5	28.3	54.5	62.7
0.5–0.74	53.0	52.7	31.4	66.5	74.4
0.75–0.99	53.6	53.5	30.2	63.4	75.9
1.0–1.9	57.2	55.2	33.7	73.1	81.0
2.0+	63.0	52.4	42.1	79.6	82.1

SOURCE: Indonesia, Central Bureau of Statistics, "Agricultural Census," 1973.
[a]Excludes Kalimantan.

Geographic Distribution of Corn Production

Corn production in Indonesia is concentrated on Java and Madura, which account for almost 75 percent of production. Two other major producing centers, South Sulawesi and Nusa Tenggara Timur, together account for another 15 percent of total production. Several pockets of production, including North Sulawesi and North Sumatra, present special

FIGURE 2.2. *Corn production on Java, January–December*

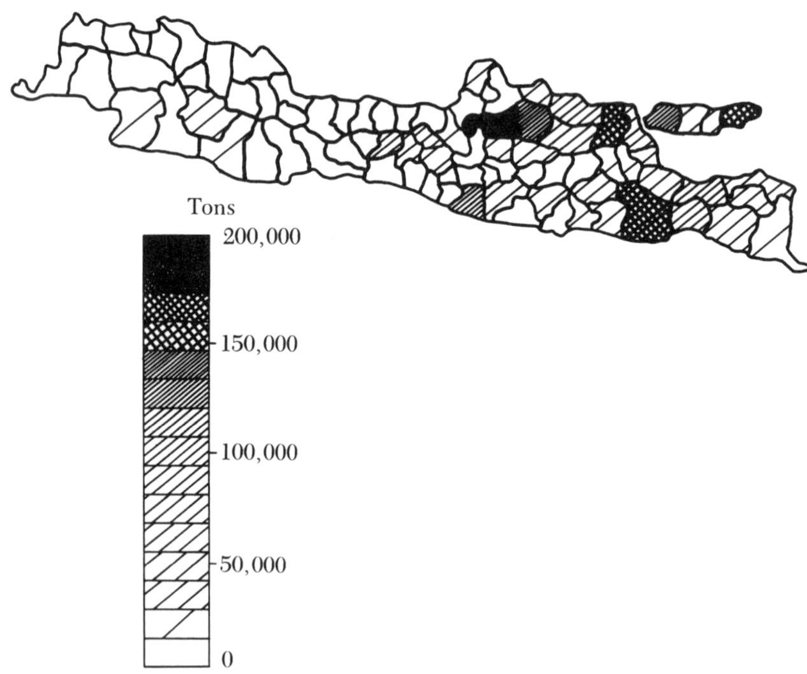

SOURCE: Indonesia, Central Bureau of Statistics, "Production of Annual Food Crops: Java and Madura" (1981).

FIGURE 2.3. *Total foodcrop land on Java planted with corn*

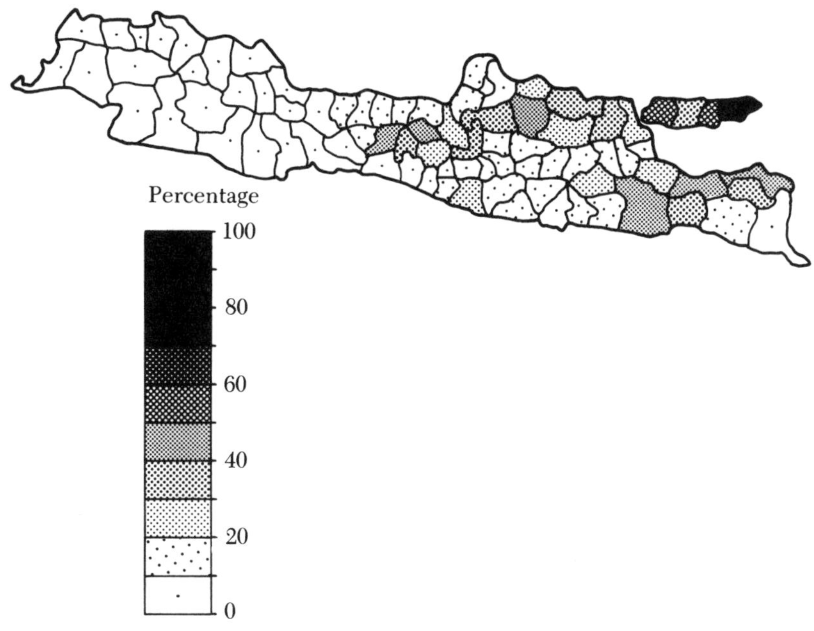

SOURCE: Indonesia, Central Bureau of Statistics, "Production of Annual Food Crops: Java and Madura" (1981).

problems since good agronomic conditions for corn growth are offset by geographic isolation and ensuing difficulties for marketing surpluses. There has been very little change in this pattern of distribution through the 1970s to the present. On Java and Madura, almost all corn is produced on the eastern half of the land mass, as shown in Figure 2.2. The province of East Java produces 45 percent of the nation's total output. As shown in Figure 2.3, some *kabupatens* in East Java have slightly less than half the total food crop land planted in corn. The distribution of production means that surpluses are far from the principal domestic and international markets. On Java the growing market for corn as livestock feed is centered in Jakarta, over 800 kilometers from East Java's production centers. Distant surplus-producing areas, such as South Sulawesi, North Sulawesi, and North Sumatra, have difficulty competing with cheaper Lampung corn in Java's markets when inter-island "imports" are needed. North Sumatra is close to Singapore and Malaysia, and North and South Sulawesi participate in these markets as well. However, international trade requires that merchants bulk corn into larger lots, make more complicated legal arrangements, and meet higher standards of quality than are necessary for the domestic market. These factors hamper disposal of the small surpluses of 10,000 to 30,000 tons per year which these areas periodically produce.

Seasonality of Production

The seasonality of rainfall is the major determinant of the distribution of corn production throughout the year. The west-to-east order of regional peaks in production, which is apparent in Figure 2.4, is a consequence of the western monsoon's spread across the islands. The rains arrive in Central Java in October or November and follow slightly later in East Java. Relative to West Java, average annual rainfall amounts decline, and the length and intensity of the dry season increase in East Java and along the northern coast. Dry months with less than 100 millimeters of rainfall number fewer than four in Central Java, but increase to five or six as one moves through East Java to Madura. As a consequence, corn plantings in the dry (third) season (June–September) in Central and East Java are risky, and farmers compensate by leaving fields fallow, planting short-duration varieties, or providing supplemental irrigation water.

In general the pattern of peak rainfall across the rest of the archipelago follows the spread of the western monsoon. The rains arrive last in Nusa Tenggara Timur and allow a single corn crop in February. Several of the other islands' corn areas, such as parts of North Sumatra and South Sulawesi, are affected by the southeast monsoon as well, which causes another peak in rainfall in May. For these regions, the total rainfall is less than on Java. But this lower level comes mostly through lower averages during months of heavy rainfall rather than an increase in critically dry months and hence does not greatly reduce the number of potential growing seasons.

Despite the potential in most areas for three corn crops a year, the first crop, which occupies land from October to March, is by far the largest. The peak harvest period is defined by the East Java crop because of its size, and thus peak production occurs between December and March. The provinces differ in the temporal concentration of their production. Harvests in Yogyakarta and Nusa Tenggara Timur are the most sharply concentrated in one season; over 85 percent of total production occurs with the principal harvest in the first crop season. East and Central Java have more important secondary harvests; the main first crop harvest provides less than 60 percent of annual output. In these two provinces, the sizable off-season harvests occur on a variety of land types, which include *sawah* and both low- and high-altitude rain-fed land. The common feature on both types of land is a pattern of rainfall or water control insufficient for a rice crop, but adequate for corn and other *palawija* crops. The frequen-

FIGURE 2.4. *Seasonal distribution of corn production and area occupied by corn, September 1980–September 1981*

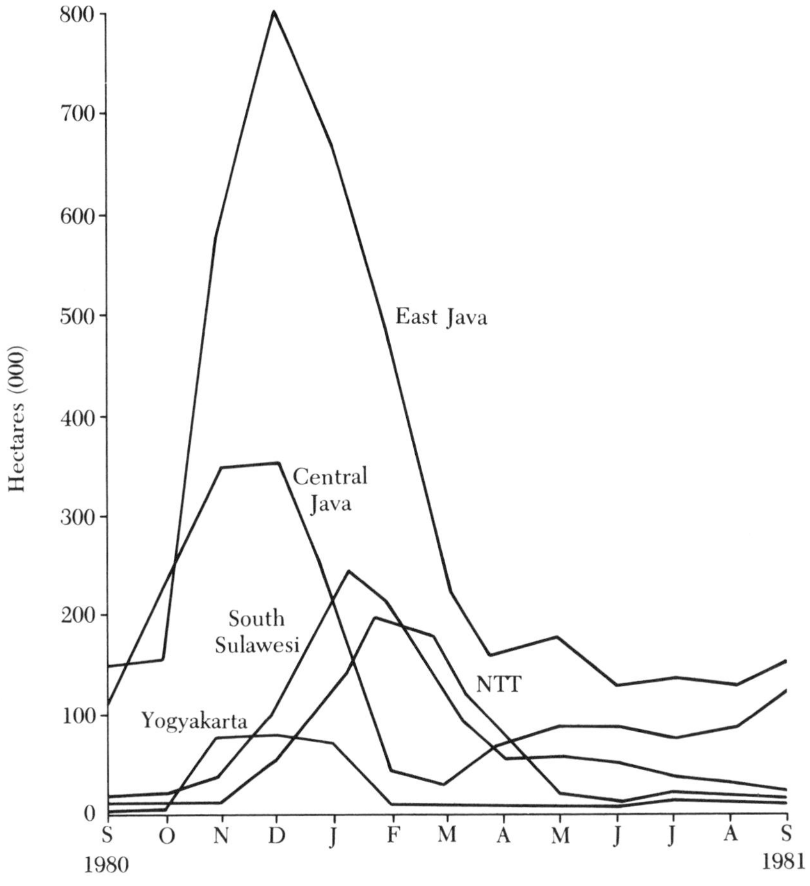

	Trimester Distribution of Production (percent)		
	December–March	April–July	August–November
East Java	60	20	20
Central Java	56	18	26
Yogyakarta	93	2	5
South Sulawesi	76	19	5
NTT[a]	86	8	6

SOURCE: Indonesia, Central Bureau of Statistics, "Production of Annual Food Crops: Java and Madura" (1981).
[a]For Nusa Tenggara Timur, the trimesters are February–May, June–September, and October–January.

cy of corn harvests on Java has important implications for purchase and storage strategies of corn users and traders. Storage for more than three or four months becomes risky because of uncertainty about the size of the next harvest. Even storage for purely operational convenience by industrial users can be kept to low levels because of the nearly continuous availability of newly harvested corn from somewhere on Java.

With most of corn production dependent on rain, the exact timing of planting the first-season crop, which is generally October on Java and November on the outer islands, depends on the arrival of the rainy season. For the major crop this can vary by as much as a month. Consequently, the principal harvest, which straddles the end of the calendar year, can shift back and forth across this recording divide. As a result, harvest data by calendar year often show dramatic year-to-year fluctuations, which are largely recording aberrations arising from two principal harvests being squeezed into one calendar year. Figure 2.5 demonstrates

FIGURE 2.5. *Total corn area harvested, by calendar and crop year, East Java, 1967–1983*

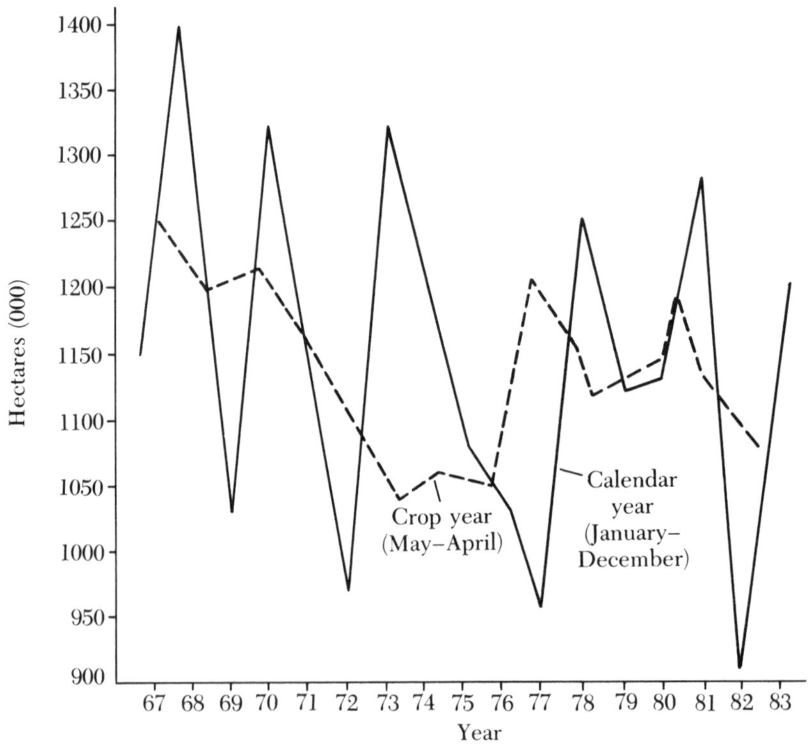

SOURCE: Data from the Agricultural Service in East Java.

this phenomenon with data on area harvested annually in East Java. Use of a crop year (May–April) rather than a calendar year clearly reduces annual crop fluctuations and lowers variance by 80 percent for the period 1967–1983. Adjusting the record-breaking national harvest in 1983 of 5.1 million tons to a crop year results in a shift of about 0.5 million tons to adjacent years.

Agronomic Determinants of Production

The range of conditions under which corn will grow and produce some yield is extremely diverse and much wider, for example, than that of either rice or wheat. Some conditions are much more hospitable for high yields than others. The major determinants of corn's ability to thrive are soil types, nutrient availability (whether from natural or synthetic sources), water availability, temperature and day length, and pests and diseases. As the following discussion emphasizes, important interactions exist among these variables, not all of which are fully understood even in the controlled environment of research stations. The interactions on farmers' fields in the tropics are just beginning to be studied.

Soil Types

Corn grows well on a wide range of soils in various parts of the world, but the highest yields are on loamy soils with good aeration and drainage. Heavier clay soils permit good growth as long as initial plowing or hoeing is deep and soil is cultivated to avoid compaction. Light sandy soils, gravelly soils, and soils with a clay pan result in poorer development and penetration of roots, which under normal conditions reach one to two meters, and corn stands on these soils are subject to inadequate moisture, lodging, and poor nutrient uptake.

Corn in Indonesia is grown on diverse types of soil, from lowland alluvials to upland volcanic soils and from rich *sawah* soils on Java to leached hillside laterites on other islands. Differences in natural fertility and in soil management practices greatly affect the agronomics and economics of corn production between areas. One result of this diversity is the need for decentralized experimentation and extension programs so that production recommendations can be tailored to local conditions.

About three-fourths of Indonesia's corn area is on rain-fed land, which occurs in hillier areas. This land class is frequently sloped and often terraced. The structure and natural fertility of *tegalan* soils vary tremendously. On volcanic hillsides, which are common in Java and parts of other islands, the soils can be rich, deep, and finely textured. In the uplands of south-central Java, as well as parts of South Sulawesi and Nusa Tenggara Timur, corn is grown on leached, limestone-based soils. Gravelly, thin soils and steep slopes contribute to poor plant canopy and high erosion from water runoff.

The remainder of corn production is on level, bunded *sawah* in lowlands or on terraced hillsides, and almost all these areas are on Java. This corn area is generally of two types: irrigated land where insufficient water prevents year-round rice cultivation; and rain-fed *sawah* which is planted with rice only when the heavy rainy season floods the fields. The former is excellent for corn production, but the latter, which is subject to both flooding and drought, requires use of short-duration corn varieties, which have limited yield potential.

Corn tolerates acid soils better than most other *palawija* crops, and good yields are obtained with soil acidity in the range of pH 5.3 to 7.3. On more acid soils, the macronutrients required for plant growth—nitrogen, phosphorus, and potassium—as well as the micronutrients—calcium, manganese, and sulfur—become less available for absorption by the plant. Other soil nutrients, such as aluminum, iron, and magnesium, become more soluble at higher acidity and become toxic to the corn plant. Where soils are highly acid, below pH 5.5, lime can be used to reduce acidity and improve yields.

The causes of acidity for *sawah* and rain-fed land are different. On *sawah*, high fertilizer applications, especially of urea, have increased soil acidity, although this process is counteracted by regular flooding of the land. *Tegalan* soils, especially those of the outer islands, become acid as limestone components are leached from the soil, which proceeds more quickly where cultivation is more intense and inadequate attention has been given to maintaining the organic content of the soils. Acidity of soils on rain-fed land and *sawah* is a major but as yet unquantified constraint to raising corn yields. Increased attention has been focused on this problem as part of programs to promote soybean production. Farmers and extension agents are usually uninformed about the impact of acidity on corn production, however, and liming is rarely practiced.

Nutrients

Corn needs an adequate supply of nutrients for good yields, and this supply depends on water availability, management practices such as timing and placing of fertilizer, and soil characteristics such as natural nutrient content and capacity to release the nutrients for plant use. Estimates of nutrient uptake during corn plant growth are presented in Table 2.5 for different levels of grain yield. For a 4-ton grain harvest, urea, triple superphosphate (TSP), and potassium chloride (KCl) are absorbed at 230 kilograms, 48 kilograms, and 118 kilograms, respectively. This uptake of nutrients by the plant indicates minimum amounts of fertilizer supplements needed to replenish soil fertility. Provision of just these

TABLE 2.5. *Estimates of soil nutrients removed by corn*

Dry corn grain harvested (tons)	Nutrients removed by total plant for various yields of dry corn harvested[a] (kilograms)				
	N (urea)	P_2O_5 (TSP)	K_2O (KCl)	Ca	Mg
1	25.9 (57.6)	5.4 (12.0)	17.7 (29.5)	1.9	2.2
2	51.8 (115.1)	10.8 (24.0)	35.4 (59.0)	3.8	4.4
3	77.7 (172.7)	16.2 (36.0)	53.1 (88.5)	5.7	6.6
4	103.6 (230.2)	21.6 (48.0)	70.8 (118.0)	7.6	8.8
5	129.5 (287.8)	27.0 (60.0)	88.5 (147.5)	9.5	11.0

SOURCE: Derived from results of Sayre (1955).
NOTES: Figures in parentheses show the amount of the indicated commercial fertilizer needed to supply the respective nutrient levels. Urea and triple superphosphate (P_2O_5) are chemical fertilizers commonly available in Indonesia's rural areas.
[a]Total nutrients removed in stems, leaves, and grain. Excludes roots in soil.

minimum levels for repeated plantings will barely support stable yields, since leaching, oxidation, and soil bonding will make a part of added nutrients unavailable to plants. In addition, the rate of nutrient uptake is not constant through the growth cycle. It is highest between the 10 days before and the 25 to 30 days after tasseling. There is also a translocation to the grain of nutrients already contained in the stalks and leaves.

Water Availability

Because nutrients to the plant must be in solution, the availability of water is particularly important during this period when nutrient requirements are the greatest. Through much of the growth cycle the corn plant uses 4 millimeters of water per day, but during silking and grain formation (soft dough) stage, 6 to 8 millimeters per day may be absorbed from the soil. Inadequate water during this period can reduce yields 20 to 50 percent.

Water requirements for normal corn growth are roughly equivalent to the level of evapotranspiration, that is, the loss of water to the atmosphere through aerial parts of the plant. An estimate of this loss for a 125-day duration variety is shown in Table 2.6. Total water needs for 125-day varieties are slightly more than 400 millimeters, which indicates that for Indonesian short-duration varieties of 90 days, 300 millimeters or roughly 100 millimeters per month are required. Actual rainfall requirements on rain-fed soils vary with the intensity and timing of rainfall, as well as with the soil's capacity to retain water.

Indonesia's major crop systems are located in areas with 1,400 to 2,500

TABLE 2.6. *Corn plant water loss through evapotranspiration during different growth stages*

Growth stages	Days	Evapotranspiration (millimeters)
Initial	20	40
Developing	35	108
Full canopy	40	168
Ripening	30	96
TOTAL	125	412

SOURCES: Olman and Sjarifuddin (1977), p. 11, citing J. Doorenbos and W. O. Print, "Guidelines for Predicting Crop Water Requirements," FAO Irrigation and Drainage Paper no. 24 (Rome: Food and Agriculture Organization of the United Nations, 1975).
NOTES: Assumes a reference crop evapotranspiration rate of 4 millimeters per day and a frequency of rain once a week for the initial stage. The reference crop evapotranspiration rate is based on representative solar radiation, temperature, altitude, wind speed, and relative humidity.

millimeters of annual rainfall, but precipitation is highly seasonal. Since almost 90 percent of Indonesia's corn is grown on land dependent on rainfall to supply water to the crop, crop choice and planting time depend critically on rainfall patterns. This timing varies with the spread of monsoon weather, as described previously.

In almost all regions, the main corn planting in October or November occurs with the first rains after the dry season. The heavier rainfall patterns during the second crop season that begins by February on Java are less favorable for corn because the plant does not tolerate poor drainage or excess moisture in the root zone for more than three days. On rain-fed land, heavy rainfall during this season contributes to lower corn yields than those of the first harvest, and farmers sometimes delay the second planting to avoid the months of peak rainfall. There is generally too little rainfall in the third season (June–September) to obtain good corn yields, which is increasingly the case as one moves across East Java to the islands of Nusa Tenggara Timur. On rain-fed *sawah*, corn squeezed into the crop rotations before the heavy rains and the main rice crop is often lost through flooding, even though fast-maturing varieties are used.

Temperature and Day Length

Compared with other corn-growing areas of the world, temperature and day length in Indonesia's corn areas vary relatively little throughout the year. Warm days, abundant solar energy, and warm nights are good climatic conditions for growing corn. High temperatures combined with low humidity, however, can disrupt pollination and result in a high proportion of barren plants in rain-fed systems, particularly for the dry (third) season crop.

The variation in temperature from one corn area to another stems mainly from differences in altitude. Since temperature directly affects the number of days required from planting to harvest, farmers in each area, at different altitudes, must choose crop varieties that will mature before the next crop rotation in multiple cropping systems.

Temperature after seedlings emerge is important in determining the length of time to tasseling. After the tassel stage, temperature plays a less important role in the time needed for ripening. Wallace and Bressman (1937) found that each degree over 21.1°C for the 60-plus days after planting speeds the tasseling of longer-duration varieties by 2 to 3 days. An alternative adjustment of duration to altitude uses the general rule that the number of degree days required to time of tasseling is almost constant for any given variety with changes in altitude. With lower temperatures at higher altitudes, more days are required to accumulate the number of degree days to tasseling, and farmers respond by using shorter-duration varieties or shifting from three to two crops per year. At higher altitudes crop rotations tend to be more tightly constrained than those at lower altitudes.

Only 7 percent of the total land area of Java is more than 1,000 meters above sea level, however, and most of this highland is devoted to garden-type crops, such as potatoes, cabbage, leafy greens, and carrots, which benefit from cool temperatures. But even with most corn area below 1,000 meters, differences in days to silking due to altitude are significant. Between sea level and 765 meters, this duration increases perhaps 13 days—about 2 days per 100 meters of elevation—for any particular variety.

Pests and Diseases

In Indonesia, corn is damaged by a variety of pests and diseases. To establish their relative importance and regional incidence, reporting forms for extension agents have been devised and are compiled nationally each year. Extension agents are capable of distinguishing the various diseases and pests, but their responsibilities for a broad array of crops and wide geographic area make sizable underreporting of damage to *palawija* crops a probable bias. Consequently, although Table 2.7 illustrates relative sources of crop loss to diseases and pests (in 1981), it should not be read as an accurate estimate of total hectares lost. The figure shown, 13,783 hectares, is less than 0.5 percent of planted area. Since management practices rarely include use of crop protectants, these total losses must be much too low.

The *relative* importance of corn diseases and pests, however, is probably reflected fairly accurately in Table 2.7. Of all insect pests, the army worm does the most damage. Because this pest finds a suitable environment with many *palawija* crops, it is especially prevalent in intercrop

TABLE 2.7. *Area and intensity of corn crop loss, 1981*

	Area (hectares)	Intensity (percentage of hectares lost)
Pests		
Army worms (*Laphygma* spp.)	4,606	34.5
Cutworms (*Agrotis* spp.)	919	9.6
Seedling fly (*Atherigona exigua*)	670	25.7
Stalk borer (*Ostrinia furnacalis*)	297	5.9
Rootworms (*Hollotrichia helleri, Aprosterna area, Leaucophalis rorida, Hypomeces squamus*)	250	11.9
Corn borer (*Pyrausta nubilalis*)	27	83.6
Wild pigs	2,220	25.3
Rats	1,457	15.6
Diseases		
Downy mildew (*Sclerospora maydis*)	3,249	48.3
Leaf blight (*Helminthosporium turcicum*)	49	57.8
Rusts (*Puccinia* spp.)	20	50.0
Smut (*Ustilago maydis*)	15	8.5
Seedling, stalk rot (*Gibberella Fujikuroi*)	4	15.0
Total area affected by pests and diseases	13,783	
Area lost to flooding and drought	100,848	—
TOTAL	114,631	—

SOURCES: For pests and diseases: Indonesia, Central Bureau of Statistics, "Area and Intensity of Pest and Disease Damage of Food Crops in Indonesia" (1981). Includes West, Central, and East Java, Yogyakarta, North and West Sumatra, Lampung, Bali, Nusa Tenggara Barat, South Kalimantan, and South Sulawesi. For flooding and drought: Indonesia, Central Bureau of Statistics, "Production of Annual Food Crops in Indonesia" (1981).

agriculture. Farmers surveyed noted that in a corn-soybean intercrop, infestation builds up on the soybeans before the worm attacks the corn. Hence, inadequate protection of associated crops often leads to losses in the corn crop.

Animals such as wild pigs and monkeys damage significant areas of corn near forests, especially on the outer islands in both older and newly settled communities. There are few short-term prospects for control of these pests, and they will continue to present risks to corn farmers in these less densely populated regions.

The major disease that causes corn damage is downy mildew (*Sclerospora maydis*). Local corn varieties generally possess some resistance to the fungus, but most of the earlier improved varieties are susceptible. This shortcoming was made clear in the early 1970s when a large commercial corn operation in Lampung, which used the susceptible Metro variety, suffered ruinous crop losses (see Rix 1979). Indonesian corn breeders have made incorporation of downy mildew resistance into domestically available varieties a breeding priority since 1969, and by using Thai and Philippine genetic material, they have successfully achieved resistance in national improved varieties such as Arjuna and Harapan-6, which were released in the late 1970s.

Considerable field evidence confirmed that downy mildew should be a less serious problem in the future. Most farmers have been made aware of the environmental conditions that favor downy mildew early in the growth cycle—humid nights and hot, dry days—and the need to avoid these conditions by not delaying planting too long after the start of the rainy season. Most farmers are now using resistant varieties, either local or improved. A fungicide seed treatment—Ridomil—has proven very effective. At one survey site in Sumatra, Ridomil is one of the components of a corn package that reversed the losses farmers previously had experienced from downy mildew and enabled triple cropping (see Perry 1984a). But use of Ridomil is still extremely limited, and some farmers complain about the additional cash cost at the beginning of the crop season (approximately Rp 7,250 per hectare in 1984).[3] More important, some farmers are unaware of its existence or its proper use, and in many local markets it is unavailable to farmers. Effective control of downy mildew, therefore, will require that plant breeders continue to breed resistance into new corn varieties that they develop to suit widely varying local agronomic conditions.

The agronomic determinants of corn production—soil, moisture, temperature, pests and diseases—are the basic conditions with which farmers must deal. Constraints posed by some of these conditions are just beginning to be addressed in Indonesia through plant breeding for such factors as drought resistance, shorter maturity, tolerance to cool temperatures, or reduced fertilizer requirements. Breeding for other desirable traits, such as higher yield in a white corn variety or in a short-stature variety used as an intercrop, would be useful to fill other niches in regional corn systems. The important role of such corn varieties, particularly in giving farmers a wider choice of crops, a broader base for economic decision making, and greater potential to raise yields and income, can be seen as the vastly different types of corn production systems are looked at in greater detail in Chapter 3.

[3]The appropriate foreign exchange rate for this period is about 1,100 rupiahs per U.S. dollar.

3. Corn Production Systems

Stephen D. Mink, Paul A. Dorosh, and Douglas H. Perry

To evaluate the potential for increases in corn yields and to provide a basis for characterizing different production systems and their constraints, the authors carried out farmer surveys in seven major corn-producing areas. Tremendous diversity was found, but, as shown in Table 3.1, survey results can be organized into a typology of four corn systems, defined by the following summary categories: land type (soil characteristics, water control), crop system (monoculture, intercrop, multiple cropping, rainfall patterns, crop duration constraints, intercrop profitability), and management choices (fertilizer and other input choices).

The land types used for corn production are *tegalan* (rain-fed) and *sawah* (floodable rice land). The two *tegalan* systems differ from each other in the frequency of corn harvests and are classified as systems with multiple or single corn crop per year. The two *sawah* systems are identified by the degree of water control. Irrigated *sawah* has permanent irrigation infrastructure, and rain-fed *sawah* is irregularly flooded by rainfall runoff. The *tegalan* systems cover large areas and are fairly heterogeneous; it is thus useful to define high- and low-productivity subsystems. The *sawah* systems are more uniform, although rain-fed *sawah* is a low-productivity corn system and irrigated *sawah* a high-productivity one.

The production systems are scattered in a mosaic across the Indonesian landscape. While any region may be dominated by one system, there are still pockets of the other systems. A region's individual farmers, whose plots are representative of several different types, thus make management decisions for corn under a single set of economic variables (such as prices for fertilizer and corn) on plots with dissimilar production characteristics. For this reason alone, changes in price signals cannot be expected to have a uniform impact across farmers in a region.

An economic profile of each production system is sketched by highlighting the elements of costs and returns of corn and competing crops. In most corn-producing areas, farmers must make basic agronomic and economic decisions—what crops to grow, what inputs to purchase, and how to allocate the land—for three crop seasons a year. Farmers compare the cost of producing the crops—costs for seeds, for the fertilizer they require, and for labor to plow, plant, weed, and harvest—with their expected returns. The profitability of growing different crops can vary enormously among the production systems and seasons, and farm households

TABLE 3.1. *Corn systems in Indonesia*

	Multiple corn crop *tegalan*		Single corn crop *tegalan*		Rain-fed *sawah*	Irrigated *sawah*
	High productivity	Low productivity	High productivity	Low productivity	Low productivity	High productivity
Percentage of total corn area	16	39	4	20	10	11
Land type						
Yields (tons per hectare)	2.2–3.8	1.0	1.0–1.5	<0.5	1.0	3.0
Management choices						
Chemical fertilizer (kilograms per hectare)	300–425	0–50	225–275	0–25	75–125	400+
Seed color	yellow	white (yellow)	yellow	mixed	white	yellow
Crop system	monoculture	monoculture	intercrop[a]	intercrop[a]	intercrop[b]	monoculture
Representative regions	EAST JAVA Malang Kediri	SOUTH SULAWESI Bone	LAMPUNG	YOGYAKARTA Gunung Kidul	EAST JAVA Bojonegoro	EAST JAVA Kediri Malang
	NORTH SUMATRA Karo Asahan	EAST JAVA Madura	EAST JAVA Kediri	CENTRAL JAVA Wonogiri	CENTRAL JAVA Grobogan Blora	
		CENTRAL JAVA		NUSA TENGGARA TIMUR (NTT)		
Marketings (percentage of production)	30–80	40	60–85	15	40	50–80

[a]Cassava, upland rice.
[b]Soybeans, mung beans.

choose a mix of crops that meets their need for food and income and that is also suitable for the land type and growing conditions. While there is a broad range of input use, yields, and profitability for crop production, only a selection of competing crop returns are presented here; more complete comparisons can be found in background working papers (see Dorosh 1984a, 1984b, 1984c; Mink 1984a, 1984b; Perry 1984a).

To avoid ambiguity in the meaning of crop profit in Tables 3.2 through 3.6, two calculations are presented in each cost-and-return table. Profit I is the value of output less cash costs (for hired labor, fertilizer, pesticides, seed, and taxes). It represents the return to land, family labor, capital, and management. Profit II is Profit I less wages for family labor (imputed at 50 to 80 percent of the region's prevailing wage for hired labor) and gives the return to land, management, and capital. Profit II probably comes closer to farmers' rough calculations of returns to a crop. Farmers usually have a precise idea of cash outlays for a crop and have at least a general idea of the relative labor intensity of various crops. In the profit calculations shown in Tables 3.2 through 3.6, input and output prices have been allowed to differ by site and season to reflect prices in markets located in the various survey regions. Appendix table A3.1 summarizes the values used.

Multiple Corn Crop *Tegal* System

The largest corn cropping system in Indonesia, which comprises about 55 percent of the area planted in corn each year, is on rain-fed land, where two or three corn crops a year may be included in the crop rotation. It is a heterogeneous grouping and encompasses diverse soil types, climatic zones, altitudes and preferences for corn color. But it is fairly uniform in its suitability for long-duration varieties and the nature of its water constraints.

Although corn may be planted three crop seasons a year in this system, by far the most hectarage is planted in the first rainy season. As shown in Figure 3.1, a region's potential to grow corn in the dry (third) season declines in relation to seasonal decreases in rainfall. In particularly dry parts of the country, crops with lower water requirements, such as hot red peppers, are planted instead of corn or the fields are left fallow.

Longer-duration varieties, which have higher yield potential than fast-maturing traditional seeds, have done well in this system, and varieties that require 95 and even more than 100 days are increasingly popular for the major crop grown in the first season. Some farmers also plant a long-duration variety for the second season before they shift to a short-maturity, local seed for the dry (third) season. Use of longer-duration varieties

FIGURE 3.1. *Typical monthly rainfall and cropping patterns in multiple corn crop* tegal *systems*

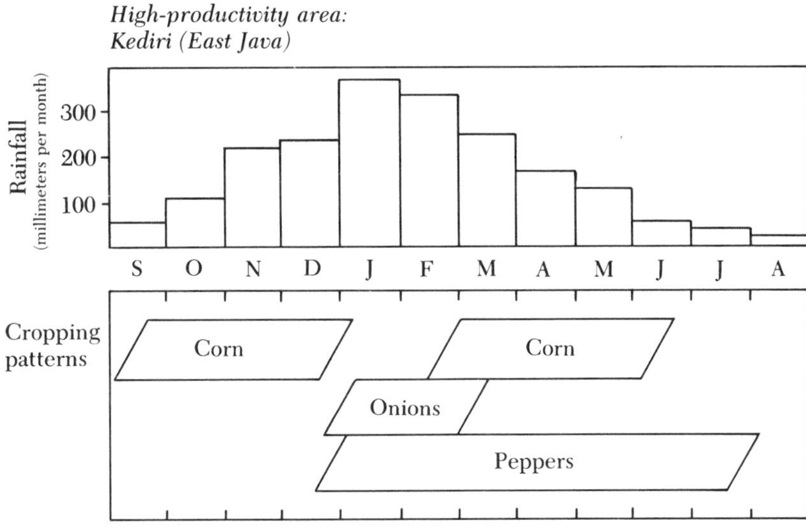

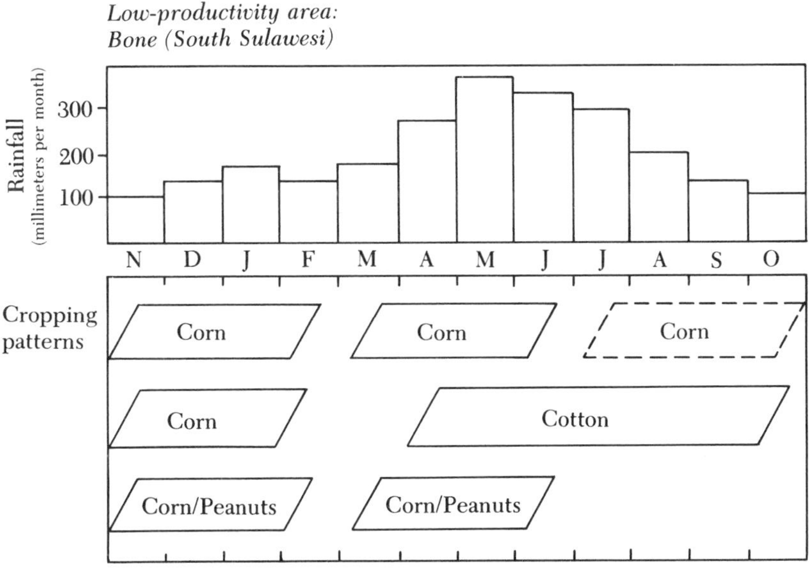

TABLE 3.2. *Costs and returns for multiple corn crop* tegal *systems: high productivity*

Location	Malang			Kediri			Karo		Asahan	
Planting season Crop	Oct corn	Feb corn	June corn	Oct corn non-hybrid	Oct corn hybrid	Jan corn/pepper/ onions	Sept and Feb corn	Aug/Sept upland rice	Sept and Feb corn	June/July upland rice
Labor use (days)[a]										
Male	76	64	58	44	69	163	41	101	52	143
Female	8	8	9	5	14	131	1	7	7	6
Hired labor (percent)	52	55	53	79	92	76	11	38	57	76
Bullock power (pair per day)	22	13	8	17	13	—	—	—	—	—
Tractor power (days)	—	—	—	—	—	—	1	1	1	1
Fertilizer (kilograms)[b]										
Urea	356	366	352	358	401	355	217	184	153	147
Ammonium sulfate	14	14	20	7	16	666	—	—	—	—
TSP	1	1	—	77	108	317	235	232	160	186
KCl	—	—	—	1	19	7	—	—	—	—
Manure	8,700	—	—	7,800	—	—	10	10	—	—

Non-labor cash costs							71	74	76	80
(000 Rp)										
Fertilizer	32	33	32	51	47	93				
Seed	8	8	8	4	33	423				
Pesticides	1	1	1	1	—	45				
Taxes	2	2	2	1	2	3				
Other	2	—	—	—	—	—				
Yields										
(tons per hectare)										
Corn	2.28	1.90	1.57	3.10	5.50	1.30	3.02	—	3.00	—
Peppers	—	—	—	—	—	2.27	—	—	—	—
Onions	—	—	—	—	—	2.83	—	—	—	—
Rice[c]	—	—	—	—	—	—	—	1.87	—	2.35
Total output value (000 Rp)	267	228	196	285	563	2,072	281	318	252	404
Profit I (000 Rp)[d]	159	148	127	168	402	1,310	203	170	136	187
Profit II (000 Rp)	130	122	99	155	398	1,259	147	82	105	153
Sample size	21	20	12	13	5	9	8	7	20	9

NOTES: Costs are for a single season and include inputs for intercrops, wherever these exist. Returns include value of intercrops. All values are on a per hectare basis.

[a]Workdays for labor, animal traction, and tractors have been standardized to an 8-hour day. Across survey sites, the workday for human labor ranged from 5 to 8 hours, draft animals were usually worked 4 hours, and tractor needs were 3 hours per hectare.

[b]The major fertilizers used in Indonesia by principal nutrient are: nitrogen (urea and ammonium sulfate), potassium (KCl), and phosphorus (TSP).

[c]Yield figures for rice refer to milled output unless otherwise stated.

[d]Profit I is return to land, family labor, capital, and management. It is defined as value of output cash costs (wage labor and non-labor inputs). Profit II is the return to land, management, and capital. It is defined as Profit I less imputed costs of family labor.

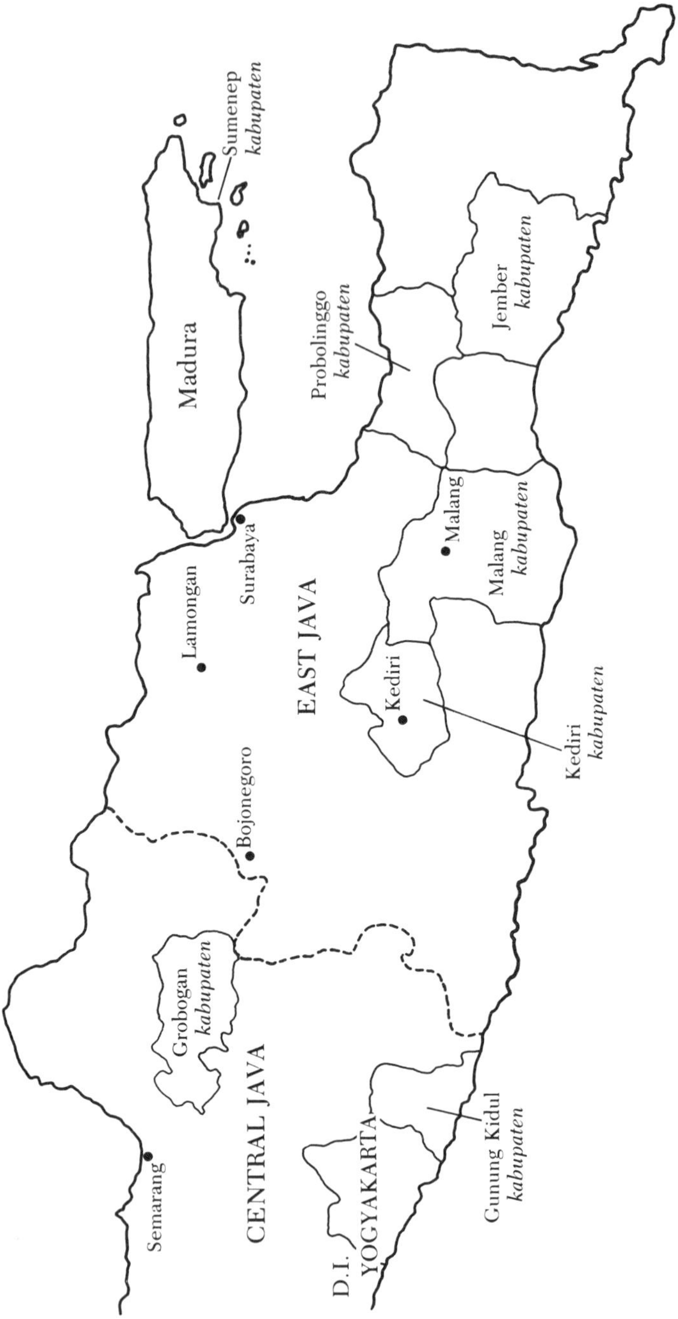

FIGURE 3.2. *Corn-producing areas on Java and Madura*

during the second season may be limited if a region's dry season is long, in which case a short-duration variety is planted in both the second and third seasons or the dry season crop is dropped. In Karo in North Sumatra and North Sulawesi, a bimodal rainfall pattern allows long-duration varieties to be grown in both rainy seasons.

High-Productivity Areas

Corn area in the high-productivity subsystem is about 16 percent of total corn plantings. Concentrations are located in East Java (see Figure 3.2), along with pockets in the Karo and lowland areas of North Sumatra. Survey results for these areas are shown in Table 3.2. Farmers are rapidly switching from traditional to longer-duration, improved varieties such as Arjuna and Harapan-6. These seeds generally provide the best yields as long as fertilizer use is near recommended levels. Since there is a broad range of growing environments and management practices, however, it is not surprising that the new varieties in some places do little better than improved local varieties, particularly if fertilizer applications are low. This performance of currently available varieties is not as important in the long run as the demonstrated willingness of farmers in these productive areas to experiment with longer-duration varieties and higher levels of fertilizer use. They are looking for appropriate crop technologies that improve their returns.

Low-Productivity Areas

Low-productivity, multiple corn crop areas comprise about 39 percent of annual corn plantings. Most of them are located in Indonesia's two major white corn regions—Central Java's highlands and South Sulawesi—although the yellow corn systems of Madura and other parts of East Java are also included. Figure 3.1 illustrates the rainfall and cropping patterns for the region of Bone in South Sulawesi (see Figure 3.3), and Table 3.3 presents the survey results.

Central Java is included in this low-productivity group because of the likely limits to future gains in yields. Through the end of the 1970s, the area kept pace with the yield increases of East Java largely because of increased fertilizer use. But farmers have not responded enthusiastically to government production programs that require use of improved yellow varieties. The local white varieties do not respond well to larger applications of fertilizer, and thus it is difficult to increase yields. Unlike producers of yellow corn, who have a range of improved varieties from which to choose, farmers who grow white corn are increasingly at a disadvantage. The narrow choice of improved white seeds is a barrier to increased production also in South Sulawesi. Farmers in these areas will not be able

FIGURE 3.3. *Major corn-producing* kabupaten *in South Sulawesi*

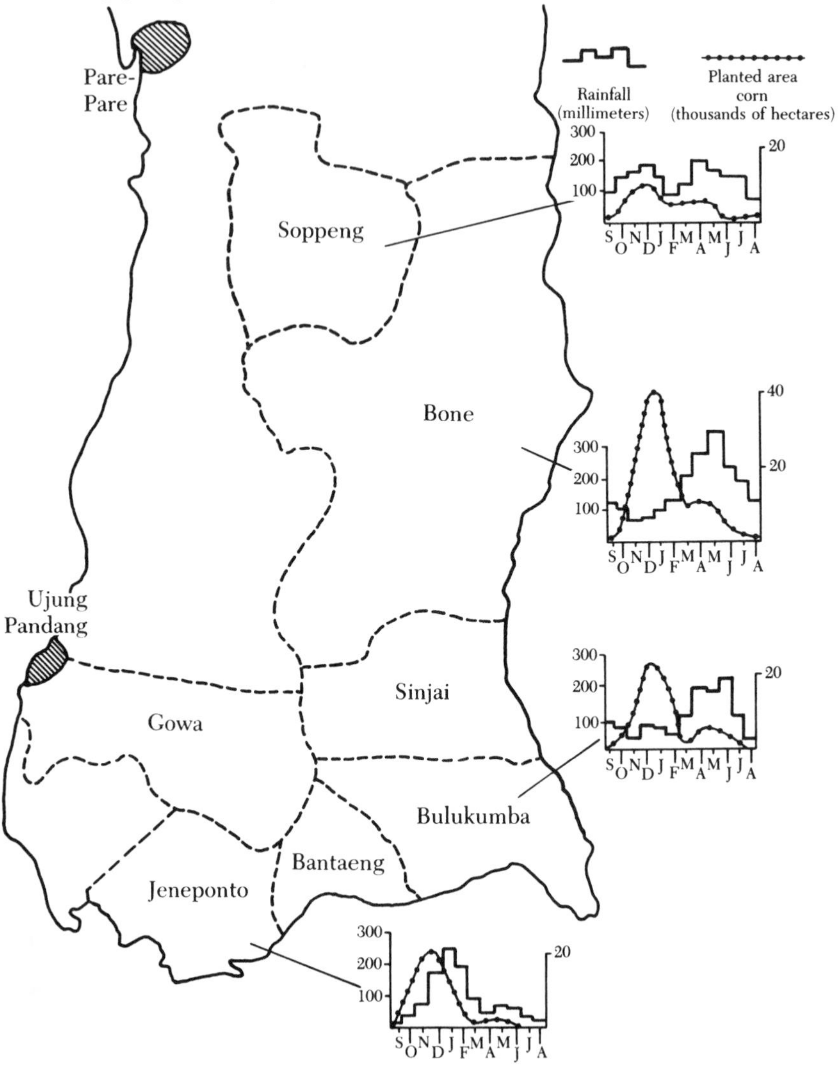

to match East Java's decreased costs of production so long as they continue planting the local white varieties currently available.

Throughout the white corn, multiple-cropped areas, varietal use need not be restricted to short-duration varieties. Although most local white varieties in use at low altitude require 90 days or less, rotations are flexible enough to accommodate varieties up to 10 days longer without difficulty. In fact, in pockets of South Sulawesi, where crop calendars are

TABLE 3.3. *Costs and returns for a multiple corn crop* tegal *system: low productivity*

Location	Bone					
Planting Season Crop	Nov corn	Mar corn	Nov corn/peanuts	Mar corn/peanuts	Mar and June corn/mung beans	Mar cotton
Labor use (days)						
Male	65	46	67	40	67	99
Female	18	18	33	22	40	15
Hired labor (percent)	11	9	29	28	15	7
Bullock power (pair per day)	5	—	5	3	2	2
Fertilizer (kilograms)						
Urea	49	61	80	78	63	50
Ammonium sulfate	—	—	—	—	—	100
TSP	—	—	—	—	—	100
Non-labor cash costs (000 Rp)						
Fertilizer	4	6	7	7	6	23
Seed	1	1	21	21	6	3
Pesticides	—	—	—	2	2	18
Taxes	1	1	1	1	1	4
Yields (tons per hectare)						
Corn	1.05	0.75	1.60	0.75	0.60	—
Peanuts	—	—	0.50	0.30	—	—
Mung beans	—	—	—	—	0.06	—
Cotton	—	—	—	—	—	0.70
Total output value (000 Rp)	84	60	167	88	71	197
Profit I (000 Rp)	56	45	101	52	43	142
Profit II (000 Rp)	−16	−11	31	8	−9	39
Sample size	19	10	5	4	8	14

representative of much of that province's corn region, farmers have shifted without trouble to yellow varieties that require 95 days or more.

For the white corn areas, it appears that much of the current reluctance to shift to yellow varieties has resulted from past difficulties in marketing corn of this color. The local markets supply corn to consumers who strongly prefer white corn, and buyers for feed from other regions have been slow to build up contacts with farmers since it is easier to bulk large lots of yellow corn elsewhere. But where market channels are developing, producers of white corn seem to be slowly shifting to yellow varieties. Most of the farmers in South Sulawesi who are growing yellow corn mention the development of assured feed demand from urban poultry raisers as a major factor in their switch. This changeover is generally not complete; farm households estimate their home consumption and continue to plant enough white corn to meet this need and plant the remaining land in yellow corn for sale. Whether the ongoing growth of the feed industry will cause a general shift to yellow varieties in these areas is not yet clear.

Costs, Returns, and Alternative Crops

As shown in Tables 3.2 and 3.3, in high-productivity areas the returns from growing monoculture corn exceed those in low-productivity areas by more than Rp 100,000 per hectare, and the intercropped system in the third season in Kediri is the most profitable of all. Profit II for monoculture corn in Malang ranges from Rp 99,000 to Rp 130,000 per hectare, whereas in Bone, returns are marginally negative once imputed costs of family labor are included. Continued cultivation of corn under such circumstances suggests that opportunity costs of family labor are significantly below the reported local wage rates.

The difference in return is partly due to more intensive use of inputs. Total fertilizer use is uniformly high in the more productive areas and averages over 350 kilograms per hectare for locations in East Java. The mix varies by region: applications are almost entirely urea in East Java, whereas phosphorus (triple superphosphate, or TSP) is used more extensively on soils in the outer islands. Fertilizer trials have shown that many of Java's soils have a low response to phosphorus, and thus urea is a more appropriate fertilizer. Application of fertilizer is quite efficient, and farmers are well aware of the importance of timing and placement. In many low-productivity areas of South Sulawesi, however, fertilizer use on corn began only in the late 1970s. By the mid-1980s, farmers applied less than 50 kilograms of urea per hectare on average and even less TSP. These rates are well below those that give optimal returns, even if local corn varieties are used. Farmers are still learning what yield responses can be achieved under various growing conditions. Compared with high-productivity areas, other factors such as more limited opportunities to market corn and a less developed private market for fertilizer also constrain fertilizer use. In addition, year-to-year variations in corn yields may be more substantial in the low-productivity areas, thus leading to more risk in using large amounts of fertilizer. The surveys were unable to measure the degree of yield variations.

Total labor input is in the range of 50 to 85 workdays per hectare for monoculture corn. The exception is in Karo, North Sumatra, where tractors are used for land preparation and only 42 workdays per hectare are used. The difference between labor use in Malang and Bone is not large, despite extensive use of draft animals in Malang for land preparation and seeding, which normally would allow savings on labor. But Malang's higher yields are associated with use of more labor to apply fertilizer, to weed, and to harvest.

Yields of monoculture stands in the first crop season range from 2.3 to 3.1 tons per hectare in high-productivity areas, while low-productivity areas obtain yields of about 1 ton. In high-productivity areas, best yields from local, 90-day varieties are about 2.5 tons per hectare, although longer-duration varieties usually have higher yields (see Dorosh 1984a). In East Java, a subsample of Kediri farmers who used a new, 105-day hybrid obtained an average of 5.5 tons per hectare for the first-season crop.

Some farmers plant the second corn crop at the peak of the heavy rains, but others delay the second planting until the rains begin to moderate because they attribute reduced yields to too much moisture. A further decline in yield in the dry (third) season is due to drought stress. The poor performance of corn in the second and third seasons induces farmers to seek replacement crops. In Bone, cotton growing has been spreading since its introduction by the government in 1979, and the crop tolerates dry weather well. Even though cotton replaces two *palawija* crops, its returns are higher. Cotton has also been promoted as a dry-season crop on poorer soils in parts of Central and East Java and Nusa Tenggara Timur.

The returns from corn grown in monoculture stands cannot compare, however, with those from systems possible at higher altitudes where monoculture vegetables, or vegetables intercropped with corn, can be grown. The Kediri intercrop of corn, red peppers, and onions is representative of a range of alternatives to corn. Other major examples are potatoes in parts of Malang and cabbage on the Dieng Plateau of Central Java. These are highly profitable crops, although they are risky and require very intensive use of labor and purchased inputs. In Kediri the cost of pesticides, fertilizer, and seeds alone can exceed the gross value of a normal corn crop, and labor inputs can be three times as great. For these crops to make major inroads on corn area, channels for marketing the output, farmers' access to resources, and their agronomic skills need to be well developed.

At slightly lower altitudes, fruit crops are often the major competition for corn. This is true both in high-productivity areas such as Malang, where smallholder papaya gardens have spread rapidly on rain-fed land since the late 1970s, and in low-productivity systems such as Jeneponto in South Sulawesi, where citrus plantings have increased dramatically.

Single Corn Crop *Tegal* System

The single corn crop system is found scattered throughout the Indonesian archipelago and occupies about 24 percent of total corn area. Its productivity can be either high or low, although the latter is more the case. A common feature is the intercropping of corn and cassava; farmers sow corn after the first rains and plant cassava a month later. After the corn harvest, the cassava stands alone in the field. Farmers occasionally interplant upland rice before the cassava and harvest the rice shortly after the corn. Legume crops may be sown after the cereals are harvested, and they continue growing with the cassava into the dry season.

This season is not constrained to use short-duration corn varieties. Where upland rice is included as an intercrop, its cycle of 120 days or more provides time for farmers to grow long-duration corn varieties and does not delay planting of subsequent, optional bean crops. In later stages of the rice crop, increased shading and competition for nutrients from corn are not major problems. Likewise, long-duration corn varieties can be used when corn and cassava are intercropped.

High-Productivity Areas

Centers of high-productivity are found in East Java and in the southern Sumatra province of Lampung, whose rainfall and cropping patterns are illustrated in Figure 3.4. Lampung's corn production declined sharply in the 1970s because of large losses to downy mildew, which were partly due to use of a nonresistant variety (Metro). But farmers have shifted land back into corn since 1980 when the Department of Agriculture began to distribute Harapan-6, a resistant variety. Although this variety requires 118 days to harvest in the Lampung environment, it has been readily accepted by farmers.

Low-Productivity Areas

The low-productivity single crop systems on rain-fed land are most concentrated on Java's southern coast, from D.I. Yogyakarta through

FIGURE 3.4. *Typical monthly rainfall and cropping patterns in single corn crop* tegal *systems*

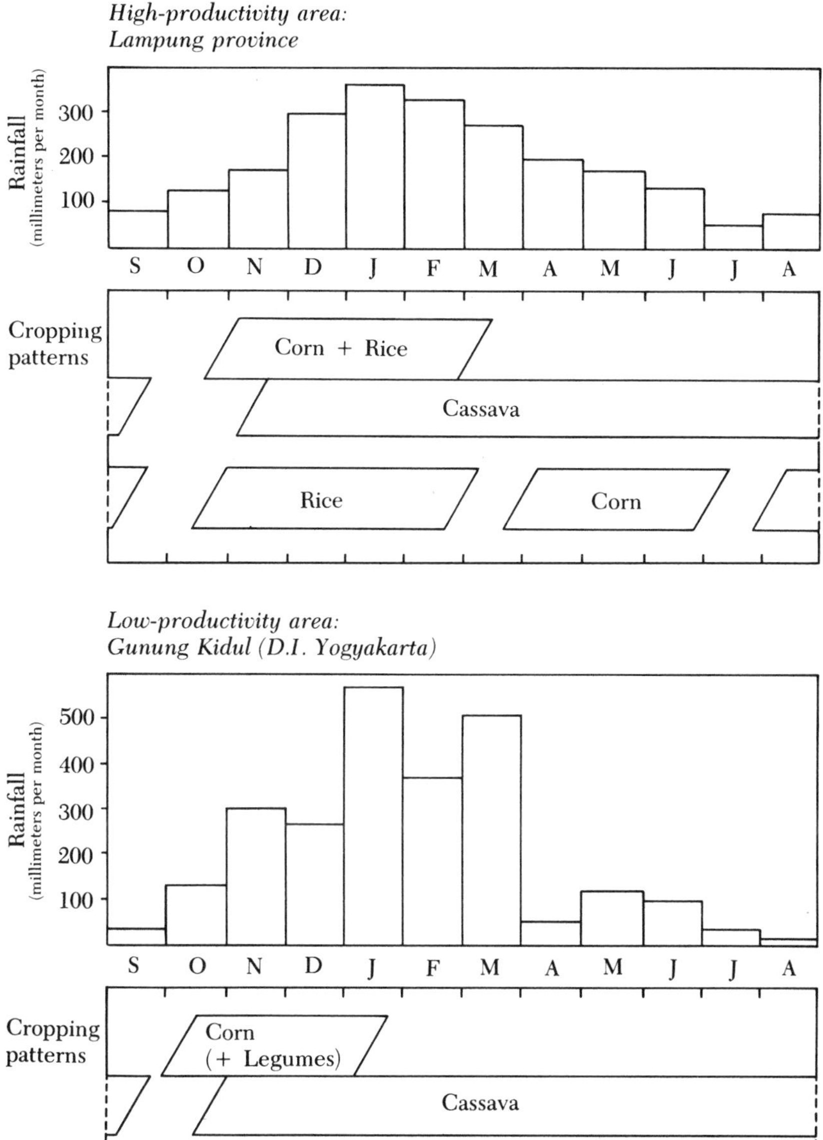

Central Java into East Java.[1] Examples exist elsewhere, such as on Madura and along the southeast coast of South Sulawesi. In Nusa Tenggara Timur, corn and cassava are intercropped as part of swidden agriculture. Figure 3.4 illustrates the rainfall and cropping patterns for one of these low-productivity systems, Gunung Kidul in the D.I. Yogyakarta region in south-central Java.

In these areas corn yields are very low even when allowance is made for reduced densities because of intercropping. Practically no fertilizer is applied, and soils are naturally poor or have become so through erosion. The light, limestone soils that predominate have very poor capacity for retaining water, and nutrients are rapidly leached out of the soil.

Costs, Returns, and Alternative Crops

As shown in Table 3.4, the corn and cassava intercrop system in high-productivity areas is reasonably profitable. But returns to this crop pattern of ten to twelve months do not compare favorably with returns to common crop rotations of similar duration in high-productivity areas of other production systems unless conditions permit the intercropping of upland rice as well. Returns from a corn-cassava intercrop in low-productivity areas, even with upland rice, are among the lowest for corn production systems anywhere in Indonesia.

In Gunung Kidul, yields of both corn and cassava are extremely low. Almost no fertilizer is used, and hillsides, both terraced and unterraced, have very poor soils due to erosion and rapid leaching. The high-productivity areas of Kediri and Lampung, where total fertilizer use is over 250 kilograms per hectare, have relatively stable yields of 0.8 and 1.7 tons per hectare, respectively, which are respectable in view of the lower corn densities of these intercropped systems.

Labor use differs sharply across regions of this system, with workdays ranging from 89 to 363 per hectare each season.[2] The main use of labor is to weed and harvest cassava. In Lampung, poorer soils reduce weeding, and cassava is harvested by using *borongon*, or piecework organized by traders. In Kediri, bullock-drawn harrows reduce the need for weeding labor, but harvesting is most frequently done with family labor. In Gunung Kidul, all labor needs are met within the family and are fairly evenly split between the sexes. The high labor input in the Kediri and Gunung Kidul regions significantly reduces profitability.

There are few crops to compete with corn, cassava, and upland rice in this system. Extension workers promote intensification by encouraging farmers to add upland rice to the corn-cassava intercrop where possible

[1]D.I. Yogyakarta is a special administrative district, which in this book is treated as a province.

[2]Results for Kediri and Gunung Kidul are adapted from Roche (1983).

TABLE 3.4. *Costs and returns for single corn crop* tegal *systems: high and low productivity*

Location	High productivity			Low Productivity	
	Lampung		Kediri[a]	Gunung Kidul[a]	
Planting Season Crop	Nov corn/cassava	Nov corn/cassava/ upland rice	Sept/Oct corn/cassava	Sept/Oct corn/cassava	Sept/Oct corn/cassava/ upland rice
Labor use (days)					
Male	75	77	239	189	224
Female	14	12	21	157	139
Hired labor (percent)	40	30	57	—	6
Bullock power (pair per day)	—	—	13	—	—
Fertilizer (kilograms)					
Urea	165	110	369	—	1
TSP	101	153	—	—	—
KCl	2	—	—	—	—
Manure	—	—	6,129	—	174
Non-labor cash costs (000 Rp)	34	34	49	2	5
Yields (tons per hectare)					
Corn	1.69	1.17	0.78	0.20	0.11
Cassava	9.86	10.60	16.44	2.64	2.27
Rice[b]	—	1.10	—	—	0.20
Total output value (000 Rp)	394	480	501	100	120
Profit I (000 Rp)	258	375	205	98	107
Profit II (000 Rp)	181	283	131	6	15
Sample size	10	7	27	4	13

[a]Data from Roche (1983).
[b]Milled output.

and to follow corn in the dry season with a fast-maturing bean crop, which is grown largely on residual moisture. Farmers can vary the planting densities in intercropping to favor the plant that offers the best return in any given year. Long-term investments in improving soils or in shifting to perennial crops on soils prone to erosion could benefit from targeted credit and extension programs. Otherwise, raising farm incomes to levels comparable to other regions will rest on government efforts to reduce population density through transmigration programs, which will allow remaining farmers to manage larger units. But in general, Gunung Kidul soils are too infertile to support more demanding crops. Even where tree crops such as clove, coconut, and banana are more profitable, most farmers cannot easily make the shift since they need the plot to provide the families' food needs before the tree crops become productive.

Rain-fed *Sawah* System

The rain-fed *sawah* system, which comprises about 10 percent of total corn area, predominates on the floodplains of the northern coast of Java between Semarang and Surabaya. It is also found on a limited basis in South Sulawesi, primarily on the inland plain around Lake Tempe. Lack of irrigation on this system's otherwise fertile soils limits rice to one crop a year, to the time of peak rainfall, which floods the level, bunded plains. Rains during the first and third crop seasons are insufficient to grow flooded rice, but they permit growing *palawija* crops on either end of the main rice crop, as shown in Figure 3.5. Hence, two corn crops per year are possible in this system, and the first is frequently intercropped.

Lack of water control prompts farmers to use very short-duration corn varieties of 75 to 80 days. The unpredictability of heavy rains and field flooding toward the end of the first season's corn intercrop presents a serious risk of crop loss, which would be even greater if farmers shifted from the local, 75-day variety to longer-duration, higher-yielding varieties. Furthermore, the onset of the dry season during the second corn crop requires the use of the short-duration local variety, since longer-duration varieties would need additional irrigation. Additional water is available only through onerous hand application from shallow, temporary field wells. It is highly unlikely that farmers in this *sawah* system will be able to take advantage of recently released, longer-duration corn varieties, which have the potential to improve yields. The inability so far to develop a very short-duration variety that is responsive to fertilizer adds to the difficulty of increasing productivity in this system.

Costs, Returns, and Alternative Crops

Returns to corn rotations on rain-fed *sawah* increase with the value of intercrops. Table 3.5 presents the survey results for Grobogan in Central

FIGURE 3.5. *Typical monthly rainfall and cropping pattern in a rain-fed* sawah *system*

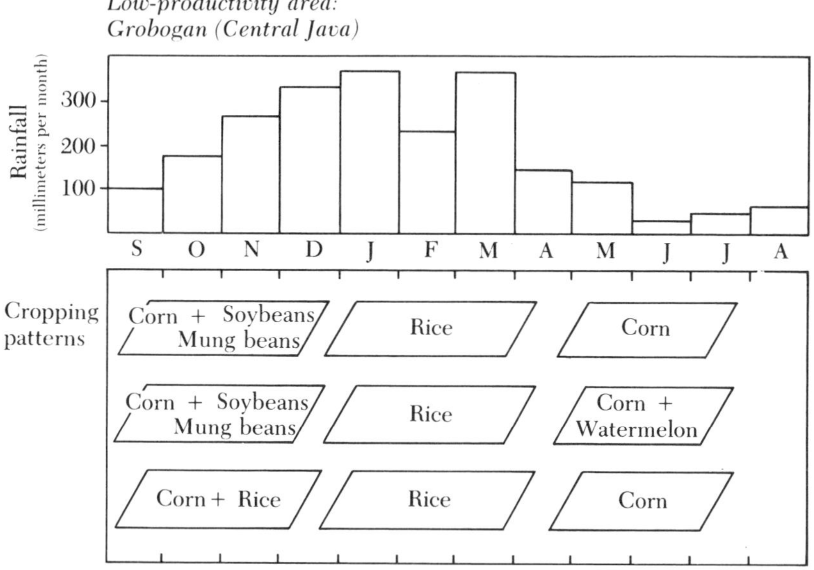

Java. Monoculture corn production, which is most common in the dry season, gives the lowest return among alternative crop selections in the Grobogan sample. As shown in the Profit II figure in Table 3.5, the farmer barely breaks even on the crop. The returns from the intercrop alternatives are higher and even compare favorably with those from other production systems, such as monoculture corn grown on *sawah* or high-productivity corn grown on rain-fed land. However, returns from the corn-soybean and corn-mung bean intercrops on rain-fed *sawah* entail higher risk because of the pests that attack bean crops.

Compared with other systems, fertilizer use is fairly low, but more tends to be used in the dry season. By applying fertilizer at that time, farmers run the risk of "root burn," but they minimize the risk by dissolving fertilizer in irrigation water. The low levels of application for the first season's crop may be connected to the risk of crop loss through flooding. Organic fertilizer, however, is applied more heavily in the first season because the onset of rain assures better decomposition and incorporation into the soil.

In Grobogan, total labor use on different crops varies between 116 and 222 days. Land preparation in the first season requires more labor because the soil is too dry and hard for animals to plow, and it is thus hoed manually. In the second season, oxen can be used. During the dry condi-

TABLE 3.5. *Costs and returns for a rain-fed* sawah *corn system*

Location Planting Season Crop	Grobogan Sept/Oct corn/soybean	 Sept/Oct corn/mung bean	 Sept/Oct corn/rice	 May/June corn/melon	 May/June corn
Labor use (days)					
Male	135	100	166	97	111
Female	42	16	56	40	16
Hired labor (percent)	26	53	47	38	27
Bullock power (pair per day)	—	1	—	2	7
Fertilizer (kilograms)					
Urea	65	23	507	158	127
TSP	12	16	78	88	67
Manure	455	585	2,409	278	197
Non-labor cash costs (000 Rp)					
Fertilizer	7	4	53	22	18
Seed	18	9	10	10	2
Pesticides	4	3	4	4	—
Taxes	1	1	1	1	1
Yields (tons per hectare)					
Corn	0.96	1.11	0.45	1.03	0.96
Soybeans	0.57	—	—	—	—
Mung beans	—	0.36	—	—	—
Melon seeds	—	—	—	0.36	—
Rice (*gabah*)[a]	—	—	4.41	—	—
Total output value (000 Rp)	296	232	442	396	120
Profit I (000 Rp)	229	164	291	315	65
Profit II (000 Rp)	151	132	212	264	9
Sample size	23	7	2	9	16

[a]*Gabah*, or unhulled rice, converts to milled rice at a ratio of 1:0.65.

tions of the second season, labor is needed for burdensome hand irrigation, but weeding requirements are somewhat reduced. Labor inputs specifically for the bean or melon crop—planting, spraying, harvesting, and processing—account for 20 to 40 workdays out of the total. Planting and harvesting in the intercrop systems are the major activities that involve "hired" labor, which in Grobogan consists mostly of *gotong royong* (exchange labor).

When corn is grown as a monoculture or intercropped with beans, corn yields are consistently 1 ton per hectare in both growing seasons. Similar spacing of plants in the two cases contributes to this result; even without a bean intercrop, corn is not planted more densely in the dry season due to the drier growing conditions and the need for hand irrigation. The exception is for a rice-corn intercrop, in which corn seeds are spaced farther apart to favor the growth of rice, which is a preferred staple over corn in the farm household's own consumption.

The prospects are poor for improving corn yields in this system, and farmers are on the lookout for potentially more profitable crops.[3] The choice of crop to intercrop with corn depends largely on rainfall. In the first season, rainfall is adequate for either soybeans or mung beans. Of the two, mung beans mature about 15 days faster and are used especially in areas where the risk of late season flooding is greater. In higher areas, a new longer-duration soybean variety which gives higher yields has been distributed through a government intensification program. But neither of the bean crops currently replaces corn area or reduces corn density in intercrop plantings. Major pest problems with bean crops have yet to be resolved, and unlike corn, beans do not provide a starchy staple for the farm household.

A recently introduced and quickly expanding crop for the first season is *padi gogo rancah*. Farmers directly seed the rice on land that is subject to flooding by heavy, late season rains. This practice has become feasible since the development of short-duration rice varieties suitable to areas where early rains are likely and soils retain moisture. Farmers thus have reduced risks and costs of reseeding the rice. It might be possible for this technique to expand into much of the corn area in the first season, but it is too recent an innovation for firm projections to be made.

The choice of intercrops in the dry season also depends on soil mois-

[3]Corn hectarage might well decline in Grobogan in the 1990s. As part of the JRATUN-SELUNA watershed district irrigation development plans, Grobogan is slated to receive 7,400 hectares of technical irrigation by the end of the Fourth Development Plan in 1988. The Department of Agriculture's policy is to use water distribution to restrict the annual crop rotation on irrigated land to two rice crops, followed by a *palawija* crop. Some farmers will nevertheless try to replace the *palawija* crop with a rice crop, dependent on residual moisture and rainfall. Thus Grobogan could lose somewhere between 7,400 and 14,800 hectares of corn plantings to rice.

ture. On low, heavier soils, moisture from the water table is occasionally sufficient for melons, which are grown for their profitable seeds (*kwaci*). The dry season is more severe in the eastern part of this system on Java, and sorghum, a more drought-tolerant crop, is often interplanted with corn. Investment in dry-season irrigation would significantly alter the crop pattern, but prospecting for ground water has confirmed that supplies are inadequate for major tube-well irrigation projects. Portable pumps may be feasible, but they are more likely to be used to pump water to irrigate specialty or bean crops rather than corn.

Irrigated *Sawah* System

Corn area on irrigated *sawah* accounts for about 11 percent of total corn plantings. This system is in use almost entirely on Java, with concentrations in East Java's *kabupatens* Kediri, Malang, Jember, and Probolinggo. Figure 3.6 illustrates the rainfall and cropping patterns of Kediri and Malang. Over 20 percent of crop area classified as irrigated *sawah* in these areas is generally planted in corn, and in Kediri the figure rises to 50 percent. As shown in Table 3.6, the *sawah* system has the most intensive use of inputs of any corn production system in Indonesia, and yields are twice the national average. Corn is grown as a monoculture, fertilizer applications often exceed recommended rates, use of improved yellow varieties is common, and irrigation is provided.

The degree of water control and availability determines whether corn is grown once or twice in this *sawah* system. Flooding for rice is assured only in the first season for much of Malang and Kediri, where the rice crop is followed by two corn seasons. Where better water control permits two rice harvests, only one corn crop is grown. It is not unusual to find a dry-season corn crop on *sawah* that is technically irrigated (with full water control), which could grow three rice crops a year.[4] In systems with technical irrigation, the Department of Agriculture often reduces water supplies to farmers in the dry season to permit canal maintenance and to control pest build-up through enforced breaks in continuous rice cultivation. Residual moisture and limited irrigation supply are sufficient for corn and various competitive *palawija* and vegetable crops.

On *sawah*, farmers have to a large extent shifted to 100-day, improved corn varieties such as Arjuna and Harapan-6 for one or both crops. The introduction of short-duration rice varieties in the 1970s made this possible. The choice of rice variety determines the time available for the other two crop seasons. For instance, use of the rice variety Cisadane, a longer-

[4]Technical irrigation provides maximum control over water flows by using a reliable source year-round and equipping each parcel with an independent inlet and drainage outlet.

FIGURE 3.6. *Typical monthly rainfall and cropping patterns in irrigated* sawah *systems*

High-productivity areas:
Kediri (East Java)

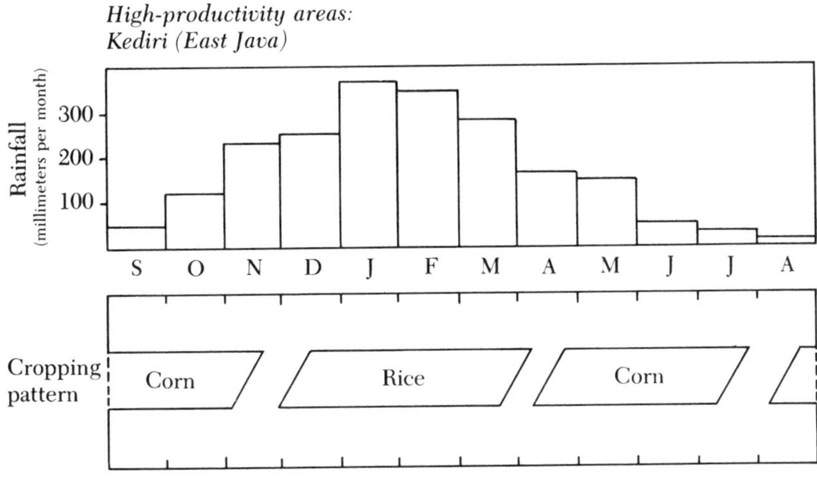

Malang (East Java)

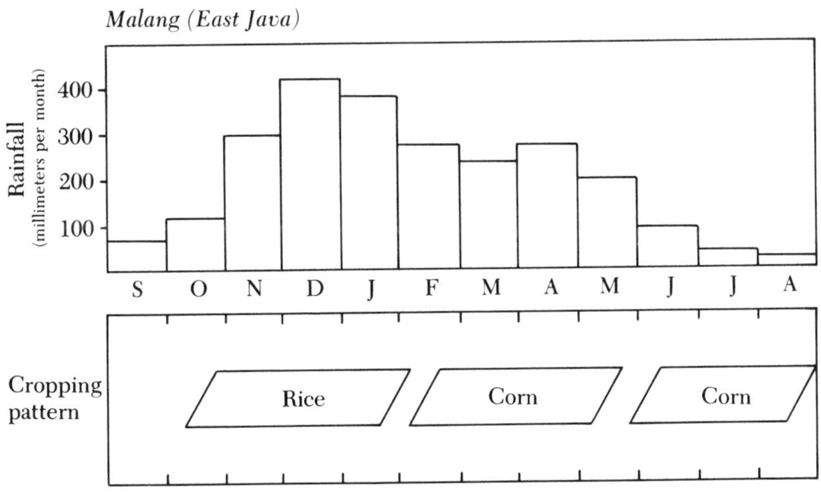

TABLE 3.6. *Cost and returns for irrigated* sawah *corn systems*

Location	Malang		Kediri	
Planting Season Crop	Feb corn	June corn	Apr corn	Aug corn
Labor use (days)				
Male	127	121	82	68
Female	15	19	5	7
Bullock power (pair per day)	26	15	26	20
Fertilizer (kilograms)				
Urea	660	614	454	438
TSP	10	13	27	24
Ammonium sulfate	26	30	7	0
Manure	—	—	—	—
Non-labor cash costs (000 Rp)				
Fertilizer	59	61	42	36
Seed	9	8	4	4
Pesticides	1	1	1	1
Taxes	4	4	2	2
Yields (tons per hectare)				
Corn	3.29	3.14	2.40	2.60
Total output value (000 Rp)	383	383	272	306
Profit I (000 Rp)	164	183	117	161
Profit II (000 Rp)	155	178	100	144
Sample size	14	10	10	9

duration high-yielding variety preferred for its taste, makes it difficult to squeeze in two long-duration corn crops, although two corn plantings—one long-duration, followed by a short-duration local variety—fit the crop calendar. After choosing a shorter-duration rice variety such as IR 36, farmers usually grow two improved, long-duration corn varieties. How the recently released, 105-day hybrid may fit into the rotation is still uncertain, since farmers have little experience with it. It will be used at least for the first corn crop following rice. Discussions with farmers owning *sawah* make it clear that experimentation with longer-duration, higher-yielding corn varieties in the crop rotation has only recently begun. But the switch to corn varieties of 100 days or more has already proven possible and profitable, and the trend will continue.

Costs, Returns, and Alternative Crops

Returns to land, management, and capital (Profit II) range between Rp 100,000 to Rp 178,000 hectare, and the average is not much higher than net returns from high-productivity systems on rain-fed land. This result is partly explained by the barely sufficient availability of irrigation water in the dry season on *sawah*, whereas high-productivity rain-fed land receives plenty of rainfall in the first planting season. Yields in the two seasons are thus quite similar.

High fertilizer applications and widespread use of improved corn varieties contribute to yields that range from 2.4 to 3.3 tons per hectare. Use of 450 to 650 kilograms of urea per hectare is in fact well above recommended rates based on fertilizer trials, and these high rates may be attributable to farmers' calculations of the fodder value of plants thinned out from purposely dense plantings. Farmers might also lack efficient application methods or compensate for fertilizer losses through runoff of irrigation water. Although yields from *sawah* are generally high, they are quite variable. *Sawah* yields in Kediri are below not only those in Malang but also those from Kediri's systems on rain-fed land.

Total labor use on *sawah* systems is 75 to 142 workdays. The small size of some *sawah* plots precludes the use of bullocks for land preparation and weeding, and labor needs are therefore slightly higher than those for plots on rain-fed land (*tegal*), which are larger. Land preparation in the first season, even with bullocks, takes longer because the soil is still wet and heavy. Remaining rice stubble is difficult to plow under, and thus total labor needs are greater for the first corn crop than for the second crop, in which land preparation is often minimal. Work by women, who mostly plant and harvest, represents about 10 percent of total labor use.

Much nonfamily labor is used to grow corn on *sawah*, and the types of arrangements are of greater variety than those in other systems. In Malang, almost one-half of the *sawah* farmers in the sample who use nonfamily labor provide inputs to sharecroppers who do all the manual labor and receive 20 percent of the harvest as payment. For the other half, wage labor predominates, and farmers pay harvest laborers for piecework or by the hour. Some farmers simply sell mature standing crops to merchants who organize work crews for harvesting on their own accounts. Noncash arrangements such as *gotong royong* (exchange labor) or in-kind payments are becoming rare as this *sawah* system becomes increasingly commercial.

The diversity of Indonesia's corn production environment cannot be overemphasized. This chapter has categorized this diversity in terms of broad production systems, highlighting agronomic and economic differences, whereas Chapter 1 used commercialization as an organizing theme. The economics of input use are examined in the next chapter, and an understanding of the diversity of the corn systems is essential background to the economic analysis. For government policies that are intended to have a country-wide impact, as with fertilizer pricing or the support price for corn, the diversity of corn systems will cause farmers to have widely varying responses, even when they are in the same geographical region. Increased commercialization tends to make responses somewhat more homogeneous because household characteristics and preferences play less of a role. Even in fully commercial corn operations, however, the diversity of soil types, water availability, altitudes, and alternative potential crop choices can lead to a wide range of responses to apparently uniform policy changes. Chapter 4 examines this range of potential responses and attempts to provide rough guidelines to aggregate response of corn farmers to key pricing changes.

TABLE A3.1. *Price assumptions for calculating costs and returns, 1982–1983*

	Malang	Kediri	Grobogan	Gunung Kidul	Bone	Lampung	Karo	Asahan
Output prices (rupiahs per kilogram)								
Corn	120	105/120[a]	100/125[a]	105	80	95	93	84
Rice (*gabah*)			90		130	125	170	172
Peanuts				200	80			
Melon seed			750					
Onions		350						
Mung beans			340		400			
Peppers		400						
Gaplek		30		30	45	23		
Cotton					280			
Tobacco					1,098			
Soybeans			350					
Input prices								
Seed (rupiahs per kilogram)								
Corn			120		80	186	141	135
Rice (*gabah*)			285		140	185	248	256
Peanuts					100			
Soybeans			500					
Mung beans			680		400			
Cotton					125			
Melon			1,500					
Tobacco (rupiahs per seedling)					2			
Labor (rupiahs per 8 hours)								
Nonfamily: M	720	880	800	400	1,300	2,880	2,020	1,575
F	640	800	800	300	1,300			
Family[b]: M		660	600	300	975	1,440	2,020	1,575
F		600	600	220	975			
Bullock (pair per 8 hours)	2,720	1,920	3,000	2,000	2,000	6,167		
Fertilizer (rupiahs per kilogram)	85	85	90	90	90	90	90	90
Pesticide (rupiahs per liter)					1,500	1,500	1,500	1,500
Interest (percent per month)	10	10	10		2	10	10	10
Tractor (rupiahs per 8 hours)							110,174	112,613

SOURCE: Dorosh, Mink, and Perry (1984).
[a]First-season harvest price/other-season harvest price.
[b]Imputed cost.

4. The Economics of Input Use

Stephen D. Mink

In most of Indonesia's corn production systems, farmers have an increasingly wider choice of inputs for growing corn. A variety of fertilizers and pesticides is usually available at reasonable prices; two-wheel tractors, which are sold through private channels and supported by adequate servicing, are increasingly visible in rural areas; new seed varieties are appearing yearly; and government programs are beginning to promote use of lime on acid soils. Farmers' selection of inputs and levels of use differ dramatically across the corn-producing regions, and these decisions affect yields and Indonesia's total corn production. This chapter focuses on analyzing the economic factors behind these choices and discusses some of the aggregate consequences for the agricultural sector.

Fertilizer Use

The economics of fertilizer use for corn production can be pieced together into a nearly complete, but still unfinished, picture. The first part of this chapter presents evidence on aggregate fertilizer use for corn and marginal physical output response to fertilizer at current levels of use, under reasonable assumptions about fertilizer prices and the price elasticity of demand for fertilizer by corn farmers. This information is used to estimate the likely shifts in fertilizer use and corn output if fertilizer prices change—particularly if the subsidy to farmers for fertilizer, which was in place in the mid-1980s, is lifted in favor of a price policy that would allow domestic fertilizer prices to rise to levels more in line with prices on world markets.

Aggregate use of fertilizer on corn is shown in Table 4.1. Average fertilizer applications per hectare are taken from annual agricultural surveys conducted by the Central Bureau of Statistics, the last of which was published in 1981. In that year, total use of fertilizer on corn was 339,825 metric tons, or about 12 percent of the total use for all food crops. Although the aggregate figure includes urea, triple superphosphate (TSP), potassium chloride, and several other minor fertilizers, it is largely urea that is used. On Java, 90 percent of fertilizer applied to corn in 1980 was urea.

The increase in corn production which results from additional fertilizer use (or marginal physical product) depends critically on field-level variables—corn variety, absolute levels of fertilizer use, management tech-

TABLE 4.1. *Fertilizer use on corn, Indonesia*

Year	Area harvested (000 hectares)	Fertilizer per hectare[a] (kilograms)	Total fertilizer on corn (tons)	Total nutrients on corn (tons)	Total nutrients on food crops (tons)	Share of nutrients used on corn (percent)
1970	2,938	21.9	64,349	28,957	197,000	14.7
1971	2,652	31.1	82,471	37,112	244,400	15.2
1972	2,160	32.3	69,770	31,396	308,100	10.2
1973	3,433	25.0	85,829	38,623	379,200	10.2
1974	2,667	40.2	107,208	48,244	393,300	12.3
1975	2,445	44.6	109,041	49,068	422,600	11.6
1976	2,095	48.7	102,029	45,913	415,600	11.0
1977	2,567	52.7	135,281	60,876	556,800	10.9
1978	3,025	55.2	166,959	75,131	617,600	12.2
1979	2,594	43.7	113,341	51,004	698,700	7.3
1980	2,735	76.2	208,402	93,781	1,012,200	9.3
1981	2,955	115.0	339,825	152,921	1,240,600	12.3
1982	2,061	NA	NA	NA	1,364,700	—

SOURCES: For area harvested: Indonesia, Central Bureau of Statistics, *Statistical Pocketbook of Indonesia*, various years. For fertilizer per hectare: Indonesia, Central Bureau of Statistics, "Agricultural Census," various years. For total nutrients for food crops: Harvard Institute for International Development (1983).

[a]Figures for fertilizer per hectare are calculated by dividing total use of fertilizer on corn by the area harvested.

niques such as fertilizer placement, and limiting factors such as soil and climate. Table 4.2 presents a sample of results from five of the study's survey sites. Several factors contribute to the differences in marginal physical product, which range from 1.4 to 4.7 units (kilograms) of additional corn output per unit of urea. One is the differing rates of improved and local seeds in use by region. Seed type is important because corn varieties differ in the efficiency with which they use fertilizer. In contrast to improved seeds, the yield response of local varieties to fertilizer is lower and levels off at lower rates of application.

Use of fertilizer on corn is new for farmers in many areas of Indonesia; for them to apply economically optimal amounts, they need to experiment with fertilizer and gain experience. In theory, profit-oriented farmers are expected, as a simple approximation, to increase the use of an input until the cost of an additional unit no longer results in an increase in output sufficient in value to pay for that unit of input. By this logic, farmers with the same production environment and seeds, who face the same input and output prices, through profit seeking, should end up at similar levels of input use and marginal physical products. This result is less likely in a real-world setting where farmers do not have equal experience using an input. East Java farmers with over a decade of experience using several types of fertilizer on a number of corn varieties confidently use high levels of fertilizer, whereas South Sulawesi farmers have had fertilizer available for corn only since 1979 and are still cautious in its use.

TABLE 4.2. *Marginal physical product and management choices*

Location	Marginal physical product[a]	Average fertilizer use (kilograms per hectare)	Predominant corn variety
East Java, Malang	1.4	462	improved
East Java, Kediri	2.8	464	improved
Central Java, Grobogan	2.1	194	local
West Sumatra	4.7	267	local/improved
South Sulawesi, Bone	3.3	51	local

SOURCES: Dorosh (1984a, 1984b); Mink (1984a, 1984b); Perry (1984a).
[a]Output of shelled corn per unit of extra urea applied.

If farmers face different prices for the output, they will adjust levels of inputs in such a way that marginal physical products may diverge. Fertilizer prices are fairly uniform across Indonesia, but the prices that farmers receive for corn can vary. Surplus-producing areas off Java, such as North and South Sulawesi, often encounter lower corn prices than Java's because of transport costs to markets off the island. A profit-oriented farmer who faces lower output prices will typically cut back on fertilizer use.

From this perspective, the regional differences in marginal physical product reported in Table 4.2 are understandable. In comparing the areas that plant local white varieties—Grobogan and Bone—farmers in Grobogan have lower marginal physical products. This result is due partly to their greater experience and higher level of fertilizer use and partly to higher output prices. Farmers in Bone remain at lower input levels, where output response is greater. In West Sumatra, farmers have begun to shift to improved corn varieties but lag somewhat behind in adjusting fertilizer amounts to the higher levels appropriate to these varieties. The combination of fertilizer-responsive seeds and suboptimal fertilizer use thus results in a very high marginal physical product. The generally lower figures for the two sites in East Java are the result of very high fertilizer rates and extensive use of improved corn varieties. The difference in marginal physical product between Malang and Kediri is not entirely understood, but it may be related to less water control and less use of improved varieties in Malang. At any of these survey sites, macro- and micronutrient imbalances may also help explain different rates of fertilizer efficiency, and this possibility deserves greater attention in fertilizer trials.

A rough estimate of a national average for marginal physical product can be made by taking the results of the sample as representative of the various regions and weighting them by regional production. The result is about 2.5 (or a corn-to-nitrogen marginal physical product of 5.5). How this value for marginal physical product evolves over the next several years will depend on the relative rates at which various kinds of fertilizer and improved seeds spread. High fertilizer use would reduce the value, whereas more extensive use of improved seeds would increase it.

The price elasticity of demand for fertilizer on corn is still largely a matter of speculation. Econometric analysis of average applications per hectare shows trend growth of 12 percent per year (which indicates farmers' learning processes) but gives implausible price coefficients (the wrong sign and insignificant). In the absence of better data on corn-specific fertilizer applications, an alternative is simply to adopt the price elasticities, which range from −0.7 to −1.0, which were estimated for fertilizer use on rice in Indonesia by Timmer (1985a). Since rice is grown by many of the same farmers who grow corn and has a marginal physical product similar to corn's, this estimate can serve as an imperfect proxy for the price elasticity of fertilizer on corn.

The domestic price of fertilizer is subsidized by the government at high cost to the government budget. This policy is coming under increasing scrutiny as the government attempts to adjust to stagnant oil revenues. One possibility is a move toward world prices, which would cause urea prices to farmers to rise from Rp 90 in 1984 to over Rp 150 per kilogram. Because the vast majority of fertilizer is used for rice, any change in fertilizer price policy will be judged primarily for its effect on rice output. And although consequences for *palawija* production—including corn—are important, they are likely to be overshadowed.

With a price elasticity of demand for fertilizer in corn production of −0.7, an increase in fertilizer price from Rp 90 to Rp 150 per kilogram leads to a decline in demand for fertilizer of 46 percent, assuming the elasticity holds over this substantial price change. If it is assumed that fertilizer use on corn increases about 12 percent per year due to trend factors, fertilizer use in 1982 should have been 380,000 tons, and a price increase would have decreased this by 174,000 tons. With a marginal physical output coefficient of 2.5, a decline in corn production of roughly 437,000 tons would be expected. Similar calculations that use a price elasticity of −1.0 result in a decline in fertilizer use of 253,000 tons and a drop in corn production of 633,000 tons.

The consequences of raising the fertilizer price to levels in world markets are equally dramatic for the individual farmer. For an East Java farmer who brings in a 3-ton harvest and uses 400 kilograms of urea per hectare, the increased cost of fertilizer would cut the fertilizer application to 215 kilograms and cause output to drop by one-half ton. Net return (Profit II) drops from about Rp 160,000 per hectare to Rp 115,000 per hectare, or a 30 percent fall as a result of the increase in fertilizer price. In

TABLE 4.3. *Marginal physical output of corn from liming at different levels of phosphate applications, Sukamandi, Java*

Phosphate (P_2O_5) (kilograms per hectare)		Lime (tons per hectare) 3.3	6.6	9.9	13.2
	Additional output (tons)				
0	First season	1.2	0.5	0.4	−1.0
	Second season	0.5	0.7		
45	First season	1.1	−0.1	0.2	−0.1
	Second season	1.0	0.6		
90	First season	1.1	0.2	−0.1	−0.2
	Second season	1.0	0.6		
135	First season	0.4	−0.2	−0.1	0.5
	Second season	0.7	0.6		
180	First season	0.6	0	0.2	−0.5
	Second season	0.2	0.6		
	Average for first season	0.9	0.3	0.1	−0.3
	Average for second season	0.7	0.6		

SOURCE: Indonesia, Department of Agriculture, "Annual Report 1981–82" (Bogor: Central Research Institute for Agriculture, 1982).
NOTE: Minus signs indicate a decrease in physical output. All numbers for additional output of corn are in tons per hectare.

practice this would be offset somewhat by trend growth in fertilizer use and by any rise in output prices which might follow aggregate decreases in production.

Use of Agricultural Lime on Corn

A critical constraint to food crop production—especially on outer-island rain-fed soils—is soil acidity.[1] Research on appropriate management of these soils, which are under continuous cultivation by smallholders, began only recently. Since the benefits of such practices as green manuring and liming are relatively long term, the design and interpretation of experiments are thus complicated, and results that are available are tentative and incomplete. Moreover, inadequate mapping of the affected areas and degree of soil acidity hinders the planning and economic feasibility analysis of government programs to remedy the problem. In 1984 the Department of Agriculture had to rely on spot testing to plan a liming program that would cover 1.85 million hectares of soybeans over the course of the five-year plan (REPELITA IV).

Tests were carried out in both Java and West Sumatra to evaluate the responsiveness of the corn variety Harapan-6 to several inputs, including lime (see Table 4.3). A second set of data was collected over three corn seasons at Sitiung transmigration area in West Sumatra, where trials

[1]For the complete analysis of agricultural lime on tropical soils, see Perry (1984b).

TABLE 4.4. *Marginal physical output of corn from liming, Sitiung, Sumatra*

Lime (tons per hectare)	Additional output (tons per hectare)	
	Season 2	Season 3
2	1.7	1.3
4	0.2	0.1
6	0.3	0.65

SOURCE: Perry (1984a).

tested the response of Harapan-6 to inputs including lime on soils of original pH of 4.1 (see Hakim 1984). Results for the second and third seasons are shown in Table 4.4.[2]

From these two data sets, the additional corn production from increased applications of lime—the marginal physical product—can be estimated. At moderate levels of phosphate application, use of 2 to 3 tons of lime results in yield increases of at least a ton. At this level of lime application, marginal physical product is lower at Sukamandi than at Sitiung, perhaps because the initial acidity constraint at Sitiung was not so severe. Above the level of 3 to 4 tons of lime applications, marginal physical product declines sharply. The output responses to applications of 2 to 4 tons of lime per hectare are well above results on tropical soils in other countries, which suggests that further regional testing is needed to determine whether the data are representative of other regions in Indonesia.[3] Longer-term experiments are required since little can be concluded from these two trials about the length of time lime applications remain effective. Many factors can influence the time curve of effectiveness, such as depth of plowing, amounts leached out by rainfall, and size of the lime granules.

Despite incomplete agronomic results, the profitability of adding lime to soils specifically used for corn production can still be roughly estimated. Acid soils planted in soybeans on the outer islands will receive lime applications according to plans prepared by the Bureau for Food Crop Production Development in 1984. The initial application will be 2 to 3 tons of lime per hectare. Five years later an additional 500 kilograms per year are to be applied. The price of lime delivered to the farm level is Rp 60 to Rp 70 per kilogram, of which Rp 35 to Rp 40 is the cost of

[2]The first-season harvest was severely affected by bad weather and is not included in this analysis; for an analysis of the Sitiung data, see Perry (1984b).

[3]Agronomists at the International Center for the Improvement of Maize and Wheat (CIMMYT) suggest that tropical, clay loam soils that are acid, with aluminum toxicity, need 6 to 7 tons of lime per hectare to raise the soil pH by one unit.

TABLE 4.5. *Costs and returns to liming corn*

	Quantity	Value (rupiahs)
Costs per application		
Lime	2.5 tons	162,500
Application labor	17.5 workdays	22,750
Total		185,250
Benefits per harvest		
Additional corn	1 ton	105,000
	Net return to liming (rupiahs)	Discounted Benefit–Cost Ratio[a]
Year 1	24,750[b]	0.90
Year 2	234,750	1.52

[a]Benefits occur at harvest, in the sixth and ninth months of each year, beginning with the initial application. Discounting is at 3 percent per month.

[b]Two crops at Rp 105,000 each = Rp 210,000 minus liming costs of Rp 185,250 equals Rp 24,750. No liming costs are incurred the second year.

producing it and the remainder is the cost of transporting it to the village. In the government program, farmers are to receive the lime free.

There are few farm-level data to estimate the additional costs for labor to transport lime from the home to field and to apply it. Results from field surveys suggest that about 1.5 workdays (workday = 8 hours) are required to apply 150 kilograms of fertilizer per hectare, but this average includes many farmers who carefully dibble the fertilizer near the root zone. In most cases lime is simply broadcast before plowing or hoeing. To carry 2 to 3 tons of lime from home to the fields is not so prohibitive a constraint as one might imagine. Many corn farmers already use shoulder poles to haul, in loads of about 50 kilograms each, over 2 tons of animal manure to the fields one season a year. If it is assumed that after a large initial application, lime is applied thereafter in smaller quantities, say the 500 kilograms per year of the government program, this amount is little more than the weight of chemical fertilizer that many corn farmers already haul by shoulder pole to their fields every season. One estimate, therefore, is that it takes 7 workdays to apply a ton of lime. If it is assumed that family labor does the work, a shadow wage of Rp 1,300 per day (75 percent of the market wage in Sumatra, which is Rp 1,750 per day if the value of food is included) is applicable for Sumatra.

An economic analysis of the costs and benefits of lime applications is presented in Table 4.5. In addition to the above assumptions for marginal physical product and labor costs, the output price for corn is Rp 105 per kilogram, and two corn crops per year are harvested. The results in Table 4.5 show that farmers who pay the full cost of lime would nearly recover their investment after only two crops of corn. After two years, the discounted benefit-to-cost ratio is 1.52, which indicates that liming is a very worthwhile investment for corn. The results clearly indicate that although the government hopes to have farmers lime at least once every five years for soybeans, the frequency could increase to every two years for corn grown on acid soils, if necessary, and still provide an attractive return to farmers.

The government's decision to provide lime free to soybean farmers in selected regions may initially be justifiable while farmers become familiar with its use and while supplies are still very limited. But the earlier analysis shows that the potential for profit from lime use could cause demand to surpass by far the government's ability to finance a full subsidy. Indonesia's abundant but undeveloped lime resources and the eventual need for substantial capacity for transportation and marketing indicate that the government will soon need to evaluate its role in providing this input and consider the extent to which the private sector, which handles fertilizer so successfully, should expand its role. A move away from full subsidies for lime will be required if the private sector is to make a significant investment.

Choice of Corn Variety

Several new corn varieties have been released since 1979, including a hybrid variety, which require 95 days or more to maturity. Where supplies of the new seeds have been adequate, many corn experts have been surprised at the speed with which these varieties have been adopted. Especially surprised were plant breeders who previously thought most corn systems in Indonesia were constrained to use short-duration local varieties of 85 days or less. The national rate of increase in yields will be tied closely to the speed with which these improved varieties spread. Present levels of adoption of higher-yielding corn varieties are poorly documented, but potential use can be estimated from the production system typology described in Chapter 3 (Table 3.1) by identifying which systems can use longer-duration varieties. Corn varieties appropriate to climate and current crop rotations are broken down in Table 4.6, which

TABLE 4.6. *Use of corn variety, by duration*

Crop duration (days)	Percentage of area planted		
	Total	Yellow	White
<85	10	—	10
86–95	25	15	10
96+	65	50	15
TOTAL	100	65	35

SOURCE: Author's estimates.

shows the percentage of total corn area planted in corn varieties of short, medium and long maturities. Long-duration, improved yellow varieties appear readily suitable for 50 percent of Indonesia's corn area. The spread of improved varieties through the white corn regions will be significantly slower because breeding research for this color type has been minimal in Indonesia and strong consumer preferences preclude a rapid shift to yellow varieties.

Factors other than duration are important in farmers' choice of seed variety. The recent introduction of potentially higher-yielding hybrid seed in Indonesia drew attention to factors such as cash flow, end use, credit needs, and farmers' perception of risk and their influence on adopting new varieties. The potentially large effect of these factors was demonstrated in two of the survey sites. In Lampung, farmers had tried hybrid seed but thought its extra output "was not worth the effort." Kediri farmers weigh these factors differently, and their use of hybrid corn is rapidly expanding.

At these survey sites, the main alternative to hybrid seed was Arjuna. Table 4.7 shows an economic comparison of the two varieties based on practices of the farmers in the survey. The cash costs of using the hybrid are substantially higher than those for Arjuna. In the Lampung sample, cash costs were Rp 82,500 per hectare for the hybrid compared with only Rp 30,200 per hectare for Arjuna. The major additional cost is for the seed itself. Costs are also greater for seed treatment (protection against downy mildew), fertilizer, and labor to apply the fertilizer.

Many farmers continue to face a considerable cash constraint at the beginning of the main corn season. It follows the dry season, when income from field crops drops severely. Cash outlays for the hybrid are not only greater but also earlier in season, as farmers must pay for the relatively expensive seed and an early application of fertilizer. For Arjuna, most of the cash outlays would come a month later when that variety receives the major fertilizer application.

For several seasons, the shift to hybrid seed entails greater risks for farmers as they learn new management techniques. They must space hybrid seeds differently and sow only one seed per location instead of the usual several seeds. Some farmers have had trouble gauging correct depth of planting. Unlike clusters of Arjuna seedlings, which can lift the soil as they sprout, a single hybrid seed may not be able to break the soil surface unless it is planted less deeply than Arjuna. In addition to this risk of a poor stand, farmers face a more general risk early in the season. Crop damage from poor rains, insects, or rats, which forces replanting, requires a large additional cash outlay for additional seed if the farmer chooses to replant—costs that are higher than those of reseeding Arjuna.

Output risk—the susceptibility to loss, or difficulty selling the harvest

TABLE 4.7. *Comparison of two seed technologies in two survey locations (per hectare)*

	Kediri				Lampung			
	Arjuna		Hybrid		Arjuna		Hybrid	
	Quantity	Value (000 Rp)	Quantity	Value (000 Rp)	Quantity	Value (000 Rp)	Quantity	Value (000 Rp)
Inputs								
Seed	35 kg	4.5	20 kg	30.0	20 kg	3.2	20 kg	30.0
Seed treatment	—	—	75 g	4.0	—	—	75 g	4.0
Fertilizer	436 kg	39.2	544 kg	48.9	250 kg	22.5	450 kg	40.5
Fertilizer labor[a]	4.36 wd	4.5	5.44 wd	5.7	2.5 wd	4.5	4.5 wd	8.0
Output[b]	3.8 tons	399.0	5.5 tons	577.5	4.0 tons	380.0	5.0 tons	475.0
Simple net return		350.8		488.9		349.8		392.5
Simple net return advantage of hybrid technology			138.1				42.7	
Net return advantage of hybrid technology if incremental opportunity cost and risk factor of input value included[c]			126.5				27.4	

[a]Fertilizer labor estimated as 1 workday per 100 kilograms. Other labor inputs are considered the same across technologies.
[b]Kediri output value = Rp 105 per kilogram. Lampung output value = Rp 95 per kilogram (1984 values).
[c]Opportunity cost on input value is 3 percent per month for 3 months. Risk factor evaluated as 20 percent of additional hybrid input cost.

at a reasonable price—is not substantially different between Arjuna and hybrid corn. They have similar taste and milling characteristics, and both varieties are acceptable to consumers or the feed industry. Both varieties have a tendency toward poor husk cover and thus are prone to pest infestations, which begin in the field and increase during storage, particularly if stored in traditional ways on the farm. Although there is little difference in output risk between these two varieties, they do present farmers with an additional risk factor through storage loss, so greater *field* yields may not translate into greater *food* yields. If farmers are able to market their production quickly, this problem disappears.

Simple net returns shown in Table 4.7 are adjusted for both the higher opportunity cost of planting hybrids, which reflects the additional cash requirements, and the greater risk. One method of representing the former is to add an interest cost applied over the duration of the crop—here, 3 percent per month—to the differential cash needs of the hybrid. Similarly, an arbitrary risk premium of 20 percent of the difference in the cost of inputs to plant hybrids is added to the "cost" of growing the hybrid. This risk premium is expected to decrease after several seasons of farmer experience with the hybrid.

Once cash constraints and risk have been included, the shift from Arjuna to hybrid seed results in a gain of Rp 126,500 per hectare in Kediri, but in Lampung the gain is only Rp 27,400 per hectare. With the improvement in return quite modest for hybrid use in Lampung, the lack of enthusiasm farmers expressed for the new variety is not surprising. The main difference in result between Lampung and Kediri arises from improvement in yields, which is much larger in Kediri. Extrapolation from this very small sample is not warranted, but it appears that at these two sites the increased cash requirements of the hybrid, though substantial, are less critical for farmers' choice of variety than the degree of expected yield gains. Credit programs for input purchases would thus not have much effect on the farmer's choice of variety. This impression, however, may be more characteristic of areas where farmers already use substantial amounts of purchased inputs such as fertilizer, as in the two sites here. Farmers who are not accustomed to large cash outlays and who want to shift directly from local varieties to hybrids are more likely to be deterred by the cash costs. They are used to much lower cash inputs for corn production and would be a good target group for a rural credit program aimed at financing adoption of profitable new technology.

Choice of Technique in Corn Production

Farmers who face different costs of inputs for corn production choose different techniques for producing corn. This difference in choice of technique is especially evident across the corn regions of Indonesia as farmers choose different means of preparing land, seeding, and weeding. In all the corn systems in Indonesia, the largest variable input cost per hectare is for human labor. But in some regions there is substantial substitution away from human labor in favor of animal traction and two- or four-wheeled tractors, a shift frequently constrained by nonprice factors such as small plot size or rocky soils, which make animal or tractor power impractical. But where such considerations are not important, farmers make their choices largely on the basis of comparative costs of alternative techniques.

Choice of technique is a particularly relevant issue in rural economies with substantial underemployment. Government interventions, such as fuel or credit subsidies or overvalued exchange rates, distort farmers' incentives and promote the use of tractors and other labor-displacing techniques. The use of tractors and the effects on rural employment are important social issues in Indonesia's labor-surplus economy. The effect of the government's macroeconomic policy on the corn economy through factor prices is discussed in Chapter 10.

The limited evidence on factor substitution suggests that Indonesian farmers are sensitive to labor costs, and in regions where wages are at the upper end of the current range, farmers shift when possible to animal and mechanical power. Table 4.8 demonstrates this impact of different input prices for manual labor, draft animals, and mechanical power on the mix of production techniques currently in use. Tractor use is most common in North Sumatra, where rural wage rates are high, and thus labor use is

TABLE 4.8. *Choice of technique for monoculture corn*

	North Sumatra		East Java		Central Java	South Sulawesi
	Karo	Asahan	Malang	Kediri	Grobogan	Bone
Inputs (per hectare)						
Labor (workdays)	42	59	76	49	127	76
Draft power (pair per day)	—	—	15	17	7	3
Tractor (days)	0.375	0.375	—	—	—	—
Costs (per day)						
Labor[a]	1,500	1,200	710	1,016	1,300	800
Draft power (per pair)	—	—	1,920	2,720	3,000	2,000
Tractor	110,174	112,613	—	—	—	—
Total costs of power (per hectare)	104,315	113,029	82,760	96,024	122,600	104,800

SOURCE: Survey data cited in Dorosh, Mink, and Perry (1984).
[a]Includes wages and food. All costs are in rupiahs per day.

only about 50 workdays per hectare. Wage rates are high in South Sulawesi as well, but rocky, hilly fields make plowing with tractors or animals difficult. Farmers have not been able to economize on labor costs by switching to other power sources; they have simply kept labor use at a low level (with resulting low yields).

Of the survey sites on Java, Kediri has the highest wage rate and the lowest use of human labor; draft animals supply much of the power. In Malang, wage rates are about 20 percent lower than those in Kediri, and use of human labor is correspondingly higher. Grobogan has the highest cost for renting draft animals, and although their use is not eliminated, farmers substitute human labor to reduce costs of cultivation. It is apparent from these observations that where wages have risen, substitution away from human labor has been essential in maintaining production costs at competitive levels.

Corn Production in the Future

Summarizing the future of the corn production story in the mid-1980s is as tempting and as risky as guessing the ending of a half-read book. The direction of the plot has been established, the characters introduced, underlying conflicts uncovered, and past events put in perspective. These elements define a general direction for the future, but much depends on events yet to come.

A primary conclusion of the corn story to date is that significant progress has already occurred in raising productivity. Many participants in the corn production system have been involved in this success. The first push to increase yields in the early 1970s would have been impossible without establishment of a fertilizer distribution system capable of timely deliveries to most parts of the country. Although the main focus of fertilizer promotion in the 1970s was rice, corn producers benefited as well. Through fertilizer trials and extension efforts, the Department of Agriculture was able to assist farmers with information about fertilizer doses, timing, and application methods, all of which differed from recommendations for rice.

Government corn breeders succeeded in incorporating some resistance to downy mildew in varieties appropriate for many local corn systems. With the development of new medium-duration corn varieties, they also achieved increases in yield potential over that of local corn varieties. Very recently, private sector breeders have opened a new chapter by introducing Indonesia's first hybrid corn seed, which has proven superiority in yields for numerous locations. Even though this seed has a relatively long duration, it has been accepted by farmers whose cropping patterns are representative of large areas of corn production.

Turning potential into reality required, and still requires, decisions by millions of farmers to use fertilizer on corn. They increased their use on average over threefold since the mid-1970s and have adjusted their crop rotations and management practices to take advantage of higher-yielding varieties whenever they were available and economically advantageous. The combined efforts of these corn system participants have resulted in steadily rising yields, which in 1980 were 50 percent higher on average for the country than a decade earlier. A national yield average of 2 tons per hectare is well within reach by 1990.

Behind these generalizations, however, are production techniques that are tremendously diverse across the systems in Indonesia. The elements of diversity are striking, and each cuts across the production systems in a different way. Fertilizer use in different systems ranges from 0 to 600 kilograms per hectare, corn color is white or yellow, duration to maturity of favored varieties is anywhere from 75 to 120 days, and hybrid seeds add to profits in some areas but not significantly in others. Major end uses include both home consumption and animal feed, which in turn determine preferred grain characteristics. In some places, production operations are carried out entirely by hand, but elsewhere they are performed with large contributions from tractors. These variations are important complications because they explain why the most productive crop technology currently available may be inappropriate for many farmers. They highlight the interplay between agronomic and economic factors that influence management choices, point to research needs, and qualify unguarded optimism about future production increases.

Diversity also creates dangers in generalizing about future trends for Indonesia's corn system. Forecasting on the basis of the largest production system (high-productivity rain-fed land) is bound to overstate overall production potential. Small systems, such as found in Nusa Tenggara Timur and on the northern floodplains of Java, are highly constrained and have little technology available that is capable of accelerating growth in corn production. Generalizations about priorities in research or production intensification also tend to focus resources on the larger systems. Unequal access to breeding advances is particularly evident with regard to seed color. About 35 percent of Indonesia's corn area is planted with white varieties. Yet very little emphasis is placed on this color group in national breeding programs, and only one white variety has been released since 1970. Moreover, generalization hides the fact that in several regions where corn is an important element of corn rotations, farmers are quite clearly not participating in the overall increase in productivity. If the high degree of price integration that exists between major surplus areas and wholesale markets is extended to other regional corn markets, further expansion of this productivity gap will force farmers in the stagnant areas to deal with decreasing profitability from growing corn. If technological breakthroughs in *these* regions are not imminent, new policies may be needed to alter the income potential of other farm or off-farm activities.

How the corn story in Indonesia unfolds depends on the ability of system participants to address a number of needs, particularly for seed development and distribution. Since the problem of developing corn varieties resistant to downy mildew is largely solved, priorities must focus on yields, duration, color, and seed multiplication and distribution. A very significant finding of this study is the extent to which farmers in several of the systems are adopting varieties of 95 days or more. This finding is in contrast to much of the literature on plant breeding, which assumes that the 85-day maturity of local varieties is a tight constraint in all production systems. A clear constraint does exist at about 85 days in the northern floodplain system of Java and occasionally on *sawah* and rain-fed land for second- or third-season plantings. But for the primary harvest on both rain-fed land and *sawah*, durations of 95 to 105 days (at medium altitudes) are acceptable in the majority of crop rotations.

The appropriate emphasis on color in corn breeding cannot be determined independent of assumptions about the future marketing potential for white corn. Specific demand for white corn is primarily for household consumption, which will decline on a per capita basis as incomes continue to grow. The main international market and the most rapidly growing component of the domestic market is for yellow corn demanded by the livestock feed industry. The Indonesian market will increasingly demand yellow corn, with white reduced to a staple food largely consumed by farm households without ever being marketed. An increased emphasis on white varietal breeding, however, may be justified for two reasons: the number of farmers who rely on white corn will remain substantial at least through the 1990s; and white corn farmers tend to grow yellow corn on land that is in excess of what is needed to grow white corn for home consumption. Higher white corn yields would allow farm households to meet their need for white corn with less land and permit more land to be shifted to yellow corn.

The capacity of seed programs to develop and multiply improved varieties needs to be expanded. Even with open-pollinated varieties, replacement of farmers' seed every three or five years is advisable; genetic mixing with inferior local varieties is a continuing problem on farmers' small plots where neighbors use different varieties. Many survey farmers, who mentioned a noticeable decline in yields after three or four years of recycling seed of open-pollinated varieties, showed strong interest in renewing their seed. Hybrid seed must be bought anew for each planting season. Insufficient multiplication and distribution remains a major problem for both seed types, and farmers often complain about unavailability.

Distribution of other inputs also poses certain problems. For fertilizer, availability is inadequate only in specific regions such as South Sulawesi and Nusa Tenggara Timur. The private market in these two regions is not well established, and fertilizer that is distributed by cooperatives (KUD) continues to be channeled mainly to farmers who participate in rice intensification programs. In the main corn-producing areas of Java, fertilizer availability has generally ceased to be a concern. Ridomil, the fungicide most commonly used to protect against downy mildew, is not widely known among farmers and even more rarely available. It is sometimes part of the BIMAS package and provided through a cooperative, but it is rarely found in stores of private merchants who sell agricultural inputs. Agricultural lime is generally unavailable and quite expensive. Its importance in raising yields on acid soils is increasingly recognized by the Department of Agriculture, but new programs are limited to soybean production. If the distribution channels to be established restrict lime to soybean production, the major contribution it can make to corn profits in many regions will be forgone.

In addition to the physical availability of inputs in rural areas, farmer access to inputs includes the ability to pay for them. Insufficient cash flow at the beginning of a growing season is a common constraint, particularly for buying hybrid seed and fertilizer. BIMAS credit programs have only partially solved the problem. In many cases, the complete package is unavailable, is inappropriate for farmers' needs, or does not have wide participation. A recent innovative, general credit program does not require that agricultural loans be applied to specific input packages, and this program could thus give farmers much more flexibility in their management decisions.[4] Although the size of the agricultural loan program is still small in comparison to BIMAS, it is growing rapidly and could provide important experience on alternative means of providing production credit.

Agronomic recommendations by the Department of Agriculture are on the whole appropriate; they focus on such factors that limit yields as seed spacing, regularity of plant stand, fertilizer levels and placement, and timely planting to avoid downy mildew. Progress on these practices is often interrelated. For example, farmers usually do not work to improve the regularity of plant stands until they begin to use fertilizer at high enough rates that efficiency of fertilizer use becomes noticeable. One issue that has not received much attention is moisture conservation for the dry-season crop. Mulching with crop residues can reduce evaporation and water stress and thus contribute to higher yields. On the other hand,

[4]The new credit program, KUPEDES, is also administered through village units of Bank Rakyat Indonesia, which was originally responsible for administration of BIMAS loans.

weed competition, which is a major problem in many parts of the world, does not appear to be a serious problem in Indonesian corn production. Weeding by hand early after corn seedlings emerge is generally followed by another round before silking, and this is usually sufficient to maintain a clean field.

One major gap in knowledge is the interaction of intercrops and the optimal management of these systems. Where long- and short-duration crops, such as corn and cassava are mixed, the benefits of intercropping stem from better control of erosion, maintenance of ground cover, and an economic yield from the corn long before the cassava harvest. These advantages are less important where crops of more equal duration, such as corn and beans, are mixed. The contribution of beans to soil fertility through nitrogen fixation may play a small positive (if often overstated) role. It is difficult to formulate from experimental evidence a set of fertilizer and pest-control practices that is clearly superior in managing this intercrop. In several survey sites, farmers themselves showed little consistency in basic practices. As individual commodity systems become more intensive and use greater amounts of fertilizer, the intercrop may give way to side-by-side monoculture plots, which permit more specific refinements for each crop.

Price incentives and guaranteed markets can encourage farmers to accept technology that they might otherwise perceive as risky. In areas that historically have produced white corn, farmers have had difficulty trying to market yellow corn. With marketings from only small farms, merchants from outside the area have not found it worthwhile to arrange the bulking of corn purchases. But where market channels have been established and fair prices guaranteed—for example, through support of the floor price for yellow corn by cooperatives (KUD) in parts of South Sulawesi—farmers have rapidly shifted part of their production into high-yielding yellow varieties. A floor price not only influences the adoption of new technology but also meets the government's stated objective of supporting farm incomes. To date, the government has set floor prices at comparatively low levels, however, in part so that it can dispose of any acquired corn without excessive budget losses.

Chapters 2, 3, and 4 have demonstrated the diversity of corn systems in Indonesia and the complicated links that exist between production increases and improvements in the off-farm elements of the corn system. Developing the substantial potential of Indonesia's corn system will depend on sensible policies not only for farm production, but for marketing, trade, and manufacturing as well.

PART THREE

End Uses for Corn

Corn has a remarkable diversity of end uses, even in a food system as relatively underdeveloped as Indonesia's. For example, soybeans—the "miracle crop" of the twentieth century—do not serve as flexibly as corn in satisfying the variety of different functions that corn fulfills. Unlike rice, which serves almost entirely as a human foodstuff, corn serves commercially somewhere in the world as a staple food, as feed for livestock, as the source of a high-quality vegetable oil, as the raw material for fructose-based sweetener, as a base to produce ethyl alcohol, which can be used to fuel motor vehicles, and as the raw material for a variety of industrial processes, especially ones that use starch as an ingredient.

Chapter 3 has already demonstrated the high degree of competition corn faces in most Indonesian farming systems. Many crops serve as profitable substitutes, depending on price relationships and the available technology. The consumption story is no less complicated. In each of its potential end uses as a commodity, corn faces a variety of substitutes, each of which might displace corn or be replaced by corn. This introduction presents a framework for understanding commodity substitutions in alternative end uses on world markets and corn's role within this framework. Three end uses for corn are of particular importance in Indonesia: its direct consumption by humans, its use as livestock feed, and its use as the raw material for a fructose-based liquid sweetener industry. In the mid-1980s the latter end use is only a potential one in the Indonesian setting.

Framework of End Use Substitutions

To understand the mechanisms by which one commodity might substitute for another in a particular end use, it is helpful to identify key links among the following three important factors: (1) the eight commodities that form the core of the world food system; (2) the six end uses for these commodities; and (3) the primary causal forces that provide the impetus for change. These forces—population growth, income changes, and energy prices—are exogenous to a food system in the short run, but in the long run they are linked to performance in the food system itself.

The eight commodities are rice, wheat, corn, soybeans, palm oil, sugar, cassava, and petroleum. Except for petroleum, these commodities account for nearly all international trade in food staples. Livestock and dairy products, cotton and other natural fibers, and tropical fruits and beverages make up the rest of agricultural trade, but their market behavior is very specialized. Petroleum is included because its price, through its impact on international financial flows, macroeconomic performance, and the foreign exchange rate of oil importers and exporters is an important factor in explaining the dynamics of the world grain economy (Timmer 1984b).

Six major end uses for these eight commodities are shown in Table I3.1 (the six *F*'s): food, feed, fuel, fructose (and other sweeteners), fats (and oils), and factories (the manufacturing sector). Based on a world perspective, each commodity is allocated to an end use according to its primary end use (P), any secondary end uses (S), and potential future end uses (F). If a commodity does not fit any of these three roles, it is classified with a dash (—) to indicate a minor or no end use in that category.

By this classification, the eight commodities are seen to have great diversity. Rice is consumed almost entirely as human food; only minor amounts go for livestock feed or industrial use. Sugar is used primarily as a sweetener, and much enters the industrial sector as an ingredient in soft drinks and processed foods. A secondary use of sugar as a base for alcohol fermentation has emerged, especially in Brazil and other sugar-surplus countries. Wheat also has limited end uses. Most wheat is consumed as food, with a large proportion passing through a commercial baking industry, although roughly one-third of the world's wheat, primarily of low quality, is fed to livestock. The proportions of wheat fed to livestock varies dramatically from country to country, but most of this use occurs in Europe, particularly the Soviet Union.

Petroleum is a commodity in a class by itself, but it does have multiple end uses. Its primary use is obviously as fuel, but significant quantities are used as industrial raw material, especially if natural gas is included under petroleum. Natural gas is the raw stock for much of the petrochemical industry, from fertilizers to synthetic fibers and plastics.

Cassava, a tropical root crop, is consumed primarily by humans in Africa, Brazil, Indonesia, and South Asia. It is the source of tapioca and a growing starch industry. Its high efficiency in producing carbohydrates on marginal lands makes it a potential source of alcohol and, as Chapter 7 shows, a fructose-based sweetener syrup. Cassava has also found an important niche in world trade as a cheap livestock feed used primarily in the European Community countries in combination with soybean meal as a substitute for corn. Since corn is artificially expensive in these countries because of import levies, the combination of cassava and soybean meal,

TABLE I3.1. *Framework for understanding demand linkages in the world food system*

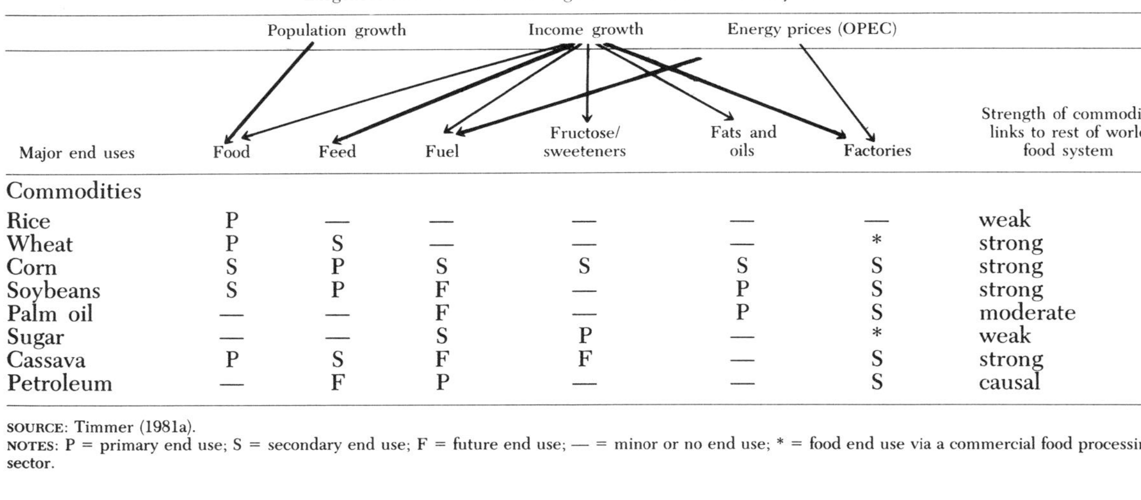

Exogenous causal forces influencing demand for each commodity end use							
	Population growth		Income growth		Energy prices (OPEC)		
Major end uses	Food	Feed	Fuel	Fructose/ sweeteners	Fats and oils	Factories	Strength of commodity links to rest of world food system
Commodities							
Rice	P	—	—	—	—	—	weak
Wheat	P	S	—	—	—	*	strong
Corn	S	P	S	S	S	S	strong
Soybeans	S	P	F	—	P	S	strong
Palm oil	—	—	F	—	P	S	moderate
Sugar	—	—	S	P	—	*	weak
Cassava	P	S	F	F	—	S	strong
Petroleum	—	F	P	—	—	S	causal

SOURCE: Timmer (1981a).
NOTES: P = primary end use; S = secondary end use; F = future end use; — = minor or no end use; * = food end use via a commercial food processing sector.

which enter at low tariffs or duty free, has a cost advantage over corn. Cassava exports, primarily from Thailand with smaller amounts from Indonesia, thus depend on the cost and availability of corn (see Nelson 1983). When the Soviet Union was embargoed from U.S. corn exports, for example, it began to import cassava from Thailand and corn from Argentina for its feed industry. Chapter 6 demonstrates that Indonesia's pricing policy for imported soybean meal significantly limits the potential use of cassava for local feed rations and thus increases domestic demand for corn. Such substitutions for commodity and source are now characteristic of Indonesia's food system.

Palm oil is the most rapidly growing source of vegetable oil in Indonesia, and modern plantations and smallholder nucleus estate investments provide low-cost supplies for both the domestic and world markets. Some palm oil is used in industry. It may have a future use as a low-grade fuel for diesel engines if the price relationships become suitable. Palm oil is included in the framework not because of these specific interests but because it shows yet another form of substitution possible via international trade, as illustrated in the cases of India and China. Both countries have used the increased availability of vegetable oils in world markets, which is largely a result of very low-cost production of palm oil in Asia and Africa, and their lower price relative to wheat and rice as a means of increasing domestic acreage of food grains at the expense of domestic oilseed acreage. This shift reduces import demand for food grains (in the mid-1980s India was self-sufficient) and increases import demand for vegetable oils (to the extent that India and China were two of the world's largest importers in the early 1980s). The possibilities for commodity substitution can thus be quite roundabout.

Soybeans begin to show the potential complexity and interrelatedness of a country's food system. In the early stages of development, soybeans tend to be grown as a food crop for direct family consumption or as an important cash crop for sale in local markets. Throughout Asia, and especially in Indonesia, a small-scale processing industry produces a wide variety of soy-based food products. At a later stage, soybeans are processed for their oil and meal. From an Asian perspective, it is surprising that only about 15 percent of the world's soybeans are used directly for consumption by humans and that very few of these enter world trade. The rest, some 80 million metric tons, are crushed for their oil and meal, which is used as a high-quality livestock feed. Like palm oil, soybean oil may have a potential use as a low-grade fuel in diesel engines if price relationships permit.

It has been argued that anyone who can understand the world market for soybeans can understand the entire food economy because soybeans serve so many end uses. But Table I3.1 shows that corn serves even more important end uses than soybeans. Indeed, it is the only commodity with a primary or secondary end use in all six categories, from food to factories. Cornstarch and corn oil from the wet-milling process, high-fructose corn sweeteners, and corn syrup are important end uses for corn in the United States and, as Chapter 7 shows, potentially in Indonesia as well. But the United States produces so much of the world's corn that these end uses are secondary and do not provide the primary market forces driving world corn prices. Corn for direct consumption by humans is important, as a breakfast cereal in the United States and as a basic starchy staple for millions in Latin America, Africa, and Asia. In Indonesia, corn for direct consumption by humans remains the dominant end use by a substantial margin. As with soybeans, however, corn as human food is not important enough in world markets to provide the primary impetus for price formation.

The majority of the world's corn, and nearly all of the corn that enters international trade, is fed to livestock. Since the early 1960s, corn has emerged as the lowest-cost source of a nutritionally well-balanced feedstuff for several important categories of livestock. Sophisticated livestock feed blends supplement the protein, vitamins, and minerals in corn, but corn is the base for much of the emerging feedlot meat production around the world, including, as Chapter 6 shows, the livestock feed industry in Indonesia.

Price Links among Commodities

How the prices for the basic food commodities shown in Table I3.1 are linked depends on supply and demand factors. The figure shows the three primary causal factors that exogeneously influence demand for these commodities in the short run: population growth; income changes; and the level of energy prices (led by OPEC). The heavy arrows drawn in the table illustrate primary influence; the lighter arrows show secondary influence. Many dashed arrows showing roundabout, indirect, or less important causal influences are omitted for clarity, but population growth, for example, increases the demand for sweeteners or fats and oils. Likewise, energy prices have an important indirect influence on demand for most commodities through macroeconomic effects, but these links are not illustrated in the figure.[1]

For the 1980s in Indonesia and in many other economies, the most important force determining commodity price linkages is likely to be income-led demand for meat and its resulting ramifications on demand for livestock feed. Roughly 10 grain calories are required to produce 1 calorie of edible meat using intensive beef feedlot technology, and perhaps one-third of that for highly efficient poultry operations. A single addition to

[1]These effects are discussed in Timmer, Falcon, and Pearson (1983), pp. 263–269.

the world's population at a poverty level consumes about 180 kilograms of grain per year directly as a starchy staple. But if that individual is combined with adequate income to consume a diet with large amounts of meat, consumption of grain rises to more than 700 kilograms per year. About 3 tons of grain per year would be needed to run a European automobile on grain-based alcohol.

The implication is that population growth adds to food demand slowly and steadily. Since much of the population growth is among the poor, not all of the added food needed will show up as effective demand in grain markets. An inherent characteristic of income growth, however, is that it can be converted directly to market demand. Income growth from Indonesia's current average—about $500 to $600 per capita per year—tends to cause rapid increases in demand for meat, and income declines would cause equally sharp falloffs. Despite much attention given in Indonesia to the shortcomings of economic development and concerns for the very poor, a rapidly growing proportion of the population has emerged from subsistence-level poverty since the mid-1960s and is seeking improved standards of living, especially through a better-quality diet with more animal protein. More animal protein at the margin means more grain fed to livestock, and this emergence of a significant fraction of Indonesia's population into the relatively affluent middle class creates a multiplied demand for livestock feeds. Income growth in the 1980s is the major driving force explaining the dynamics of consumption and price formation in Indonesia's grain markets.

Substitutions among commodities in end uses will then transmit much of that driving force to other commodities that are strongly linked within the system itself. The links in Indonesia are even stronger than in world markets. Table I3.1 shows that, in world markets, rice and sugar are weakly linked to the other commodities, primarily because of very thin markets and short-run rigidities in alternative supply sources, especially for sweeteners. In Indonesia's domestic economy, the rice and sugar sectors are closely linked to the corn economy, as the following three chapters make clear.

Corn as a potential source of liquid fuel is unlikely in the Indonesian setting, with its abundant sources of petroleum, natural gas, and firewood. Industrial end uses other than the potential for fructose-based sweeteners are similarly unimportant. The following chapters examine in considerable depth the key end uses for corn: its direct consumption by humans as food, which has been its primary role since the grain was introduced by the Portuguese in the early sixteenth century; its consumption by livestock, an end use of importance only since the 1970s; and its use as the raw material for fructose sweeteners, which is only a potential in the mid-1980s.

5. Household Corn Consumption

Richard T. Monteverde and Stephen D. Mink

Three-quarters of Indonesia's corn production is consumed directly by humans as a staple foodstuff. Until recently, who consumes this corn and when, where they live, and how their consumption patterns change when incomes and prices change has been poorly understood. Sporadic efforts at analysis of corn consumption patterns have been frustrated by inconsistent data and by the sheer diversity and complexity of the patterns themselves. This chapter makes yet another effort to understand these patterns. The goal is to finish with a knowledge of the structural parameters that explain the dynamics of household corn consumption.

The chapter begins with a discussion of the role of corn in the Indonesian diet. The surprising importance of corn in particular regions is highlighted, along with the crucial role corn plays for the rural poor during *paceklik*, the "hungry season" before the main rice harvest on Java. The diverse forms in which corn is consumed are also stressed because they reveal strong regional preferences for white or yellow corn as well as for flinty or starchy varieties. The complexities presented to corn breeders and extension agents by these taste preferences have already been noted in Chapter 2; the problems created for the marketing sector are described in Chapter 8.

The overall quantitative significance of corn in household consumption patterns is developed in the second part of this chapter. Particular attention is focused on conflicting evidence of average corn consumption per capita from SUSENAS (the National Socio-Economic Survey of Indonesian households) and the food balance sheet, which is based on aggregate estimates of corn production. Understanding this conflict helps one judge the results presented in part three of this chapter, where key parameters that explain changes in corn consumption are estimated.

Income and price elasticities for corn demand quantify the response of households to changes in their economic environment. Earlier efforts at estimating these elasticities reported perverse results: positive price elasticities and inconsistent income elasticities that were sometimes positive, sometimes negative. These problems have not disappeared, but the results reported in this chapter are notably more successful in confirming significantly negative price elasticities.

Corn in the Indonesian Diet

Although corn is a secondary foodstuff to rice, it is a major source of calories and protein in the Indonesian diet. According to food balance sheet data in Table 5.1, corn directly consumed by humans accounts for about 10 percent of all calories and protein available for consumption. By the 1980s, increasing amounts of corn were also consumed indirectly in the form of poultry meat and eggs, pork, and dairy products.

While survey data show that average availability of corn per capita ranges from about 15 to 20 kilograms annually, this average disguises corn's importance as a staple in certain regions, at particular times of the year, and for low-income consumers. As shown in Tables 5.2 and 5.3, corn is consumed almost entirely in rural producing areas; urban consumers account for less than 3 percent of total consumption. In terms of

TABLE 5.1. *Daily per capita consumption of calories and protein, by commodity, 1980*

Commodity	Calories	Share of total calories (percent)	Protein (grams)	Share of total protein (percent)
Rice	1,310	51.0	22.92	47.3
Coconuts	230	8.9	2.30	4.7
Corn (dry forms)	225	8.8	5.87	12.1
Cassava	191	7.4	1.36	2.8
Refined sugar	111	4.3	—	—
Copra oil	87	3.4	—	—
Wheat flour	69	2.7	2.22	4.6
Soybeans	51	2.0	4.50	9.3
Groundnuts	45	1.8	1.94	4.0
Palm oil	44	1.7	—	—
Other sugar	42	1.6	0.12	0.2
Sweet potatoes	33	1.3	0.31	0.6
Bananas	21	0.8	0.27	0.6
Marine fish	14	0.5	2.43	5.0
Sago flour	9	0.4	0.03	0.1
Fresh corn	8	0.3	0.25	0.5
Pork	7	0.3	0.17	0.3
Imported milk	7	0.3	0.38	0.8
Tapioca	7	0.3	0.02	—
Beef	6	0.2	0.38	0.8
Chicken	5	0.2	0.27	0.6
Eggs	7	0.2	0.53	1.1
Inland fish	4	0.2	0.76	1.2
Other fruits	14	0.5	0.18	0.4
Other vegetables	13	0.5	0.65	1.3
Other meat	7	0.3	0.55	1.1
Other fats	2	0.1	—	—
Cow milk	1	0.0	0.04	—
TOTAL	2,570	100.0	48.45	100.0

SOURCE: Indonesia, Central Bureau of Statistics, "Food Balance Sheet for Indonesia," 1980.

TABLE 5.2. *Corn-consuming households, by residence, 1976 and 1978*

	Corn consumption (percent of households)	
	1976	1978
Residence		
Rural	97.9	97.5
Urban	2.1	2.5
TOTAL	100.0	100.0
Island Group		
Sumatra	3.1	1.3
Java	70.6	78.8
Nusa Tenggara	10.1	8.2
Kalimantan	0.5	0.5
Sulawesi	15.4	11.2
Maluku–Irian Jaya	0.4	0.0
TOTAL	100.0	100.0
Province		
Central Java	21.4	30.0
East Java	47.4	45.1
Nusa Tenggara Timur	7.3	7.1
North Sulawesi	4.7	3.6
South Sulawesi	7.0	5.0
Other	12.2	9.2
TOTAL	100.0	100.0

SOURCES: Indonesia, Central Bureau of Statistics, National Socio-Economic Survey (SUSENAS) raw data for 1976 and 1978.

total amounts of corn consumed, East Java is the most important center, followed by Central Java and South Sulawesi in proportions that closely approximate their shares in total production. On a per capita basis, however, corn is a much more important staple in Nusa Tenggara Timur, North Sulawesi, and Southeast Sulawesi; in these regions corn consumption per capita is from three to four times the national average. With the exception of transmigration populations, almost no corn is consumed on other major islands such as Sumatra, Kalimantan (Borneo), and Irian Jaya.

Provincial averages are similarly deceptive. In all of the provinces where overall levels are important, corn consumption is concentrated in subpopulations. These areas of high corn consumption in Java, Sulawesi, and Nusa Tenggara Timur are shown at the *kabupaten* level in Figures 5.1, 5.2, and 5.3. Figure 5.4 shows the share of corn in calories provided by starchy staples among ecologically similar regions of Java.

While almost all corn is consumed in producing areas, Table 5.4 shows that less than one-half is consumed by producers from their own production. That just over one-half of consumption comes from market purchases is an important consideration in evaluating altered consumption patterns in response to changes in consumer incomes and food prices. In most provinces, consumers are connected to markets, if not dependent upon them, in meeting their desired levels of corn consumption. To some extent poor farmers with severe cash constraints sell corn in one season and buy corn for home consumption in another. But landless agricultural laborers and other poor groups in rural areas account for much of the consumption from market sources. Yogyakarta, with only 7 percent of consumption originating from market purchases, is exceptional for major producing areas on Java. Farm households in Gunung Kidul, an area of poor subsistence farmers who rarely engage nonfamily labor, produce almost all the corn in that province. In the past, most corn production in this area has been needed for household consumption; landless laborers migrated to neighboring rice-growing areas when seasonal employment prospects were brighter. By contrast, East Java has the highest proportion of consumption from market sources. This province has the most trading activity, shows the strongest taste preference for corn by nonfarming households, and has the most assured flows of corn to the market because of the off-season harvests on irrigated *sawah*.

TABLE 5.3. *Weekly per capita consumption of corn (grain equivalent), by residence, 1976 and 1978*

	Corn (grain equivalent) (grams)	
	1976	1978
Residence		
Rural	292	322
Urban	27	36
Island Group		
Sumatra	41	19
Java	271	334
Nusa Tenggara	445	398
Kalimantan	26	29
Sulawesi	517	408
Maluku–Irian Jaya	—[a]	8
Province[b]		
Nusa Tenggara Timur	939	1,017
Southeast Sulawesi	1,070	796
North Sulawesi	782	636
East Java	552	583
Central Java	286	446
South Sulawesi	388	301
Central Sulawesi	316	277
D.I. Yogyakarta	73	187
Nusa Tenggara Barat	81	112

SOURCES: Indonesia, Central Bureau of Statistics, National Socio-Economic Survey (SUSENAS) raw data for 1976 and 1978, unadjusted for underreporting.

[a]No estimate since Irian Jaya was not in the 1976 sample.

[b]In other provinces corn consumption was less than 60 grams per capita per week in 1978.

FIGURE 5.1. *Average weekly household consumption of corn grain in Java*

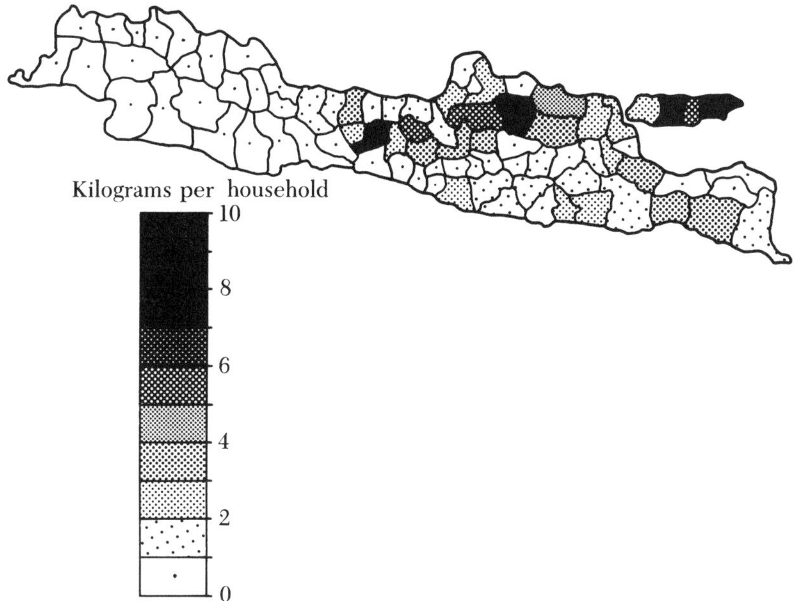

SOURCE: Indonesia, Central Bureau of Statistics, National Socio-Economic Survey (SUSENAS) raw data for 1978.

The importance of corn is accentuated by the large niche it fills in the *paceklik*, or preharvest "hungry season," which falls between the dry-season corn harvest, with its reduced yields, and the main rice harvest of March–April. The strong seasonality of consumption of corn is evident from Table 5.5. Corn consumption on Java is greatest in the period from January to March because of greater consumption per capita as well as additional numbers of people eating corn. The seasonal adjustment is largely the consequence of shifts in relative prices among the main staples. Corn consumption peaks around the main harvest, a time when corn prices fall, but declines in subsequent months as rice from the main harvest reaches the market and its price declines relative to that of corn. Some of the lower consumption of corn toward the end of the year is probably due to a seasonal decline in overall consumption of starchy staples. While the *paceklik* season is not so serious a problem as it was prior to the mid-1970s, it is still a difficult time of year for many people.

Some of the seasonality of corn consumption is determined as much by the special difficulties of storing corn as by the seasonal patterns in production and consumption of the other principal staples, rice and cassava. As Chapters 2 and 8 point out, corn is difficult to dry since the main harvest occurs during the rainy season and thus cannot be stored for more

FIGURE 5.2. *Average weekly household consumption of corn grain in Sulawesi*

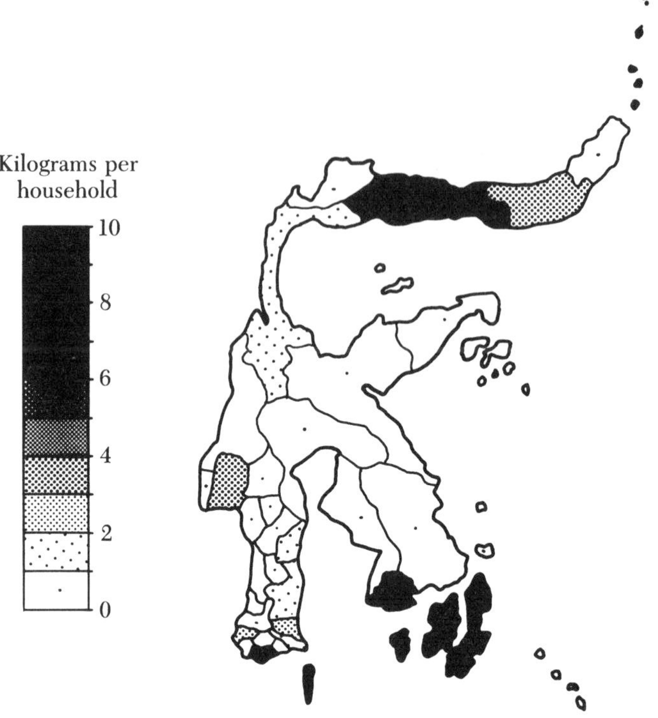

SOURCE: Indonesia, Central Bureau of Statistics, National Socio-Economic Survey (SUSENAS) raw data for 1978.

than a few months. Losses in storage by farm households are high, and thus they usually store only a minimum of corn beyond a necessary security stock. Consequently, the seasonal pattern of corn consumption corresponds with a slight lag to the seasonal production pattern.

Among the Javanese, preferences for corn are strongest in East Java. Table 5.5 shows that, compared with other provinces on Java, East Java has a larger proportion of people consuming corn and a smaller seasonal drop-off as consumers switch to other staples in response to relative price changes. A larger proportion of people remain corn consumers throughout the year in the centers of consumption in the outer islands, partly because of limited access to rice, which is the preferred staple, in these areas which are not well suited to rice production. On the outer islands, the peak in corn consumption, which corresponds to the major harvest in these regions, usually comes later in the year than for Java.

From the perspective of Indonesian consumers, corn is not a homogeneous commodity, and ways of preparing grain corn for consumption as a staple food differ across the major consuming regions of Indonesia. Most methods involve breaking the grain to make it more palatable and digestible. Because of differences in flintiness, starchiness, or ratio of germ to starch, varieties of corn differ in their yield of edible product. Where higher-yielding corn varieties have been introduced, farmers occasionally discounted the increased production if it did not lead to corresponding

FIGURE 5.3. *Average weekly household consumption of corn grain in Nusa Tenggara Timur*

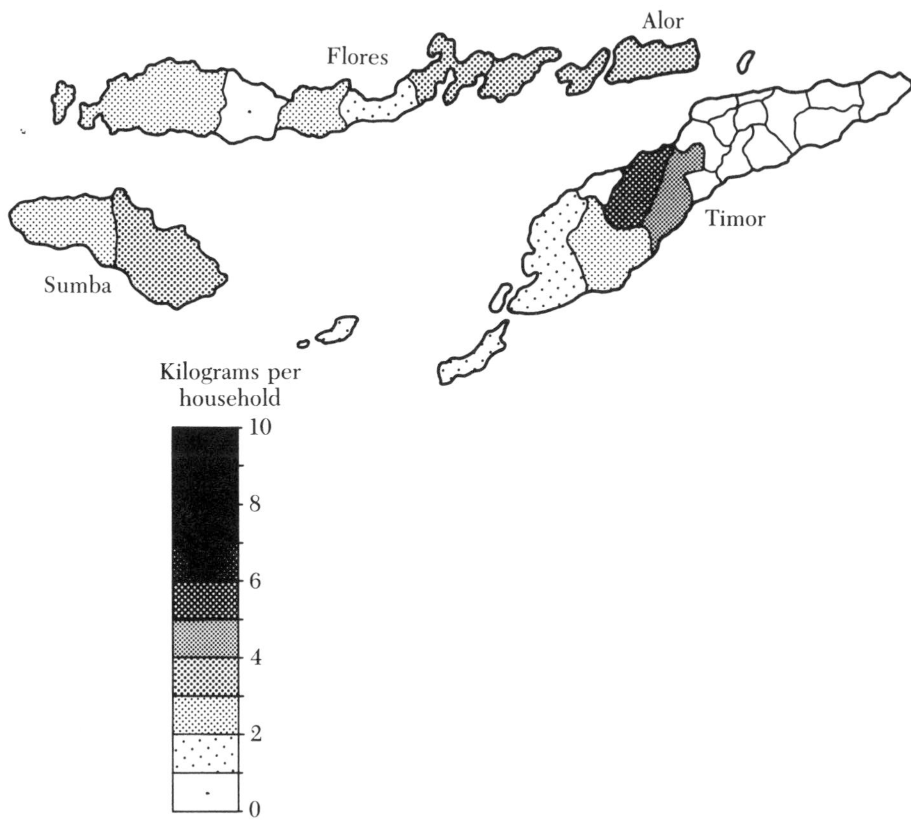

SOURCE: Indonesia, Central Bureau of Statistics, National Socio-Economic Survey (SUSENAS) raw data for 1978.

FIGURE 5.4. *Percentage of staple food calories from corn for* kabupaten *in Java with agroclimatic similarity*

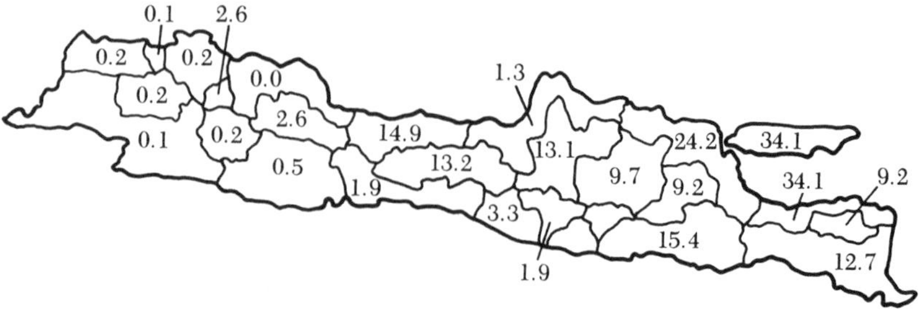

SOURCE: Sajogyo et al. (1980), using data from Indonesia, Central Bureau of Statistics, National Socio-Economic Survey (SUSENAS) for 1976.

increased consumption, due to the corn variety's not being suited to the preferred methods of preparation.

Table 5.6 shows that most households begin with dry, shelled corn, which they process before eating as a starchy staple. In some regions, notably West Java and rural areas in the outer islands, fresh ears of corn are consumed as a vegetable. Cooking with corn flour is rare, except for rural East Java, where it is an ingredient for baked goods eaten as snacks and prepared for holidays. Households produce much of this flour as a by-product in processing cracked corn, the major way they consume corn in that province.[1]

In East Java and South Sulawesi, most corn is consumed as cracked corn that is steamed until it has the approximate size and texture of rice. Indeed, households frequently mix the corn with rice (*beras jagung*) to reduce the cost of eating this preferred staple. The proportions vary as the relative cost of the two grains shifts with the harvest seasons and as the income level of the family changes. In the past, women in the household cracked the corn with small, hand-turned grinders; while this method is still common in South Sulawesi, many households in East Java now rely on diesel-powered grinders operated by private business. For this method of preparation, flintier corn is best suited for grinding since softer varieties with more starch result in excess flour by-product.

In Central Java, consumers prefer varieties of corn with greater starch content since they prepare the staple corn product from flour. To produce the flour from grain, households first soak the dry kernels in water for

[1]In some households, corn flour is simply a by-product of cracking corn, and not all consumption of corn flour reported in the SUSENAS surveys should be added to reported corn grain since the same grain is the basis for cracked corn and flour consumption in such households. However, much of the corn flour consumption reported in the 1978 survey was from Malang and was probably purchased for use in baked goods. If so, it was not a joint product of home processing.

TABLE 5.4. *Percentage of corn (grain equivalent) by acquisition source for major corn-consuming provinces, 1976*

Province	Source of Acquisition			
	Purchased	Own-produced	Others (gifts)	Total
Central Java	56.4	42.0	1.6	100.0
D.I. Yogyakarta	7.2	91.4	1.5	100.0
East Java	62.6	35.3	2.1	100.0
Nusa Tenggara Timur	18.8	78.6	2.6	100.0
North Sulawesi	42.0	55.3	2.7	100.0
Central Sulawesi	29.5	67.1	3.5	100.0
South Sulawesi	26.4	70.6	3.0	100.0
Southeast Sulawesi	21.2	78.7	0.1	100.0
All Indonesia	50.8	47.0	2.2	100.0

SOURCE: Indonesia, Central Bureau of Statistics, National Socio-Economic Survey (SUSENAS) raw data for 1976.

several days until soft, pound them by hand into a mash, and sun dry it. They screen out the chaff, germ, and gritty particles to produce a flour which is steamed until fluffy. Rarely do households mix corn directly with rice; they tend to alternate between the two staples, depending on their financial means to buy rice. Consumers in these regions do not favor flint types of corn because they are harder to process into flour when the traditional method of preparation is used and they yield more grit by-product. In Nusa Tenggara Timur, corn is consumed primarily as porridge. The household simply boils the grain until soft and palatable and adds other condiments, such as sugar, according to taste. The porridge may also be mixed with dried cassava (*gaplek*) or fresh cassava (see Dorosh 1984c).

Although there is some consumption of fresh ear corn as a vegetable in urban areas, it is mostly farm households that consume fresh corn. It provides these rural families with an important source of energy several weeks before the main harvest, and thus it is an important component of

TABLE 5.5. *Seasonal variation in percentage of corn consumers, by quarter, 1978*

Province	Share of population consuming corn (percent)				
	1st quarter	2d quarter	3d quarter	4th quarter	Annual average
Central Java	38.2	21.0	10.0	12.9	20.5
D.I. Yogyakarta	31.5	10.3	3.4	1.1	11.6
East Java	42.6	26.7	27.3	30.5	31.8
Nusa Tenggara Timur	36.4	45.7	62.6	48.5	48.3
North Sulawesi	26.7	36.4	37.6	44.0	36.2
Central Sulawesi	14.7	17.3	15.2	18.1	16.3
South Sulawesi	25.9	24.9	14.9	14.2	19.9
Southeast Sulawesi	34.5	52.3	38.9	39.9	41.4

SOURCE: Indonesia, Central Bureau of Statistics, National Socio-Economic Survey (SUSENAS) raw data for 1978.

TABLE 5.6. *Corn consumption by form and region*

	Corn consumed (grams)					
Form	All Indonesia	All Java	East Java	Central Java	West Java	Off Java
Fresh						
Rural	43	18	1	6	36	88
Urban	13	10	21	0	23	17
Dried corn with husk						
Rural	25	10	18	8	4	52
Urban	3	1	2	1	0	6
Grain corn						
Rural	296	369	589	508	12	168
Urban	28	25	84	22	2	34
Flour						
Rural	18	20	54	4	0	16
Urban	2	1	0	0	1	4

SOURCE: Indonesia, Central Bureau of Statistics, "National Socio-Economic Survey: Java, Madura, and Off Java" (SUSENAS), February Sub-round 1979 (March 1982).
NOTE: Figures represent average weekly consumption per capita.

the diet during the *paceklik* season. Boiling or roasting the ears is most common, but households sometimes strip the ears so that the grains can be added to a flour mixture for making a fritter-like snack. Corn is also a primary input in some types of commercially prepared noodles. The noodle industry requires extra-white varieties of corn for color purity in clear noodles, and several areas that grow local varieties in Central Java and South Sulawesi are the main suppliers. Since noodle factories first process the corn into starch before forming it into thin noodles, they prefer starchier corn varieties. Noodles are typically consumed as a snack food bought from roadside food stalls, and thus they are more commonly found in urban areas or upper-income class diets.

Within a region, consumers give generally uniform reasons for preferring white or yellow corn varieties and cite consumption characteristics, such as taste, texture, and odor, and economic factors, such as proportions of processed output, much as they do in stating preferred qualities of rice varieties. Across regions, however, no simple, consistent logic exists for preferences based on milling characteristics. On Java, farmers claim yellow varieties yield more cracked corn when home processed, although they believe yellow varieties produce a higher proportion of flour to grit. But farmers in South Sulawesi commonly observe that local white varieties are preferable to introduced yellow varieties, partly because white corn mills into a higher proportion of the cracked corn that is preferred locally. Meanwhile, noodle manufacturers in Central Java specifically cite the South Sulawesi varieties as superior for flour content when processed for starch. It may be that habit and consumption characteristics of the varieties are more important factors than milling qualities in determining preferences in each region.

Quantitative Significance of Household Corn Consumption

The average figures for corn consumption drawn from the food balance sheet and shown in Table 5.1 appear to indicate that corn is the third most important source of calories in the Indonesian diet, far behind rice but nearly on a par with coconuts and only slightly ahead of cassava. This average pattern of Indonesia as a multi-staple food economy based on a heavy dominance of rice is a useful first picture of food consumption preferences and patterns, for it suggests high rates of potential substitution among alternative sources of staple calories.

Such potential substitution, however, also suggests that actual consumption patterns are likely to be highly diverse at any given time and reflect seasonal, geographical, income, and price differences facing individual households. This diversity does not show up in time series data for consumption, based as they are on food balance sheet calculations for all of Indonesia. Cross-section data from SUSENAS, the National Socio-Economic Survey of Indonesia's households that has been carried out two or three times each decade since the mid-1960s, show the diversity clearly along each of the dimensions indicated. Unfortunately, the figures for average consumption of corn per capita drawn from the food balance sheet data do not agree with the average figures determined from SUSENAS results, either for absolute values in any given year or for trends in consumption per capita since the mid-1970s or so.

Because all analysis of Indonesia's patterns of corn consumption is drawn from one or both of these basic sources of data, it is important to reconcile the differences and, to the extent that crucial problems remain, to remember the tentative nature of any conclusions drawn on the basis of these data. With this proviso, this chapter proceeds with four tasks: an examination of the importance of corn in the Indonesian diet; a comparison of food balance sheet data with SUSENAS data for corn consumption by humans; an attempt to estimate basic parameters for corn consumption that reflect the flexibility of household decision making when incomes or corn prices change; and a reconciliation of the important differences between income elasticities for corn consumption estimated from time series data and those from cross-section data. Since the income elasticity drawn from time series data is positive, and from cross-section data negative, the reconciliation is essential to projections of household corn consumption.

The Importance of Corn Consumption

Average direct per capita consumption of corn as food is between 15 and 20 kilograms per year in Indonesia, and corn provides roughly 10 percent of the 150 to 200 kilograms of grain-equivalent calories needed annually as a minimum by a normal working adult. The next section tries to make this estimate somewhat more precise and to determine trends over time in the total, but it is important at this stage not to treat the aggregate as representative of some "average" Indonesian consumer. The corn-consuming population in Indonesia is in fact relatively small, perhaps only one in seven people, and for that population, corn is the primary food staple during at least part of the year.

Table 5.7 shows how much corn is consumed in the seven leading corn-consuming provinces by the part of the population that reported corn consumption in the 1978 SUSENAS. These provinces, which include East and Central Java, accounted for 46 percent of Indonesia's total population in the 1980 census of 147.5 million. Even though these are the primary corn-consuming areas, on average only 27 percent of the population in these seven provinces reported consuming corn. If there were no corn consumers in any other province, only 12.5 percent of Indonesia's total population would be corn consumers, or one in eight. Small numbers elsewhere probably bring the total up to about 14 percent.

For these consumers, corn plays a very important role in the diet. Table 5.7 shows that consumption per capita is over 100 kilograms per year in Southeast Sulawesi, Nusa Tenggara Timur, and North Sulawesi and over 90 kilograms per year in Central Sulawesi, East Java, Central Java, and South Sulawesi. Since individuals rarely consume more than 150 to 200 kilograms of grain directly in a year, corn must be the primary calorie source for most of these households.

In total, more than 18 million people in Indonesia consume corn as their staple foodstuff. A comparison with Kenya, where corn is by all accounts the staple foodstuff in the diet, shows the importance of corn in Indonesia. In 1980, 17.4 million Kenyans consumed roughly 1.8 million metric tons of corn, for an intake per capita of just over 100 kilograms per year (USDA 1981). At about the same time, 18.4 million Indonesians were consuming 1.7 million tons of corn, for an intake per capita of about 95 kilograms per year. If Indonesia's corn consumers were all gathered in one locale, they would represent a corn-based society as large as Kenya's.

Incomes and seasonal variations serve to concentrate corn consumption even further, making it yet more important to particular households at key times during the year. Table 5.7 shows that the ratio between the share of population consuming corn in the highest quarter relative to the average share ranges from 1.11 in Central Sulawesi to 1.86 in Central Java. A ratio of 1.00 would indicate an even seasonal distribution of corn consumption, whereas the higher values indicate substantial concentration of corn consumption in one or two quarters of the year. The seasonality is sharpest in Central Java, where corn's role in bridging the "hungry season" for the poor is critical. But seasonal peaks are also the pattern in East Java, South Sulawesi, and Nusa Tenggara Timur.

TABLE 5.7. *Importance of corn to particular populations*

Province	1980 population of province (millions)	Proportion of corn eaters[a] (percent)	Corn-eating population (millions)	Annual per capita consumption by corn eaters (kilograms)	Quarterly high share by corn eaters relative to average share
Southeast Sulawesi	0.942	41.1	0.387	118.0	1.27
Nusa Tenggara Timur	2.737	48.2	1.319	105.5	1.30
North Sulawesi	2.115	36.2	0.766	101.8	1.22
Central Sulawesi	1.290	16.3	0.210	94.6	1.11
East Java	29.189	31.8	9.282	92.8	1.34
Central Java	25.373	20.5	5.201	92.8	1.86
South Sulawesi	6.062	19.9	1.206	90.0	1.30
TOTAL	67.708		18.371	94.5	

SOURCE: Based on data in Monteverde (1987).
[a]Average proportion over an entire year.

FIGURE 5.5. *Per capita corn consumption per week, by form of consumption and income group, 1976 and 1980*

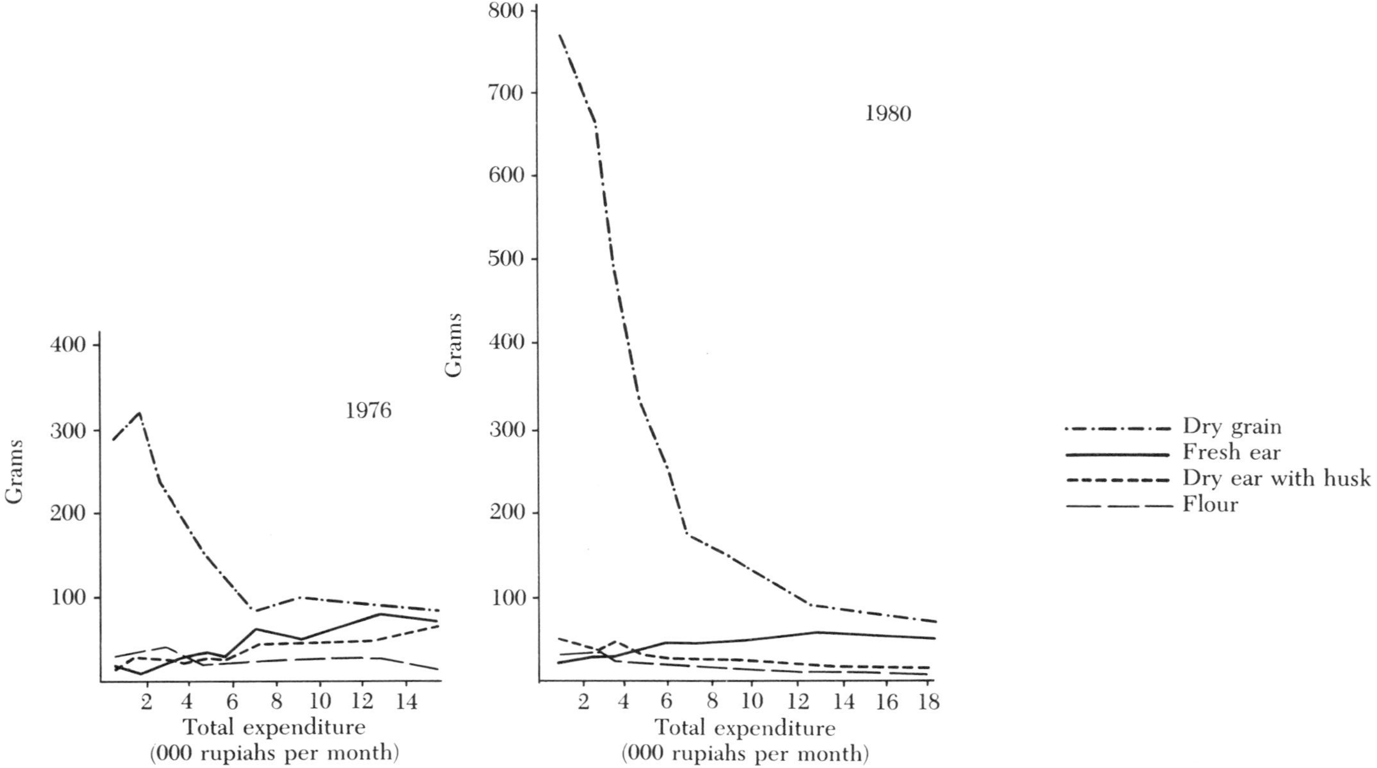

Income is also a major determinant of corn consumption. Figure 5.5 shows a strong downward trend in consumption of corn at higher incomes.[2] There is an important difference in this pattern, however, between the two SUSENAS samples shown in Figure 5.5. The 1980 SUSENAS shows a decline in consumption of corn grain and dry grain equivalents through the entire range of income—in contrast to the 1976 SUSENAS, which shows an *increase* in corn consumption from the first to second income groups before a steady decline in consumption sets in with increasing levels of income. The 1970 SUSENAS also shows this pattern, which suggests that in the early part of the 1970s, corn grain for the poorest segments of the society was a normal good, with its consumption rising with income. At the time of the 1976 SUSENAS survey, these were about 17 percent of the population, and the group for whom corn represented a normal good would probably have been an even larger percentage in 1970.

For all income groups, dry corn grain is the most important base for household preparation, but its proportion of total corn consumption at different income levels varies considerably. For the poorest income strata, dry corn grain accounts for close to 80 percent of total quantities, but at higher income levels this proportion falls, as flour and fresh and dry cob preparations claim almost 50 percent of a consumption level that is smaller in total. This is consistent with the general tendency for diets to include more vegetables and foods requiring more preparation as incomes increase. Fresh corn, served in a variety of ways as a vegetable, is generally consumed in greater amounts as income rises, though the 1980 SUSENAS gives some indication that at higher income levels other vegetables also substitute in the diet. Consumption of corn flour, which is used for baking, similarly increases through median income groups until it is replaced by wheat flour. In both cases, corn appears to shift from a normal good to an inferior good at about the income range that enables households to purchase higher-quality substitutes and enliven the basic diet.

Determining Aggregate Levels of Corn Consumption

The two major sources of data on per capita consumption of corn—the food balance sheets and the SUSENAS surveys—provide conflicting estimates. Comparison of the two sources in Table 5.8 shows that food balance sheet figures are generally higher than SUSENAS estimates by as much as 85 percent. The gap between the two sets of figures is partly due to the two different approaches to estimating consumption.

[2]The SUSENAS surveys report data only on total expenditures rather than on income, and the difference is attributed to savings. For our purposes, the difference between total expenditures and income is slight, and the two terms are used interchangeably in this chapter.

TABLE 5.8. *Corn availability per capita: official food balance sheet and SUSENAS estimates*

Year	Production	Imports	Exports	Seed[a]	Losses[b]	Feed[b]	Industry	Available for consumption	Available per capita	SUSENAS estimate[c]
	(000 tons)								(kilograms)	
Grain										
1968	3,166	—	66	66	62	62	—	2,910	26.18	
1969	2,293	—	156	70	43	43	—	1,981	17.43	
1970	2,825	—	253	50	51	51	—	2,420	20.83	22.0
1971	2,606	—	219	66	48	48	—	2,225	18.70	
1972	2,254	—	78	56	44	44	—	2,032	16.71	
1973	3,690	—	181	72	70	70	—	3,297	26.46	
1974	3,011	—	197	60	56	56	—	2,640	20.69	
1975	2,903	—	51	46	57	57	—	2,692	20.61	
1976	2,572	54	3	66	52	52	—	2,451	18.34	9.9
1977	3,142	9	10	72	62	63	—	2,943	21.52	
1978	4,029	26	21	64	81	81	—	3,808	27.21	18.20/21.22
1979	3,724	70	7	65	189	75	—	3,458	24.14	13.00/14.51
1980	3,991	34	15	65	197	237	—	3,443	23.55	13.00/14.51
Fresh ear[d]										
1968	556							556	5.00	
1969	568							568	5.00	
1970	581							581	5.00	
1971	594							594	5.00	
1972	608							608	5.00	
1973	623							623	5.00	
1974	638							638	5.00	
1975	653							653	5.00	
1976	299							299	2.24	
1977	306							306	2.24	
1978	233							233	1.66	6.24
1979	283							283	1.98	2.08
1980	327							327	2.24	2.08

SOURCES: Indonesia, Central Bureau of Statistics, "Food Balance Sheet for Indonesia," for 1968–74, 1975, and 1980. Indonesia, Central Bureau of Statistics, "The National Socio-Economic Survey: Java, Madura, and Off Java" (SUSENAS), February 1979 Sub-round (March 1982).

[a]Seed use is estimated at 23.838 kilograms per hectare.

[b]Losses and livestock feed use are estimated at 2 percent of production for the period 1968–1978.

[c]Where two figures are presented, the first includes corn grain and corn grain equivalents of dry ears with husk. The second figure includes corn grain equivalents of corn flour as well. To convert the SUSENAS recording of the four forms of corn consumption, the authors have used dry weight equivalents of grain of 1.0, 0.45, and 0.35 for flour, dried ear corn with husk, and fresh ear corn, respectively. These weights are based on relative prices for the respective commodities in wholesale markets in East Java. An attempt to measure the physical conversion coefficients by weighing samples purchased in one village in Central Java yielded a factor of 0.8 for dried ear corn with husk and 0.7 for fresh ear corn.

[d]For the period 1968–1975, fresh ear consumption was estimated from consumption surveys at 50 ears per capita per year, at 10 ears per kilogram.

The official food balance sheet figures for availability of corn grain per capita averaged almost 22 kilograms through the 1970s and rose toward the end of the decade, although not to the peaks seen in 1968 or 1973. Major year-to-year swings in availability are evident; from 1972 to 1973 the figures show a 59 percent increase. Several difficulties with these data lead to overestimation of corn's availability for household consumption and of variability from year to year. Food balance sheets calculate availability per capita as a residual after other sources of disappearance are deducted, and errors in these other components bias the figures for household corn consumption. As Chapter 2 shows, official estimates of corn production are too high by as much as 15 percent because of estimates of corn yields that exceed the more reliable ones from the provincial Departments of Agriculture. Reinforcing this bias, official estimates of corn use as livestock feed are very low because they are apparently based on direct use of corn by feed mills. They omit both corn that livestock raisers mix with purchased feed concentrate and corn fed to village chickens. As Chapter 6 indicates, these amounts are greater than those picked up in the food balance sheet. The food balance sheet also probably underestimates the disappearance of corn through losses and industrial uses other than the livestock feed industry, but these components are small and less significantly bias the figures for availability per capita of corn.

The food balance sheet also presents data for consumption of fresh ear corn as a vegetable, and through 1975, it estimated consumption on the basis of 5 kilograms per capita per year. It is not clear what method was used for subsequent revision of estimating fresh ear consumption, but the results are not stable as a proportion of production or on a per capita basis. Farm families in rural areas consume most of the fresh corn, taking the ears from corn fields where dry ears will be the main harvest. Results from Corn Project farm surveys in several production areas indicate that farmers harvest notable quantities of fresh ear corn. In parts of Central Java and South Sulawesi, farm households harvest up to 6 percent of a field's yield in ears for their own consumption.

Table 5.9 presents an adjusted food balance sheet that accounts for some of these factors. Availability per capita is substantially reduced from official figures as they were adjusted for lower corn production and greater absorption by livestock feed use and losses. Annual consumption of dry corn grain is reduced to 13.7 kilograms per capita as an average for the 1970s, and consumption apparently increases at the turn of the decade. The adjusted food balance sheet figures are not corrected for year-to-year variability in production. As discussed in Chapter 2, this variation is partly a statistical creation and stems from reporting of crop production on a calendar-year basis, which occasionally captures parts of two principal harvests at year's end. To correct for variability would require crop pro-

TABLE 5.9. *Adjusted food balance sheet for corn grain*

Year	Production[a]	Imports	Exports	Seed[b]	Losses[c]	Feed[d]	Industry[e]	Available for consumption[f]	Available per capita[f]	Population
	(000 tons)							(kilograms)		(millions)
1970	2,224	0	282	66	222	129	30	1,495	12.70	117.7
1971	2,105	0	217	54	211	150	30	1,443	11.98	120.4
1972	1,753	0	79	86	175	164	30	1,219	9.89	123.2
1973	2,951	142	180	67	295	186	30	2,335	18.51	126.1
1974	2,296	0	197	61	230	212	35	1,561	12.10	129.0
1975	2,315	0	51	52	232	243	60	1,677	12.70	132.0
1976	2,430	54	4	64	243	284	92	1,797	13.30	135.1
1977	2,573	10	10	76	257	296	70	1,874	13.56	138.2
1978	3,393	26	21	65	339	352	98	2,544	17.99	141.4
1979	2,853	70	7	68	285	385	73	2,105	14.54	144.7
1980	3,419	33	15	74	342	452	30	2,539	17.15	148.0
1981	3,858	2	5	70	386	599	30	2,770	18.30	151.3

[a]Official data on area × adjusted yields. See Chapter 2.
[b]Seed calculated at 25 kilograms per hectare × area harvested in the subsequent year.
[c]Losses are estimated at 10 percent of domestic production.
[d]Estimates of livestock feed use are taken from Chapter 6.
[e]Calculated on a base of 30,000 tons per year for medium- and large-scale firms producing mostly processed foods and beverages, plus use by the corn oil factory P.T. Indocorn, which operated using domestic corn between 1974 and 1979.
[f]Comparable to grain equivalent of dry forms of corn consumption reported by SUSENAS, that is, dry ear with husk, corn flour, and dry grain.

duction figures by crop year, which are not available on a national level. Table 5.9 also does not attempt to include use of fresh ear corn; the SUSENAS figures for individual years are the best available.

SUSENAS estimates of corn grain consumption by humans for selected years are generally lower than either the official or adjusted food balance sheet estimates. They show annual consumption of 13 kilograms per capita in 1978, down sharply from the 22 kilograms per capita in 1969–1970. On the other hand, SUSENAS estimates for 1976 are less than one-half the 1969–1970 level and only slightly more than one-half of the reported 1978 level; so there are also major problems with these data. The SUSENAS reliance on recall survey techniques probably results in underreportage of consumption both through unintentional omissions and conscious underreporting of what is considered an inferior good. Offsetting this bias in the 1978 and 1980 SUSENAS figures reported in Table 5.8 is their derivation as annualized consumption from the results of the February sub-rounds of the survey. This is a season of greater corn consumption since it corresponds to the principal corn harvest. If average annual consumption of corn is taken to fall somewhere between the SUSENAS and adjusted food balance sheet estimates, it would be substantially below official estimates. At the end of the 1970s, it probably remained above 13 kilograms per capita for dry corn grain.

Parameters of Change: Estimating Income and Price Elasticities

A detailed description of corn consumption patterns is important for revealing the groups that rely most heavily on corn as a staple food, but additional information is needed to understand how these patterns may change in the future. Two major factors—incomes and prices—bear directly on levels of consumption and are of particular interest since ongoing economic growth and specific government policies influence both.

What happens to corn consumption when incomes and prices change? Although price changes are roughly comparable for all corn consumers, if allowance is made for quality differences and transportation margins, the same is obviously not true of income changes. Since income data tend to be from aggregate national income statistics, a difficult but crucial question concerns how incomes of corn consumers are linked to aggregate changes in income. Answering this question requires an intensive effort to determine who the consumers of corn are. With this knowledge it may be possible to make at least rough judgments about the links between incomes of corn-consuming households and the performance of the overall economy.

Linking changes in corn consumption to future changes in income and price is straightforward in concept, but in practice it requires a careful choice among the four forms these parameters can take. These forms differ by the period of adjustment and disaggregation of the population to which the parameters are applied, and they correspond to the cells in the following two-by-two matrix.

Period of Adjustment	Aggregation level	
	National	Household
short run	time series	?
long run	lag models aggregated	cross section

Which form of the parameters one uses depends on the nature of the question asked. Year-to-year changes in market demand because of a change in price can best be projected from short-run, national aggregate parameters. Adjustments after several years by low-income households, for example, are reflected from disaggregated long-run parameters. National, long-run parameters show full adjustment responses in aggregate, whereas short-run, disaggregated parameters attempt to capture immediate behavioral responses of specific types of households.

Two types of information are available—time series and cross-section data—for estimating price and income parameters for each of the four cells. A cardinal rule of statistical analysis is that no information can be derived from data that were not generated using such information in the first place. Consequently, disaggregated parameters of consumer decision making—income and price elasticities by income class, for example—cannot be estimated from national aggregate data. Time series data on corn consumption are made up from food balance sheet calculations and do not contain any information suitable for estimating disaggregated parameters. But these data do show year-to-year changes and can be used for estimating short-run parameters of change with respect to changes in incomes and prices. By estimating distributed lag models with time series data, it is also possible under certain circumstances to derive long-run elasticities.

SUSENAS data, on the other hand, reflect a wealth of household-specific characteristics during a specific time period such as a year. This wealth of variability permitted Monteverde (1987) to estimate income-class specific price and income elasticities for corn which had eluded earlier investigators. These disaggregated consumption parameters do not reflect year-to-year changes in household behavior when prices and incomes change but rather long-run adjustments to differences in these variables among different households in the same time period. Although the historical existence of certain general consumption patterns argues that households with low incomes will tend to behave like present high-income households when the former reach the income levels of the latter, many intervening variables argue for caution in using this interpretation of such parameters too rigorously. Still, by aggregating the parameters derived from household data using share in consumption as weights, it is possible to get long-run parameters compatible with those from time series distributed lag models.

Despite the richness of Indonesian data on corn consumption, some parameters are difficult to obtain. Direct estimation of parameters disaggregated by income class for the short run is infeasible in the absence of representative, cross-section panel data over time. For now, intuitive insights gained from patterns that link the other three cells are likely to provide the best guidance for filling the remaining cell. For all the cells, the cross-price elasticity of corn consumption with respect to the price of rice is probably important in explaining consumption behavior. Unfortunately, cross-price elasticities are notoriously difficult to estimate, especially by income class, and thus the focus here is primarily on estimates of income and own-price elasticities.

Time Series Estimates of Corn Consumption Parameters

Time series analysis of Indonesian corn data is possible using adjusted food balance sheet data shown in Table 5.9. A simple double logarithmic consumption function is used, with several alternative specifications and variable definitions examined. The general estimating form is:

$$Q = a_0 + a_1 P_c + a_2 P_i + a_3 Y + e,$$

where

Q = log of per capita availability of corn for human consumption;
P_c = log of wholesale price of corn deflated, and
  P_{c1} = log of 12-month average of P_c,
  P_{c2} = log of January–April average;
P_i = log of wholesale cross price, deflated, and
  PGAB = log of rough rice (*gabah*) price,
  PCSV = log of fresh cassava price;
Y = log of real income per capita, with
  Y_1 = log of non-estate agricultural GNP per capita, and
  Y_2 = log of P_{c1} × adjusted corn production;
e = an additive logarithmic error term with the usual assumed distribution.

Two alternative own-price series were compared; the four-month average corresponded to the period when most corn is consumed during the year. Two income series were also tried. Total GNP was considered inappropriate for deriving income per capita since it is strongly influenced by oil and other nonagricultural components which are felt by the rural, corn-consuming population only with considerable lags. One alternative was agricultural national product per capita, with estate crops excluded. Also used was a proxy for corn income to see whether income fluctuations due to corn were a significant explanatory factor in corn consumption. Since about one-half of corn consumption is from market purchases and many of these are made by noncorn farmers, this latter specification was used tentatively, although it performed well in statistical terms.

Simplest specifications performed best, as can be seen in Table 5.10. The most striking result was the consistently significant and positive income elasticity parameter across the equations, which ranged from 0.72 to 1.77. This strong result from the time series is not consistent with the income-related corn consumption patterns already presented or with the cross-section results to be discussed next. Inclusion of rice and fresh cassava prices gave sharply conflicting results, depending on which income term was included in the equation. The corn-related income term performed best, at least in terms of plausible signs and magnitudes for the other coefficients. For example, Equation 4 or 8 in Table 5.10 has highly significant and negative own-price elasticities of between 0.5 and 0.6; negative cross-price elasticities with rice, which indicates the important role of rice prices in determining the real income of corn consumers; small but positive cross-price elasticities with cassava, which indicates its role as a substitute for corn; and positive income elasticities for corn of about 0.8. The problems with this positive income elasticity have already been noted and will be returned to again.

The time series analysis is obviously hampered by extensive problems with the adjusted food balance sheet data and by the severely limited number of observations. Only the twelve years from 1970 to 1981 can be used with any confidence. Factors such as distribution of income and perceived availability of corn at the household level may not be reflected in the data, since these are derived from relatively fixed assumptions about several alternative end uses. More important, these factors are difficult to include as independent variables in explaining the time series trend. If ignored, prices and average changes in incomes per capita are left to account for all the changes. This they do quite robustly, but the income coefficient in particular may be biased.

Attempts were made to include other potential variables in the demand function to test whether the time series result was a consequence of misspecification of the demand relationship, but these were not suc-

TABLE 5.10. *Time series estimates of income and price elasticities for corn*

Equation	Constant	P_{C1}	P_{C2}	PGAB	PCSV	Y_1	Y_2	R^2	Statistics F	Statistics Durbin-Watson
1*	−3.64 (−0.79)	−0.05 (−0.13)				0.85 (1.61)		.76	4.2	2.0
2*	−13.52 (−4.90)	0.25 (0.82)		0.66 (2.61)	0.03 (0.14)	1.32 (5.38)		.89	6.7	2.6
3*	−3.62 (−3.84)	−0.54 (−3.43)					0.72 (12.40)	.96	55.7	2.1
4*	−2.13 (−2.44)	−0.59 (−4.88)		−0.32 (−3.20)	0.08 (1.21)		0.79 (16.67)	.99	83.5	2.1
5	−12.93 (−3.68)		0.71 (1.74)			1.77 (4.67)		.67	11.0	2.1
6*	−13.27 (−5.42)		0.32 (0.97)	0.58 (2.24)	−0.02 (−0.02)	1.39 (2.24)		.89	7.2	2.6
7	−5.19 (−7.04)		−0.54 (−3.46)				0.85 (13.86)	.96	96.3	2.0
8	−4.56 (−6.29)		−0.54 (−5.03)	−0.16 (−1.57)	0.18 (2.98)		0.80 (14.20)	.99	101.9	2.3

SOURCE: Estimated from data in Table 5.9.
NOTES: PGAB = price of rough rice (*gabah*); PCSV = price of cassava; *T*-statistics are in parentheses. Starred equations are corrected for first order serial correlation.

cessful. A squared income term was tried in order to capture changes in the income elasticity that might result from changing distribution of income, but the term was generally insignificant. A time trend contributed little to explaining consumption, which indicates that tastes were not changing radically during the period under review. Lagged consumption was also included in an effort to measure potential friction in adjustment to desired levels of consumption upon changes in independent variables. Lack of explanatory power of this term across the equations suggests that consumers adjust levels of corn consumption quickly—within a year—to changes in prices and income.

Cross-Section Estimates of Corn Consumption Parameters

Extensive work on food consumption in Indonesia has been conducted with the cross-section data from the various SUSENAS surveys. Cross-section data have typically been used to estimate income elasticities or highly restricted forms of price elasticities using the Frisch technique for estimating a full system of demand parameters. A quite different approach was used by Timmer (1978a, 1978b) and by Timmer and Alderman (1979) to coax directly estimated price elasticities out of cross-section data. They exploited price variance existing in the SUSENAS data not only from differentials in transportation costs between market areas but also from seasonal price changes across the three sub-rounds conducted for the 1976 SUSENAS survey.

One difficulty with using cross-section data for such analysis is that constant tastes are assumed across the sample; corn consumption is highly regional, as has been noted previously. This problem was alleviated to a degree in the work by Timmer and his colleagues by using cell means—often with more than one thousand households averaged together—as observations. These groupings were still disaggregated by income class, province, urban or rural location, and sub-round. Averaging within each cell homogenized some of the interhousehold taste differences across cells; the inclusion of dummy variables for income group and province also helped account for regional taste differences.

The general estimation model used for this analysis is

$$Q = a_0 + a_i + a_1 TX + a_2 TX^2 + a_{3i} P + a_{4i} XP + a_{5j} R_j + a_{6k} T_k + a_{7h} D_h + e,$$

where

Q = log of corn (or other commodity) consumption per capita in kilograms per week for each cell mean (Q has i, j, and k subscripts);

a_0 = overall intercept;
a_i = intercept for the ith income class;
TX = log of total expenditure per capita for each cell mean;
TX^2 = TX squared;
P = log of own price, calculated as the value of expenditures on the commodity divided by the quantity, for each cell;
XP = log of cross-price terms, similarly defined;
R_j = zero-one dummy variables for island groupings or provinces;
T_k = zero-one dummy variable for each of the three sub-rounds for which data were reported (January–April, May–August, September–December);
D_h = other dummy or interaction variables; and
e = an additive logarithmic error term with the usual assumed distribution.

In this form, the Engel function relating consumption to income is double log quadratic, which gives an income elasticity of $a_1 + 2\,a_2TX$. If a_2 is negative, the income elasticity declines at higher incomes for goods with positive income elasticities. This choice of specification is pragmatic; it seems to fit the data best for lower-income groups. The model also estimates price elasticities separately for four income groups. Differences in price elasticities are likely to result from the Slutsky relationship because budget shares and income elasticities for basic foods vary with income as well as because systematic variations occur in the compensated price elasticities (Timmer 1981b).

The model was estimated by Timmer and Alderman (1979) for rice, fresh cassava, and total calories from these two staples plus corn. Since commodity coverage was so limited, no opportunity existed for testing homogeneity and adding up restrictions from consumer demand theory, nor was symmetry of cross-price elasticities imposed. The approach was a pragmatic effort to estimate a portion of the full matrix of price and income elasticities and did not attempt to link demand equations via demand theory.

Results from this model were robust, but unfortunately separate results for corn were inconsistent and not reported. The model was subsequently modified by Monteverde (1987) and reapplied to derive parameters for corn. To clarify the corn consumption parameters, Monteverde applied the framework of Timmer and Alderman (1979) directly to the more than 24,000 household observations in the 1978 SUSENAS survey. This approach yielded the negative own-price elasticities for corn grain consumption which had eluded all previous analysts. The results shown in Table 5.11 reveal that poor consumers of corn are responsive to price changes. The positive own-price elasticity of the highest income quartile is not significant. The standard errors of the estimates increase with income and reflect the decline in the number of corn consumers (and thereby the sample size) as income increases. The limited sample sizes of the higher income groups result in standard errors too large to make comparisons of the elasticities across all income groups with confidence. A comparison of the elasticities of those who consume most of the corn—households in the bottom two quartiles—suggests that poor consumers of corn are more responsive to price changes than richer consumers (Alderman 1985; Timmer 1981b).

From the specification used to find the price elasticities, expenditure (income) elasticities for 1978 were also obtained. Unfortunately, the standard errors in all but the lowest quartile were too large to make meaningful estimates. The large standard errors were a result of the smaller sample size of corn consumers in higher-income groups and likely collinearity between prices and income. For the poorest quartile, the expenditure elasticity for corn grain was −0.63 and was highly significant.

Separate estimates of expenditure elasticities for several forms of corn consumption by urban and rural populations based on the 1980 SUSENAS survey are reported in Table 5.12. These estimates were derived from aggregate data and avoid the problem of multicollinearity. The consistent downward slope in consumption with respect to income by 1980, as presented earlier in Figure 5.5, reveals the uniform negative income elasticity across income groups for the consumption of corn as a starchy staple.

Several important results can be taken from the cross-section analysis. First, because of the sheer massiveness of the data and the nature of the econometric techniques applied to the data, the analysis is overwhelm-

TABLE 5.11. *Own-price elasticities for corn grain in rural Indonesia, by income quartile, 1978*

Income quartile	Own-price elasticity
Poor	−0.58 (0.12)
Low	−0.29 (0.29)
Middle	−1.25 (0.47)
High	0.16 (0.56)

SOURCE: Estimated by Monteverde (1987) from Indonesia, Central Bureau of Statistics, National Socio-Economic Survey (SUSENAS) raw data for 1978.
NOTE: Standard errors are indicated in parentheses.

TABLE 5.12. *Income elasticities by corn type, 1980*

Corn type	Rural	Urban
Corn grain	−0.75	−0.82
Fresh corn	0.39	1.20
Dried corn with husk	−0.34	insignificant
Corn flour	−0.53	insignificant

SOURCE: Estimated by Monteverde from National Socio-Economic Survey (SUSENAS) raw data for 1980.

ingly complicated and seemingly endless. The results discussed here are the tip of an iceberg involving dozens of years of professionals' time in collection of data, organization, analysis, and interpretation. The patterns seen as a result of this massive effort are elusive, and *some* econometric result is consistent with virtually any hypothesis. In such a situation, the guidelines from consumer theory are especially helpful. The results presented here are not the last word.

Second, after years of trying it is now possible to say with some confidence that corn consumers respond to changes in the price of corn in a manner predicted by this consumer theory and corroborated earlier for other commodities in the Indonesian food economy. Most corn consumption occurs in the bottom quartile of the rural population, and these consumers have a long-run price elasticity of about −0.6. This is an important result because it confirms the economic rationality of corn consumers and simultaneously indicates the real welfare consequences that can be transmitted to the rural poor through market price linkages.

Third, and most perplexing for understanding the future path of consumption, the income elasticity for corn estimated from recent cross-section data is negative for all income classes. Although this is consistent with results from other countries in stages of development similar to Indonesia's, it is strikingly inconsistent with the significantly positive income elasticities estimated from the time series data.

Reconciling the Estimates of Income Elasticities

Whether the income elasticity of demand for corn is positive or negative is crucial for any estimate of corn consumption by humans in the future because the projections differ radically depending on the value used. Given the apparent shakiness of the estimated corn consumption parameters, it might appear preferable simply to extrapolate past trends in corn consumption. But in probing for potential explanations of the discrepancy between time series and cross-section results, confidence in the accuracy of trend extrapolation diminishes. Dynamic elements of the corn system that help reconcile the seemingly contradictory cross-section and time series income elasticities undermine the basic premise of trend extrapolation—that whatever structure generated the trends will remain essentially unchanged over the period of projection. Although simple trend projections can be used as a base reference, it is possible to clarify how these dynamic factors may interact and to incorporate them in a more satisfying explanation of consumption of corn by humans.

To a very large extent, the positive income elasticity estimated from the time series data is a result of positive corn production trends that cannot be corroborated from external sources. More important, these trends are not consistent with trends in consumption per capita derived from the various SUSENAS rounds, which show corn consumption *declining* from 1970 to the late 1970s (with the exception of the very poor in the 1976 round). Such declining consumption per capita would, of course, be consistent with a negative income elasticity from the time series data because average incomes per capita rose sharply during the decade.

It may well be that one data source is right, and the other is wrong, in which case comparative and historical evidence would have to favor the SUSENAS data. Fortunately the choice is not so extreme. A combination of several factors, some interrelated, might account for the apparent paradox and allow a reconciliation of the two econometric estimates. No attempt is made here to determine the "right" combination of factors that achieve this reconciliation because the evidence is so spotty that the most plausible combination will be in the eye of the beholder.

The key to reconciling the two estimates is understanding exactly what each of the underlying data sources represents. As Table 5.8 shows, the time series data are derived from aggregate estimates of corn production, adjusted for all other domestic end uses and foreign trade, and divided by total population to yield a figure for average consumption per capita for each year. By contrast, the SUSENAS data are aggregated from a sample of individual households that are surveyed during a particular year. Even if the sample is truly representative—and evidence suggests the SUSENAS surveys have not become more representative of the Indonesian population during the 1970s and early 1980s—these figures for consumption per capita will reflect all of the changes from one survey year to the next in distribution of income, numbers of corn-consuming households, and perceived availability of corn at the household level.

Although the impact from all these factors should also be reflected in the time series data, none of the factors is included as an independent variable to explain the time series trend. This biases the income coefficient, even to the point of having the wrong sign, and thus the following issues must be factored into the interpretation of the estimation results.

First, and perhaps most essential, income distribution may change during the period of analysis. For example, if incomes per capita of the rural poor, who are the primary consumers of corn, declined during the 1970s, no problems exist in reconciling the time series and cross-section estimates of income elasticities. They will both be sharply negative. It is indeed tempting to read consequences *for* income distribution into the rising trend in corn consumption per capita: because the income elasticity for corn is negative, the incomes of corn consumers must have declined during this period. Such an inference is not a necessary one, however plausible for purposes of econometric consistency, because the share of corn consumers in the population might also have been changing.

Evidence presented in the cassava study showed that dried cassava (*gaplek*) is the least preferred staple food in Indonesia (Dixon 1984). If incomes of the very poor rose during the 1970s, many of them may have switched from dried cassava to corn as a source of relatively cheap calories, and thus the share of corn consumers would increase in the total population. In this circumstance, consumption of corn per capita *by corn consumers* would fall as their incomes rose, but the influx of new corn consumers would make average consumption of corn per capita for the total population appear to rise. This effect obviously has a much more positive welfare interpretation than the deteriorating income distribution outlined above.

Another possibility is that producers treat increases in corn output differently than if it were converted directly into cash values. The sharp rise in corn consumption per capita at the turn of the decade—from 13.56 kilograms per capita in 1977 to 18.3 kilograms in 1981 (Table 5.9)—corresponds to an equally sharp rise in production. If the elasticity of consumption out of own production is positive, much of the difficulty in explaining this result disappears.

Economists have problems with such an explanation, however, for it requires compartmentalizing household decision making into commodity and monetary subsets, with only limited mapping from one to the other. This would be plausible if corn could not be sold readily in rural markets, and thus the opportunity costs of added home consumption out of increases in production were very small. It is as if the corn from changes in production had a price of nearly zero for household decision makers but "trend" production levels were evaluated at their market price. Constraints to drying unexpectedly large harvests or discontinuities in marketing have existed for many farmers, but if these contributed to the rise in corn consumption since the mid-1970s, they are likely to play a diminished role in the future.

Recent increases in corn production may have incurred high losses since drying and storage facilities for corn have undergone few changes. Some of these increases may also have been stored by farmers, perhaps as a form of savings. In the derivation of the time series data, the quantities possibly absorbed in this way cannot be measured and are thus attributed to consumption by humans. Quite small quantities attributed to either factor could cause a negative income elasticity from time series data over the past decade. Quantifying losses and on-farm storage for the future is particularly difficult, however, since these two sources of absorption are undergoing substantial change in Indonesia's transition to surplus production of corn.

An additional factor that may account historically for the apparent paradox in income elasticities, but that will play little role in the future, is the positive income elasticity for corn consumption documented for the very poor in the first part of the 1970s. Dixon (1982) has noted that for several SUSENAS rounds the lowest income group had a positive income elasticity, although the weighted average for the whole population was always negative, even for the first round in 1963–1964. A combination of notably higher incomes for the rural poor with a positive income elasticity for corn for this subset of consumers could help explain rising corn consumption per capita. The evidence from 1978 and 1980, however, seems to show significantly negative income elasticities for corn even for the lowest income class. This is a very positive result in terms of rural welfare: very few households are so poor that they will consume more corn when their incomes rise. But the result also suggests that the underlying structure of corn demand is changing, and thus simple trend extrapolation is inappropriate.

The Importance of Corn to Indonesian Consumers

Corn has long been one of the least understood commodities in the Indonesian food economy. Since production efforts were often ignored by agricultural agents more concerned with rice, and consumption levels were determined to a large extent by on-farm production, the role of corn as Indonesia's second or third most important staple foodstuff was badly documented and little analyzed. The two basic sources of data for such analysis, SUSENAS reports and annual food balance sheet estimates, do not even agree on whether consumption per capita increased or decreased during the 1970s. Analysis in the face of such fundamental discrepancies in the basic data must be tentative at best.

Even so, analysis is revealing. The aggregate picture of corn consumption presented in the food balance sheet is very misleading and hides the fact that more than 18 million Indonesians consume corn as their primary staple food for at least major parts of the year. This corn-eating population tends to be poor and rural but grows only one-half the corn consumed by their households. Many corn consumers are landless and purchase their supplies from rural markets.

Before 1975, many corn consumers were so poor that they seem to have increased their consumption of corn when household incomes rose, apparently substituting away from cassava but also increasing total intake of calories. Because of higher living standards among the rural poor, this pattern is no longer seen. By 1978, even the lowest-income groups reported by SUSENAS reduced their corn consumption as incomes rose. A negative income elasticity of perhaps −0.4 is appropriate at present and in future years for estimating direct consumption of corn in Indonesia. The positive income elasticity estimated from time series data must be explained by a combination of factors involving income distribution, proportion of corn eaters in the overall population, and a tendency for a high proportion of increases in corn production to "disappear" within the corn-producing households.

Perhaps the most encouraging statistical result reported in this chapter is the significantly negative own-price elasticity of demand for corn of about −0.6. Based on extensive analysis by Monteverde of raw SUSENAS data, the negative price elasticities are notably larger in absolute value for the very poor, which is consistent with patterns for other basic food staples in Indonesia and other countries. A reassuring similarity of these cross-section estimates of price elasticity with the time series analysis should also be noted.

Despite corn's clear status as an inferior good for all income classes of the population, roughly three-quarters of Indonesia's corn production is consumed directly as a staple food by rural households. Other end uses for corn may be more dynamic in relative terms—as livestock feed or potentially as the base for a fructose sweetener—but the dynamics of household consumption will remain the largest factor in determining the domestic balance between production and consumption of corn.

6. Corn in the Livestock Economy

Stephen D. Mink

During the 1970s, a changing pattern of end uses for corn in Indonesia seemed to create a serious dilemma. The growth in consumption of livestock products, which was associated with rapid increases in personal income, aroused concern that corn-fed livestock were competing for tight domestic supplies with low-income consumers of corn. Government planners could not look to expanded corn production to increase supplies, since improvements in agricultural technology in the 1970s resulted in only modest growth in output. Imports appeared to be the only recourse for supplying corn to the industrial feed-mixing sector, which was growing about 15 percent per year at the end of the decade.

By the mid-1980s, concerns over the direction of the feed-livestock economy have changed. Slower growth of incomes has translated into less rapid expansion of corn's use in feed rations. New technology in corn production promises increases in output sufficient to meet the needs of both consumers and livestock. Higher incomes and the government's success in regulating rice prices combine to shift many low-income consumers from corn- to rice-based diets. Real corn prices have not risen significantly, which indicates that corn consumers are not worse off because of the greater amounts of corn fed to livestock. Availability of protein sources for animal feeds has become a major difficulty, but prospects are good for adequate supplies of corn for domestic needs.

Four issues concerning the use of corn in livestock feed and the future of the corn economy are addressed in this chapter. The focus of the first section is on current levels of corn use and likely future growth of corn-based livestock feeds. In the second section, the shift from corn to substitute feed grains in response to changes in relative prices is analyzed. In the third section, the modern feed industry's use of corn in seen to affect corn market integration, which is considered from three facets—geographical, temporal, and quality. The role of government policy in the feed and livestock sector is examined in the final section.

Current and Projected Use of Corn for Livestock Feed

Two approaches can be employed to estimate the total use of corn feed grain by the livestock sector. One approach considers the demand derived from the consumption of livestock products, which is dependent upon factors such as income growth, tastes, relative product prices, and population growth. Alternatively, if supply constraints are likely to dominate demand characteristics in determining the rate of growth in the livestock sector, historical trends of growth in the animal population can be used to indicate likely future growth of feed requirements. Both approaches are followed in the subsequent analysis, and the resulting range in projections suggests that these numbers should be interpreted as less than precise. Although the two methods start with different assumptions, they both require substantial practical knowledge about animal production systems and feeding efficiency in Indonesia because numbers of animals or amounts of animal products must be translated into feed requirements and finally into use of corn feed grain.

Consumer demand for a wide range of animal products increases with income. In the *derived demand approach*, specification of this relationship, which is typically done with income elasticities of demand, allows projection of growth in demand per capita for a product as a consequence of expected increases in consumer income. Such growth in consumption per capita, multiplied by population, reveals the increase in total demand in the domestic economy.

Indonesia's demand for various meat, fish, and dairy products is shown in Table 6.1. Not all these products use corn as an input, and those that do comprise only 15 percent of nonvegetative protein, and less than 2 per-

TABLE 6.1. *Per capita consumption of animal products in the Indonesian diet, 1980*

Product	Amount consumed (kilograms per year)	Protein (grams per day)	Calories (per day)	Total Indonesian consumption[a] (000 tons)
Meat				
Chicken (village)[b]	0.55	0.17	3	80
Chicken (commercial)[b]	0.33	0.10	2	48
Pork[b]	0.59	0.17	7	86
Beef	1.00	0.38	6	146
Other meat	0.83	0.29	7	121
Offal	0.60	0.26	2	88
Eggs				
Chicken (village)[b]	0.18	0.06	1	26
Chicken (commercial)[b]	1.00	0.32	4	15
Duck	0.47	0.15	2	69
Milk[b]	4.46	0.42	8	652
Fish	9.93	3.19	18	1,452
Total protein (non-vegetative sources)		5.51	60	
TOTAL IN DIET	—	48.45	2,570	—

SOURCE: Indonesia, Central Bureau of Statistics, "Food Balance Sheet for Indonesia, 1980" (August 1982).
[a]Population in 1980 was 146.2 million.
[b]Corn is part of the livestock feed.

TABLE 6.2. *Estimated income elasticities for meat, eggs, and dairy products for Indonesia*

Product	Income Elasticities
Chicken eggs	1.6[a]
Meat	
Chicken	2.2[b]
Pork	1.4[b]
Milk (liquid equivalent)	1.5

SOURCE: Calculated by Monteverde (1987) from Indonesia, Central Bureau of Statistics, National Socio-Economic Survey (SUSENAS), February 1979 Sub-round (1982). Elasticity for milk estimated from Directorate General of Livestock, "Potential Domestic Needs for Animal Feed" (1984).

[a]Double-log quadratic.

[b]Double log.

cent of total protein, in the average diet. The low base level of consumption of corn-fed animal products implies that the additional use of corn for livestock feed will be limited, even with rapid rates of growth in incomes.

The responsiveness of demand for animal products per capita to income growth can be estimated from the Central Bureau of Statistics' National Socio-Economic Survey (SUSENAS). Income elasticities for corn-using products are presented in Table 6.2. Since the SUSENAS results are derived from cross-section data, they should be interpreted as long-run income elasticities, which are usually higher than short-run estimates. It would be preferable to have separate elasticities for village and commercial chicken products, since Indonesians express taste preferences for the former, which are reflected in higher market prices. Unfortunately, the SUSENAS data are not sufficiently disaggregated to analyze the extent to which village and commercial poultry products are differentiated.

With these income elasticities and base year data for consumption per capita, consumption of livestock products can be estimated on the basis of growth in population and incomes. Projections through 1988 are shown in Table 6.3 for products that use corn. The largest relative increase in consumption will be for poultry products—commercially produced meat, village chickens, and eggs. Consumption of pork, milk, and commercially produced eggs will grow more slowly.

The derived demand approach has several weaknesses. First, domestic demand is no indication of domestic supply capacity—for example, 85 percent of milk supplies are imported. It is difficult to assess the impact of the government's dairy intensification programs on reducing imports, but it is clear that product demand is poorly linked to use of corn in livestock feeds. Second, data that identify the demand characteristics for commercial, as opposed to village, poultry meat and eggs are not available. Some

TABLE 6.3. *Estimated consumption of livestock products and projected annual growth in per capita income, 1981–1988*

Livestock product	Total consumption (000 tons)							
				Fourth Development Plan[a]				
	1981	1982	1983	1984	1985	1986	1987	1988
Pork	98	101	104	110	117	124	132	140
Village chicken meat	96	99	103	111	121	131	142	155
Commercial chicken meat	58	60	62	67	72	79	85	93
Village chicken eggs	30	31	32	34	35	38	40	43
Commercial chicken eggs	169	173	179	191	204	218	232	248
Milk	747	768	791	842	897	916	976	996
Total population (millions)	151.3	154.7	158.1	161.6	165.1	168.7	172.2	175.9
Annual growth of national per capital income (percent)	7.1	0.4	0.5	2.79	2.83	2.82	2.93	2.85

SOURCES: Author's estimates. Population projections are taken from Indonesia, Central Bureau of Statistics "Indonesian Population Projections 1980–2000" (1983).
[a]The GDP growth rate of 5 percent per year projected in the Fourth Development Plan is assumed to hold for national income as well.

TABLE 6.4. *Livestock populations, 1970–1982 (000 head)*

Year	Village chickens	Commercial layers	Commercial broilers	Ducks	Swine	Milk cows	Cattle	Water buffalo	Goats	Sheep	Horses
1970	66,305	474	—	9,035	—	—	—	—	—	—	—
1971	71,575	1,291	—	7,459	—	—	—	—	—	—	—
1972	88,700	1,685	—	13,991	—	—	—	—	—	—	—
1973	97,457	2,234	—	14,671	2,599	—	6,311	2,243	—	—	632
1974	100,721	3,499	—	14,975	3,765	41	6,531	2,735	7,283	3,272	651
1975	112,593	3,695		17,190	3,431	47	6,542	2,756	7,762	3,280	671
1976	123,520	5,185	—	17,922	3,466	48	7,673	2,798	7,497	3,336	641
1977	122,798	7,001	—	18,166	3,824	53	6,917	2,799	7,625	3,518	659
1978	126,741	11,599	—	18,401	4,019	58	7,022	2,847	6,216	3,585	651
1979	127,918	15,412	—	17,953	4,088	64	6,996	2,862	7,716	3,629	683
1980	134,693	21,658	4,030	18,775	4,391	82	7,402	2,944	8,094	3,993	659
1981	145,678	27,837	8,032	22,503	4,558	116	7,773	2,998	7,968	4,292	668
1982	143,258	41,655[a]		24,058	4,041	142	7,654	3,037	8,424	4,694	676

SOURCE: Directorate General of Livestock worksheets of provincial animal populations. These figures differ from aggregate, national data presented by the DGL elsewhere.
[a]Combined figure for commercial layers and broilers.

able. Some argue that village chickens and eggs are preferred because of beliefs about their better taste and greater nutritional value, which suggests imperfect substitution with commercial meat and eggs. Others hold that these preferences are weak or fast breaking down. If taste preferences for village products disappear over time as commercial poultry products become more widely distributed or as incomes increase, there would be an accelerating shift to commercially produced meat and eggs, which use more corn. These shortcomings of the derived demand approach suggest it would be useful to calculate the use of corn in livestock feed through the alternative analysis of historical and expected trends in animal populations.

In the *animal population approach,* rate of increase in the population of each livestock group is estimated on the basis of past trends. Growth in various animal populations from 1970 to 1982 is shown in Table 6.4. Simple linear trends estimated from these time series data for annual livestock populations were found to give the best results for projecting the size of animal populations, except for dairy cows. The diary cow population is projected on the basis of the government's major campaign to import improved breeding stock. The projected populations of poultry, swine, and dairy cows are shown in Table 6.5.

These total animal populations can be used to project the rate of growth in use of corn-based livestock feed, but, except for commercial poultry, which have relatively standard feed rations, the animal populations must first be disaggregated by husbandry methods since feeding practices vary widely. The appendix to this chapter presents the detailed analysis for estimating the animal population. Table 6.6 shows, for each of the livestock groups and type of production system described in the Appendix, the projected use of corn as livestock feed. In the mid-1980s, livestock feeding absorbed over one-fifth of annual corn production. As the table shows, the derived demand approach has the livestock sector's use of corn growing from 580,000 tons in 1983 to 826,000 tons in 1988, a rate of 7.3 percent per year. The supply approach starts from a higher base, 733,000 tons in 1983, and projects an increase to 1,008,000 tons in 1988, a rate of 6.6 percent per year. Taken together, the alternative projections are close to the annual growth rate of 7 percent used in the Fourth Development Plan. The two estimates of growth rates for the sector's use of grain corn based on derived demand and animal population growth differ by less than 10 percent.

The figures for commercial poultry account for the main difference between the two estimates. The derived demand estimates indicate lower total use by the commercial poultry industry and slower growth in use of corn for egg production and faster growth in use for broilers than do the estimates based on animal populations. The significance of commercial

TABLE 6.5. *Projected livestock population (000 head)*

	1983	1984	1985	1986	1987	1988	1989	1990
Corn-fed livestock								
Poultry								
Commercial								
Layers	26,328	28,663	31,088	33,513	35,938	38,363	40,788	43,213
Broilers[a]	43,730	47,772	51,813	55,855	59,897	63,939	67,980	72,022
Village[b]	74,023	76,906	79,789	82,672	85,554	88,437	91,320	94,203
Total	144,081	153,341	162,690	172,040	181,389	190,739	200,088	209,438
Swine[c]								
Modern	237	250	263	276	289	301	314	328
Traditional	1,628	1,714	1,801	1,887	1,974	2,060	2,146	2,233
Total	1,865	1,964	2,064	2,163	2,263	2,361	2,460	2,561
Dairy cattle[d]								
Lactating cows	63	69	85	104	120	135	148	160
Total livestock population								
Poultry								
Commercial								
Layers	26,328	28,663	31,088	33,513	35,938	38,363	40,788	43,213
Broilers	43,730	47,772	51,813	55,855	59,897	63,939	67,980	72,022
Village	147,056	154,703	162,747	171,210	180,113	189,479	199,332	209,697
Total	217,024	231,138	245,648	260,578	275,948	291,781	308,100	324,932
Swine	5,132	5,409	5,700	6,008	6,332	6,673	7,033	7,412
Dairy cattle	155	169	208	254	293	329	362	390

SOURCES: Author's estimates from historical trends. Annual animal population data from worksheets of the Directorate General of Livestock.

NOTES: Within each livestock group, the total numbers of animals that receive corn as part of their feed rations is termed corn-fed. Animals raised in corn-producing areas—which generally have corn storage facilities and processing of corn for household consumption—are most likely to be fed corn.

[a]It is assumed that at the time of any given census, broilers comprise 25 percent of the commercial flock. If broiler flocks are sold and replaced every ten weeks, the annual production of broilers is five times the number given at the time of the census.

[b]Feeding corn to village chickens is assumed to be significant only in areas where households consume corn and thus store it; it was assumed that village chickens were fed corn in provinces with corn consumption by humans of 15 kilograms per capita per year.

[c]Only the provinces with significant swine populations and corn production are included.

[d]Corn fed to dairy cows is almost entirely milling by-products, which are most common in East and Central Java.

TABLE 6.6. *Projected use of corn for livestock feed (000 tons)*

	1983	1984	1985	1986	1987	1988	Average annual growth (percent)
			Derived demand approach				
Poultry							
Commercial							
Layers	198	213	227	242	258	275	6.8
Pullets	50	53	57	61	65	69	6.7
Broilers	96	102	111	122	131	142	8.1
Village							
Layers	165	177	180	195	207	222	6.1
Meat[a]	28	30	36	39	44	49	11.8
Swine							
Modern	20	21	22	23	25	26	5.4
Traditional	7	7	8	8	9	9	5.2
Dairy cows	16	18	22	27	31	34	16.3
TOTAL	580	621	663	717	770	826	7.3
			Supply approach				
Poultry							
Layers	280	306	331	358	384	409	7.9
Pullets	70	76	83	89	96	102	7.8
Broilers	70	76	83	89	96	102	7.8
Village	222	231	239	248	257	265	3.6
Swine							
Modern	57	60	63	66	70	73	5.1
Traditional	18	19	20	21	22	23	5.0
Dairy cows							
Lactating	16	18	22	27	31	34	16.3
TOTAL	733	786	841	898	956	1,008	6.6

SOURCE: Author's estimates.

[a]Calculated on the basis of numbers of birds needed in addition to spent hens such that demand for village chicken meat is met.

poultry is clear, however, as this industry uses roughly 60 percent of the total corn feed grains.

This study also found that village chickens, usually considered scavengers, are fed surprisingly large amounts of corn. They are fed by-products from the processing of corn for the household's own use since these residuals rarely have markets or alternative uses. Aggregate use of corn for village chickens is substantial and constitutes one-quarter of all grain fed to livestock.[1]

These projections for corn use are marginally above estimates made by the World Bank in which demand for corn feed grains was set at 920,000 tons in 1990, and they are slightly below the government's projections of 1.05 million tons by the end of the Fourth Development Plan in 1988

[1]It is not clear how much of the corn fed to village chickens is a by-product of corn processed and consumed in the household, and hence already counted in the food balance sheet, and how much is in addition to rural household use.

TABLE 6.7. *Estimated regional use of corn for livestock feed, 1983 (000 tons)*

	Commercial poultry	Village poultry	Swine	Dairy	Total
Central Java	31	70	15	5	121
East Java	51	80	9	10	150
West Java/Jakarta	139	—	—	—	139
D. I. Yogyakarta	10	—	3	1	14
Total Java	231	150	27	16	424
North Sulawesi	10	4	5	—	19
Central Sulawesi	1	4	—	—	6
Southeast Sulawesi	1	5	—	—	4
South Sulawesi	9	44	12	—	65
Total Sulawesi	21	57	17	—	94
North Sumatra	33	—	27	—	60
Lampung	45	—	—	—	45
Total Sumatra	78	—	27	—	105
Bali	10	8	2	—	20
Nusa Tenggara Timur	1	8	2	—	11
Kalimantan	42	—	—	—	42
Others	2	—	—	—	2
TOTAL	385	223	75	16	698

SOURCE: Author's estimates.

(World Bank 1984; Indonesia, Directorate General of Livestock 1984). The three estimates differ in the assumptions they make for feed-to-product conversion coefficients and for proportions of total animal populations fed various corn rations. Similar to the government's estimates, the analysis here uses a feed conversion ratio of less efficiency for improved poultry husbandry than does the World Bank. The World Bank's estimate also omits corn use for village chickens.

Table 6.7 shows the estimates for regional use of corn feed grains. One surprising feature is that although Java is the dominant user, its proportion of total use of feed grains—58 percent—is less than its proportion of total production, which averages around 70 percent. Other islands are also significant users of corn feed grains and raise almost one-half the improved chickens and a majority of corn-fed swine. Comparison of regional use of corn feed grains with average regional production indicates only two regions that are chronic deficit areas: the region of Jakarta and West Java, which has a high concentration of poultry, and Kalimantan. Both these areas meet the demand for corn feed grain with grain imports,, interregional grain, or prepared feed shipments. Inter-island corn shipments, which link the centers of animal and corn production, are increasingly important.

Price Response and Corn Use in Livestock Feed

Seasonal fluctuations in the amount of corn used as livestock feed occur because livestock producers adjust to shifting commodity prices. The extent to which corn is replaced by substitute feeds as a result of a rise in corn prices can be summarized in a price elasticity of demand. Several feed manufacturers indicated that the amount of corn in their mixed feed rations varies from 35 to 45 percent in response to seasonal changes in the price of corn, which typically ranges from Rp 115 to Rp 150 per kilogram. The price elasticity of corn use implied by this adjustment is −1.0 for the modern feed industry. But this figure needs to be adjusted for the livestock sector as a whole. Raisers of village chickens and traditionally fed swine show much less responsiveness to price because they seldom have available the range of energy feeds that large-scale operations do, nor do they balance nutrition and cost of inputs with output prices as assiduously as commercial poultry raisers do. This informal livestock sector may be taken to have a price elasticity in the range of −0.1 to −0.3. If modern swine and poultry operations account for about 65 percent of use of corn for feed, the weighted elasticity becomes −0.7 for the livestock sector. In 1984, total use of corn feed grain was 786,000 tons (animal population approach), and the seasonal rise in corn prices was about 30 percent, from Rp 115 to Rp 150 per kilogram. Monthly use of corn correspondingly varied between a peak of 72,400 tons and a trough of 58,600 tons.

Results from these calculations reveal little of the complexity of management choices that face livestock owners and feed mill operators and that affect overall use of corn. Rising corn prices, for example, may cause not only substitution away from corn in the ration but also a cutback in animal populations. In modern swine operations, if the feed-to-pork price ratio is unfavorable, sows are not bred. In commercial layer and broiler operations, purchases of day-old chicks decline when the feed-to-output price ratio rises. Further cutbacks in the poultry population occur, since fewer layers are fed through the molting period and a greater number of unproductive birds is culled from the flock. If these adjustments in herd and flock size are considered in addition to the straightforward substitution between feed ingredients, demand for corn as feed will be more elastic than −0.7 in the intermediate run.

The degree of substitution among feedstuffs may be reduced, however, by the availability of both complete feed rations and feed concentrates produced for the modern poultry sector. Use of complete feeds is more common in urban than in rural areas, where producers mix feed concentrate, a feed base with high protein content, with energy sources, usually rice bran and corn. Unlike complete feed in which the corn component varies with seasonal price changes, the proportion of corn to be mixed with concentrate is generally fixed at about 40 percent. More concentrate is sold when corn is cheap and available to poultry raisers, and more complete feed is sold when feed mills are granted access to cheaper imported corn. Several feed firms suggested, as a rough guess, that about 65 to 70 percent of the market on average was supplied by whole, com-

TABLE 6.8. *Price comparison of commercially available energy and protein sources for livestock feed, 1984*

Product	Cost (rupiahs per kilogram)
Energy	
Rice bran	80
Rice brokens	155–175
Sorghum	100–150
Wheat pollards	95
Cassava chips	70
Molasses	50–70
Protein	
Soybean meal (41%)	335
Palm kernel meal	100
Fish meal (55%)	550–600
Copra meal	90
Kapok meal	89
Peanut meal	300
Peanut cake (40%)	400
Leucaena leaf meal (15–20%)	100
Rapeseed meal	240

SOURCE: Feed industry representatives.
NOTES: Price ranges indicate typical seasonal movements. Exchange rate = Rp 1,100 per U.S. dollar. Percentages indicate the protein content of the feed supplement.

plete feeds. If it is assumed that users of concentrate adhere closely to the fixed ratios of corn use that are recommended, the overall price elasticity of demand could drop as low as −0.5 for the livestock sector.

Indonesia's livestock producers are able to shift out of corn feed grain when corn prices are unfavorable because alternative energy feedstuffs are available. Table 6.8 shows market prices of energy substitutes for corn and complementary protein supplements. Under current conditions of the livestock sector, practical solutions to nutritional balance and problems, such as handling, quality variability, and rancidity, often place limits on the use of such alternatives.

Rice bran is readily available in most rural areas in Indonesia. Rice bran from the majority of Indonesia's small-scale rice milling units is a mixture of pericarp, husk, and polishings—their proportions vary widely. Good-quality bran is low in crude fiber and free of rancid fat. If used up to 45 percent of the poultry ration, it can support rapid weight gain in broilers, and it can also be substituted for corn in rations for swine and dairy cows. Poorer-quality rice bran has more husks, and thus more crude fiber, which acts as a laxative and can cause scours in all species; crude fiber varies between 6 and 45 percent. The fat content of rice bran is a major drawback since its tendency to go rancid quickly precludes storage much beyond two weeks. Despite these disadvantages, feed mills still try to use rice bran in formulations as a cheap energy source.

Rice has energy close in value to corn, and slightly greater protein, but generally only the lowest qualities, such as broken or spoiled rice, are cheap enough for rice to be a substitute energy feedstuff. Rice brokens are used in commercially mixed feeds in modest amounts from September to December when corn prices rise to their highest level in relation to rice. Use of rice is limited by its lack of carotene, which is often regarded by poultry raisers as too costly to add as a supplement, and thus rice is usually used in combination with yellow corn.

Although cassava is an important food crop found throughout Indonesia, its domestic use in livestock feed is currently very limited, mostly because of high relative costs. Indonesia exports dried cassava chips *(gaplek)* and pellets to Europe, where relative prices of livestock feeds favor the import and use of cassava; this export market has served to establish a floor price for domestic dried cassava above the level at which it would be used domestically as a livestock feed (Nelson 1983). Although cassava is a good energy source, it is very low in protein, and feed rations with cassava require even more protein supplements than cereal-based feeds. The costs of complementary protein supplements—chiefly imported soybean and fish meals—are increased by protective trade policy in Indonesia, and this adds to the cost of using cassava.

To illustrate the relative costs, cassava is essentially equivalent to corn in energy value, but, ton for ton, cassava has 70 kilograms less crude protein. The cost of crude protein is 82 cents per kilogram (soybean meal of 41 percent protein at $335 per ton c.i.f. Jakarta). Cassava must thus sell at a discount to corn of at least $57.40 per ton (82 cents per kilogram × 70 kilograms) before it will be used in livestock feed rations. If the cost of soybean meal dropped to $200 per ton, the protein discount for cassava would be only $34 per ton.

In practice, there are additional constraints to using cassava as a corn substitute. Variable quality caused by molds, dirt, other additives, and fermentation leads most feed mixers to restrict cassava to 15 to 20 percent of poultry rations. Crude fiber levels are more than twice that of corn, and for cassava to be used extensively, producers would need to shift to low-fiber protein ingredients—from soybean meal, for example, to more expensive fish meal in the feed mixture. Unpelleted cassava is very dusty when ground for rations and is an operating nuisance for feed mills that do not have modern processing machinery.

Fresh cassava peelings are produced domestically in large quantities as a by-product, but their use in commercial feed is limited. Almost all uses of cassava in Indonesia—for starch, dried cassava for export or consumption by humans, or fresh roots for consumers—are preceded by the peeling of fresh roots, which is normally done within the farm household. Inefficient peeling techniques result in removal of 20 percent of the weight of fresh roots. The peels are either used or sold as feed, mostly for ruminants. It is not economical to bulk quantities from the village level for use by larger commercial livestock producers. Starch manufacturers with medium- and large-scale operations, however, frequently buy unpeeled roots at harvest and produce sufficient flows of fresh peelings to establish market outlets. The starch industry on Java may produce between 75,000 to 125,000 tons of fresh peelings a year, which replace corn in pig and dairy rations.

Wheat pollards are a by-product of wheat flour milling. Indonesia imports wheat grain and mills it domestically to fulfill its needs for wheat flour. By 1983–1984, grain imports had risen to 1.7 million tons, and from food balance sheet data, the milling conversion rate to flour appears to be 72 percent. Annual production of by-products from wheat milling, of which wheat pollards is the main one, would thus be 475,000 tons. Because there are no other domestic industrial uses for wheat pollards, they are absorbed by the livestock sector or re-exported, but in what quantities is undetermined since data on end uses of wheat by-products are difficult to acquire.

Wheat pollards have more crude fiber and a protein value almost 60 percent higher than corn, but have only about one-half the energy value. If wheat pollards are substituted for corn in poultry rations, they must be supplemented with an energy source—most frequently liquid fat despite its expense. Some swine raisers in a main corn-producing area of Central Java found that at current relative prices, it was profitable to replace corn completely with wheat pollards.

Sorghum is grown during the dry season in parts of Central and East Java. It has 95 percent of the feed value of corn and can be used as a partial or complete replacement for corn in rations. Some care must be taken in poultry rations, however, especially with dark pericarp varieties, since these are high in tannin, which is a mild toxin and depresses weight gain in broilers and egg production. Much of Indonesia's sorghum harvest is of light pericarp varieties, which pose a lesser problem. Since sorghum is low in the pigment carotene, the yellow color in egg yolks, skin, and shanks of poultry becomes pale if sorghum replaces all corn in the feed ration. Nutritional quality of Indonesian sorghums is quite variable, especially in crude protein, and greater care must thus be taken to ensure a balanced ration.

Ground sorghum is currently used in both swine and commercial poultry rations in Indonesia, especially following its harvest in the dry season when sorghum's relative price drops. Lack of market outlets has kept sorghum area to as low as 20,000 hectares in recent years, however, and many feed mills are reluctant to adjust their feed mixtures to include sorghum if favorable supply and prices are expected to be temporary.

The range of crops and agricultural by-products that can substitute for corn as an energy source is quite broad in Indonesia. Most feedstuffs have some drawback to their use—quality variability, high fiber content, seasonal unavailability, rancidity if stored—which may be overcome at certain relative prices. Within the current range of domestic prices, however, corn has advantages, such as reliability of supply, relative ease of handling, and manageable variance in quality, that make it the prime energy source in mixed feeds. Because of seasonal movements of relative prices of feedstuffs, the proportion of corn in feed rations does vary, but generally corn remains the most important energy source in livestock feeds.

The Livestock Feed Industry and Corn Market Integration

The livestock feed industry in Indonesia consists of over fifty firms that mix complete feeds and produce feed concentrates. Over 90 percent of output is for domestic poultry, and the rest is divided among swine, dairy cows, ducks, and fish. In this analysis, the feed industry is distinct from the thousands of rural and urban rice milling units, which produce rice bran as a by-product, and from the pelleting industry, which processes cassava as a feed for export to Europe. The modern feed industry was established in 1972 upon separate investments by two foreign firms, and it expanded rapidly through the end of the decade. The early 1980s brought slower growth and an altered structure to the industry. Smaller, less efficient firms have been confronted with declining profit margins, and their portion of total output has been shrinking. Larger foreign firms diversified into related fields, such as poultry breeding farms. Some moved into input technology and set up corn seed operations because of the government's attempt to make production of livestock feed a domestically owned industry.

Among livestock feed firms there remains a wide range in scale of operations. The more efficient and better-financed firms, in which annual output ranges from 20,000 to over 100,000 tons per year, consist of seven foreign firms and five domestically financed firms. There is also a group of five to ten medium-sized domestic firms, as well as over thirty small firms, which produce on average 500 tons per year. The large firms are concentrated in four urban areas—Jakarta, Surabaya, Semarang, and Medan—whereas the medium- and small-sized firms tend to be located in secondary urban centers, such as Yogyakarta, Bandung, Cirebon, and Padang.

Despite the strong growth of the modern feed industry, it is still not the dominant user of corn. It absorbs just over one-fifth of annual marketed corn from domestic production and from 35 to 40 percent of total grain corn that is used in all of its derivatives for feed. The modern feed industry is the most rapidly growing component, but it is not the main source of demand in the corn economy.

In recent years, large firms in urban locations have tended to dominate the industry. Smaller firms, which are usually located closer to sources of domestic supply, are increasingly unable to compete; as a result, they are producing less or going out of business. Contributing to the financial woes of smaller firms are their lack of sufficient cash flow to purchase inputs, their more expensive and lower-quality feed due to rudimentary, noncomputerized formulation of rations, and their high costs incurred for imported protein feed supplements as a result of the government's distribution arrangements. As a consequence of this centralization of firms, corn used by the industry travels longer distances from producer to user, and transportation costs are a larger proportion of total product costs. In turn, feed mills have responded by selling more concentrate to rural and secondary urban markets so that livestock owners can use local corn in the feed mixture and thus not pay the higher transport costs.

Links between urban feed mills and corn-producing areas, however, are being strengthened, and demand for corn from the livestock sector significantly contributes to corn market integration. Price movements of corn in geographically dispersed locations are more tightly linked because of the feed mills' keen purchasing operations for inputs, which take full advantage of Indonesia's improving communications and transport networks. Purchasing strategies of feed mills have become more sophisticated, as they shift from simple contracts with commodity wholesalers to direct purchase of corn in truckload lots (about 10 tons) from small-scale collectors in rural areas. Administratively, this purchasing is more complex because of the necessarily larger number of contracts and the need of smaller collectors to be paid more quickly because of their cash constraints. But it does allow mills to save on the direct cost of corn. Corn that travels this path is handled by a shorter chain of market participants than is typical for rural-to-urban commodity flows and is diverted from the traditional wholesaler network. As a result, there is stronger demand for corn in corn-growing areas.

The investment by several large feed mills in corn drying and transport facilities has also strengthened their links to corn-producing areas and altered the constraints on corn purchases. Wet corn cannot be stored or milled without prohibitive losses, and many firms will not buy corn with over 17 percent moisture. Because the main corn harvest occurs during the rainy season, feed mills have always been constrained from buying corn directly from farmers, who usually sell corn with a high moisture content. Drying has typically been done by small collectors before sale to wholesalers, who then supply corn to the feed mills. The larger mills have begun to install drying capacity, however, and this allows them to buy wetter corn closer to the farm gate at more favorable prices, even when corrected for moisture content.

Although most feed mills handle and transport grain corn in sacks, several mills are moving to bulk handling as part of a strategy of buying East Java's corn for shipment to mills in Jakarta. Incoming corn is removed from bags at a facility for drying in East Java and transported in bulk by truck to Jakarta. Bulk handling reduces shipment costs of corn to Jakarta and increases the capacity and speed of shipments on this route. Such innovation in handling promotes stronger connections between corn markets in the two regions.

The potential role of the feed mill industry in temporal price integration—storing corn from harvest to harvest, from months of low prices to months of high prices—remains undeveloped. Feed mills have invested only modestly in modern storage facilities, mostly because their incentive to store corn is reduced by several economic and technical factors and by government policy, which is discussed in the next section. As a result, most mills rarely store corn beyond their operating needs for one to two months. Most mills use flat storage for bagged corn, but several of the largest mills supplement this with 1,000-ton silos. Although no solid data exist for the feed industry's total corn storage, its capacity clearly is insufficient to play much of a role in smoothing fluctuations in market supplies and seasonal prices of corn.

Improved drying and storage facilities are also major components necessary to solve the problem of high moisture content in corn. Fungal growth in damp corn leads frequently to aflatoxin contamination, which causes serious decreases in layer production and slows weight gain of broilers. Aflatoxin contamination seems to be primarily a result of holding damp corn too long between harvest and wholesale bulking. This problem is difficult to solve because of inadequate incentives to growers and collectors of corn to invest in drying facilities and because of the millions of corn farmers and traders involved in the postharvest operations. Levels of aflatoxin can be dangerously high, especially in the rainy season corn harvest, and large mills are just beginning to develop standards and tests to reject incoming, contaminated corn.

Feed mill operators attempted to shift some of the burden of corn drying onto other marketing participants by offering a ladder of increasing prices for drier corn. But these experiments were unsuccessful, and feed mills reverted to setting a standard moisture content and refusing to buy corn that exceeded the standard. This standard is less stringent, however, in the rainy season than in the dry season and less important at mills that have driers. The feed industry has not been instrumental in developing quality standards for corn based on moisture content and thus linking quality and price, which would be essential to stimulate investment in drying facilities. Market prices for corn of different degrees of moisture remain only indirectly linked to costs of drying.

Demand for livestock feed contributes to price integration across the two principal types of marketed corn—white and yellow. Over 35 percent of Indonesia's corn production is of white varieties, and the poultry industry has traditionally refrained from using corn of this color for feed. The only nutritional difference between white and yellow corn is the reduced amount of carotene (vitamin A) in white corn, but it is technically feasible to supplement this in mixed feeds. Several small feed mill operators claim that white corn also has lower protein content, but this is not borne out in nutritional analyses. The reluctance of poultry feed producers to use white corn stems partly from consumer preferences for a yellowish poultry product and partly from poultry raisers' concern that change in feed will cause stress in the flock and reduce output. Poultry raisers are generally less willing to buy a product whose appearance fluctuates.

The feed mill industry itself has shown some reluctance to buy white corn, partly because production of white corn is more seasonal than yellow corn, and thus it might not be available at reasonable prices year-round. Because feed producers want to produce a feed acceptable to buyers, they stick to a yellow product. Several large mills find they can achieve this appearance even if white corn comprises 10 to 15 percent of the total ration. And because white corn is often cheaper than yellow corn, there are incentives to include it, particularly when selling feed to swine raisers, who are generally indifferent to color and will buy whichever is cheaper. But on the whole, unlike consumers who show little tendency to substitute one color of corn for the other, the feed industry shows some price flexibility and helps keep the two prices roughly in line. The purchasing strategies of the feed industry will increasingly contribute to the price integration of white and yellow corn as use of corn in livestock feed continues to expand and as poultry raisers learn that corn color alone causes little stress in layer and broiler flocks.

Government Policy and the Livestock Sector

Since the rapid takeoff of corn's use as livestock feed in the early 1970s, government policy has aimed to support a basically competitive, free enterprise system for inputs and animal products and to impose relatively few regulations or controls. Still, a broad range of government policies—primarily price and trade policies—influences the levels of corn use for livestock feed. The effect of government policy on the market prices of commodities other than corn may be just as critical in determining these levels in the next several years. The government controls the prices of corn's complement, soybean meal, and influences the price of one of its main energy substitutes, wheat pollards. Changes in price policy for these commodities cause significant adjustments in the amount of corn used in feed formulas. As policies continue to be sought that balance foreign exchange constraints, goals for human nutrition, and the government's objectives for farm income, participants in the livestock sector face a fair degree of uncertainty over future government action.

Some government policies have been quite limited in scope or impact on the livestock sector. In 1978 the government instituted a floor price policy for corn to support incomes of corn farmers. So far the floor price has rarely exceeded the market prices except in isolated areas where transportation costs are high. The floor price policy for corn has therefore not raised input costs to feed mills. New entrants to the feed industry have faced few restrictions, although the government reserves the right to limit licensing to prevent overinvestment in an industry or to promote production by cooperatives. Further foreign investment in the feed industry is limited because it is difficult for foreign firms to acquire licenses and in theory such industries must revert to Indonesian ownership within ten years of the initial investment. Imports of animal stock have not been restricted by duties or regulations. The government has encouraged the poultry industry during the Fourth Development Plan to develop domestic capacity to breed replacement stock by phasing out imports of parent stock, which is used for day-old chick operations. But imports of grandparent stock needed for regeneration of parent stock will continue. The extension and credit program for poultry raisers subsidizes credit through its loans to small poultry operations, but its impact has been relatively minor in the overall expansion of poultry husbandry.

There are three main areas in which government activity increasingly affects the use of corn as a livestock feed: the limits placed on size of poultry operations; price policies for protein complements to corn for feed rations; and seasonal imports of corn specifically for distribution to the urban feed industry.

In 1980 the government sought to create rural employment and income opportunities by phasing out poultry operations with more than 5,000 layers and broiler operations larger than 750 birds per week.[2] At the time, it was believed that small, labor-intensive operations would be competitive with modern, mechanized outfits by the government's deadline of May 1984. In 1984 this policy was supplemented by additional regulations meant to head off the move by large operations to abide by the letter, if not the spirit, of the policy by engaging in contract growing, in which the firms essentially provided wage laborers with birds, feed, and medicine, and all output was returned to the center. These regulations detailed a "nuclear industry" approach intended to forge stronger links

[2]The government policy was established through a Presidential Instruction, KEPPRES 50.

between poultry raisers and both suppliers of inputs and marketers of output.[3] The intent was to foster greater managerial responsibility and potential profit than were possible under the terms of contract growing. The government intends to regulate the ratio of input-to-output prices to guarantee poultry raisers a profit. Suppliers and marketers are licensed and restricted in operations to five *kecamatan*, and preferably these functions are performed by poultry cooperatives. The private sector is permitted to operate in areas where cooperatives do not yet deal with poultry. Suppliers and marketers can also be producers, but only up to 20 percent of their market total. Poultry raisers are required by contract to sell at least 75 percent of their production via their supplier at established prices, and they are free to market the remainder as desired. In its initial stage, operations were to be set up in the Jakarta area, Surabaya, Bandung, and Medan, and later expansion was planned (see *Poultry Indonesia* 1984).

These policies and regulations affect flows and overall demand for corn. Limiting the size of operating units effectively eliminates storage of corn by poultry raisers, since small operators generally do not have adequate capital resources to carry input stocks. If cooperatives that become the suppliers and marketers for the "nuclear industry" program were given access to credit for purchasing corn during the harvest, they could play a role in storing corn for later sale to poultry-raising members and possibly in investing in corn-grinding machinery as well. In some areas, cooperatives are already involved in crop processing, often producing rice bran. With the move toward small poultry units, cooperatives might take on an important role in storing and processing corn for poultry husbandry members. But at present, their impact is still minor since they account for only 5 percent of poultry product sales.

These industry regulations, in conjunction with the credit program for poultry raisers, encourage development of poultry husbandry in rural areas. As argued previously, because rural poultry raisers are physically closer than urban raisers to feed inputs such as rice bran and corn, they are more apt to buy feed concentrate and mix it with the energy feedstuffs available locally. Since concentrates are sold with recommended fixed proportions of energy inputs—corn generally at 40 percent—to be added, a shift to greater use of concentrates would mean less fluctuation in use of corn as livestock feed as corn prices change.

The government's policy has the effect of increasing average costs of

[3]Suppliers of inputs and marketers of output (INTI) form the core of the nuclear industry approach *(Perusahaan INTI Rakyat Perunggasan*, or *PIR Perunggasan)*. The goal of the policy is to have the poultry raisers (PLASMA) band together in poultry-based cooperatives (KUD) in order to consolidate ownership and management of the input and marketing functions in farmers' hands. Thus KEPPRES 50 seeks to have the KUDs become the INTI of the *PIR Perunggasan*.

production for broilers and eggs, which are shown in Table 6.9. Small operations tend to have higher feed conversion ratios, greater incidence of disease, and less effective culling of unproductive birds, often as a result of inferior management skills and physical structures that foster heat stress and feed losses. Large-scale operations generally are eligible for discounts on inputs such as chicks and feed, which reflect real economies of scale. Table 6.9 shows the decline in cost per unit that results in a shift from small to large producing units. Even if lower costs of production translate into lower prices for poultry and eggs, the human nutritional gains from the positive demand response would be negligible—less than a gram of protein per week would be added to consumption per capita. But the efficiency gains in inputs—close to 35,000 tons for corn alone—are not trivial and need to be weighed in evaluating the social value of rural job and income creation. In addition, the lower prices for poultry products will affect the rate of growth in demand, and hence the rate of growth in the feed industry.

The second area of government policy that affects use of corn feed is in the pricing of protein feed supplements. As part of the government's policy, BULOG was given responsibility for stabilizing prices and supply

TABLE 6.9. *Effect of scale on poultry production costs, product demand, and feed corn use*

Meat		
	Costs (rupiahs)	
Item	Small producer	Large producer
Day-old chick[a]	380	323
Starter ration (340 rupiahs per kilogram)[b]	452 (1.33 kilograms)	340 (1.11 kilograms)
Finisher ration (310 rupiahs per kilogram)[b]	828 (2.67 kilograms)	619 (2.22 kilograms)
Subtotal	1,660	1,282
Capital cost[c]	23	36
Total cost	1,683	1,318
Unit cost[d]	1,503 per kilogram of meat	1,178 per kilogram of meat

Effect of a shift from small to large producer units

Cost decline (percent)	Demand increase (percent)	Poultry meat consumption increase per capita (annual)[e] (kilograms)	Total poultry meat consumption increase (tons)	Change in use of corn feed (tons)
22	18	0.23	44,000	−2,400

(continued)

Eggs		
	Costs (rupiahs)	
Item	Small producer	Large producer
Day-old chick[a]	380	323
Starter ration (2 months: 1.85 kilograms)[b]	629	566
Grower ration (2–6 months: 8.15 kilograms)[b]	2,608	2,347
Layer ration (6–24 months: 60 kilograms)[b]	18,600	16,740
Subtotal	22,217	19,976
Capital cost[c]	1,154	2,074
Total cost	23,371	22,050
Unit cost[f]	1,128 per kilogram of eggs	921 per kilogram of eggs

Effect of a shift from small to large producer units

Cost decline (percent)	Demand increase (percent)	Poultry egg consumption increase per capita (kilograms)	Total poultry egg consumption increase (tons)	Change in use of corn feed (tons)
19	6	0.09	15,024	−33,200

NOTES: For poultry meat, the price elasticity of demand used in the calculations was −0.8. The feed-to-liveweight conversion coefficient used was 2.1 for large producers and 2.5 for small producers. For eggs, the price elasticity of demand used was −0.3.

[a]Large producers are given a 15 percent discount.

[b]Large producers are given a 10 percent discount.

[c]Large producers face finance charges of 18 percent per year, while small producers receive subsidized credit through *BIMAS Ayam* of 9 percent per year. The interest charge applies to an 8-week production cycle for broilers and for the first 30 weeks of a layer cycle, after which debts are assumed to be reduced, as both large and small operating units finance feed purchases through egg sales.

[d]Liveweight averages 1.5 kilograms, and broiler carcasses dress out at 70 percent.

[e]Estimated 1984 poultry consumption (under small producer units) is 1.27 kilograms per capita per year.

[f]The laying ratio over 18 months, including a 1-month molt, is taken here to be 0.6 for small units and 0.7 for large units. Hence with eggs at 60 grams a piece, a layer in a small unit lays 329 eggs over 548 days, or 19.7 kilograms per cycle.

of inputs for livestock feed. In March 1982, BULOG was granted the sole right to import soybean meal, the protein feed preferred by feed mills. Since this meal is a complement for low-protein, high-energy feeds, the price of soybean meal significantly affects the use of corn as livestock feed. Energy feedstuffs differ in their protein content, and apart from using other protein feeds, feed mills generally shift from low-protein to higher-protein energy feeds when soybean meal becomes relatively more expensive. When soybean meal is cheap, feed mixtures may include protein-poor cassava; when the price of soybean meal increases, feed mixtures include more rice bran, whose protein content is about 13 percent compared with corn's 9 to 10 percent.

Since 1982 BULOG has distributed imported soybean meal via two channels—directly to feed mills of large and medium size and indirectly to small mills through a marketing agent (ASBIMTI). In theory, small feed mills are assured the same factory-gate price large mills pay. BULOG sells to the marketing agent at a discounted price meant to reflect additional administrative, handling, and transport costs. After devaluation of the rupiah in March 1983, however, BULOG came under pressure to reduce the foreign exchange requirements of its operations and sought to reduce imports of soybean meal by 20 percent. Feed mills were advised to shift to domestic protein sources, such as copra meal, fish meal, and wheat pollards. But mills were reluctant to do so because of the lower and more variable quality and the higher costs for protein of these substitutes.

The squeeze on soybean imports had two significant consequences for use of corn as feed. First, it led to difficulties in maintaining regular deliveries at government-quoted prices because supplies leaked from licensed marketers into the free-price market. As a result, small mills faced a difficult supply situation and paid higher effective prices than did large mills. Second, the cost of soybean meal to large mills also increased in 1984 to Rp 350 per kilogram. At this cost of protein, use of cassava as an energy feed is not economical, and its substitutability for corn is reduced. Although cassava is regularly exported as an animal feed, it rarely enters domestic animal rations. The government may be willing to sacrifice some small-scale industries and cost efficiency in feed production to achieve savings in foreign exchange. But this goal has not been achieved—large feed mills have shifted to alternative, imported protein feeds, such as fish, rapeseed, and sunflower seed meal. None of these currently faces trade restrictions, and thus there has been little reduction in total expenditures of foreign currency.

Imports of corn have become BULOG's responsibility as part of its role in stabilizing prices of livestock feed. Stocks from domestic corn procurement and imports are distributed by BULOG primarily to feed mills when domestic corn prices rise seasonally—generally between the months of August and November. Table 6.10 shows annual BULOG sales

TABLE 6.10. *BULOG corn sales to feed mills*

Year	Total sales (tons)	Origin (percent)		Average sales price (rupiahs per kilogram)
		Imports	Domestic procurement	
1977–78	17,299	72	28	50
1978–79	44,455	73	27	120
1979–80	36,835	21	79	90
1980–81	72,308	15	85	105
1981–82	147,162	—	100	110
1982–83	224,653	97	3	135
1983–84	46,110	9	91	130

SOURCE: BULOG.

to feed mills and origin of its supplies—imported or domestically procured. Since 1977–1978 when corn sales to feed mills began, imports were greater than domestic procurement for three of the years and reached a peak of 217,800 tons in 1982–1983, a period of severe drought. These corn sales have generally been below market prices, and from 1981 to 1984, BULOG was confronted with substantial budgetary losses from its corn operations.

By injecting corn into the market on a seasonal basis, BULOG helps limit variation in monthly corn prices. While this market intervention accomplishes BULOG's goal of stabilizing the cost of feed to poultry raisers, it is accompanied by economic costs to the corn sector. Feed mills are less likely to make purchases of corn in rural areas in the August–November period if imported corn of good quality is available at lower prices in the port cities of their factories. This lack of demand depresses the price received by farmers who harvest corn in this period. Furthermore, by reducing interseasonal price variation, BULOG removes much of the incentive for the private sector—feed mills or commodity traders—to invest in corn storage and drying facilities to carry stocks from the months of peak harvest to those of peak prices. In effect, BULOG has taken on part of this storage function through the domestic procurements of its price support program, and it provides this service, at a loss on its own account, to feed mills.

The role that government policy plays in the livestock economy—particularly policies that affect size of poultry operations and imports of corn and soybean meal—will continue to be important. Use of corn feed grain and its by-products for livestock will remain the most rapidly growing domestic component of demand through the 1980s. Use of corn feed grain is projected to grow from about 700,000 tons in 1983 to about 1 million tons by 1988, primarily because of income-driven demand for poultry meat and eggs. Despite growth in demand for corn feed grain of over 7 percent per year, a potential increase in national corn production to over 6 million tons by the end of the Fourth Development Plan in 1988 would lead to growing surpluses. A drop in the real domestic price of corn is thus likely, as Indonesia shifts from importing corn at c.i.f. prices to exporting at f.o.b. levels.

Appendix: Animal Husbandry and the Use of Corn as Livestock Feed

Determining the demand for corn for livestock feed from the derived demand for livestock products requires an estimate of growth in meat, eggs, milk and other products consumed by households (see Table 6.3). These estimates are linked, via representative slaughter and dressed weight coefficients, to the gross output of livestock products required to satisfy the increase in demand (assuming no change in imports or exports). This output is translated into demand for corn as feed through specific conversion coefficients involved in feeding corn to each type of livestock. The details of these calculations are shown in Tables A6.1, A6.2 and A6.3 for swine, chicken meat, and chicken eggs, respectively. The use of corn by the dairy industry is still too small to be significant in these calculations. The derived demand approach does not require regional disaggregation of feeding practices because aggregate data for product demand are used to generate the projected rates of growth.

The animal supply approach, however, is considerably more complicated. The feeding of corn to livestock varies according to the type of

TABLE A6.1. *Derived demand estimates and projections of corn use as feed for swine, 1982–1988*

	1982	1983	1984	1985	1986	1987	1988
Total consumption of pork (000 tons)	101	104	110	117	124	132	140
Consumption of pork, carcass weight (000 tons)[a]	168	173	183	195	207	220	233
Swine slaughtered, liveweight (000 tons)[b]	240	247	261	279	296	314	333
Total swine slaughtered (000 head)[c]	2,400	2,470	2,610	2,790	2,960	3,140	3,330
Offtake from corn-fed swine systems (000 head)[d]							
Modern	120	124	131	140	148	157	167
Traditional	768	790	835	893	948	1,005	1,066
Corn fed to swine (000 tons)[e]							
Modern	19	20	21	22	23	25	26
Traditional	7	7	7	8	8	9	9
TOTAL	26	27	28	30	31	34	35

SOURCES: Note (a): Food and Agriculture Organization of the United Nations and the World Bank Cooperative Program (1978); note (b): Tillman (1981).

[a]Ratio of pork meat to carcass equals 0.6.

[b]Ratio of carcass weight to liveweight equals 0.7.

[c]Liveweight equals 100 kilograms per head at slaughter.

[d]Of the total Indonesian swine population in the early 1980s, corn-fed swine in the modern and traditional units were approximately 5 percent and 32 percent, respectively. The remaining population is raised either on other feedstuffs in confinement systems or as scavengers.

[e]Feed rations for the modern system are assumed to include 0.66 kilograms of corn per day per head for a period of 8 months until slaughter. Traditional systems are assumed to feed 0.03 kilograms of corn per day for a period of 10 months. Boars and breeding sows, estimated at 10 percent of offtake, are included for the purposes of feed use estimation.

TABLE A6.2. *Derived demand estimates and projections of corn use as feed to produce chicken meat, 1982–1988*

	1982	1983	1984	1985	1986	1987	1988
Consumption of poultry meat (000 tons)							
Commercial	60	62	67	72	79	85	93
Village	99	103	111	121	131	142	155
Total birds slaughtered (000,000 head)[a]							
Commercial broilers	58	60	64	69	76	82	89
Village poultry[b]	138	143	154	168	182	197	215
	(53)	(55)	(60)	(72)	(78)	(87)	(97)
Corn fed to poultry (000 tons)							
Commercial broilers[c]	93	96	102	111	122	131	142
Village poultry[d]	69	72	77	84	91	99	108
	(27)	(28)	(30)	(36)	(39)	(44)	(49)
TOTAL	162	168	179	195	213	230	250

[a]Based on carcass weights of 0.72 kilograms and 1.04 kilograms for village poultry and commercial broilers, respectively.

[b]Numbers in parentheses are calculated on the basis of head needed in addition to spent hens such that demand for village chicken meat is met.

[c]The feed-liveweight estimate uses a slaughter liveweight of 1.6 kilograms per head. The feed-liveweight conversion assumption is 2.5, with corn at 40 percent of the ration.

[d]Of total village poultry slaughtered for meat, 50 percent are assumed to be raised in areas where corn is fed. The analysis here assumes that the poultry are raised specifically for meat and are raised until 4 months, and total corn consumption is 1 kilogram. See text for consumption.

operation, whether commercial or traditional, and according to regional differences in feeding practices. Table A6.4 shows the provinces in which corn is fed to commercial poultry, village poultry, dairy cows, and swine, and Table A6.5 shows the animal populations in each province in 1982.[1] To account for the regional differences in husbandry, growth trends for each animal population are estimated by province. Each animal population is then reaggregated into systems in which corn is fed to the animal and those in which it is not. This distinction would also be important in calculating demand for feed in the derived demand approach if regional data on household demand for livestock products were available.

Commercial Poultry

Feeding practices for commercial poultry are fairly uniform across various sizes of operation.[2] Commercial poultry production, both layer and broiler, has always been basically a small-operator activity in Indonesia

[1]Other livestock species are fed corn, but in very small quantities or in limited areas or operations. Traditional feeding of corn to ducks and horses, as well as commercial feeding of shrimp and fattening of cattle, may undergo growth, but it will not add significantly to overall use of corn for livestock feed for the next several years.

[2]In this analysis, all poultry rations are assumed to be 40 percent corn. One-third of the flock was assumed to be chicks being raised as layers, and these pullets require 10 kilograms of feed per head up to the laying stage, which begins at about six months. There are two of these chick-growing cycles per year. Layers comprise the remaining two-thirds of the flock

TABLE A6.3. *Derived demand estimates and projections of corn use as feed to produce chicken eggs, 1982–1988*

	1982	1983	1984	1985	1986	1987	1988
Consumption of poultry eggs (000 tons)							
Commercial	173	179	191	204	218	232	248
Village	31	32	34	35	38	40	43
Commercial poultry required (000,000 head)							
Layers[a]	12.0	12.4	13.3	14.2	15.1	16.1	17.2
Pullets[b]	6.0	6.2	6.6	7.1	7.6	8.1	8.6
Corn fed to commercial poultry (000 tons)[c]							
Layers	192	198	213	227	242	258	275
Pullets	48	50	53	57	61	65	69
TOTAL	240	248	266	284	303	323	344
Total production of village poultry eggs (000 tons)[d]	238	246	262	269	292	308	331
Total village layers (000,000 head)[e]	85	88	94	96	104	110	118
Total village flock in corn areas (000,000 head)[f]	53	55	59	60	65	69	74
Corn fed to village poultry (000 tons)[g]	159	165	177	180	195	207	222

SOURCE: Note (d): see Kingston and Creswell (1982).

[a]Commercial layers are assumed to produce 14.4 kilograms per year (240 eggs × 60 grams per egg).

[b]The total flock is considered to be two-thirds layers and one-third replacement pullets.

[c]Layers consume 40 kilograms of feed per year, and pullets 10 kilograms in six months, with the pullet flock cycling twice in a year. Feed is 40 percent corn.

[d]Of total village egg production, 13 percent is consumed by humans, 71 percent is hatched, and 16 percent is waste.

[e]Village chickens produce about 2.8 kilograms of eggs per year (70 eggs × 40 grams per egg).

[f]Village hens are 80 percent of adult birds.

[g]Adult birds are each fed about 3 kilograms of corn per year.

despite the appearance of large, modern operations in the 1970s. Since 1981 the government has actively protected the small-scale producer through regulations that phase out operations with more than 5,000 layers or 750 broilers per week. Even before the phase-out had a widespread impact, small operators dominated, as can be seen from the ownership structure in East Java in 1982, which is shown in Table A6.6. Small-scale operations are frequently run as family operations, often for a secondary source of income. There is a wide range of managerial skills, but they are generally low. Credit constraints limit investment in physical structures, and compared with modern industry standards, productivity is lowered

---

and use 40 kilograms of feed per head per year. Output from layers is about 14.4 kilograms of eggs per year (240 eggs at 60 grams per egg). Broilers are assumed to reach a liveweight of 1.6 kilograms in 8 to 9 weeks and dress out to 1.4 kilograms. Each bird consumes 4 kilograms of feed, which represents a feed conversion ratio of 2.5 to 1. Breeders of broiler chicks claim that a more efficient feed conversion ratio of 2 to 1 is possible. But given the part-time, backyard nature of most poultry operations and the reports from several producers of conversion ratios of over 2.8 to 1, a middle figure is more realistic.

because of difficulties with sanitation, unhygienic water sources, disease control, and heat stress in backyard coops.

Large poultry operations generally buy the ingredients for mixing their own feed. But small poultry raisers do not usually have the know-how or a large enough scale of operation for feed mixing to be feasible, and they thus depend on purchased feed. As a generalization, small urban operators are most likely to buy complete feed, whereas rural producers buy commercial concentrate feed (high protein) and mix it with locally available energy sources, such as corn, and rice bran. By doing so, rural producers do not have to pay the cost of transporting the energy components of a complete feed.

For rural producers to mix corn and purchased concentrate feeds, they must store and grind corn—two operations that small-scale poultry raisers seem ill equipped to handle. Traditional storage of corn in kitchen rafters is inadequate for the quantities of corn required, but so far there is no practical alternative for storing corn on a small scale that does not entail substantial risk of storage loss to insects. For small rural producers, capital costs of stored corn are also prohibitive. The capital constraint applies as well to acquisition of grinding machinery—a single poultry raiser could not run even small milling machinery near its capacity. Storage and grinding of corn are currently provided in rural areas by the private sector, although there is room for an increased role by cooperatives (KUD), especially where these are organized to support the government's poultry credit program *(BIMAS Ayam)*.

Village Chickens

Village chickens are ubiquitous in rural Indonesia; households typically maintain a small flock of five to fifteen birds. Productivity is very low, but

TABLE A6.4. *Provinces with corn-fed livestock*

	Swine	Commercial poultry	Village poultry	Dairy cows
East Java	x	x	x	x
Central Java	x	x	x	x
D.I. Yogyakarta	x	x		
North Sumatra	x	x		
South Sulawesi	x	x	x	
Bali	x	x	x	
Nusa Tenggara Timur	x	x	x	
North Sulawesi	x	x	x	
Central Sulawesi		x	x	
Southeast Sulawesi		x	x	
Others		x		

SOURCES: Field observations, personal communications, and discussions with staff members of various Departments of Livestock Services.

TABLE A6.5. *Animal populations by province, 1982 (000 head)*

Province	Village chickens	Commercial chickens	Ducks	Swine	Milk cows	Beef	Water buffalo	Goats	Sheep	Horses
D.I. Aceh	4,565	83	2,500	8	—	353	396	322	133	15
North Sumatra	9,700	4,036	1,253	991	6	164	169	279	53	11
West Sumatra	4,357	833	920	11	—	286	151	169[b]	—	9
Riau	1,734	433	251	42	—	18	30	90	1	—
Jambi	1,323	638	123	23	—	21	41	48	19	1
Bengkulu	1,778	90	343	—	—	51	64	86	22	—
South Sumatra	5,047	479	820	79	—	252	109	338	97	2
Lampung	18,391	5,026	1,597	38	—	92	33	174	30	—
SUMATRA	46,895	11,618	7,807	1,192	6	1,237	993	1,506	355	38
D.K.I. Jakarta	364	1,689	13	71	6	—	1	21	4	—
West Java	16,976	11,337	2,341	52	39	132	448	1,012	1,969	14
Central Java	23,187	4,653	3,007	177	31	933	353	2,338	1,067	29
D.I. Yogyakarta	2,376	759	248	12	2	164	15	244	66	2
East Java	25,027	5,063	2,695	85	58	2,597	230	1,875	778	58
JAVA	67,930	23,501	8,304	397	136	3,826	1,047	5,490	3,884	103
West Kalimantan	1,265	754	208	407	—	75	2	43	—	—
Central Kalimantan	1,806[a]	—	—	192	—	45	10	28	2	—
South Kalimantan	4,531	769	2,033	12	—	58	55	64	20	4
East Kalimantan	2,110	2,683	579	59	—	14	14	45	3	—
KALIMANTAN	9,712	4,206	2,820	670	—	192	81	180	25	4
North Sulawesi	1,210	1,084	152	184	—	188	2	—	53	19
Central Sulawesi	1,350	37	83	76	—	275	36	145	16	15
South Sulawesi	14,412	846	3,957	311	—	1,109	513	533	33	243
Southeast Sulawesi	907	—	77	5	—	61	11	69	—	4
SULAWESI	17,879	1,967	4,269	576	—	1,633	562	747	102	281
Bali	89	39	9	20	—	13	38	—	—	—
Nusa Tenggara Barat	3,071	—	780	22	—	237	192	175	30	61
Nusa Tenggara Timur	2,182	75	46	726	—	466	141	323	66	181
Maluku	1,066	182	17	62	—	35	20	154	8	3
Irian Jaya	617	128	53	375	—	15	—	15	1	3
INDONESIA	149,441	41,716	24,105	4,040	142	7,654	3,054	8,590	4,471	674

SOURCE: Directorate General of Livestock worksheets, Jakarta.
[a]Includes all poultry.
[b]Includes both goats and sheep.

TABLE A6.6. *Size distribution of layer flocks, East Java*

Size of operation for layer flocks (head)	Percent of total
1–20	9
21–300	41
301–1000	28
1001–5000	13
5001+	8

SOURCE: Department of Livestock Services, East Java, "Annual Report" (1982).

because of the sheer numbers of birds, the contribution to meat and egg production is substantial. Constraints on improving productivity include poor genetic potential for feed conversion into meat and eggs, prevalence of disease, the poor quality of scavenged feed, and losses of up to two-thirds of chicks, which requires that most eggs be used for hatching. The size of the flock fluctuates widely because of losses to disease and slaughter for holiday celebrations.

In addition to scavenging, village chickens frequently receive a small supplement of corn, rice bran, and waste cooked rice. Substantial amounts of corn are fed to village chickens in areas with corn storage facilities, which provide year-round availability to consumers. Grain corn may be used, but more frequently the chickens are fed by-products of daily processing in the household. The total amounts of corn fed to an adult chicken in a year can be substantial; Corn Project surveys in several corn-producing centers found chickens consuming as much as 5 to 7 kilograms per head per year, well above the estimated 3 kilograms for

TABLE A6.7. *Distribution of swine population by type of operation*

	Modern	Traditional	
Province	Intensive (percent)	Confined (percent)	Extensive (percent)
East Java	40	60	—
Central Java	35	65	—
D.I. Yogyakarta	45	55	—
North Sumatra	7	83	10
South Sulawesi	8	82	10
North Sulawesi	8	82	10
Bali	1	4	95
Nusa Tenggara Timur	1	4	95

SOURCES: Department of Livestock Services, "Annual Report," various provinces and years; personal observations and discussions with officials; Nell and Rollinson (1974).
NOTE: In other areas, corn is replaced by substitute feeds.

village chickens generally.[3] Village chickens raised specifically for meat are considered to fill only half of total demand; the remainder is met by hens sold at the end of the laying cycle.

Swine

Because of Islamic injunctions against eating pork, commercial swine production is mostly an activity of Chinese and Christians on Java and in North Sumatra, Hindus on Bali, and the Christian Toraja in South Sulawesi. Three production systems are identifiable: intensive commercial operations, traditional confinement systems, and extensive, scavenging husbandry. Table A6.7 shows the types of systems used in the early 1980s in each province.

Intensive commercial operations, which generally range between 500 and 2,000 head, are actively improving breeding stock by importing Landrace, Duroc, and Yorkshire boars. Production efficiency has been increased with better feed. In the early 1970s a slaughter weight of 90 kilograms was not reached until 10 to 12 months in age, whereas current averages are 8 to 10 months, still almost double that in the United States. Since the pigs are totally confined, feed rations must be complete, but the composition is highly variable. In an informal survey, respondents with modern intensive operations in Central Java indicated they were feeding about 2 kilograms of feed per day up to a slaughter weight at 8 months of 100 kilograms, which yields roughly 42 kilograms of pork.[4] Corn makes up 33 percent of feed.

Swine operations on Java are frequently run in conjunction with an agricultural processing business, and by-products, such as copra meal, soybean waste, cassava waste, and rice bran, are mixed with the feed rations. Corn is a common source of energy in the ration and is included in a mash either as whole grain or as a bran by-product of corn milling. The most common substitutes for corn are rice bran, wheat pollards, and sorghum. Near urban centers, pigs in commercial operations are more frequently garbage-fed, and no corn is used in the ration.

Traditional confinement systems are most common on Java. These systems are typically no larger than one to two breeding sows and are often operated by non-Chinese villagers on the fringes of intensive operations. They may fatten pigs for local sale or sell piglets to larger firms that desire

[3]In calculating the use of corn feed in this analysis, it was estimated that village chickens were fed 3 kilograms of corn per bird per year. Hens are 80 percent of the flock and lay about 70 eggs per year (2.8 kilograms). Of the eggs produced, 13 percent are consumed, 71 percent are hatched, and 16 percent are wasted. Village chickens raised specifically for meat are marketed on average at 4 months of age, and half of them are raised in areas where corn is fed in some form.

[4]Liveweight at slaughter is 100 kilograms, of which the carcass is 70 percent. The ratio of pork meat to carcass is 0.6.

rapid expansion or are capable of raising capital for feed during the period of growing out fatteners. Breeding stock is improving, but inferior feed composition, which is only about 0.5 kilograms of mixed feed (6 percent corn) per day to which fodder and by-products are added, requires 10 to 12 months for slaughter weight to be reached. Feeding of high-quality protein and energy sources is rare, and feed rations contain corn only when it is a component of purchased complete feeds given to piglets before weaning. Pigs that have been weaned and pregnant sows are fed mostly agricultural by-products, rice bran, and green fodder.

Extensive pig husbandry, in which pigs scavenge for food, is not found on Java, but it is the predominant system for raising swine in Nusa Tenggara Timur, Bali, North Sumatra, and West Kalimantan. In this traditional system, corn is not fed to pigs. Since there has been little genetic improvement and pigs scavenge for their food, they have low efficiency of conversion and low productivity. With the exception of Bali pigs—of swayback, Chinese origin, which are in high demand among Chinese for their red meat and the distinctive cooking qualities of the fat—extensive systems are found where land is more abundant but developed markets are distant.

Dairy Cows

Dairy cow husbandry has undergone rapid development as a consequence of strong growth in consumer demand and the government's concerted efforts to replace substantial dairy imports with domestic production. Priority has gone to small-scale producers organized through dairy cooperatives (KUD), and major centers are on Java in Boyolali, Malang, Pandaan Berung, and Ujung Berung *kabupaten*. Table A6.8

TABLE A6.8. *Herd ownership distribution of dairy cooperative members, 1982*

Herd size (head)	Percentage of total cows in cooperatives
1	10.7
2–3	44.2
4–5	17.9
6–7	10.6
8–10	9.5
11+	7.1[a]

SOURCE: Speech by the Junior Minister of Cooperatives to the National Seminar on Milk Cows, Animal Husbandry Faculty, University of Gadjah Mada, December 1982.

[a]Estimated on 14 head per herd.

TABLE A6.9. *Estimated corn residues and fodder production, 1974*

	Total dry matter (000 tons)	
	Java/Madura	Indonesia
Food crop residues		
Corn residues	9,480	15,600
Rice straw	10,850	22,125
Cassava (leaves)	1,108	1,398
Other	3,275	4,429
Subtotal	24,713	43,552
Nonfood crop fodder[a]	7,900	NA
TOTAL	32,613	NA

SOURCES: For food crop residues, Muller (1974) and Nell and Rollinson (1974).
[a]Includes grasses from roadsides, estates, dikes, etc.

shows the dairy cooperatives' emphasis on small-scale production; almost 75 percent of the dairy cows in cooperatives are owned in herds of five cows or less. Almost all of Indonesia's dairy herd is on Java, and more than 50 percent of the herd belongs to milk cooperative members. Programs to improve production include imports of Friesian heifers and local breeding programs that include artificial insemination. Processing and marketing bottlenecks have been loosened through disease prevention, monitoring of market prices, and construction of several milk-processing plants, which were scheduled to begin operating in 1985.

Apart from production organized in cooperatives, there are also dairy operations classified as industrial, which consist of large private herds. They comprise about 20 percent of the Indonesian herd. In these larger operations, managerial skills are quite high, and productivity, which is

TABLE A6.10. *Estimated agro-industrial by-products used as energy feeds*

Product	Quantity (000 tons per year)
Corn bran	455
Corn chaff	25
Rice bran	2,577
Molasses	343
Cassava pomace	157
Cassava peelings	5,000
Wheat pollards	457
Coffee pulp	89
Banana fruit waste	22

SOURCES: Corn and wheat pollards: estimated by author; other: Soedomo and Sukanto (1982).

indicated by the proportion of lactating cows, the length of lactation, and average production, is well above that of smaller herds.

Most dairy cows are kept in confinement systems, and since they are ruminants, their primary feed is fodder. Fodder is cut and carried to the stabled cows, and the usual practice is to feed them dry corn stovers after the ears have been harvested.[5] Crop thinnings are a valued green fodder, and farmers at several survey locations plant corn at densities well over recommendations with the intention of thinning a fodder crop. Topping the corn stand above the corn ear once the grain has formed is a common practice in some areas. Tables A6.9 and A6.10 show the importance of corn fodder and corn grain by-products compared with other crop residues.

Despite the abundant vegetative waste from corn production, cash markets are rare for corn plant residues used as feed. In the few dairy areas, green corn fodder is sold, as it is on livestock market days when feed is needed for the cattle in transit. More frequently, corn stovers are made available free to neighbors or are burned since they are considered, like rice straw, a surplus item most easily disposed of by burning. Corn stalks and leaves are in abundant supply during harvest periods. There have been several attempts to promote corn silage in Indonesia, but its use remains unattractive to most small farmers with livestock. Making silage and maintaining it in good condition is difficult on a small scale under tropical conditions. Cooperative efforts in dairy areas to produce and store silage centrally for sale to surrounding dairy farmers have so far been frustrated by returns too low to justify costs. Greater use of these residues rests on improving feed value and storage methods to allow the supply of higher-quality corn fodder to be spread across the year.

[5]Fodder is fed twice a day for a total of 40 to 50 kilograms per day, and corn stalks are a seasonally important component. In dairy centers such as Batu, in Malang *kabupaten*, green stovers can be sold for as much as Rp 10 each, and this price has prompted many corn farmers to harvest stovers and green ears for the vegetable market rather than produce grain corn. In addition to fodder, a concentrate, often as much as 7 kilograms per day, is fed to lactating cows. In parts of Central and East Java, corn bran is used in concentrate up to 20 percent of the total feed mixture, although an overall average for these areas is probably 10 percent. In West Java, corn bran is usually replaced by rice bran and cassava. In larger operations total concentrate fed per cow appears to be less, and this is largely due to substitution of higher-quality, commercially prepared products for locally mixed feeds. Although calves, heifers, and dry cows occasionally receive concentrate feed, the quantity is insignificant, and only the feed for lactating cows is used in this analysis for projecting the use of corn feed grains. Of the dairy herd in corn areas, an estimated 63 percent is lactating at any given time, and on average, lactating cows receive 7 kilograms per day of concentrate, which is 10 percent corn by-products.

7. Prospects for Corn Sweeteners

Scott R. Pearson

Most corn currently produced in Indonesia is consumed directly as food for humans or feed for livestock. Increases in corn production in the past few years offer prospects of a significant corn surplus after domestic needs are met. Historically, surplus corn has been exported, and the potential exportable surplus could range from 200,000 to 500,000 metric tons by the end of the Fourth Development Plan in 1988. The prospect of this surplus has aroused interest in the potential to expand industrial uses of corn, particularly in the production of high-fructose corn sweeteners.

The economic feasibility of producing fructose sweeteners from corn depends almost entirely on government policy, especially on price and trade policy for sugar, corn, and cassava. Indonesia imported an average of 500,000 tons of sugar annually from 1978 to 1983; however, recent levels of domestic sugar production, together with carried-over stocks, have provided Indonesia with a small surplus of sugar supplies. Fructose sweeteners, whether produced from corn or cassava, would substitute for sugar imports (or free up domestic sugar production for export). The issue is whether it makes more sense to export surplus corn or to reduce sugar imports (or begin sugar exports). Annual production of 158,400 metric tons of fructose sweeteners from corn would require about 275,000 metric tons of corn annually, which would substantially reduce or eliminate the volume of corn exports. At a world price for corn of $120 per ton that prevailed in the mid-1980s, this amounts to a $33 million reduction in foreign exchange earnings from corn exports. In return, the fructose produced would substitute for approximately 160,000 metric tons of sugar, worth only $14 million at recent world prices.

Obviously, investing in the heavy capital costs of a plant to produce fructose sweeteners makes sense only if the sugar replaced is worth far more than it is in current world markets. The government's highly protective trade policy accomplishes precisely this by keeping domestic sugar prices more than four times those in the world market in the mid-1980s and probably double the long-run world price likely to prevail. Consequently, investors in Indonesia may well find it very attractive to build a corn-based, high-fructose sweetener plant, although the social profitability of such a venture is in serious doubt. The analysis in this chapter presents the methodology and calculations to determine the profitability of a fructose sweetener plant.

In the mid-1980s, less than one percent of Indonesian corn is used for industrial end uses. Potential industrial uses of corn could expand so that the total demand for corn as an industrial raw material would consume an important percentage of future corn output. If it did, the high substitutability between corn and cassava as sources of starch, as well as the potential for starch-based fructose sweeteners to replace liquefied sugar in many industrial processes, would strengthen food policy links among corn, cassava, and sugar.

Industrial End Uses of Corn

Four main industrial products—starch, oil, fructose sweeteners, and alcohol—can be obtained from corn. This chapter focuses principally on corn sweeteners. The potential for the three other industrial corn products in Indonesia is limited either by demand constraints or uncompetitively high costs of production. Cornstarch is used in Indonesia to produce foodstuffs and to assist certain industrial processes, such as making batteries and paper products. Domestic demand for cornstarch could increase along with population and income growth, but this end use is not expected to capture an increasing share of expanded corn production. The outlook is much the same for corn oil, which is produced as a joint product with starch and serves as a cooking oil, an ingredient in many foods, and an input in some industrial processes. Very little corn oil is currently used in Indonesia, but domestic demand for it could increase if it were priced competitively with other vegetable oils. Corn oil is likely to be a by-product of sweetener production rather than a product that will in itself be the primary reason for corn processing.

FIGURE 7.1. *Kernel of corn*

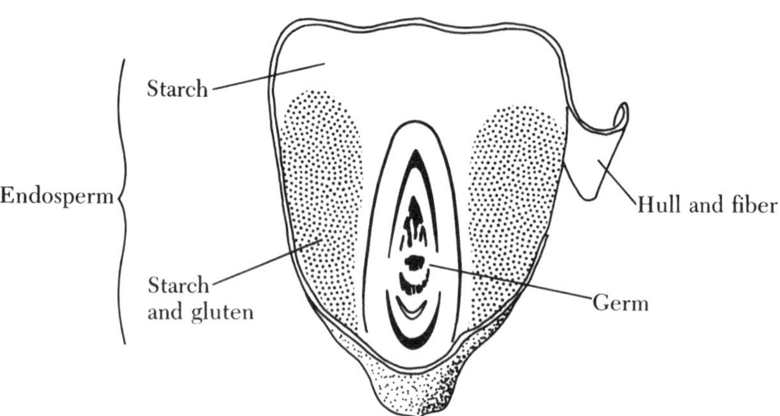

SOURCE: Corn Refiners Association (1979), pp. 12–13.

FIGURE 7.2. *Corn wet-milling process*

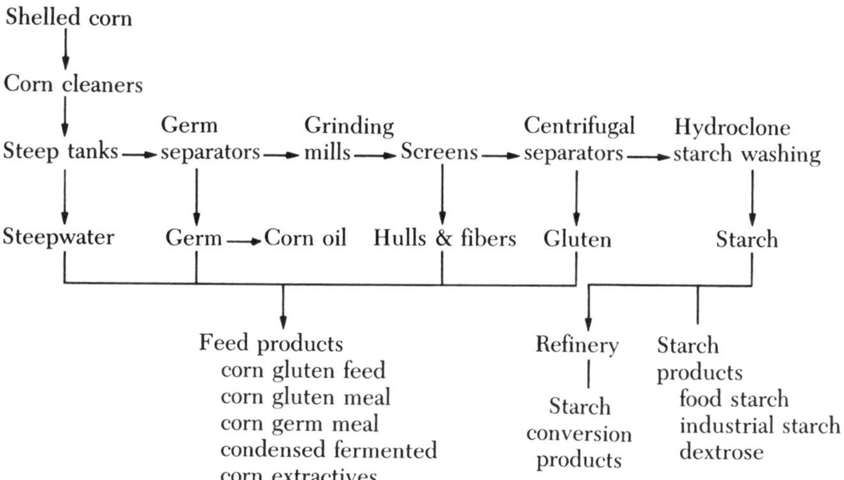

SOURCE: Corn Refiners Association (1979), pp. 12–13.

The production of alcohol (ethanol) from corn to substitute for gasoline produced from petroleum is technically feasible but highly uneconomic. Studies of corn-based ethanol production in the United States, where very large subsidies permit the process to survive, show that the world price of crude petroleum prevailing in the mid-1980s would have to double or even triple before alcohol made from corn could compete without government support (see Schrader and Tyner 1984). Because of the expectation, therefore, that future Indonesian production of cornstarch will be limited by the slow growth of demand and that future production of alcohol from corn will remain very uneconomic in Indonesia as elsewhere, the emphasis in this chapter is on nutritive sweeteners produced from corn.

Figure 7.1 shows the components of a kernel of corn. Corn sweeteners are made from the starch contained in the endosperm. Cornstarch products as well as corn alcohol are also based on the starch component, and corn oil is extracted from the germ by either an expelling or a solvent process. Most of the remainder of the corn kernel—gluten, germ meal, and fiber—is converted into livestock feed in the process of manufacturing starch, oil, sweetener, or alcohol.

The principal method used to make industrial corn products, including all corn sweeteners, is the corn wet-milling process, which is diagramed in Figure 7.2. In this process, shelled corn is cleaned and steeped in tanks containing warm water and sulfur dioxide. The steeped kernels are ground, screened, and centrifuged and thereby separated into germ, hulls and fiber, gluten, and starch slurry. Nutrients dissolved in the steep water are later concentrated and used in livestock feed. In another process, corn oil is extracted from the germ, and the residual germ meal becomes part of a feed mixture. The hulls and fiber and, most important, the gluten also are the basis for valuable feed products. Typically, the corn wet-milling process produces three main by-products: corn oil, corn gluten feed of 21 percent protein (usually containing steep-water nutrients, fiber, and germ meal), and corn gluten meal of 60 percent protein. Corn containing 15.5 percent moisture typically yields the following products: starch—55 percent; oil—3 percent; 21-percent gluten feed (dry basis)—21 percent; and 60-percent gluten meal (dry basis)—4 percent. The remaining 17 percent is accounted for by water and shrinkage.

Additional treatment of the starch slurry varies after washing, depending on the desired main product. Basic cornstarch and its products are produced by drying the slurry directly. Modified starches are made by applying particular chemical treatments before drying. The starch slurry can also be converted into various nutritive sweeteners. Corn glucose syrup results from treatment with hydrochloric acid or enzymes (chemical catalysts); this sweetener is used mainly in the confectionery, baking, jam and jelly, and beer industries.

High-fructose corn syrup (HFCS) is made by treating the starch slurry with a three-step, multiple enzyme process developed by Japanese technologists in the 1960s. In this process, dextrose is first made from cornstarch and then converted into fructose. Two standard grades of corn sweeteners—42 percent and 55 percent—are produced, and each corresponds to the level of fructose in the syrup. The remainder of the solid content of the solution is made up mostly of dextrose along with other simple sugars. Higher fructose content gives greater sweetening capacity. The sweeter, 55 percent corn sweetener (HFCS-55) is used mostly in the beverage industry, particularly for soft drinks, where it substitutes for sugar on about a one-for-one basis. The less sweet, 42 percent corn sweetener (HFCS-42) substitutes for liquid sugar in a wide variety of commercially processed foods, including dairy products (ice cream), beverages (fruit-flavored drinks), jams and jellies, canned fruits, and bakery goods. A representative list of products currently made from corn sweeteners in the United States is contained in Table 7.1. To date, uses of corn sweeteners have been restricted to industrial food processes in which the fructose corn sweetener can substitute for liquid sugar. A U.S. company has developed a technology to produce a 100 percent fructose product that would compete directly with crystal sugar in households, but the economic feasibility of this experimental process has not yet been demonstrated.

TABLE 7.1. *Applications of nutritive sweeteners made from corn*

High-fructose corn syrup			
bakery products		frozen desserts	
beverages, carbonated and still		jams, jellies, and preserves	
canned juices		pickles	
canned fruits		wine	
condiments		confectionery products	
Corn syrup			
baby and geriatric foods		industrial products:	
bakery products and supplies:		adhesives	explosives
bread	rolls	chemicals	paper
biscuits	pies	dyes and inks	textiles
doughnuts	cookies	tobacco	
cakes	etc.	jam, jellies, marmalades, and preserves	
pretzels		licorice	
beverages, brewed:		marshmallows and related products	
beer, ale, etc.		meat products (sausages, etc.)	
beverages, carbonated and still		peanut butter	
breakfast foods		pharmaceuticals	
cheese spreads and foods		pickles and pickle products	
chewing gum		pork and beans	
chocolate products		prepared mixes:	
coffee creamers		cake	
condensed sweetened milk		infant foods	
confectionery		pie fillings	
cordials and liqueurs		pudding powders	
eggs, frozen or dried		ice cream	
extracts and flavors		etc.	
frostings and icings		salad dressings	
fruit butters and juices		sauces:	
fruits and vegetables:		catsup	chili
canned	candied	tomato	seasoning
fillings	frozen	specialty	etc.
fruit drinks		seafood (frozen)	
fruit drink mixes		syrups:	
ice cream, water ices, and sherbets		table	chocolate
infant foods		cocoa	fruit
		medicinal	soda fountain
		cordials	etc.
		soups	
		toppings	

SOURCE: Corn Refiners Association (1979), p. 24.

Indonesian Market for High-Fructose Sweeteners

Whether much future corn production in Indonesia will be destined for conversion into corn sweeteners depends on three factors: the size of the domestic market for fructose sweeteners (and for the by-products of the corn wet-milling process); the ability of fructose to compete with sugar (sucrose) in Indonesia; and the competitiveness of corn versus cassava as a low-cost raw material for the starch and fructose. The first step is to determine if there is sufficient domestic demand for fructose sweeteners. Exports of fructose are unlikely due to the availability of inexpensive sugar on the world market and to protection against imports of fructose in countries that maintain high domestic sugar prices.

Domestic Demand for Sweeteners

Fructose sweeteners, whether produced from corn or cassava, are currently limited to substituting for sugar in liquid uses. In high-income economies, this restriction means that fructose sweeteners are used only in industrial food processes, producing the kinds of food and beverage items listed in Table 7.1. This limitation is not severe in high-income countries in which most food is processed. In the United States, for example, less than one-fourth of sweetener consumption (sucrose and fructose) occurs in households, and more than three-fourths is industrial. Given this wide scope for substitution, corn sweeteners accounted for 43 percent of U.S. consumption of caloric sweeteners in 1983.

The comparable breakdown of sugar consumption in Indonesia is not known exactly. Total sugar consumption in 1983 was 1.984 million metric tons or about 12.7 kilograms per capita. Direct sales of sugar by BULOG to industries, mainly those producing milk products and soft drinks, have been less than 100,000 metric tons in the mid-1980s, but this figure is known to be an underestimate of actual industrial consumption of sugar. A feasibility study for a small fructose sweetener facility using cassava estimated that industrial use of sugar amounted to about 500,000 tons in 1981 (Tate and Lyle Company 1981).

A more recent study in 1983 estimated that less than 10 percent of sugar consumption in Indonesia is industrial (Argento and Wardrip 1983). In light of the likelihood of future use of liquid sweeteners by small Indonesian vendors, food establishments, and households, that study suggested 10 percent as a workable ratio for use of fructose in total consumption of sweeteners (sucrose and fructose) in 1990. Demand for fructose sweeteners was estimated to be 280,000 tons, or 10 percent of 2.8 million tons of projected total demand for sweeteners for that year. At that level of fructose consumption, Indonesia could support production facilities of at most 220,000 tons of fructose sweeteners per year in 1985 and 280,000 tons per year by 1990. A reasonable guess for growth of fructose consumption after 1990 might be about 5 percent per year, on the assumption that incomes will grow at 5 percent per year and that fructose sweeteners will gradually take a wider market share of sweetener use as Indonesian consumers afford increasing levels of factory-processed foods.

Competitiveness of Fructose Sweeteners with Sugar

Two dimensions of Indonesia's sugar policy—the availability of licenses to produce fructose and the levels of sugar price support—are especially important for production of fructose sweeteners. Officials in charge of sugar policy in the Department of Agriculture play a major role in licensing the operation of fructose sweetener facilities; they have agreed to support decisions to license plants producing up to 300,000 tons of fructose per year. These licenses might become difficult to obtain if decision makers in the Department of Agriculture and throughout the government carry out announced investment plans to create large sugar estates in hopes of substituting domestic sugar for imports, which averaged 500,000 tons per year between 1978 and 1983 and ranged from 158,000 to 718,000 tons during that period. During 1984 a large domestic harvest of cane sugar in addition to high levels of carried-over stock resulted in a surplus of sugar supplies. If self-sufficiency in sugar is not temporary, the government will face pressures not to grant licenses to manufacture fructose.

BULOG administers price policy for sugar. In January 1984 the government's support price to farmers—BULOG's purchase price—was Rp 350 per kilogram, and BULOG's selling price for sugar ex factory was Rp 475 per kilogram. The wholesale price varied by markets but was generally about Rp 575 per kilogram (26 U.S. cents per pound). This highly protected domestic sugar price was four times the then prevailing world price for sugar and roughly double the 10 to 14 cents per pound that many analysts see as a likely trend for the world price of sugar.

Policy decisions to maintain the current degree of sugar protection and consequent high domestic sugar prices could provide an attractive investment climate for fructose sweetener production. Fructose could not compete with sugar, however, if the government expanded high-cost domestic production to replace sugar imports, which would lead to pressures to limit or even ban production of fructose. A third direction of policy would also make its production difficult or impossible, but for very different reasons. If sugar protection were reduced or eliminated and domestic sugar prices plummeted to world levels of 10 to 14 cents per pound, fructose sweeteners could not compete. The issue is whether Indonesia's sugar policy is likely to hold domestic sweetener prices high enough to place an umbrella over the costs of producing fructose. Its production quite clearly is a stepchild of sugar policy in Indonesia as it is in other countries. The following analysis assumes that the current policy of maintaining high sugar protection and issuing licenses for fructose production will continue.

Costs of Producing Corn Sweeteners

If current sugar policy is maintained, fructose sweeteners need to be produced at real costs less than 26 cents per pound (Rp 575 per kilogram) to be competitive in the Indonesian market. A discount of between 10 and 25 percent will probably be required to induce industrial users of sweet-

TABLE 7.2. *Projected costs of producing 55-percent high-fructose syrup (dry basis) from corn*

Inputs	36,000 bushels (915 tons) per day			16,000 bushels (407 tons) per day		
	270 days per year	300 days per year	330 days per year	270 days per year	300 days per year	330 days per year
Corn[a]	12,832	14,257	15,683	5,703	6,337	6,970
Chemicals[b]	7,749	8,610	9,471	3,444	3,827	4,209
Utilities, fuel, electricity[c]	6,438	7,154	7,869	2,861	3,179	3,497
Labor[d]	577	577	577	462	462	462
Miscellaneous (laboratory, supplies, overhead, insurance)[e]	1,342	1,342	1,342	997	997	997
Maintenance[f]	1,529	1,529	1,529	1,070	1,070	1,070
Working capital[g]	2,742	3,012	3,282	1,308	1,428	1,548
Depreciation[h]						
Equipment (10 years)	5,244	5,244	5,244	3,671	3,671	3,671
Buildings (40 years)	600	600	600	420	420	420
Return on investment before taxes[i]	22,935	22,935	22,935	16,055	16,055	16,055
Total costs per year	61,988	65,260	68,532	35,991	37,446	38,899
Total costs per ton of high-fructose syrup (US$)[j]	435	412	394	569	532	503
Total costs per pound of high-fructose syrup (US$)	0.197	0.187	0.179	0.258	0.241	0.228

SOURCES: Cubenas, Schrader, and Ford (1979); Schrader and Tyner (1984); and various industry sources, including factory visits and correspondence.
NOTE: All figures, unless otherwise indicated, are in thousands of U.S. dollars per year.

[a]Bushels per day × days per year ÷ by 39.36 bushels per ton × $120 per ton × 0.433 (by-product credit) = net corn costs in dollars per year.

[b]$54.40 per ton of HFCS-55 (dry basis) × bushels of corn per day × days per year ÷ by 39.36 bushels of corn per ton of corn ÷ by 1.7337 tons of corn per ton of high-fructose sweetener.

[c]$45.20 per ton of HFCS-55 (dry basis) × bushels of corn per day × days per year ÷ by 39.36 bushels of corn per ton of corn ÷ by 1.7337 tons of corn per ton of high-fructose sweetener.

[d]For 36,000-bushels-per-day plant:

Function	*Number*	*Wage rate per year (dollars)*	*Wage bill per year (dollars)*
Plant	117	1,000	117,000
Supervisors	25	5,000	125,000
Clerical	10	2,000	20,000
Laboratory	20	3,000	60,000
Administration and sales	15	7,000	105,000
Expatriate managers	2	75,000	150,000
TOTAL			577,000

For the 16,000-bushels-per-day plant, assume 80 percent of the wage bill of the 36,000-bushels-per-day plant.

[e]Laboratory cost is 20 percent of the wage bill; operating supplies are 20 percent of the wage bill; plant overhead is 60 percent of the wage bill; and insurance is 1 percent of investment.

[f]Two percent of investment of $76,450,000 (36,000 bushels per day) or of $53,515,000 (16,000 bushels per day).

[g]0.09 (annual interest rate of 18 percent charged on average for 6 months, on the assumption that working capital needs are spread evenly throughout the year) × sum of all variable costs (the first 6 lines of this table).

[h]Investment in equipment = 68.6 percent of total, in buildings = 31.4 percent of total.

[i]Thirty percent of investment.

[j]Total costs per year ÷ by bushels of corn per day × days per year ÷ by 39.36 bushels of corn per ton of corn ÷ by 1.7337 tons of corn per ton of high-fructose sweetener.

eners to switch from sugar to fructose sweeteners; a discount of 15 percent can serve as a reasonable midpoint. With this discount applied, HFCS-55 would need to be priced no higher than 22 cents per pound and HFCS-42 at or below 20 cents per pound. The less-sweet 42 percent syrup is usually priced at about 90 percent of the price of HFCS-55.

Between 1981 and 1983, prices for HFCS-55 syrup in the United States varied between 16 and 24 cents per pound, and those for HFCS-42 syrup ranged between 12 and 21 cents per pound (USDA 1984). But for two reasons these U.S. prices indicate very little about the prospective ability of new fructose sweetener plants to compete with sugar in Indonesia. First, U.S. prices for corn sweeteners are closely linked to sugar prices in the United States, which, at 28 to 30 cents per pound, were higher than those in Indonesia during 1981–1983. The critical issue, in the United States as in Indonesia, is the cost of fructose sweetener production. Cost estimates for U.S. plants producing both corn sweeteners, 42 and 55 percent HFCS, fall generally within a range of 16 to 20 cents per pound. These costs differ according to location of plant, size of facility, which allows economies of scale, and costs of corn. Second, conditions and costs for production of fructose in Indonesia might differ markedly from those in the United States. Consequently, it is necessary to analyze the costs of producing fructose sweeteners in Indonesia.

Table 7.2 contains cost estimates for producing HFCS-55 (dry basis) in Indonesia with two plant sizes—36,000 bushels (915 tons) per day and 16,000 bushels (407 tons) of corn per day. The estimates were calculated for three rates of capacity utilization—270, 300, and 330 days of production per year. Because of sizable economies of scale, operation of the larger plant is projected to incur costs substantially lower than those of the smaller factory—18.7 versus 24.1 cents per pound at 300 days per year. Whereas the capacity of the smaller plant is only 44 percent of that of the larger facility, the expected investment costs of the smaller plant are 70 percent of capital costs in the larger facility ($53.5 versus $76.5 million).[1]

Nutritive sweeteners made from corn priced at $120 per ton f.o.b. Surabaya in the larger plant that processes 36,000 bushels per day could compete with sugar in industrial uses if the real domestic price of sugar remains at or above recent levels of 26 cents per pound, even if fructose sweeteners are discounted 15 percent for competitive access. The larger plant operating 300 days per year would produce 528 tons of HFCS-55 (dry basis) per day, or 158,400 tons per year. This level of output is less than the projected upper limit of Indonesian demand for fructose sweet-

[1]Because the exchange rate between the rupiah and the U.S. dollar is changeable, data and results here are reported mainly in U.S. currency; when figures are given also in rupiahs, the assumed exchange rate is Rp 1,000 per U.S. dollar.

eners in the late 1980s—220,000 to 280,000 tons per year. The costs of production in the larger plant, running 300 days annually, are estimated at 18.7 cents per pound, well below the comparative cutoff level projected above of 22 cents per pound (26 cents discounted by 15 percent). If capacity utilization could be increased to 330 days per year, the costs would fall to 17.9 cents per pound, roughly a 5 percent cost reduction for a 10 percent increase in output. Conversely, a 10 percent decline in output (to 270 days per year) would result in a 5 percent increase in costs, from 18.7 to 19.7 cents per pound.

Corn sweeteners produced in the smaller plant that processes 16,000 bushels per day are not likely to be competitive with sugar in Indonesia, given the assumptions made for this analysis. Costs of production in the smaller facility are projected at 24.1 cents per pound if the factory runs 300 days per year. Unless the assumed discount of 15 percent off the sugar price proves much too conservative, the smaller plant's output would not be able to replace sugar in industrial end uses. In any event, investors would have a major cost incentive to build the larger plant because its costs per unit of fructose output are less than 80 percent of the smaller plant's unit costs.

The scale economies achievable with the larger plant swamp the savings in transportation costs that would result from constructing two or more smaller plants. The ton per kilometer costs of moving corn and fructose sweeteners (and feed by-products) are approximately equal, but the water content differs. Corn is usually shipped with about 15.5 moisture content, HFCS-55 is transported in a solution containing 23 percent water, and gluten meal or feed each have about 10 percent moisture when moved to market. Less water is moved by siting fructose sweetener plants near areas of consumption. But the savings are small, amounting to only about 5 percent of the transportation cost of moving corn (or product) from the main corn production region to the principal location of fructose sweetener consumption.[2] This potential saving amounts to only 90 cents per ton of fructose (5 percent of $18, the cost of transporting each ton by truck for the 780 kilometers from Kediri, East Java, to Jakarta at a cost Rp 18 per kilometer). This saving is only 2 percent of the unit costs of fructose sweetener production in the larger facility. In short, scale economies, which allow unit costs of the larger plant to be about 22 percent lower than those in the smaller plant, are far more important than potential savings in transporting water, a cost that increases the larger plant's unit costs by less than 1 percent relative to those of the smaller plant.

[2]The water premium is 0.155/(1−0.155) or 0.183 of the costs of transportation for corn and 0.234 of transport costs for products (0.68 × 0.23/0.77) + (0.28 × 0.10/0.90), where 0.68 and 0.28 are dry basis proportions of fructose sweeteners and gluten products, respectively, in corn.

TABLE 7.3. *Value of by-products from corn sweetener production*

	Per ton of corn wet milled			Per 36,000-bushels-per-day HFCS facility (at 300 days per year)		
By-products	Quantities (kilograms)	Prices (rupiahs per kilogram)	Values (rupiahs)	Quantities (tons)	Prices (rupiahs per ton)	Values (millions of rupiahs)
Corn oil	30.0	660	19,800	8,232	660,000	5,433
Corn gluten feed (21% protein at 10% moisture)	227.7	110	25,047	62,479	110,000	6,873
Corn gluten meal (60% protein at 10% moisture)	47.3	490	23,177	12,979	490,000	6,360

When corn products—starch, oil, sweeteners, or alcohol—are manufactured, valuable by-products are produced, mostly for use as livestock feed. These feed by-products typically are worth half or more of the cost of corn used as an industrial input. The costs of corn reported in Table 7.2 are net costs of corn, that is, total corn costs less the by-product credits, the value of corn oil, gluten feed, and gluten meal produced in the wet-milling process. As shown in Table 7.3, these valuable by-products are estimated to constitute about 57 percent of the total corn costs: corn oil makes up 3 percent by weight and 16.5 percent by value of corn input charges; gluten feed accounts for 20.7 percent of the weight (dry basis) and 20.9 percent of the value of corn; and gluten meal is 4.3 percent of the weight (dry basis) of corn and 19.3 percent of its input cost.

Given the projected levels of output of these by-products, two—corn oil and corn gluten meal—should not have difficulty finding markets in Indonesia at the prices shown in the table. Corn oil competes with other vegetable oils; an additional 8,200 tons per year should be absorbed easily in the face of growing incomes and demand for oils. Corn gluten meal (60 percent protein) is a substitute for soybean meal and other high-protein ingredients in mixed feeds. Mink analyzed the growth of the livestock feed industry in Chapter 6. With continued rapid growth in the consumption of poultry meat and eggs, corn gluten meal products can be expected to find a ready market in Indonesian feed mills. The price for corn gluten meal reflects in part the high costs of soybean meal in Indonesia—about $335 per ton c.i.f. Jakarta in 1984. The large tonnage of corn gluten feed, however, might be difficult to sell at the projected price. Because of its high crude fiber content (8 to 9 percent), gluten feed is typically fed to dairy and beef cows or hogs, not to poultry—the source of most demand for compound feed in Indonesia. Consequently, some special arrangements might have to be made with Indonesian dairy or beef operators to dispose of 62,000 tons of gluten feed annually.

Corn's Competitiveness with Cassava in Sweetener Production

Either corn or cassava can be used as a source of starch from which to make fructose sweeteners. To be competitive, corn sweeteners from the larger facility, produced at a projected cost of 18.7 cents per pound, must be both cheaper than sugar and lower cost than fructose sweeteners made from cassava.

In late 1982, one plant in East Java (P. T. Saritani) began producing about 7,500 tons of HFCS-42 syrup per year (25 tons per day for 300 days), processed from fresh cassava roots at a reported production cost of about 20 cents per pound (Rp 440 per kilogram in early 1984 prices). This plant interrupted production in mid-1984 while awaiting imports of parts and chemicals.

Table 7.4 presents summary data from a recent study that projected costs of producing 100 tons of fructose per day from cassava starch. If the

TABLE 7.4. *Projected costs of producing 100 tons per day of 55-percent fructose syrup from cassava starch*

	Days of operation		
Inputs	270	300	330
Cassava starch[a]	6,750	7,500	8,250
Chemicals and utilities[b]	2,076	2,307	2,538
Labor	45	45	45
Miscellaneous (laboratory, supplies, overhead, insurance)	139	139	139
Maintenance[c]	196	196	196
Working capital[d]	829	917	1,005
Depreciation[e]			
Equipment (10 years)	840	840	840
Buildings (40 years)	35	35	35
Return on investment before taxes[f]	2,940	2,940	2,940
Total costs per year	13,850	14,919	15,888
Total costs per ton of high-fructose syrup (US$)	513	497	485
Total costs per pound of high-fructose syrup (US$)	0.233	0.266	0.220

SOURCE: Industry communications.
NOTE: Unless otherwise indicated, figures are in thousands of U.S. dollars per year.
[a]25 cents per kilogram.
[b]$7,690 per ton.
[c]Two percent of investment of $9.8 million.
[d](Annual interest rate of 18 percent charged on average for 6 months, on the assumption that working capital needs are spread evenly throughout the year) × the sum of all variable costs (the first 5 lines of this table).
[e]Investment in equipment is $8.4 million and in buildings is $1.4 million.
[f]Thirty percent of investment of $9.8 million.

TABLE 7.5. *Costs of fructose sweetener production: corn and cassava compared*

	F.o.b. export price (US$ per metric ton)	Cost of sweetener (US$ per pound)
Base case		
Corn	120.00	0.187
Cassava		
Dried pellets (fresh root equivalent = $32.60)	110.00	0.219
Break-even case		
Corn	214.00	0.219
Cassava		
Dried pellets (fresh root equivalent = $22.80)	77.00	0.187

prospective plant operated 300 days per year, the fructose sweeteners would cost 22.6 cents per pound, over 20 percent higher than the sweeteners made in the larger corn-processing facility. This result is based on an assumed cost of cassava starch of 25 cents per kilogram (11.4 cents per pound), a figure similar to one calculated by Nelson (1984) in an independent analysis of cassava starch manufacturing (11.6 cents per pound for medium-scale production including bolting mill costs). Fructose sweeteners can be produced from cassava or cassava starch in small facilities that have limited opportunities to reap economies of scale. Unlike sweeteners based on corn wet milling, which require very large investment and scales of production to achieve minimum cost levels, sweeteners from cassava can be made competitively in smaller facilities that enjoy reduced transport costs of inputs and products.

The above analysis of production of corn fructose sweeteners is based on a corn price of $120 per ton f.o.b. Surabaya (about $2.40 per bushel f.o.b. Chicago), the expected long-run trend price for corn. The comparable long-run world price for cassava is $110 per ton of dried pellets, which is used for animal feed mostly in Europe. This figure implies a fresh root price of $32.60 per ton and a cassava starch price of $236 per ton.[3]

The analysis reported in Table 7.4 assumes a fresh root price of $34.50 per ton ($250 per ton for starch × 0.69/5), about 6 percent higher than the expected long-run price. At the lower fresh root price of $32.60 per ton, the cost of producing a pound of fructose from cassava in the facility with an output of 100 tons per day is 21.9 cents, or 17 percent higher than the

[3]The conversion ratio for fresh cassava roots is 0.74 × $110 per ton/2.5, where 0.74 is the proportion of fresh root costs in pellet costs and 2.5 tons of fresh roots are used for 1 ton of pellets. For cassava starch, $32.60 per ton × 5/0.69, where 0.69 is the proportion of fresh root costs in starch plus by-product costs and 5 tons fresh roots are used for 1 ton of starch. These conversion ratios are somewhat arbitrary because they depend on assumptions concerning moisture content, use of peels, quality of processing, and foreign exchange rates.

18.7 cents per pound cost of the larger corn-processing plant. The corn price would have to rise by 78 percent, to $214 per ton, for the costs of producing sweeteners from corn to increase to 21.9 cents per pound. At a corn price higher than $214 per ton, cassava would be the cheaper raw material to produce fructose. For a cassava-processing plant to produce fructose as cheaply as a corn-processing plant that buys corn at $120 per ton, the fresh cassava price would have to fall by 30 percent, to $22.80 per ton, before its costs of producing sweeteners would decline to 18.7 cents. These break-even results are summarized in Table 7.5.

Future Policy for Sugar, Cassava, and Corn

The potential demand by a fructose sweetener industry for corn is unlikely to be more than 6 percent, or 275,000 tons, of an Indonesian corn crop of 4.5 million metric tons. The industry would use correspondingly less if corn output in the late 1980s increases more rapidly than demand for corn sweeteners. Given the expected ranges of production costs, the required sugar prices to protect fructose sweeteners, and the price ranges within which corn or cassava is likely to be the raw material, the economic viability of a potential industry depends directly on government policies affecting domestic prices of sugar, cassava, and corn.

This section tests the vulnerability of fructose sweetener profitability to alternative combinations of commodity policies. Four alternative sets of policies are chosen to represent both likely and extreme outcomes. The assumptions and results are summarized in Table 7.6. At one unlikely extreme, domestic protection might be removed on all three commodities, permitting Indonesian prices to be set by world prices. At the opposite end of the policy spectrum, trade policy and tax and subsidy policies could provide significant protection to domestic production of all three crops by raising Indonesia's prices well above comparable world price levels. In the two intermediate cases, sugar is assumed to receive protection, cassava is not, and corn is protected in one case but not in the other. For each potential policy set, the issues are whether fructose production would be competitive and whether corn or cassava would be the less expensive raw material.

In the "world price" assumption, the government sets domestic producer prices in accordance with expected long-run trends in world prices of sugar, cassava, and corn.[4] This assumption does not imply free trade, however, because the government could intervene for purposes of price stabilization. Floor and ceiling prices maintained by BULOG would be

[4]These price trends are: sugar at $265 per ton c.i.f. Jakarta; cassava at $110 per ton for dried pellets f.o.b. Surabaya; and corn at $120 per ton f.o.b. Surabaya. All prices in this section are quoted in real terms.

TABLE 7.6. *Domestic commodity prices and sweetener costs under alternative policy assumptions*

	Policy assumptions			Domestic commodity prices (rupiahs per kilogram)				Sweetener cost (dollars per pound)		
					Cassava					
Policy set	Sugar	Cassava	Corn	Sugar	Pellets	Fresh	Corn	Sugar	Cassava-based sweetener	Corn-based sweetener
World price	no policy	no policy	no policy	265	110	32.6	120	.12	NP	NP
Most likely	protection	no policy	no policy	575	110	32.6	120	.26	NP	.18
Corn protection	protection	no policy	protection	575	110	32.6	>214	.26	.219	NP
Full protection	protection	protection	protection	575	>111	>32.8	>216	.26	NP	NP

SOURCE: Tables 7.2 and 7.4; author's estimates.
NOTE: NP = No production. Exchange rate is Rp 1,000 per U.S. dollar.

established around the trend price, thereby providing no long-run protection or taxation to Indonesian producers (and no long-run subsidization or taxation of domestic consumers). With world prices in effect, sweetener demand in Indonesia would be met by local and imported sugar, which is assumed in this analysis to be available at 12 cents per pound (Rp 265 per kilogram). No fructose sweetener production, Indonesian or foreign, could compete with sugar at this price.

In light of the high domestic costs of growing and processing sugar and the political influence of sugar interests, the most likely future policy for sugar is continued protection that would maintain domestic wholesale prices at least at 1984 levels of 26 cents per pound (Rp 575 per kilogram) or more than double the expected world price level. Current policies of no price intervention for cassava and stabilization of corn prices around long-run world price trends would continue. Domestic cassava prices would follow the trend for world prices. With this "most likely" set of policy assumptions, one plant that processed 36,000 bushels of corn per day would produce fructose sweeteners at a cost of 18.7 cents per pound (Rp 411 per kilogram). The annual output of 250,000 tons could substitute for about 160,000 tons of sugar. This level of output would use about 275,000 tons of corn. Corn would be the raw material for fructose sweeteners if the long-run world price relative, comparing corn to cassava pellets, is 1.09 (120/110). At these prices the cost of producing sweeteners from corn is 85 percent of that from cassava, or 18.7 versus 21.9 cents per pound. If investors, licenses, and experienced management were forthcoming, the "most likely" set of policies would support a small, but growing, corn sweetener industry in Indonesia.

Corn policy in Indonesia might return to its earlier protectionist stance if high-yielding seeds do not give the hoped-for reductions in costs of corn production and increases in yields and total production. A third policy alternative thus combines the "most likely" assumptions for sugar (high protection) and cassava (no price policy) with high protection for corn. Corn protection could occur through a tariff or quota if corn were imported or through an export subsidy if corn were exported. If the domestic producer price for corn were above $214 per ton (Rp 214,000 per ton), cassava would substitute for corn in sweetener production (214/110 = 1.95, the break-even price relative, comparing corn to cassava). The cost of sweeteners based on cassava priced at $110 per ton would be 21.9 cents per pound, which would be marginally competitive with sugar. About 800,000 tons of fresh cassava would be needed to replace 160,000 tons of sugar. If fructose sweeteners require a 15 percent discount for market access, cassava-based sweeteners costing 21.9 cents per pound would just be able to compete with sugar costing 26 cents per pound.

The final policy combination is the "full protection" alternative, in which all three commodities receive high protection so that expected long-run domestic prices greatly exceed their world price counterparts. Because cassava is exported from Indonesia, an export subsidy would be required to raise the domestic price above the world price. If any level of export subsidy were provided to cassava pellets, domestic cassava prices would be too high to permit profitable use of cassava as a raw material in sweetener production—as the above price comparisons show. Production of sweeteners from corn would become unprofitable if protection increased the price of Indonesia's corn to $216 per ton or higher, because sweeteners from corn would then cost more than 22 cents per pound. Under a "full protection" policy, fructose sweetener production would occur only if protection of corn were not excessive.

The government can thus control the future of fructose sweetener production in Indonesia directly, by licensing construction and output levels of facilities, and indirectly, by changing the relative prices of sugar, cassava, and corn through application of varying levels of protection for these three commodities. With no protection of sugar, no fructose sweeteners would be produced. With protection of sugar and no protection of either corn or cassava, sweeteners could be produced using corn as the raw material. This set of policies appears to be the most likely. Protection of corn or cassava could alter this result. High protection of corn could cause a switch to cassava for sweetener production, and high protection of both corn and cassava could make production of fructose sweeteners unprofitable, despite a very large degree of protection of sugar.

The analysis in this chapter has focused on combinations of policies that might lead to the private profitability of manufacturing high-fructose corn syrup. When the government considers whether turning corn into sweeteners is an efficient use of Indonesian resources, the answer is influenced critically by expected trends of world prices for sugar, corn, and cassava. If the world prices assumed here turn out to be approximately correct, fructose production—from corn or cassava—could be socially unprofitable because it could not compete with sugar valued at 12 cents per pound. The prospect for fructose manufacturing thus depends on the government's maintaining a high degree of protection of sugar and on the reemergence of domestic deficits in sugar supplies. From both economic and political viewpoints, only burdens would result from a decision to use corn sweeteners to replace domestic sugar that would in turn have to be exported with a heavy subsidy.

PART FOUR

Marketing, Trade, and Price Formation

Both corn production and domestic corn consumption have risen rapidly since 1970, and the net outcome in any given year has been delicately balanced between a small volume of exports or imports. The apparent tendency in the late 1970s for regular imports of corn to displace regular exports provided much of the impetus for this study. But the bright potential for continued gains in corn yields, coupled with a slowing in the rate of growth of demand from feed mills and household consumers, suggests this concern was misplaced. With facilitative government policies, trends apparent in the mid-1980s point toward potential exports of corn on a regular, if seasonal, basis. If realized, these exports would place Indonesia in a desirable, but anomalous, standing relative to other rapidly growing, middle-income countries. These countries—Taiwan, South Korea, Mexico, Brazil, and Nigeria, for example—became substantial importers of corn in the 1970s to meet the demand for high-quality animal feed as income levels moved into the range of $600 to $1,000 per capita. If Indonesia is able to counter such a trend in imports while it supplies corn at stable prices to its own developing livestock industry, it will mark a second major agricultural success story—in addition to rice—from which other countries can learn valuable technical and policy lessons.

The potential switch back to regular exports, along with significant shifts in the relative shares of different domestic end uses, implies new and more complicated tasks for the marketing sector. As a base for understanding these tasks, Table I4.1 shows a disaggregation of corn flows in 1981. Table I4.2 shows the changes in volume between 1970–1971 and 1980–1981 for each category shown in Table I4.1. The figures are averages of the two years shown in order to smooth out the noticeable "up-and-down" pattern of annual corn production.

A comparison of the data on production and end use for 1980–1981 with the data for 1970–1971 reveals two striking facts: corn production grew very rapidly over the decade—5.3 percent per year—despite nearly stable acreage; and domestic end use rose even more rapidly—6.7 percent per year, leading to the disappearance of the substantial exports at the

TABLE I4.1. *Corn flows, 1981 (000 tons)*

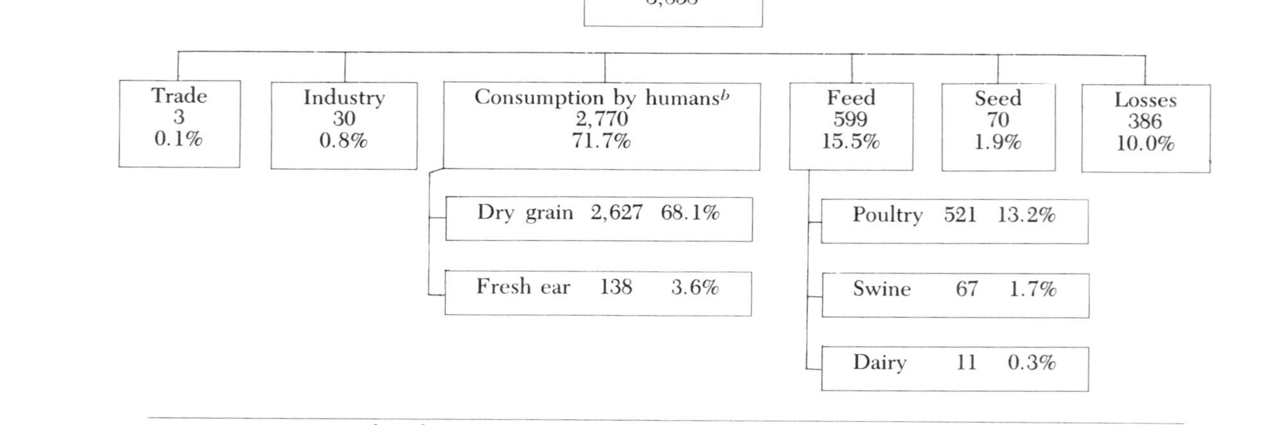

Marketed		
Industry	30	
Trade	3	
Feed	309	(3/4 of commercial poultry, plus swine and dairy)
Consumption by humans	1,410	
Total	1,752	(46%)
Nonmarketed		
Seed	75	
Feed	290	(Village chickens plus 1/4 of commercial poultry)
Consumption by humans	1,355	
Total	1,720	(44%)
Losses	386	(10%)

SOURCE: Estimated by Stephen Mink and Paul Dorosh.
[a]Adjusted from official data.
[b]Dry grain equivalent.

TABLE 14.2. *Disaggregation of end uses for corn, 1970–1971 and 1980–1981*

Variable	1970–71 average (000 tons)	1980–81 average (000 tons)	Annual percentage change
Corn production	2,165	3,639	5.3
International trade	− 250	+ 7	NA
Total domestic end uses	1,915	3,646	6.7
Components of End Use			
Seed[a]	70	71	0.1
Industry	20	25	2.3
Humans, on-farm	703	1,300	6.3
Humans, market source	786	1,330	5.4
Livestock, on-farm	126	290	8.7
Livestock, market source	61	300	17.3
Waste[b]	149	330	8.1
TOTAL	1,915	3,646	
Marketed share[c]	0.57	0.52	

SOURCES: Table 14.1 and author's estimates.
NOTES: A minus sign (−) indicates exports. A plus sign (+) indicates imports.
[a]Seed is calculated at 25 kilograms per hectare.
[b]Waste in 1970–1971 is calculated as 5 percent of on-farm use, 8 percent of international trade, and 10 percent of end uses from market sources. The low on-farm value is accounted for by the practice of feeding corn "waste" to household livestock, especially chickens and ducks. In 1980–1981, waste is calculated as 15 percent of end uses from market sources to allow for increased storage losses, and other losses are factored the same as in 1970–1971.
[c]Corn available in markets (plus exports) as share of corn production (plus imports).

beginning of the decade and the appearance of a very small level of imports at the end. Although the total amount of corn marketed more than kept pace with population growth during this decade—it increased 4.5 percent per year—the *share* of corn marketed fell from 57 percent in 1970–1971 to 52 percent in 1980–1981.

The picture sketched by these statistics, however, is not easily made consistent with the change in household consumption of corn from domestic production implied by the income and price elasticities calculated in Chapter 5. Since there were substantial gains made by the overall rural economy—not to mention the improvements in human welfare indicators, such as infant mortality rates—a rapid rate of growth in household consumption is plausible only if the income elasticity of demand for corn-consuming households is positive. But there is no evidence from cross-section data that this is so. Apparently much of the increase in corn produced during the 1970s was kept by the farm households themselves, which contributed to increased corn consumption, perhaps along with greater accumulation of household stocks and higher storage losses. Alternatively, corn production statistics might have significantly overestimated the rate of growth during the 1970s, but this cannot be confirmed or denied from available data.

The outlook for marketings from increased production in the 1980s would seem to be quite different from the pattern of the 1970s, and the role of the marketing system in stimulating increased output through more efficient price formation and exchange of inputs and output is likely to be crucial. As Chapters 2, 3, and 4 indicate, most of the promising outlook for production comes from high-yielding seed varieties and the potential for further increases in fertilizer use and measures for disease control. All of these sources of growth require substantial cash investments on the part of the farmers, and increased cash flow from their harvests is necessary to finance them. In addition, farmers adopting the full range of new corn technology are likely to have saturated their household demand for corn and may even wish to substitute rice from market purchases for corn from home production.

This outlook for the future pattern of corn production suggests that corn-producing households will be less subsistence-oriented and will behave more like other rural households that purchase their corn from the market. Accordingly, the share of corn production that is marketed should be larger. In the 1970s, marketed supplies grew by 4.5 percent per year while corn production grew by 5.3 percent, for a marketing share from increased output of 0.85. For the rest of the 1980s and the early 1990s, this share is likely to exceed 1.0. Although unanticipated stock increases and storage losses probably accompanied production increases in the 1970s and early 1980s, farmers have learned that higher yields are now reliable. Future increases in corn production will tend to be marketed shortly after harvest, or appropriate investments will be made in improved household drying and storage for later marketing. Either way, the share of corn marketed will tend to rise, thus placing a proportionately larger burden on the marketing system to reach farmers and give them opportunities to sell their output at remunerative prices. If the marketing system, through lack of responsiveness or high costs, fails in this task, corn production will not increase at the rate possible on technological and economic grounds.

The efficiency of the marketing sector may well determine whether Indonesia imports or exports corn at the end of the 1980s. With the availability of new seed technology, both hybrid and open-pollinated, more intensive fertilizer applications, and continued improvements in farming practices, production potential for the remainder of the 1980s is bright. For comparing the balance between future production and domestic end uses in order to determine if the marketing system should be oriented toward imports or exports, a continuation of the rate of growth in production in the 1970s of 5.3 percent might be taken as a lower bound, placing the average for 1988–1989 at 5,500,000 metric tons (using adjusted production figures as the base). If all the potential is realized, corn production in 1988–1989 could reach 6,000,000 metric tons, a growth rate of 6.5 percent per year from the 1980–1981 average base of 3,639,000 metric tons.

Whether these production levels result in imports or exports depends on growth in the various categories of domestic consumption. Production levels themselves affect levels of on-farm consumption by humans and livestock, but other components of domestic end use must be calculated from income and price elasticities along with population trends and any shifts in industrial end uses. The total (including waste) can then be compared with production. The net result is the surplus available for export or the deficit to be covered by imports. So long as trade is an option in either direction, the domestic price of corn is bounded by the world price. The price depends on whether net trade will be oriented toward exports, in which case an f.o.b. price that is competitive in world markets is required, or oriented toward imports, in which case a c.i.f. price derived from the same expected world market price is required.

The results of these calculations are shown in Table I4.3. As indicated in the upper part of the table, total domestic end uses do not seem likely to grow quite so rapidly as production at either the low or the high end of the range. Consequently, exports on average in 1988–1989 could replace the small volume of imports that were required during the 1980–1981

TABLE I4.3. *Projections of corn supply and demand balance, 1988–1989 average*

Variable	1980–81 average (000 tons)	1988–89 average (000 tons)		Annual change (percent)	
		Low	High	Low	High
Corn production	3,639	5,500	6,000	5.3	6.5
International trade	+ 7	− 235	− 489	NA	NA
Total domestic end uses	3,646	5,265	5,511	4.7	5.3
Components of End Use					
Seed	71	73	75	0.3	0.7
Industry[a]	25	30	35	2.3	4.3
Humans, on farm	1,300	1,869	1,815	4.6	4.3
Humans, market source	1,330	1,754	1,831	3.5	4.1
Livestock, on-farm	290	492	464	6.8	6.1
Livestock, market source	300	555	743	8.0	12.0
Waste	330	492	548	5.1	6.5
TOTAL	3,646	5,265	5,511		
Marketed share	0.52	0.54	0.59		

SOURCE: Author's estimates.

NOTE: A minus sign (−) indicates exports. A plus sign (+) indicates imports.

[a]No allowance is made for installation of a corn sweetener plant, which would utilize 275,000 tons of corn if constructed, according to estimates in Chapter 7.

base period. The volume of exports might be substantial, approaching 500,000 tons per year if the high production potential is reached and if the associated calculations for end uses are realistic.

Table I4.3 also provides disaggregated patterns of these end uses, to match the historical patterns presented in Table I4.2. Use of corn for livestock feed from combined farm and market sources provides the most dynamic component of domestic end use. The total increases from 590,000 metric tons in the 1980–1981 base period to 1,047,000 to 1,207,000 metric tons in 1988–1989, a growth rate of 7.4 to 9.4 percent. The low end of this range is nearly identical with the projections shown in Chapter 6 for use of corn for livestock feed at constant prices by the end of the decade. The high end corresponds closely to Chapter 6's projections based on falling corn prices through the decade.

Demand for corn as the raw material in a high-fructose corn sweetener industry could also expand domestic consumption rapidly. According to estimates in Chapter 7, if sugar policy and intent to license fructose sweetener plants remain as in 1985, it would be privately profitable to construct a corn-processing plant with a potential demand for 275,000 metric tons of corn by the end of the 1980s. Such potential demand is not deducted from the export supplies projected in Table I4.3. If this plant were built and fully utilized, *imports* of 40,000 tons of corn would be required under the low projection, whereas exports of 214,000 tons would still be possible under the high projection.

The continued growth in consumption of corn by humans at a relatively rapid rate, both on the farm and from market sources, is driven by the rapid growth in corn production, by continued declines in the real price of corn, and by continued, although slower, growth in the number of people who eat corn. The growth in production that generates these higher levels of end use must be consistent with emerging corn technology and with levels of incentives to corn farmers, which depend to a substantial extent on rural prices communicated to farmers by the marketing system. The prices that are generated in rural markets are determined primarily by the marginal end uses—exports or feed for the domestic livestock industry—if the marketing system is efficient and well-integrated geographically. If it is not, local supply and demand conditions play a far more important role in price formation and, consequently, in the outlook for growth in corn production.

Determining the future balance between domestic production and consumption thus requires a careful assessment of how well the corn marketing system works. To sketch a consistent picture of the future path of the Indonesian corn economy, all three pieces of the story must be assembled: end uses, local markets, and price formation via central or export markets. At one level, assembling the pieces is easy because the domestic price is determined exogenously by the f.o.b. export price. No complicated simultaneous model of domestic price formation is needed. Implicit in this approach, however, is the assumption that price signals from world markets are communicated effectively to farmers and end users. But at both ends of the corn system in Indonesia, decisions are made about production and consumption on the basis of the price signals actually prevailing in local markets at the relevant time. What relationship these local market prices bear to world market prices is an empirical question that must be answered in two steps.

First, the efficiency with which farmers and consumers in Indonesia's corn economy are connected by a domestic marketing system must be determined. For largely subsistence corn farmers, the question does not arise because they "market" their own corn within the household. But Chapter 5 shows that about one-half of Indonesia's corn consumed directly by humans is purchased from rural markets, and Chapter 6 calculates that over 50 percent of corn used for livestock feed comes from marketed supplies. Chapter 8 analyzes this domestic corn marketing system. The analysis is based on both field interviews and econometric models of market integration.

One of the striking findings of Chapter 8 is the close correspondence between the interview and the econometric approaches. In locations where traders spoke of intense competition, rapid communications, and good transportation facilities, the econometric model showed excellent integration of the nearest rural market with the central wholesale market in Jakarta. Similarly, when interviews and observations revealed a lack of competition, thin markets, and poor infrastructure, the model also showed poor price integration. Although the main corn-producing areas in Indonesia seem quite well served by the marketing system, many areas with small or just emerging surpluses of corn do not yet benefit from efficient marketing services. In these locations, the cooperatives serve a useful function in establishing a stable and guaranteed outlet for those corn farmers wishing to enter the commercial market.

The second major issue is how well corn prices in international markets are transmitted into the Indonesian corn economy. Chapter 9 reviews the history and patterns of Indonesia's corn trade and traces its switch from regular exports in the early 1970s, to irregular imports in the latter part of the 1970s, and to renewed exports in 1984. The chapter notes that corn has virtually never been freely traded across Indonesia's borders in either direction, and the various direct and indirect instruments used by the government to control corn trade are explained in some detail. Given the findings that regular export surpluses are possible if government policy is facilitative, Chapter 9 focuses mainly on understanding the ramifications of government policies that are not designed specifically as elements of a corn policy. Foremost among these is the foreign exchange rate, but interest rates and the structure of trade policy in general also contribute significantly to the potential competitiveness of Indonesia's corn surpluses in the world market.

8. Corn Marketing

C. Peter Timmer

Roughly half the corn produced by Indonesian farmers is sold for consumption off the farm. Many of the country's most productive corn farmers in fact consume none of their crop at all and prefer to sell it for cash income. Their families' food consumption needs are met from other home-produced commodities, especially rice, or from market purchases of preferred foodstuffs. Such fully commercial farmers are characteristic of agriculture in developed countries, and they are already a major and growing feature of Indonesia's agriculture as well.

For commercial agriculture to develop, a country needs an efficient marketing system for moving produce from farm gate to consumer. This marketing system must perform several important functions: (1) the *engineering* functions of transformation of the product in time, space, and form through storage, transportation, and processing; (2) the *economic* function of matching costs for these activities with various price margins over time, space, and form; and (3) the *price discovery* function of the market per se, which buyers and sellers can use as an arena for exchange and agree on the price of the commodity in the process. Each of these functions has a dynamic element as well as the more easily measured short-run static dimension. Providing stable expectations about new economic opportunities is the key dynamic function.

Indonesia's corn system seems roughly midway in the evolution from largely subsistence-oriented cultivation toward fully commercial production for the market. The extent of this evolution varies widely from region to region. A major task in the first part of this chapter is to examine the institutional structure of the marketing system and to understand the diversity of corn marketing in terms of both farm and market characteristics.

This chapter analyzes local corn markets at the farm level and identifies several key factors that contribute to fuller commercialization of corn production. Regular, large-scale marketings stimulate more competition among traders and provide better opportunities for farmers to receive a fair price. Similarly, low transportation costs and good market information contribute to efficient markets, but attempts to market yellow corn in areas that traditionally use white corn often generate low returns. From the field observations, price formation seems to be very much a function of scale, transportation costs, market information and communications, and corn color relative to local market demand.

The second part of this chapter examines the efficiency with which corn prices in rural markets are transmitted to other participants in the corn system. These participants are primarily other rural households purchasing for their own consumption, rural purchasers for small-scale livestock feeding, and urban operators of livestock feed mills. The econometric analysis of price margins for corn uses a logarithmic first difference model. The statistical evidence from this model confirms many of the impressions from the field. In particular, the results emphasize the importance of long-distance marketings—from Central and East Java to the Jakarta wholesale market—to price formation in rural markets. It seems likely that regular export marketings will play a similar role.

The picture sketched in Chapter 5 of future patterns for corn consumption suggests that corn-producing households can be expected to behave much more like other rural households that purchase their corn from the market. Accordingly, marketed supplies are likely to grow faster than corn production for the rest of the 1980s. The issue is whether the corn marketing system has the capacity to absorb much more rapid growth in supplies from corn-farming areas than it did in the 1970s.

These issues are addressed by surveying the existing marketing system and conveying some sense of its dynamic path. There is a pervasive feeling among policymakers in Indonesia that any time corn production rises significantly, the marketing system is incapable of absorbing the surplus. Each of the major functions the system must perform—purchasing from farmers, transporting to consumers, and storing until the supplies are needed—requires economic resources for them to be carried out. Such resources are not committed without expectation of profit. If competition, widely accessible information, and ease of entry into marketing activities keep these profits at normal levels, the system is functioning efficiently even if actual marketing costs are high. Just as farmers can be "poor but efficient," marketing systems can be "costly but efficient" in both static and dynamic dimensions. An overview of the corn marketing system should thus primarily be a review of costs of the various marketing functions and of competition among the economic agents who perform them. Appropriate government policy initiatives will then depend on identifying areas in which marketing costs can be effectively reduced by investments in marketing infrastructure, including information systems that provide the basis for investors' expectations, and on determining if added competitive pressures need to be brought to bear on particular market functions or in special geographical circumstances.

The Corn Marketing System

Indonesia's corn marketing system should be pictured in terms of corn flows from farmers to consumers. These flows result from the decisions of market participants—farmers, traders, processors, and consumers—acting in their own self-interest. The flows must thus be matched with economic costs and returns for the various marketing functions. Corn processing for human consumption has not been a major topic of research for this study as it remains a fairly simple process, but both storage and transportation of corn are critical functions integrating the corn system. How costly they are and how efficiently they are performed are important factors that determine the success of future efforts to increase corn production. Previous intensification programs for corn in Indonesia are thought to have foundered partly because of the marketing system's lack of capacity to handle sizable increases in marketed volumes of corn at remunerative prices to farmers. Consequently, it is necessary to understand the system's current capacity and cost structure and the potential of government policies and investments to stabilize or even reduce these costs in anticipation of higher volumes of corn to be moved from farm to feed mills and export facilities in the late 1980s.

Diverse Patterns of Corn Marketing

Any description of corn marketing flows is bedeviled by the same diversity of patterns seen in the corn farming systems—diversity that has both geographic and temporal dimensions. Part of the diversity is indeed caused by the variation in corn farming systems. The commercial corn farmers in Kediri and Malang in East Java use quite different marketing channels than those of the isolated corn farmers in Bulukumba in South Sulawesi or the much more subsistence-oriented farmers in Nusa Tenggara Timur. A persistent lesson from each of the field surveys was that *scale* of marketings was an important determinant in efficiency and competitiveness of the local marketing system. Farmers tend to find thin and irregular markets when quantities of less than a truckload are bulked in relatively small areas.

While thin markets present start-up problems for farmers just moving into substantial commercial marketings, the system does seem to locate trading opportunities fairly quickly. Most traders deal in multiple commodities and are always on the lookout for a profitable new trading activity. Those corn-growing regions where commercial sales are currently small and the marketing system fairly thin can thus expect reasonably competitive private marketing activities to develop as greater volumes of corn become available to the market if transportation costs are not prohibitive. Consequently, for policy purposes the important marketing issues are focused on East Java, South Sulawesi, North Sulawesi, and North Sumatra, where the bulk of Indonesia's corn for long-distance marketing is currently produced.

Because of the diversity with which marketing functions are performed in different corn systems in Indonesia, this chapter provides a synthesis of these functions noting important regional variations, by tracing the flow of corn from the farm household to local and provincial markets. From nearly all the regions, several general issues emerge, including high losses during storage, the importance of the demand for livestock feed in integrating regional markets, and the difficulty of integrating the markets for white and yellow corn. Some of the region-specific details on the local marketing systems are cited to illustrate diversity observed in the field. Because East Java so clearly leads in market volume for corn, it is used as the comparative reference. Marketing in the other important corn-producing regions—Central Java, Sumatra, South Sulawesi, and Nusa Tenggara Timur—is judged relative to the East Java model.

Figure 8.1 shows an overview of the corn marketing system in East Java. Although probably less than one-quarter of total corn produced in East Java ends up in either the Surabaya or Jakarta feed mills, interviews

FIGURE 8.1. *Corn marketing channels in East Java*

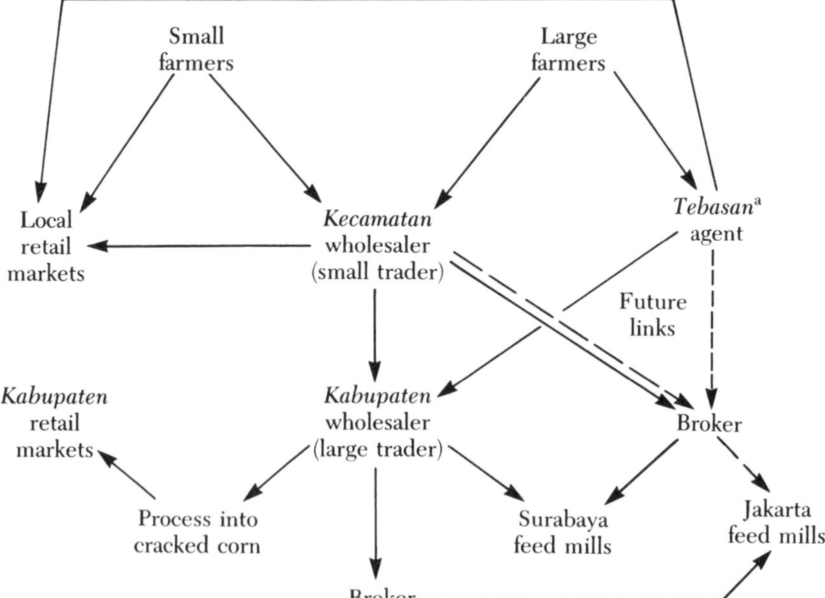

SOURCE: Interview data obtained by Paul Dorosh, Richard Monteverde, and Peter Timmer.

[a]*Tebasan* is the purchase of a standing crop by an agent who assumes responsibility for harvesting and marketing.

with traders at all levels depicted in Figure 8.1 indicate that demand from these mills is the key to price formation. Especially when feed mills in Jakarta have access to imported corn through BULOG at internationally competitive prices, their price demands of traders operating in East Java force local prices to competitive levels.

Marketing Participants and the Competitiveness of Farm Sales

As a general pattern, farm marketing of corn in Indonesia is characterized by significant competition on both sides of the transactions—many buyers and sellers. Exceptions exist, of course. In South Sulawesi, for example, Mink reported the following:

> Although there are several different channels of first sale by farmers, in any one village the options could be quite limited. Options also tend to decrease further away from the major Ujung Pandang market. In nearby Jeneponto, many traders pass through, and KUDs [cooperatives] buy corn as well. But in eastern Bulukumba, the farmers must sell to a single trader at the *kecamatan* level or use public transport to carry small quantities directly to the capital city's markets. Farmers sometimes strengthen their bargaining position by bulking their corn up to truckload lots collectively, which makes it easier to find buyers apart from the local-based trader. But this option is constrained in more remote areas by poor price information and by the need for a strong village head to coordinate the activity. (Mink 1984b, p. 38)

In Central Java, corn is often marketed in very small volumes on an almost daily basis, with some farm households carrying the day's sales to the local markets on foot or by public transportation. In Grobogan *kabupaten*, the site of Mink's field surveys in Central Java, corn is grown primarily for household consumption, although sales are the second most important source of cash income, after rice (Mink 1984a). Mink's description of the marketing process in Grobogan illustrated how different it is from South Sulawesi or East Java:

> Corn is sold as shelled grain, generally in small quantities. No corn is sold *tebasan* (as a standing crop to a middleman), nor does any move directly from the field into marketing channels. All enters the farmer's house first, stored in the rafters as ear corn with husks. From there, amounts to be sold for cash needs are husked and shelled. As a consequence of the storage method and small sales quantities, there is little farmer interest in mechanical shelling, and no shelling machines are found locally. Instead, husked ears are simply placed in a burlap bag and beaten with a stick to loosen the grains, a process that farmers claim is very quick.
>
> Corn reaching the market is generally of low quality due to inadequate drying and slow movement to market. Only a few farmers sun dry their corn before hanging it in the rafters. The drying period is limited to one or two days for the rainy-season crop, and the dry-season harvest is not dried at all. Since the husk is not yet removed, moisture reduction is minimal. Further, although farmers consider that further drying occurs in storage, where rafters are above the heat of

kitchen fires, harvests usually exceed kitchen space, and corn is often stored elsewhere in the home.

Marketed corn moves off the farm very slowly. Very few farmers are able to move harvested corn to market in fewer than five days. Furthermore [as Table 8.1 shows], almost 40 percent of marketed corn spends a month or more in the rafters first. This, combined with high moisture content, implies that corn moving to market is held for significant periods under conditions favorable for aflatoxin development and insect infestation. Tests of farmer stores following the dry season harvest gave minimum moisture content levels of 17 percent, indicating that this is indeed a major problem facing efforts to increase corn quality in this area.

Farmers' incentives to improve quality are minimal. They rarely store corn for more than four months, either for own consumption or for sale, and they do not perceive losses within this time as a major problem. Furthermore, although moisture content at higher bulking levels becomes a basis for price differentials, the first buyer of farmers' corn rarely offers a better price for drier corn. Farmers recognize that dry-season corn sells for a higher price than wet-season corn, partly because of lower moisture content; but at any given moment the market available to the farmer signals almost no quality premium for lower-moisture corn. Further, at the moment when wet-season corn ought to be dried, most farmers are busy planting the major rice crop and are less available to keep an eye on the drying corn and threatening rain clouds.

Road development and increasing numbers of small, four-wheeled, motorized vehicles in rural areas are changing the organization of primary marketing channels. Where *kecamatan*-level grain middlemen could previously be assured of grain delivery by farmers to their bulking locations, now farmers frequently have the option of selling their grain directly to small-scale dealers who travel to the village with small vehicles. These dealers often come from urban centers and do not have any fixed location or bulking station in the producing area. They are highly mobile, competitive, and sensitive to daily changes in urban-rural price spreads. As they in turn often sell directly to urban wholesalers, their bypassing of

TABLE 8.1. *Farm storage-to-sales flows, Grobogan sample averages, 1982–1983*

Month	Share of annual sales (percent)	Producer[a] price (rupiahs)	Price[b] index
August[c]	28.4	135	107.6
September	10.1	140	107.4
October	3.9	150	105.8
November	2.0	150	107.3
December	1.1	150	106.1
January[c]	29.5	150	89.9
February	13.4	125	87.9
March	7.5	100	90.4
April	3.9	100	92.1
May	0.2	100	95.9
June	0.0	110	101.8
July	0.0	135	107.6

SOURCE: Mink (1984a), p. 33.

[a]Actual producer price, Grobogan *kabupaten*, 1982–1983.

[b]Producer price index, constructed as a three-month moving average, from 1970 to 1983, Grobogan *kabupaten* producer prices.

[c]Harvest month.

kecamatan and *kabupaten* middlemen shortens the marketing chain. This may increase the speed with which corn is bulked and moved out of rural areas. If this trend continues, the type of drying and storage technology that would be relevant for introduction would shift from the village farther along the bulking chain. It also implies that local monopsonies by corn buyers, if they exist now, are facing higher levels of competition from buyers from outside the local areas. (Mink 1984a, pp. 22–23, 28)

Where large quantities are marketed immediately during and after the harvest, as in East Java, small traders in mini-trucks (Colts) call regularly on farmers in search of supplies. Some of these traders operate on their own account and will resell to *kabupaten* wholesalers or even directly to feed mills in Surabaya. Others operate as agents for *kecamatan* or *kabupaten* wholesalers and are financed by them.

In the Kediri area, farmers usually harvest and husk the corn with hired labor and transport it to the household for several days of sun drying. The ears are then shelled, usually by placing them in a bag and pounding with a stick or sometimes by using a simple shelling tool made up of a nail protruding from a board. Dorosh noted that in the Kediri corn system, the shelled grain may be dried further before it is sold or placed in farm storage for family consumption.

Farmers who shell their own corn typically wait for a local collector to come to the house to offer to buy it. No prior agreement is made with any particular merchants, and merchants looking for corn discover which farmers have corn for sale by word of mouth. A few farmers take their own corn to Pare, a marketing center, using public transportation. Little of the husked corn sold in Kepung is dried and shelled in the village itself. Instead, local collectors often purchase corn using credit obtained from merchants in Pare and rent use of the drying floors at warehouses there.

On-farm storage usually is limited to corn consumed within the household. Many farmers sell the majority of their corn at harvest time for several reasons. First, corn prices at harvest time for the second season *tegal* and the *sawah* corn crops are not lower than at other times of the year, so there is no anticipated profit from storing corn and selling it later. For example, retail prices of corn in Pare fluctuated between Rp 100 and 110 per kilogram in the first five months of 1982. They varied between Rp 150 and 170 per kilogram from June to February of the following year, and then dropped again to Rp 120 per kilogram at the time of the 1982–83 *tegal* harvest. Second, corn from the first *tegal* and second *sawah* crops often is sold to meet immediate cash needs for the following onion and pepper crops on *tegal* or the rice crop on *sawah*. Third, some farmers do not have drying space or sufficient family labor available to dry and shell the corn. However, the farmer who shells corn himself has the advantage of using cobs as fuel for household cooking. (Dorosh 1984b, pp. 26–27)

In summary, where substantial volumes of corn are already being marketed, farmer access to the marketing system seems quite good. This characterizes most of East Java, the parts of South Sulawesi close to Ujung

Pandang and Pare-Pare, and probably some areas in Central Java. On the other hand, where harvest supplies are not immediately marketed or where only small surpluses are available for sale, transaction costs seem significantly higher. This is especially true if the color of corn being marketed—white as opposed to yellow—does not correspond to local tastes, which is the case in Central Java and South Sulawesi. Local markets historically have developed to sell white corn to local residents who do not produce their own supplies. In the absence of effective demand for yellow corn from a local livestock or feed industry or from traders intending to transport the yellow corn to such markets in other regions, little market demand for yellow corn exists. The pioneering farmer who tries new corn technology may achieve higher yields but face disastrous prices at harvest. The environment in Central Java raises a complex set of problems with respect to income distribution and the potential of corn farmers to participate in the higher productivity of new corn technologies (see Mink 1984a). In South Sulawesi's less constrained farming system, expansion of yellow corn production could occur rapidly if ready markets for the output were available (see Mink 1984b).

Drying and Storage

Many corn farmers in the two East Java *kabupaten* surveyed, Malang and Kediri, sold all the corn at or even before the harvest. Some drying on the ear after husking is performed at the farm household, depending on space and household labor available, but most drying seems to be carried out on traders' drying floors. Mechanical dryers are seldom used although a variety of different types are available in the province. A few cooperatives have Lister dryers provided under aid financing, but none seems to be in operation. Private traders have often rigged makeshift dryers when sufficient corn supplies were available at prices competitive for export markets. Local corn markets for household consumption have lenient moisture standards, which are possible to meet through sun drying—deliveries between 15 and 17 percent moisture usually are not discounted. Feed mills without drying capacity often reject corn with more than 17 percent moisture, and others discount corn above 15 percent moisture during the dry season. BULOG tends to enforce its 14 percent standard when buying to support the floor price, and export buyers also insist on 14 percent moisture. Most traders agree that this standard cannot be met reliably through sun drying even in the dry season, and it is difficult to reach 17 percent moisture reliably through sun drying in the rainy season.

Mechanical drying seems to cost roughly twice as much per kilogram as sun drying—perhaps Rp 2 to Rp 4 per kilogram rather than Rp 1 to Rp 2 per kilogram on Java, although costs seem to be higher on the outer islands. There is also the problem of mechanical skills and spare parts needed to keep mechanical dryers operating. Visitors to cooperative (KUD) operations where Lister dryers are installed, for example, find that they are not operating for one or more of three reasons: lack of trained personnel to operate the fairly complicated machines, lack of spare parts and expertise in repairs, and the high cost of operations relative to sun drying.

Dryers installed by private traders seem to operate primarily under the pressure of peak harvest volume when drying floors are full and when the corn is ultimately destined for export or longer-term storage, where low moisture content is essential. A 10-ton batch dryer operated by P. T. Sumber Tani in Dampit, 45 kilometers south of Malang, for example, dried corn to 14 percent moisture for the export market via Surabaya, as well as for those feed mills that insisted on the same moisture standard (presumably because they intended to store the grain for several months and did not have sufficient drying capacity of their own).[1]

The moisture level at which corn moves into storage and the length of time it is stored without large losses are obviously related. Although traders in several provinces report successful storage of corn for six months or even a year, this practice requires very careful attention to initial moisture conditions and regular fumigation for pest management. Few feed mills store corn for more than a month; traders seldom keep the commodity even that long. Given that roughly 60 percent of Indonesia's annual corn harvest occurs in just four months, December through March, how and where is the corn stored?

Part of the answer can be seen in the striking evidence shown in Figure 8.2. By matching SUSENAS data for seasonal consumption of corn in East Java with data for seasonal harvest patterns for the province reported by the Department of Agriculture (with consumption lagged one month after production), it is possible to compare the two seasonal patterns. The match is very close: much of the corn is consumed within a month of when it was produced; there is no need for subsequent storage. Seasonal fluctuations in corn consumption by humans can be offset by compensating intake of other commodities whose seasonal availabilities are more stable or may even match, in mirror image, those of corn.

Such seasonal fluctuations are not desirable for the livestock feed industry, however, which requires much more regular supplies of its major energy source than is implied by Figure 8.2. Chapter 2 emphasizes that

[1]The Dampit operation bought corn directly from farmers at 20 to 30 percent moisture and dried it in one hour to 14 percent, at a cost of about Rp 4 per kilogram, not including handling costs or depreciation. The dryer, purchased for cash for Rp 20 million, was manufactured by American Drying Systems, Inc., of Miami, Florida. It is also used for drying rough rice *(gabah)* during the rice harvest.

FIGURE 8.2. *Corn produced and consumed in East Java over time, 1978*

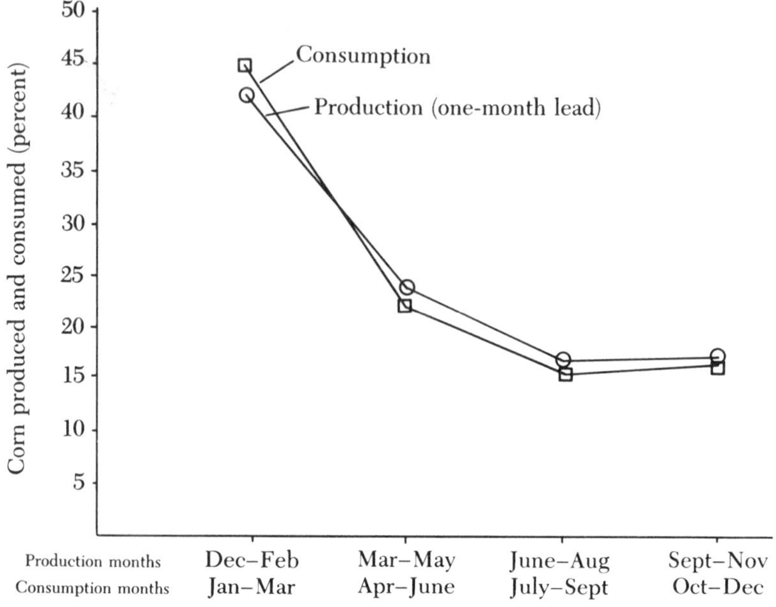

SOURCE: Data from the Department of Agriculture and from Indonesia, Central Bureau of Statistics, National Socio-Economic Survey (SUSENAS), for 1978, assembled by Monteverde (1987).

corn is harvested somewhere in Indonesia every month. The inverse of the seasonal peak of 60 percent of the harvest in four months is that 40 percent of supplies are fairly smoothly stretched out over the other eight months. Roughly 5 percent of annual production, or about 180,000 metric tons, is thus harvested each month *at a minimum.* At current levels of corn utilization, the feed industry needs only about 25,000 tons per month from the market. Corn storage is thus not yet a critical issue for the feed industry if significant quantities of this "off-season" corn are marketed and so long as transportation facilities from the major corn-surplus regions are efficient and low cost.

This situation could change quickly, of course. The feed industry is expected to grow rapidly through the mid-1990s and is likely to compete more intensively with other end users for its regular monthly supplies from the domestic market. Furthermore, new technology for corn production may well add to the seasonal peak in harvest supplies, and better drying and storage facilities are thus required if ruinous prices to farmers are not to result. These issues are treated more fully at the end of this chapter.

Transportation and Regional Market Integration

Especially in East Java, where substantial corn surpluses are routinely moved out of rural areas to local markets and to feed mills in Surabaya and Jakarta, the transportation and communications network seems remarkably efficient. Interviews with wholesalers at the *kabupaten* level revealed that nearly all conducted their business by telephone, both "up" to feed mills in Surabaya and Jakarta and "down" to small traders at the *kecamatan* level. Some operated their own fleets of trucks; others used a very competitive rental market. There was widespread agreement on transportation costs between various locations, and when petrol prices went up during the interviewing period (January 1984), new marginal costs were factored in immediately in the new transportation rates after the price increase. Such behavior is indicative of a transportation system that is competitive and operating near the bottom of its average cost curve.

With efficient transportation and communications, price information between different markets should be conveyed very quickly, with actual shipment taking place whenever profitable. Mink made the following observations about conditions in South Sulawesi:

Since 1978, parallel marketing channels have competed in South Sulawesi. One consists primarily of private participants, while the recent addition has been DOLOG purchases, mostly from KUDs [cooperatives].[2] In both cases, the marketing chain is short, frequently with only one intermediary between the producer and the port collectors who are engaged in inter-island trade or export.

The private channel begins with farmers selling to a locally based, large collector, capable of arranging transactions by the truckload. In the more remote areas of the corn crescent, there are three or four large collectors in each *kabupaten*, while closer to Ujung Pandang and Pare-Pare, competition between collectors is more intense. For example, one collector in eastern Bulukumba had few competitors and handled over 1,300 tons per year, while the typical collector in Jeneponto or Soppeng was one of a dozen in the area and handled approximately 100 tons per year.

Collectors do not deal solely in corn. Seasonality of harvests and similar marketing requirements for most *palawija* crops allow collectors to shift among these crops according to which offers the best profit margin.

Price movements are followed on a daily basis by private market participants down to the large collector level. The current Ujung Pandang or Pare-Pare price is known in rural areas through phone contacts or returning truckers who relay the information to potential customers. Large collectors generally know of price changes in the port city within a day. Price movements are especially important since there is almost no forward contracting. Most contracts are made and filled within days.

Traders in the port cities are equally careful in following trade prices in Surabaya and in world markets when South Sulawesi corn is competitive. One trader

[2]A DOLOG is a regional office of the national food logistics agency, BULOG.

active in exports routinely received price information by telex, while inter-island traders rely on phone contacts.

As a result of close price monitoring, South Sulawesi corn prices quickly reflect external prices all the way down the marketing chain. For the DOLOG marketing channel participants, market prices are relevant only if they are above the floor price, which has not been the case in recent years. Corn price variation still occurs in this channel, but it depends largely on quality. DOLOG's floor price applies to corn meeting the standard 14 percent moisture content and 3 percent damaged kernels. Cooperatives will accept lower quality corn if they can process it up to the DOLOG requirements, and a standard price conversion table is used by cooperatives for this corn. For example, at 18 percent moisture and 6 percent damaged kernels, farmers receive about 93 percent of the corn support price. As DOLOG has only been buying corn in substantial volumes since 1983, farmers are still becoming familiar with this pricing system. (Mink 1984b, pp. 51–52, 53–54)

Perry found similar efficiency of regional market integration in Sumatra (Perry, Ali, and Daniel 1984; Perry 1984a). Farmers in West Sumatra produce corn specifically for the Medan market, whereas farmers in Lampung produce for a local poultry market and the feed mills in Jakarta. In his sample, 85 percent of corn production was marketed.

The obvious failures of regional integration occur in special circumstances: where corn marketings are very small and do not justify the attention of more than one or two traders; where the color of corn marketed does not correspond to local demand; and where the producing areas are far removed from consuming areas *and* where high transportation costs exist between the two. Small volumes of marketings are a significant and continuing problem in Nusa Tenggara Timur, in parts of Central Java and South Sulawesi, and probably in the low-yield areas of East Java, such as on Madura. The color problem is primarily an issue in South Sulawesi and Central Java. The long distances in combination with high transportation charges are an important problem for Nusa Tenggara Timur, South Sulawesi, North Sulawesi, and some parts of Sumatra.

The combination of distance *and* costs is stressed because distance alone does not impede corn marketing. American corn produced in South Dakota moves by truck, rail, or river barge to New Orleans and then by ocean freighter to Japan or Malaysia, in direct competition with corn exports from nearby Thailand or even Indonesia. Similarly, corn produced in Malang can be trucked directly to Jakarta for about Rp 20 per kilogram, a road distance of about 800 kilometers. By contrast, it is about twice as far from Bulukumba via Ujung Pandang in South Sulawesi to the Jakarta market. Total marketing costs, however, would be closer to Rp 50 to Rp 60 per kilogram even though most of the distance would be by ocean freighter, normally much cheaper than truck transportation for long hauls. On the other hand, loading Bulukumba corn over the beach onto

Buginese proas for shipment to Kalimantan, Nusa Tenggara Timur, and Nusa Tenggara Barat can probably be accomplished for only Rp 15 to Rp 25 per kilogram.

The ultimate test of short-run regional corn market integration is how well price movements in connected markets track each other. To interpret the models designed to carry out this test, however, it is necessary to have some sense of the system itself. This is especially true if the results indicate wide variation in market integration. Specific reasons must then be sought. It is preferable to be aware of the potential problems and reasons before looking at the model, rather than raising them in ad hoc fashion later to explain awkward results.

The Efficiency of Price Formation

Traders earn their livelihood by purchasing a commodity when and where its price is low and selling it, they hope, when and where its price is high. In the process they tend to raise the low price and lower the high price and thus contribute to the welfare of both farmers and consumers. The extent to which traders improve the economic welfare of others while earning a living for themselves is an empirical question. This chapter has so far addressed this question descriptively; the operation of the market was observed directly for any insights that could be had on how well traders were performing their tasks.

The task at hand is to address the question of market performance indirectly. If traders actually compete with one another for supplies from farmers and similarly compete to sell the commodity in a different time, place, and form to consumers, farm prices should bear a functional relationship to consumer prices. When changes in supply or demand conditions are transmitted rapidly and competitively to other participants in the marketing chain, prices at each level are connected by the economic costs of transforming the commodity at each stage. Since price data at various levels of the marketing chain are frequently available, it is possible to test the extent to which markets are connected by analyzing statistically the price margins between levels.

Statistical analysis of price margins requires a carefully specified model of how the individual market prices are likely to be connected. Historically, simple correlation coefficients have been used to test market integration, but this approach has been shown to have serious flaws (Harriss 1979; Timmer 1974a, 1974b). A more robust model that incorporates generalized distributed lags has been used by Ravallion (1986), and this approach serves as the starting point for the model developed here.

A Statistical Model of Price Integration

The Jakarta market for corn to supply the expanding feed mill industry was repeatedly cited by traders as the focal point for price formation throughout Java and on several of the outer islands as well. Although local consumption requirements are met from local production first, surpluses that can be moved to the Jakarta market serve as the marginal supply and hence the ultimate determinant of price. This role of the Jakarta corn market is central to the statistical model tested here and is analogous to the role of the export market for cassava price formation (Unnevehr 1984a, 1984b).

The price in the corn market in Jakarta serves as the focal price to which prices in local markets adjust if the two markets are connected by traders. The price integration model tests two aspects of this potential market integration: the extent to which prices in the local market are *integrated* into the Jakarta market over the long run; and the extent to which short-run changes in the local market are caused by similar short-run changes in the margin between the local and the Jakarta market. The latter indicates short-run market *connection*. It is entirely possible for general economic and market forces to integrate the two markets in the long run (and hence account for a high correlation coefficient), even though traders fail to connect the two markets through commodity flows in the short run.

The model developed here explains the change from month to month in the (logarithm of the) price of corn in a rural market, which is as close to a producer price as available statistics permit. This monthly change, or first difference, is specified as a function of the same monthly change in the urban, or Jakarta, price. This specification assumes that traders know about price conditions in the central market quickly enough for local prices to be influenced in the same month by that information. The widespread use of telephones and overnight truck shipments from East Java to Jakarta certainly support this assumption for local markets on Java, and it probably is realistic for the Medan and Ujung Pandang markets as well.[3]

In addition, local price changes could be influenced by the change in the spatial margin in the previous month between the central and local markets. If the margin widened and transaction costs remained the same, traders would have an incentive to move more corn from the local market to the central market and thus push up local prices and push down the central prices. The coefficient attached to the change in the temporal

[3]Using a two-month lag model similar to the one-month model developed here, Mink (1986) has confirmed this assumption for Java, but he finds it does not hold for the connection between rural markets in South Sulawesi and the Jakarta wholesale markets.

margin in the central market is the key to judging long-run market integration, whereas the coefficient attached to changes in this spatial margin is a major factor measuring the strength of market connections.

Several other factors might also contribute to local changes in prices. Seasonal movements in local supplies, such that insufficient volumes are available to be shipped to the central market, could easily sever the normal long-run market relationship. Similarly, marketing costs themselves could change, as labor, trucks, or warehouse space are bid for by alternative users. These changes may be specific to a locality or occur seasonally. Lastly, the *level* of prices in the central market may influence the changes in prices in the local market. This effect is most likely to occur if the economic environment is strongly inflationary or if interest charges are a large component of marketing costs. Since the model tested here is for month-to-month changes, the latter factor is not likely to be important, but the inflation factor may well be. This effect might alternatively be tested by adding time trends (multiplicatively) to the temporal and spatial margin variables.

In its simplest specification, the statistical model explains the first difference in logarithms of monthly prices of corn in local markets as a function of four independent variables:

$$P_t - P_{t-1} = d_0 + d_1 * (P_{t-1} - R_{t-1}) + d_2 * (R_t - R_{t-1}) + d_3 * R_{t-1} + d_4 * X + e_t, \tag{1}$$

where

P_t= the logarithm of the rural or farm price for corn, for month t,
R_t= the logarithm of the central or urban market price for corn, for month t,
X= a matrix of exogenous seasonal, regional, or other special variables that might influence local price formation independently of central prices,
d_i= estimated parameters, and
e_t= random error term.

After estimation, Equation (1) can be rearranged in such a way that interpretation of the parameters is clearer:

$$P_t = d_0 + (1 + d_1) * P_{t-1} + d_2 * (R_t - R_{t-1}) + (d_3 - d_1) * R_{t-1} + d_4 * X. \tag{2}$$

In this form it is more apparent that the coefficient d_2 measures the extent to which changes in prices in the central market *R* are transmitted to local market prices *P*. If $d_2 = 1$, transmittal is neutral in proportional terms. If marketing costs are calculated in absolute rather than percentage terms, of course, d_2 need not be 1, even if information on price changes in the central market is being fully transmitted to local markets.

The other coefficients in Equation (2) can best be interpreted when the term $R_t - R_{t-1} = 0$, that is, when the central market is in equilibrium from month to month. The impact of d_2 then drops out. If the special impact of *X* is also held in abeyance, the remaining two variables are local price and central price, both lagged one month. The coefficients attached to each of these two price terms, $(1 + d_1)$ and $(d_3 - d_1)$, respectively, reflect the relative contributions of local and central price history to the formation of the current level of the local price. Markets where previous central prices are the primary determinants of local prices, rather than previous local prices, are well connected in the sense that supply and demand conditions in the central market are communicated effectively to local markets and influence prices there, whatever the previous local conditions and history of local prices.

This information can be used to compare the degree to which different local markets are connected to the Jakarta market. Equation (3) introduces an Index of Market Connection (IMC) that is the ratio of the local market coefficient to the central market coefficient:

$$IMC = \frac{1 + d_1}{d_3 - d_1} \tag{3}$$

Values of the Index of Market Connection that are small, for example, IMC < 1, indicate a high degree of market integration. In the extreme case when local conditions have no influence on local prices, $d_1 = -1$ and IMC = 0. When local conditions are a major factor in local price formation, which indicates a lack of connection to the central market, d_1 is smaller in absolute size, and IMC will be significantly greater than 1.

A large value of IMC can occur even when $d_2 = 1$, that is, when price changes in the central market are, on average, transmitted to the local market, which indicates full long-run price integration. The difference between d_2 and IMC reflects the difference between long-run and short-run price integration. The former can be caused by broader economic forces that influence both the local and the central commodity markets. Short-run price integration has been termed market connection here and reflects how successful the activities of traders are in linking markets that are geographically separated through information and commodity flows. The Index of Market Connection is designed to measure how well this linkage is established. It should be noted that if $d_3 = 0$, as expected when short time periods are examined, then IMC reduces to the simple ratio of

$(1 + d_1)/ -d_1$. Since the econometric model is specified in such a way that $0 > d_1 > -1$ under normal conditions, this ratio is normally positive.

Both short-run and long-run aspects of corn market integration are of interest in this study. The data to be analyzed here are all for rural corn markets on Java; their integration into the wholesale market in Jakarta is to be tested. Given how tightly knit the rural economy of Java is, with its good road and communications network and regular flow of commodities, workers, and money to and from the countryside, it will be surprising if *long-run* price integration is not quite good. Both Mink (1984a) and Dorosh (1984a, 1984b) noted conditions in Central and East Java, however, where short-run price integration may not be complete. It is now possible to address empirically the degree to which this may be a problem.

Data and Analysis

The statistical model developed in Equation (1) requires price data from local and central markets for intervals short enough that both price integration in the long run and market connection in the short run can be tested. Monthly data are used here; weekly or even daily data might also be appropriate for markets that are very closely connected. Averages over periods longer than a month will almost certainly hide important intraperiod variations that would provide evidence on how well the short-run market connection is established.

The local price data used to test market integration are taken from rural markets at the *kecamatan* level, six in East Java and three in Central Java. (The time series for rural corn prices in South Sulawesi were not long enough to test price integration with this model.) As Figure 8.3 illustrates, the nine local markets are well distributed throughout important corn-growing areas of these two provinces. The names of both the *kabupaten* and the specific *kecamatan* are identified in the figure. Statistics from SUSENAS and the Department of Agriculture can be paired for these nine *kabupaten* with data for corn production and consumption shown in Table 8.2. This table also includes the numerical code used by the Central Bureau of Statistics for each *kabupaten* and a simple code used in this chapter for quick reference to each location. Sumenep *kabupaten*, on Madura in East Java, is thus denoted EJ1, and Saronggi is the *kecamatan* from which price statistics were taken. Several *kabupaten* names will already be familiar. Malang (EJ2) and Kediri (EJ6) were the sites for Dorosh's field studies in East Java, and Grobogan (CJ2) served as the location for Mink's study in Central Java.

These disaggregated data shown in the table provide a useful glimpse of the nature of the corn economy immediately surrounding the market sites chosen for analysis. All the markets are located in *kabupaten* where corn is an important field crop; area planted with corn ranges from nearly 70

FIGURE 8.3. *Locations of rural market sites on Java and Madura for price integration analysis*

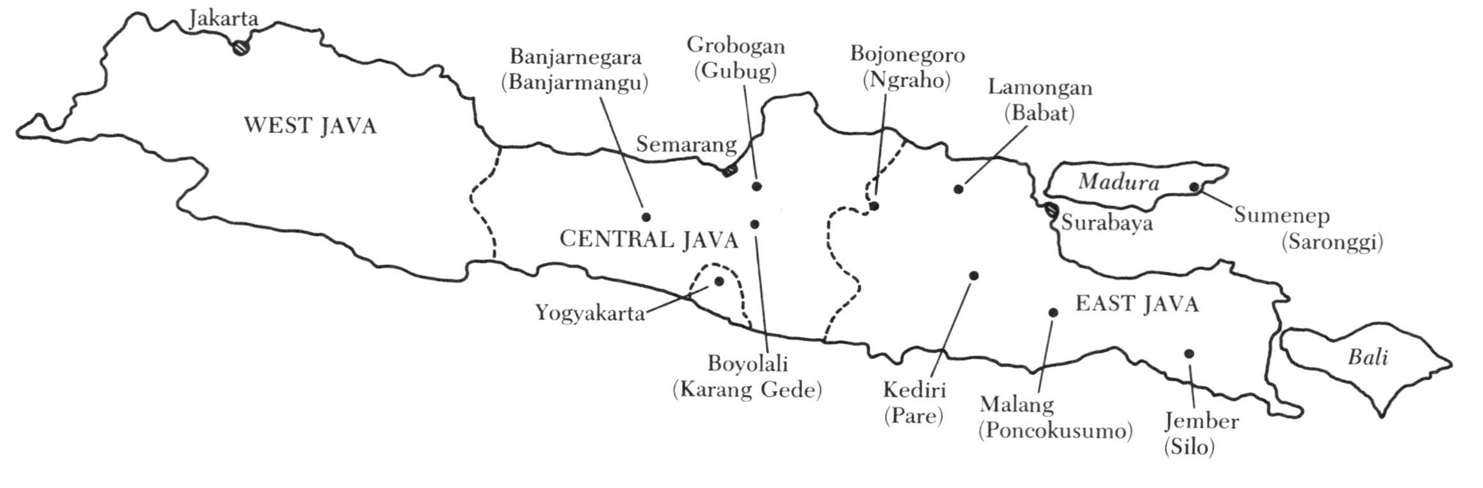

TABLE 8.2. *Characteristics of* kabupaten *used for price integration analysis of rural corn markets, late 1970s*

Province *kabupaten* *kecamatan*	Code[a]	Share of total food crop planted with corn (percent)	Average corn consumption per household per week (kilograms)	Average corn price[b] 1973–1982 (rupiahs per kilogram)
East Java	3500	29.1	2.50	74.6 (27.0)
Sumenep	EJ1	68.1	6.43	79.2
Saronggi	3529			(36.5)
Malang	EJ2	42.9	4.81	76.3
Poncokusumo	3507			(30.7)
Lamongan	EJ3	36.9	2.95	76.5
Babat	3524			(36.3)
Bojonegoro	EJ4	26.7	3.53	72.1
Ngraho	3522			(31.3)
Jember	EJ5	14.0	3.81	68.2
Silo	3509			(29.3)
Kediri	EJ6	25.9	2.18	75.5
Pare	3506			(34.8)
Central Java	3300	19.7	2.09	75.3 (30.7)
Boyolali	CJ1	31.3	5.15	84.2
Karang Gede	3309			(32.1)
Grobogan	CJ2	38.0	5.27	80.4
Gubug	3315			(32.8)
Banjarnegara	CJ3	48.7	9.12	82.3
Banjarmangu	3304			(32.5)

SOURCES: Indonesia, Central Bureau of Statistics, National Socio-Economic Survey (SUSENAS) for 1978, and Department of Agriculture.

NOTE: The average price of corn in the Jakarta wholesale market for the 1973–1982 period was 97.6 rupiahs per kilogram, with a standard deviation of 40.5.

[a]The four-digit code is used by the Central Bureau of Statistics to identify provinces and *kabupaten* in its national surveys.

[b]Standard deviation is given in parentheses.

percent in Sumenep to 14 percent in Jember. Corn is important for consumption as well. Only Kediri is below the average in East Java, which has the highest level of provincial corn consumption on Java. (Nusa Tenggara Timur has the highest level of consumption per capita in all of Indonesia.)

Monthly price observations were available from January 1973 to December 1982 for all locations used in the analysis. The average prices for this period are also shown in Table 8.2 (standard deviations are in parentheses). One pattern is immediately apparent: roughly, average prices tend to decline the farther the market is from Jakarta. The average wholesale price in Jakarta was Rp 97.6 per kilogram during the ten-year period. In Banjarnegara (CJ3) in Central Java, the average price was Rp 82.3 per kilogram, and in Jember (EJ5), at the eastern end of East Java, it was only Rp 68.2 per kilogram. Such a pattern suggests that the Jakarta market is indeed the focal point of price formation; the statistical model is designed to test this hypothesis.

As noted earlier, the simplest approach is to examine simple correlation coefficients for prices in various markets. These are shown in Table 8.3, for the period from 1973 to 1982. It is difficult to determine what these correlations mean. The correlation coefficient of 0.973 certainly seems to suggest that the market in Kediri (EJ6) is well connected to the Jakarta market. In inverse fashion, Boyolali (CJ1) seems poorly connected—its coefficient is only 0.555. All the other markets, however, have correlations with the Jakarta market of between 0.885 and 0.929, a narrow range that suggests equally "good" market connection. But there is neither a real sense of how good the connection is nor a way to identify the nature of any poor market connection. The more carefully specified model in Equation (1) is required for a more sensitive indicator of market connection.

In the Appendix to this chapter, Table A8.1 shows the statistical results from estimating Equation (1) for prices in each of the nine local markets as a function of price changes in the Jakarta market, margin changes from the local to central markets, and the level of Jakarta prices. The full set of seasonal dummy variables only occasionally contributed in a significant way to the overall explanatory power of the regressions, and even then the other coefficients were little changed. Consequently, no runs with seasonal dummy variables are reported. Similarly, no runs with time as an exogenous variable are reported. No consistent pattern emerged when it was included either independently or multiplicatively, and, again, the other coefficients were little changed.

Short-run market connection. Table 8.4 reports the important results of the test of short-run market connection. For each of the nine local markets, two parameters are shown for the 1973–1982 period of analysis: the d_2 coefficient, which is interpreted as an indicator of long-run market integration (perhaps through common but external economic forces); and the Index of Market Connection. This index, derived from Equation (2), is the ratio of the coefficient attached to lagged local price to the coefficient attached to lagged central price, when central prices are in equilibrium from month to month. It provides a much more sensitive indicator of the influence of the central price on local price formation in the short run than does a simple correlation coefficient between the two markets. The right-hand column of the table shows the values of the index on the basis of the 1973–1982 data.

Not surprisingly, the Kediri (EJ6) market has the best market connection in the short run, with an IMC value of only 0.54. This market also had the highest simple correlation with the Jakarta wholesale market. The Boyolali (CJ1) market has the worst connection in the short run with the

TABLE 8.3. *Price averages and simple correlation coefficients for corn markets on Java, 1973–1982*

Location of price observation		Average price (rupiahs per kilogram)	Simple correlation coefficients									
			JKT	EJ1	EJ2	EJ3	EJ4	EJ5	EJ6	CJ1	CJ2	CJ3
Jakarta (wholesale)		97.6	1.000									
East Java (rural markets)												
Sumenep	EJ1	79.2	0.885	1.000								
Malang	EJ2	76.3	0.925	0.854	1.000							
Lamongan	EJ3	76.5	0.929	0.913	0.878	1.000						
Bojonegoro	EJ4	72.1	0.892	0.880	0.880	0.896	1.000					
Jember	EJ5	68.2	0.898	0.795	0.813	0.836	0.755	1.000				
Kediri	EJ6	75.5	0.973	0.860	0.920	0.913	0.897	0.860	1.000			
Central Java (rural markets)												
Boyolali	CJ1	84.2	0.587	0.516	0.555	0.511	0.528	0.521	0.556	1.000		
Grobogan	CJ2	80.4	0.905	0.767	0.837	0.841	0.795	0.880	0.878	0.575	1.000	
Banjarnegara	CJ3	82.3	0.914	0.887	0.860	0.898	0.884	0.819	0.902	0.612	0.869	1.000

TABLE 8.4. *Integration of rural corn markets in East and Central Java with Jakarta wholesale market*

Local Market		Long-run market integration 1973–1982	Short-run market connection IMC[b]
East Java			
Sumenep	EJ1	1.088[a]	2.22
Malang	EJ2	0.480	0.60
Lamongan	EJ3	1.144[a]	1.14
Bojonegoro	EJ4	0.909[a]	2.81
Jember	EJ5	0.356	1.86
Kediri	EJ6	0.993[a]	0.54*
Central Java			
Boyolali	CJ1	0.235	5.50
Grobogan	CJ2	0.663	1.74
Banjarnegara	CJ3	1.074[a]	0.70*

NOTE: Markets are listed by *kabupaten*, with codes corresponding to those in Table 8.2.

[a]The value 1.0 falls within plus or minus 2 standard errors of the coefficient d_2.

[b]Index of Market Connection = $\frac{1 + d_1}{d_3 - d_1}$ for 1973–1982 coefficients.

An asterisk (*) indicates d_3 was significant and was used in the calculation.

Jakarta market, with an IMC of 5.50, nearly twice as large as the next worst coefficient, that for Bojonegoro (EJ4) in East Java.

What is surprising, however, is that Malang (EJ2) is nearly as well connected to Jakarta in the short run as Kediri. While this is consistent with field observations by various members of the project team, there was little in the simple correlations to set Kediri apart from all the other locations (except the more obviously well connected Malang and the poorly connected Boyolali). The discriminating power of the model is thus beginning to be seen.

Two other local markets seem to be poorly connected to the Jakarta market in the short run: Bojonegoro (EJ4) and Sumenep (EJ1), both in East Java. There are physical reasons for this relative lack of connection. Sumenep is on the island of Madura, at the end of a fairly primitive road and communications network. Bojonegoro is in the northern limestone hills of East Java, where corn markets are much smaller than those of Kediri and Malang. The *kecamatan* sampled, Ngraho, is in fact quite close to Central Java and is equally isolated from both Semarang and Surabaya. The site has some of the characteristics that Mink (1984a) observed in Grobogan, and the combination of smaller marketings and longer distances to provincial capitals, which serve as alternative markets for corn if insufficient quantities can be bulked for a regular Jakarta trade, has prevented a reliable market connection. It is possible that Bojonegoro is well connected to the Jakarta market for several months each year, during the harvest, but this hypothesis has not been tested.

Three other local markets are only moderately well connected to the Jakarta market: Lamongan (EJ3) and Jember (EJ5) in East Java and Grobogan (CJ2) in Central Java. A combination of distance, transportation costs, and smaller regular marketings seems to account for this pattern of short-run market connection.

Long-run market integration. The model used to test short-run market connection also permits a direct test of long-run market integration. This measure is reflected by how close the value of d_2 is to 1, which indicates that a given percentage change in central market prices is exactly transferred to local markets, causing their prices to change by the same percentage. The logarithmic specification yields the percentage change interpretation, which is more likely to reflect the actual structure of marketing costs in an inflationary environment than in circumstances in which long-run price stability permits absolute marketing changes to play a larger role. In the latter environment, d_2 need not be equal to 1 even if markets are fully integrated. It is also possible that longer-run forces take more than a month to be fully reflected in local markets.

The evidence for the long-run integration of local corn markets with the Jakarta market can also be seen in Table 8.4. Only five of the local markets have values of d_2 not significantly different from 1, and four markets—Malang, Jember, Boyolali, and Grobogan—reflect significant lack of long-run connection. Only Malang is a surprise in this grouping, since it registered strong short-run market connection. The results for Malang might be explained by much stronger connections in the 1978–1982 period, when corn production and marketings rose particularly sharply.

Measures of long-run market integration, whether from simple correlation coefficients or from the d_2 coefficient in the first difference model used here, provide little insight into how well *connected* markets are with each other. Long-run integration is important, of course, for it shows that the cellular nature of subsistence economies is breaking down. But this is mostly a function of broader trade interaction rather than specific linkages among commodity markets. The statistical model presented here shows that rural corn markets on Java still show a very wide diversity in this more specific measure of market performance.

What Drives Price Formation?

Corn markets in rural Java are clearly set in a network of economic interactions that serve to integrate individual commodity markets with broader structural changes in the entire economy. In other words, corn markets are influenced in the long run by rice prices, interest rates, wage rates, and changing perceptions of the opportunity cost of land. The corn economy is thus part of the overall economic development effort and should not be thought of as an isolated and separate component. Because consumers, producers, and traders interact in rural markets to determine corn prices, it is equally true that these individual decision makers must also be seen as set in the broader economic forces that surround them. It is perhaps a truism, but no less important for being true, that corn producers, consumers, and traders respond to their economic environment. It is this response that integrates the corn economy with the rest of the food system and the macro economy in the long run.

The question is quite different in the short run. If an unexpected supply of corn arrives on the Malang market, for example, does it depress prices until local consumption is stimulated enough for the market to clear? Alternatively, will traders immediately seize the opportunity to move several additional truckloads to the Jakarta wholesale markets and to feed mills or perhaps even attempt to make an export contract for delivery to Singapore or Hong Kong? The evidence is considerably more mixed here. Even on Java there appear to be many rural markets where local supply and demand conditions—hence local price formation—are not closely tied to the major outside wholesale markets.

The markets least well connected to the Jakarta market are not surprisingly those where relatively small volumes are available to be shipped out of the local area and where transportation is difficult and costs are high. On the other hand, the regular commercial sources of corn—Kediri, Malang, and Banjarnegara—are extremely well connected to the Jakarta market. Both statistical and field data confirm this. The econometric results point to close short-run market connections in precisely those localities where field interviews indicate that traders compete for regular commercial marketings and use telephones, modern truck fleets, and a sophisticated array of field intelligence techniques to maintain a competitive edge.

The consistency between information from field interviews and econometric analysis of price data is important. Often in marketing research it is not possible to do both, and it is desirable to have some confidence that either approach will be illuminating about actual market conditions. In this case, both approaches point to a similar and highly important conclusion: price formation for corn in rural markets on Java is determined primarily by what happens in the Jakarta wholesale market. This is especially true in the long run. There are some clear exceptions in the short run, but for understanding price formation for corn in Indonesia, it is legitimate to focus on the Jakarta market.

A national market for corn does function in Indonesia, a market whose price formation is determined largely by the commercial demand for livestock feed relative to the volume of marketings from several important supplying regions. Imports and exports can also play a major role in this price formation. In the past few years, imports have been used primarily to maintain stable corn supplies to feed mills near Jakarta and influence price formation directly. Exports, on the other hand, require a set of price linkages from the port of shipment back to the rural markets. These price linkages have already been shown to be quite effective for exports of cassava (see Unnevehr 1984a, 1984b).

For the period of price analysis undertaken here, 1973 to 1982, corn was not regularly imported or exported. It is thus difficult to test directly the hypothesis for price linkages stemming from international trade in corn. Substantial volumes of corn were exported in 1971 and 1972, however, and these exports may have contributed to better long-run price integration in the early 1970s than is reported in Table 8.4. More important, corn was exported in quantity again in 1984, and field observations would confirm that export prices play a significant role in rural price formation. This role of export prices is crucial for understanding price formation during the late 1980s, when regular export supplies are likely if the policy environment is conducive.

Policy Environment for an Export-Oriented Corn Marketing System

If Indonesia is to become a regular exporter of corn, domestic prices have to be competitive with world market prices if no subsidies are to be paid. This competitiveness is partly a function of the foreign exchange rate, as Chapter 9 discusses, but it also depends on BULOG's floor price policy. Corn prices probably will have to fall by 2 to 3 percent per year in relative terms if Indonesia's f.o.b. prices are to be regularly competitive in world markets; the faster fall is associated with the larger production levels and export volumes. This may appear to be a perverse supply response on the part of Indonesian corn farmers: higher production associated with lower prices. But in this case, technological change is driving supply, costs are falling, and profits are increasing even with lower output prices. The opportunity to export provides a floor for how low the price must fall as substantial new supplies of corn reach domestic markets.

The net result of the projected balance for corn in the late 1980s is the likely export of 250,000 to 500,000 tons of corn per year. With f.o.b. export prices expected to be approximately $120 per metric ton, these exports would earn $30 to $60 million in foreign exchange.

Continued improvements in marketing efficiency and fair access by farmers to marketing channels are needed to call forth this dramatic increase in production. This will be difficult because the share of marketed output is expected to increase under both the low and high projections for production, to a range of 0.54 to 0.59 in the late 1980s from the value of 0.52 in 1980–1981. Such a rapid increase in marketings could easily depress farm prices at harvest if trade channels are not developed and marketing infrastructure, including drying and storage capacity, is inadequate.

A conducive policy environment is needed to develop this marketing capacity. As earlier parts of this chapter indicate, much of corn marketing is carried out by the private sector. The government plays an active role through the cooperatives in some regions and influences the private sector everywhere through its pricing and trade policies. For the government to play an effective role in developing the corn marketing system, it must recognize the impact of its own direct marketing activities, whether through BULOG or the cooperatives, on all other marketing participants. This role requires an important perspective. Commodity marketing systems in developing countries are both fragile and robust. They are robust in the sense that private marketing agents are always on the lookout for a profitable opportunity to trade. Despite government regulations or contrary objectives, the potential to buy a commodity at a low price and sell it at a high price will always attract the entrepreneurial and adventurous who have access to risk capital.

But the fragility of marketing systems is apparent in how easily the fabric of trust, communication, and expectations about the costs and returns of commodity trading can be ripped apart by government policy. Such government policy toward marketing and commodity price formation is often motivated by the best of intentions. Policies that control prices, regulate access to market channels, or set standards for commodity trading, however, frequently are based on only partial understanding of how marketing systems work and what the impact of government policy ultimately will be in the long run.

This chapter has analyzed how the Indonesian corn marketing system operates, with a major goal to identify government policy initiatives that will further improve the efficiency of the system, lower its costs, and enhance access to it for farmers and end users. At the same time, any government policies that impede reaching these goals need to be identified. Such policies might be justified on the basis of other benefits, or they might simply be incorrect or ineffective instruments for reaching desired goals. Understanding the impact of government policy is necessary before such judgments can be reached.

The Role of Government Policy in Corn Marketing

The government intervenes in corn marketing and price formation in several important ways. At the broadest level, foreign exchange rate and international trade policies directly influence domestic corn prices. More specifically, BULOG operates a floor price policy through the cooperatives and supplies corn to feed mills at "stable" prices. International trade in corn is involved in both of these policies; BULOG sometimes assists in the export of corn purchased at the floor price, especially in South Sulawesi, and imports corn to provide regular supplies to feed mills, especially near Jakarta. Subsidies have been required on both ends of these transactions. In the interests of raising the harvest price for farmers and lowering the seasonal high prices for feed mills, BULOG has unconsciously altered the participation of private marketing agents in the purchase and storage function. Table 8.5 presents price data that help explain why this is so.

Because of the strong seasonal pattern of corn production in Indonesia, with 60 percent of the harvest completed between December and March, a regular inverse pattern of seasonal prices occurs in rural corn markets, especially on Java. On the basis of the rural price data that were analyzed with the statistical model of market connection, a seasonal price index for corn was constructed for Central and East Java. As Table 8.5 shows, the low point of the price index occurs in March, at the end of the main harvest period. The price rises to its peak in October, before the harvest begins to pick up again. For the 1973–1982 period from which these price data are drawn, the seasonal pattern is both regular and quite pronounced: the price in October is 58.6 percent higher on average than the price in March.

This seasonal pattern implies that full storage costs exceed 8 percent of product value per month for this seven-month period. Although such

TABLE 8.5. *Seasonal price index for corn in rural markets on Java compared with BULOG selling price to feed mills near Jakarta*

Month	Seasonal index of corn prices in rural markets on Java, 1973–1982	BULOG selling price for corn to feed mills near Jakarta (rupiahs per kilogram)			
		1981	1982	1983	1984
January	1.027	105	105	140	145
February	0.876	105	105	140	145
March	0.764	105	105	140	145
April	0.766	105	135	140	155
May	0.879	105	135	140	155
June	0.987	105	135	140	
July	1.095	105	135	140	
August	1.128	105	135	140	
September	1.131	105	135	145	
October	1.212	105	135	145	
November	1.103	105	135	145	
December	1.034	110	135	145	

SOURCE: BULOG and Central Bureau of Statistics worksheets.

storage costs are high, they would be consistent with interest rates of 3 percent per month, storage losses of 3 percent per month, other monthly costs (warehouse, labor, pest control, etc.) of 1 percent, and an economic return of 1 percent per month to the trader for risk and opportunity costs of the activity. The livestock feed industry is understandably unhappy about such wide seasonal price fluctuations, even if they do reflect actual costs of storage.

BULOG's response in recent years has been to supply the feed mills near Jakarta with corn at the prices shown in Table 8.5. Although there is an upward trend to these prices, which reflects domestic inflation, there is no seasonal variation at all. In other words, by providing corn to feed mills at stable prices, often from subsidized imported supplies, BULOG has removed all incentives for feed mills to invest in corn storage, a problem that Chapter 6 emphasizes in the analysis of the livestock feed industry. More important, these distorted price signals are also communicated efficiently to most other participants in the corn marketing system and thus make the lack of storage incentives quite pervasive.

The interaction of storage costs and government policy on corn trade and prices is illustrated in Figure 8.4. The horizontal axis shows a full year of corn price formation, starting with a seasonal price decline when the harvest starts and ending at the next harvest. The figure is illustrative only and does not represent any precise Indonesian setting, since this varies considerably from year to year. But the figure is broadly representative of Indonesian circumstances.

In the absence of government intervention and in the presence of efficient and active corn marketing agents, corn prices in normal years would be bounded by the f.o.b. export price on the low side and the c.i.f. import price on the high side. In this example, these are set at $120 and $160 per metric ton, respectively, with a band of $40 per metric ton between f.o.b. and c.i.f. prices. Within this band, price formation for Indonesian corn takes place independent of world prices. When pressures of the harvest push corn prices down, however, traders start buying for export when the price reaches $120 per ton. Exports continue as long as prices stay at this level, until April in the figure, at which point smaller supplies in the market allow prices to begin rising.

How fast do prices rise? Figure 8.4 is designed to show two alternatives, and each depends critically on the costs of storing corn. One alternative corresponds to high storage costs of about $7.50 per ton per month; the second reflects storage costs of only $5.00 per ton per month. The high cost assumption is roughly commensurate with historical seasonal rises in prices observed in rural markets on Java, as shown in Table 8.5. With no market intervention on the part of the government, these storage costs cause corn prices to rise smoothly until either imports become

FIGURE 8.4. *Role of storage costs and government trade policy on corn price formation and the potential for imports and exports in the same crop year*

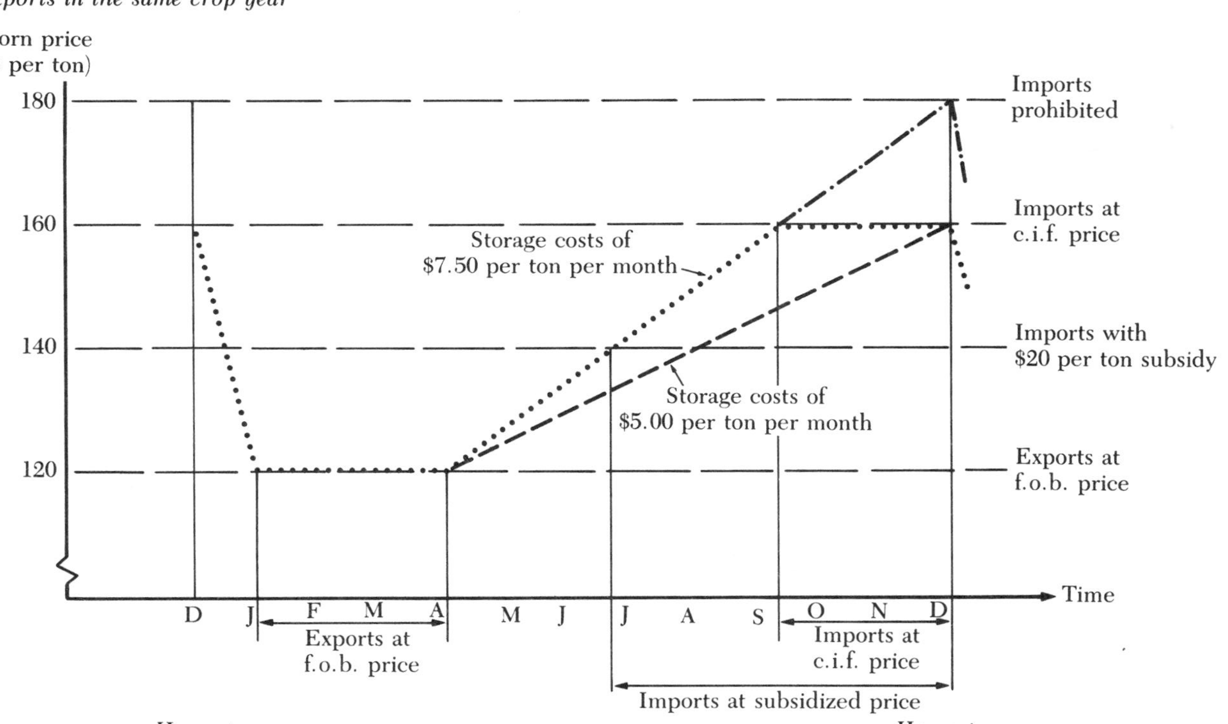

NOTE: Illustrative price and cost figures are in dollars per metric ton.

competitive and provide a ceiling to prices or the next harvest begins and sends prices down again.

With high monthly storage costs, prices rise quickly and reach the c.i.f. import price in September. From this point until the next harvest starts in December, private traders would find it profitable to import corn at the $160 per ton c.i.f. price. The seasonal pattern of corn prices has a flat floor for several months, when domestic markets are connected to export markets, and a flat ceiling for several months, when domestic markets are again connected to international markets, but this time through imports. Indonesia would be an exporter and importer of corn in the same year, and price formation between the f.o.b. and c.i.f. band is determined by storage costs.

If these storage costs were lower, $5.00 per ton instead of the $7.50 per ton just discussed, the pattern of Indonesia's trade would be sharply different. As Figure 8.4 shows, the lower storage costs permit a slower seasonal rise in price. The c.i.f. import price of $160 per ton is not reached before the next harvest begins, and imports never become competitive. In other words, the need to import is a direct function of high storage costs.

The need to import can also be a direct function of government policy. At one extreme it is possible simply to ban imports. With high storage costs, the seasonal rise in price continues past the c.i.f. import price of $160 ton to $180, before the next harvest begins. With high storage costs, banning imports widens the spread in seasonal prices.

With the lower storage costs illustrated in Figure 8.4, a government ban on corn imports is redundant since no imports are needed anyway. Even though such a ban is ineffective in influencing trade, however, it might influence market participants and price formation because of its impact on their expectations. Confidence that imports will *not* be used to prevent a full seasonal rise in price allows traders to buy corn at the harvest for storage over the long term, for six to eight months. For traders to do this without ruinous losses in storage, however, requires that the corn be well dried and free of molds and insects. Investments in drying and storage are needed to ensure such conditions, and these types of investments are very sensitive to traders' expectations about the economic return to their utilization. Cutting off the seasonal price rise arbitrarily is a sure way to dampen these expectations and, as a result, reduce storage and increase imports of corn.

Such a situation is also illustrated in Figure 8.4. Suppose the government's price policy for corn attempts to limit the seasonal movement of prices to a range of $20 per ton, from $120 per ton when exports occur to $140 per ton when imports are brought in under government auspices.

Naturally, since the c.i.f. import price is $160 per ton, the price of $140 per ton can be maintained only by subsidizing each ton of imports by $20.

With such a government policy for imports and pricing, private traders are able to hold stocks for less than three months at high storage costs and about four months at low storage costs. Imports are the main source of supply to feed mills for over five months if storage costs are high, and these imports also drive price formation in rural markets through the market connections analyzed earlier. It can thus be seen why the government's attempts to stabilize prices of corn for feed mills have such pervasive but largely unanticipated effects.

Government Policy for Efficient Markets

The goal of government policy with respect to corn marketing is not to provide price stability at all costs, but rather to develop an environment in which price stability will be one of several desirable outcomes, which include lower subsidy costs, reduced storage costs, and wider participation in corn marketing. The full set of corn policies that can reach these objectives needs to be treated in a broader food policy context. But any agenda for corn policy will include some important marketing initiatives, and the focus here is on the rationale for their design and implementation.

Government initiatives in marketing. There are two key ingredients for a successful government policy toward corn marketing: a competitive foreign exchange rate and a stable environment for trade; and a price policy that is conducive to investments by the private sector in corn drying and storage facilities. Without these ingredients, many of the specific programs and policies oriented toward the corn system are likely to have a small payoff.

With competitive exchange rates and stable trade policy in place, an additional set of initiatives would be socially profitable. First is continuing public investment in marketing infrastructure, in particular, the roads, ports, and communication networks that reduce the costs of maintaining connections between markets. The corn system is not alone in benefiting from these investments, of course. But as traders travel outside the traditional areas of large marketings of corn in search of new commercial sources of supply, farmers are among the first to benefit if roads, telephones, and rural marketplaces lower these traders' costs.

Related to these investments, but requiring somewhat different government initiatives, are actions needed to broaden access to trading activities. Markets work efficiently only when enough traders compete with each other to keep marketing margins equal to actual marketing costs, with no room for excess profits. By setting up stringent licensing arrangements, granting monopoly zones for trading companies, or otherwise restricting access to the business of marketing corn, the government can create high barriers to entry that reduce competition in the marketing sector rather than improve it. This impact is frequently unwitting; the goal is usually to achieve the results of competition through monopoly control. Often what happens, however, is a lack of competition, which leaves many markets—and farmers—unattended except by informal and higher-cost traders.

Another important role for government activity in marketing is providing market information. Nearly all private agents have significant incentives to conceal whatever market information they have and to use it for commercial profit. This works to the disadvantage of small farmers, who generally know far less about market conditions than do the traders. Such imbalance in market knowledge contributes to a widespread perception, and some reality, that traders can take advantage of farmers (and sometimes consumers).

By actively gathering and broadcasting information about daily conditions in rural, wholesale, and retail markets for a variety of commodities, the government can improve the bargaining power of small farmers. The difference is not likely to be significant in those market areas already served by a broad and competitive corn marketing system, such as those surrounding Kediri, Malang, or Ujung Pandang, because competition itself serves to spread market information. In areas with thinner markets, providing farmers and small traders with better information on market conditions could significantly improve the efficiency of marketing.

The government can also play a more direct marketing role. Purchases by government marketing agents can provide the "start-up" incentives needed to build adequate market volume for an efficient private sector to take over, especially in areas where corn surpluses are just beginning to appear in the market in large volumes, or where yellow corn is in surplus when local market demand is for white corn. This role, played primarily by the cooperatives on behalf of provincial DOLOG offices, is most clearly being served in South Sulawesi. This role requires subsidies, either explicit or implicit, because the costs of such marketing initiatives are high. Otherwise the private sector would do its marketing directly and make a profit at it.

The goal is not necessarily to make the cooperatives efficient corn marketing agents in the long run, but rather to help develop local corn farmers into commercially oriented producers and thus build the scale of corn sales to local markets. The larger scale attracts private traders, who then compete with each other for farmers' business. Whether the cooperatives can compete with such traders is not a mark of their success. The success of the cooperatives comes from encouraging the farmers to produce regularly for the market, and subsidies can be fully justified in this task. Beyond this, the cooperatives might well be expected to become efficient enough in the long run to compete with private traders in the regular business of buying and selling corn.

Finally, there is an important research role for the government in marketing. This is most clearly seen in current efforts to lower storage costs by developing a mixable, powdered pesticide of low toxicity which will be appropriate for use by farmers and the cooperatives. Additional activities might include research on low-cost dryers, efficient shelling devices, and improved on-farm storage facilities.

Understanding the nature of markets. This chapter has looked at Indonesia's corn marketing system as the set of economic activities that connect farmers' decisions about corn production and sales to the decisions of diverse end users. Two themes recur throughout the chapter: millions of private decisions are made each day with respect to corn marketing; and government policy influences the economic environment in which these decisions are made. The government itself does not make these decisions. Analysis of the corn marketing system must thus integrate the decision-making perspective of farmers, household consumers, and livestock feeders with an understanding of how government initiatives change the decision-making environment. Since much of this change turns out to be unanticipated and unwanted by policymakers, especially in the long run, the analysis is more complex than it might seem. In the end, marketing analysis of the corn system requires an understanding of the entire Indonesian agricultural development effort and, indeed, the role of markets in the overall economy.

Such is the nature of understanding markets. Their millions of participants are constantly sifting whatever information comes their way for insights into what the future holds. Participation in markets requires taking risks, and the lower the risks, the more efficient the market transactions for both parties. Risk is inherent in marketing because the future is unknowable. Governments can lower the degree of risk by articulating a consistent vision of their policy objectives and by implementing those policies in such a manner that market participants can form stable expectations about the ultimate effects of government actions.

TABLE A8.1. *Regression coefficients for test of market connection*

Rural market location		Independent variables				Adjusted R^2	Durbin-Watson
		Constant	$P_{t-1} - R_{t-1}$	$R_t - R_{t-1}$	R_{t-1}		
East Java							
Sumenep	EJ1	−0.0689 (3.5)	−0.3103 (4.6)	1.0876 (6.2)	NS	0.3061	1.72
Malang	EJ2	−0.1486 (6.2)	−0.6233 (7.6)	0.4801 (2.7)	NS	0.3522	1.88
Lamongan	EJ3	−0.1248 (5.1)	−0.4673 (5.9)	1.1439 (6.4)	NS	0.3305	1.73
Bojonegoro	EJ4	−0.0834 (3.2)	−0.2626 (3.9)	0.9088 (4.5)	NS	0.1681	1.84
Jember	EJ5	−0.1208 (4.4)	−0.3500 (5.2)	0.3555 (2.1)	NS	0.1973	2.10
Kediri	EJ6	−0.5142 (3.7)	−0.6225 (6.7)	0.9930 (6.6)	0.0754 (2.7)	0.3380	1.84
Central Java							
Boyolali	CJ1	−0.0158 (1.0)	−0.1539 (3.2)	0.2345 (1.1)	NS	0.0713	2.18
Grobogan	CJ2	−0.0726 (4.1)	−0.3653 (5.3)	0.6631 (4.2)	NS	0.2458	1.62
Banjarnegara	CJ3	0.2117 (1.3)	−0.6178 (7.1)	1.0737 (5.2)	−0.0707 (1.9)	0.3474	1.99

NOTE: *t*-statistics are indicated in parentheses.

9. International Trade in Corn

Paul A. Dorosh

The pattern of Indonesia's international trade in corn has been highly erratic. Although inter-island shipments from areas of corn surpluses to major centers of corn consumption occur regularly and have grown in response to increased corn production, substantial amounts of corn traded to other parts of Asia nearly came to a halt in 1975 and began again only in 1984 in response to a high world price for corn and the devaluation of the rupiah in 1983. This chapter describes Indonesia's unusual pattern of trade, analyzes the factors causing this pattern, and suggests government policies that can encourage further growth in corn exports.

Indonesia's corn has rarely been traded freely. Up to the mid-1980s, the government restricted corn trade by controlling export and import licenses and by taxing exports and imports of corn. In 1984, restrictions on licensing were the major policy instruments used by the government to restrict corn trade, as exporters were subject to licensing and BULOG was the sole licensed importer. There was no tax on corn exports, and the tax on imports was waived for BULOG.

In addition to trade and price policies, the government's foreign exchange rate policy had important effects on Indonesia's international trade in corn. When the rupiah became increasingly overvalued from 1972 to 1978, and again in 1982, Indonesia's corn was no longer competitive in world markets, and private traders could not profitably export corn. The devaluations of the rupiah in 1978 and again in 1983 restored the competitiveness of Indonesia's corn and contributed to at least a temporary surge in corn exports both times. Even with a constant dollar price, the border price for corn is subject to continual shifting as the rupiah's value changes in relation to the U.S. dollar and thus alters the relationship of the domestic price for corn to the world price.

The export trade is centered in Surabaya in East Java, which is the leading province in production and exports of corn. To a lesser extent, corn is exported from Medan, in North Sumatra, and from North Sulawesi and South Sulawesi; BULOG has exported corn from Jakarta. The corn-producing province of Lampung, on the southern tip of Sumatra, sells primarily to the Jakarta market. Most of Indonesia's corn is exported first to Singapore from which it is often transshipped, but smaller amounts are exported directly to Malaysia, Hong Kong, Japan, and South Korea.

This trade is highly seasonal. Private traders buy corn primarily during the main harvest, which on Java is from December to March. Since collectors and wholesalers do not have sufficient capacity to dry corn mechanically and store it for long periods of time, these supplies must be sold off within a few months. As noted in Chapter 8, this limited storage capacity and high storage costs largely account for Indonesia's importing and exporting corn in the same year.

Factors other than drying and storage capacity have significantly limited Indonesia's capacity to export corn. High marketing costs from port to export destination reduce the competitiveness of Indonesia's corn. Transportation costs are high. Port facilities have been inadequate for handling bulk cargoes and large ocean-going vessels, and corn must be bagged before shipment, which adds to labor and handling costs. Freight costs to Asian ports are high and amount to about 13 percent of the c.i.f. value. Customs procedures have often been cumbersome, and frequently private traders have not been able to obtain export licenses.

All of these factors—irregular exportable surpluses, little drying and storage capacity, and high marketing and transportation costs—have led potential overseas customers to view Indonesia as an irregular supplier of corn. To provide regular, timely exports of corn of consistent quality to the Asian market requires greater investment in public and private storage capacity, upgraded port facilities, and streamlined administrative procedures to complement the increase in corn production and sound macroeconomic policy. Inter-island trade would benefit significantly from these changes as well; private traders on the outer islands frequently encounter price discounts because of high transport costs to Java and inferior quality of corn resulting from poor storage conditions.

These issues have become increasingly important as increases in domestic corn production point to larger potential surpluses for export, with approximately 500,000 tons available for export by 1988. One-half million tons would be equal to 8 percent of total production; this figure compares with an average share of exports in total production of less than 2 percent since the mid-1960s. Export levels of approximately one-half million tons would place corn among the top ten (non-oil) earners of foreign exchange.

This chapter examines the role of government policies in corn trade, particularly as they affect the private sector and its function in corn marketing and, by extension, as they alter production incentives to farmers. The first section describes the flow of corn across Indonesia's borders and analyzes the factors, particularly government trade policies, that affect domestic and international prices and Indonesia's trade in corn. The second section examines the impact of other government policies, particularly the foreign exchange rate, on the competitiveness of Indonesia's corn in the world market. The future prospects for Indonesia's trade in corn are evaluated in the last section.

Corn Trade and Price Formation

Indonesia's corn exports come from several producing regions. East Java, the major production center, is the leading export province, but as shown in Table 9.1, outer island provinces, including South Sulawesi, North Sulawesi, North Sumatra, and Lampung, have also exported significant amounts of corn to foreign markets. These latter areas, although small in total production (less than 40 percent in 1982), typically produce a surplus over quantities demanded locally. Part of this surplus is traded within the country to other islands, mainly Java, and part of it is exported when prices permit.

Differential transport costs help explain why corn is sometimes exported abroad from the outer islands rather than shipped to Java. Typical transport costs to Jakarta from Gorontalo, North Sulawesi, in 1984 were about Rp 13 per kilogram plus an additional Rp 12 per kilogram for handling, compared with only Rp 18 per kilogram transport and handling from Kediri, a major corn marketing center in East Java. Thus wholesalers in North Sulawesi in general receive a price of about Rp 7 per kilogram less than East Java merchants receive for the same quality corn delivered to Jakarta. In some years, traders on outer islands found it more profitable to export corn to foreign markets than ship it to Jakarta, even

TABLE 9.1. *Indonesian corn exports by port, 1966–1984 (tons)*

Year	Total	East Java[a]	Lampung	South Sulawesi[b]	Medan	Other
1966	85,087	24,972	29,450	8,792	3,577	18,296
1967	155,610	61,511	27,903	39,763	2,784	23,649
1968	65,308	8,358	29,371	25,621	1,386	572
1969	153,761	87,301	38,671	18,632	5,613	3,544
1970	281,842	188,376	53,647	23,783	5,125	10,911
1971	217,139	123,321	68,087	5,337	12,534	7,860
1972	78,534	18,212	43,843	600	15,727	152
1973	180,271	73,295	54,593	32,666	14,941	4,776
1974	195,496	112,213	57,980	1,001	17,334	6,968
1975	50,553	21,471	14,905	—	13,803	374
1976	3,514	1,000	608	—	1,906	0
1977	10,450	3,350	4,089	—	3,011	0
1978	21,077	17,224	2,460	98	1,295	0
1979	6,830	4,130	1,900	—	800	0
1980	14,890	—	—	7,780	7,110	0
1981	4,786	1,600	—	1,686	1,500	0
1982	541	541	—	—	—	0
1983	17,936	2,001	702	3,000	1,594	10,640
1984[c]	164,653	43,443	33,500	21,260	1,800	64,650

SOURCES: Indonesia, Central Bureau of Statistics, "Exports" and "Imports," various years; BULOG.
[a]Includes Surabaya, Banyuwangi, Panarukan, and Probolinggo.
[b]Includes Ujung Pandang and Pare-Pare.
[c]September 1983–July 1984; all other years are calendar years.

TABLE 9.2. *Indonesia's corn exports by destination, 1966–1984 (tons)*

Year	Total	Japan	Singapore	Hong Kong	Malaysia	Taiwan	Other
1966	85,087	70,892	—	13,718	—	—	477
1967	155,610	37,502	21,691	46,131	—	—	50,286
1968	65,308	13,465	49,425	1,650	768	—	—
1969	153,761	31,991	85,910	22,316	13,522	—	22
1970	281,842	68,372	146,744	48,633	15,246	—	2,847
1971	217,139	46,347	113,177	35,803	21,711	—	101
1972	78,553	16,539	33,987	15,918	11,955	—	154
1973	180,271	43,305	63,113	14,300	8,660	47,591	3,302
1974	196,854	6,900	80,863	14,375	17,497	74,856	2,363
1975	50,553	4,350	24,512	1,653	4,133	—	15,905
1976	3,514	1,530	1,598	—	386	—	—
1977	10,450	2,800	3,309	700	3,641	—	—
1978	21,076	4,363	3,085	12,628	1,000	—	—
1979	6,830	1,000	2,758	2,922	150	—	—
1980	14,890	775	9,455	—	1,660	—	3,000
1981	4,786	1,350	3,036	—	—	400	—
1982	541	541	—	—	—	—	—
1983	17,936	1,951	6,785	3,600	3,600	2,000	—
1984[a]	32,724	1,420	10,886	4,846	4,495	2,262	8,815

SOURCES: Indonesia, Central Bureau of Statistics, "Exports," various years; Department of Trade, East Java.
[a]1984 exports are for January through April from Surabaya only.

when traders on Java were not exporting corn. The ability to trade corn freely in the world market provides outer island merchants (and farmers) with an additional outlet for their corn. As Chapter 3 shows, the availability of other markets and higher farm prices in remote producing regions may be especially important to spur adoption of new varieties and increased fertilizer use by farmers.

As shown in Table 9.2, Indonesia's corn exports have gone almost exclusively to other Asian countries, such as Singapore, Malaysia, Hong Kong, Japan, and South Korea. The world's largest importers, the European Community, the Soviet Union, and Japan, prefer large bulk shipments of high-quality corn, usually supplied by the United States or Argentina; Indonesia is not likely to break into that market.[1] Corn grown in East Java or North Sulawesi for export must normally find its way to Singapore or Hong Kong. Local collectors are the first link in the marketing chain from farmer to export market. The corn may then be sold directly to a wholesaler who is also an exporter, as is often done in East Java, or alternatively, the corn may be purchased by a broker once it reaches the wholesale level. The broker then makes the arrangements for

[1]Several small ports in Japan can handle ships of only 10,000 tons or less. Until aflatoxin problems eliminated the trade, Thailand shipped corn directly to these small Japanese ports, thus saving Japanese importers the transshipment and handling costs incurred in offloading bulk freighters from the United States. If the quality problems could be solved, Indonesia might be able to supply these ports for part of the year.

transport, licensing, and sale of the corn. Exporters make contact with foreign traders either by personal trips to neighboring countries or by telex or telephone. Through these contacts, traders are able to obtain up-to-date world price information.

Trade Policy

Export and import restrictions, licensing requirements, and taxes have had a direct impact on corn trade. Exports have been stopped several times, either by official trade bans or simply by the Department of Trade's not issuing licenses. In some cases the decision to stop exports may have been superfluous because rising domestic prices made export trade unprofitable for private merchants. The government has used export taxes and import tariffs to help raise tax revenues and to affect trade flows. In the early 1970s the Department of Trade levied a 10 percent tax on corn exports, but in 1984 neither export nor import tax policies were in effect. The import tax on corn is waived for BULOG, which was the only importer of corn in the mid-1980s. Licensing requirements for exports are designed to give BULOG and the Department of Trade better control over the domestic supply of corn. Traders who want to export corn are required to obtain an export license from the Department of Trade. Since 1978, BULOG has had responsibility for maintaining adequate domestic supplies of corn, which was at that time labeled a "guarded" (*diawasi*) commodity. Before granting approval for licenses, BULOG, with the assistance of the Department of Agriculture, first determines whether exportable surpluses exist. This calculation can take many weeks since it involves checking estimates of current corn production and estimating future corn needs. BULOG's approval is also required for private market imports, but since 1981 the government has not granted import licenses to the private market. In this way BULOG maintains a monopoly on corn imports.

After BULOG determines that an exportable surplus exists, a trader must usually wait at least a week for an export license application to be processed. The license specifies the amount of exports allowed and is usually good for several months. Destination of exports is not given on the license but is later recorded on the bill of lading registered at the Department of Trade. A check price (*harga patokan*) set by BULOG is used to calculate the value of exports. Previously, the check price also was used for determining the amount of export tax to be paid, but by 1984 the export tax rate was zero. In the early 1970s the check price was significantly less than the actual market price received by merchants, thus reducing tax liabilities, but check prices in the 1980s have more closely approximated actual export prices.

The licensing requirement adds to the uncertainty of export planning in both the short and long term for traders. Long-run trading contacts are more difficult to establish since domestic traders cannot be sure of obtaining licenses in future years, even if domestic supplies of corn are available at competitive prices. In the short run (within a few months), some traders have been frustrated in their efforts to obtain licenses to fulfill tentative trading agreements. In East Java, over fifteen traders obtained licenses for export in 1984, but in North Sulawesi some traders who had planned to export corn were unable to obtain licenses. Although the licensing requirement need not restrict the opportunities for the private sector, it can lead to rents for privileged exporters who are able to obtain licenses when profitable trading opportunities exist. Export taxes lower the price received by the trader and farmers and can reduce the competitiveness of Indonesian corn in the world market. Import tariffs serve to protect domestic producers of corn but result in higher prices for consumers. Fewer licensing restrictions, especially in Sulawesi and Sumatra, could be of substantial benefit. Frequent changes in the international corn price and local domestic supply variations make it very difficult for BULOG or the Department of Trade to know the relevant facts about trade opportunities specific to each local situation, particularly

TABLE 9.3. *Surabaya exporters' marketing costs*

Items	Components of corn export price (rupiahs)	
Components of f.o.b. price		
Price of corn, Surabaya wholesale market		128,939
Transport to harbor warehouse	920	
Harbor costs		
Unloading	305	
Warehouse rental (3 days at Rp 100 per ton per day)	300	
Transport to shipside	706	
Dock fee	100	
Loading onto ship	717	
Expediter's fee (Rp 250,000 per lot)	250	
Other administrative costs	400	
Subtotal	3,698	
Bank service charge (0.25 percent)	338	
Letter of credit interest (0.75 percent per month for 2 months)	2,025	
Total marketing costs		6,061
Price of corn f.o.b. Surabaya		135,000
Exporter's costs as percentage of f.o.b. price = 4.5 percent		
Components of c.i.f. price		
Estimated shipping cost to Singapore		20,273
Estimated insurance cost (0.3 percent)		466
Estimated price of corn c.i.f. Singapore		155,739

SOURCE: Data obtained from interview with exporters' association in Surabaya.
NOTE: Table lists typical costs per ton for a lot of 1,000 tons in 1984. All figures are in rupiahs per ton except where indicated.

TABLE 9.4. *Profitability of storing corn, 1984*

Item	Exporter's costs (rupiahs per ton) — Storage losses: 2 percent per month	2.5 percent per month
May: corn price,[a] f.o.b. Surabaya	140,465	140,465
Exporter's marketing cost	5,912	5,912
Implied wholesale price	134,553	134,553
Exporter's costs		
Storage costs		
Warehouse fee (Rp 330 per ton per month)	1,320	1,320
Interest (1.5 percent per month)	8,073	8,073
Storage losses	13,165	16,457
Total costs	22,558	25,850
Price of stored corn	157,111	160,403
September: corn price,[b] c.i.f. Surabaya	166,950	166,950
Profit for storing corn	9,839	6,547

[a]Exchange rate used for May was Rp 1,010 per U.S. dollar.
[b]Exchange rate used for September was Rp 1,050 per U.S. dollar.

in the outer islands. Quantities of corn involved may sometimes be small, and the time period in which the corn can be profitably exported may likewise be short. The policy of delaying decisions on the availability of trade licenses for private merchants until near harvest time adds unnecessary uncertainty for traders.

The Export Price

Indonesia's corn has not always been competitive in the Asian market because of high marketing and transport costs, which account for a rather high percentage of the c.i.f. price. As shown in Table 9.3, marketing costs for a representative lot of 1,000 tons, which is typical of exports from Surabaya in 1984, from the wholesale level to f.o.b. basis are only about Rp 6 per kilogram, or 4 percent of the c.i.f. value, but transport costs of about Rp 20 per kilogram to nearby Asian countries take up another 13 percent of the c.i.f. value. Dock fees, transport costs, and interest charges account for most of the cost, but expediters' fees and so-called administrative costs account for more than 10 percent of the marketing costs.

In some years Indonesia both imported and exported corn because of deterioration in the quality of stored corn and the high costs of storage. Feed mills and other industrial users of corn require steady supplies of corn to enable year-round production. Imports (sometimes subsidized) have provided a low-cost alternative to storing domestically produced corn. The profitability of storing corn is calculated in Table 9.4, which illustrates the interplay among storage costs, government policy, and imports. Even though corn exports from September 1983 to July 1984 were over 160,000 tons, BULOG imported 47,000 tons of corn in August and September 1984 for sales to feed mills. Private exports of corn had been essentially banned from Surabaya and Lampung in April, although a few small, previously licensed shipments were allowed to be exported in May and June. As shown in the table, there would have been only a small profit for a private merchant (or BULOG) who stored corn for four months rather than exported it in May. The price of imported corn in September was $159 per ton (Rp 166,950 per ton), which exceeded the cost of stored corn by about Rp 6.5 per kilogram, if storage losses were assumed to be 2.5 percent per month. Profit earned from storing corn would have been essentially zero, however, if the exchange rate versus the dollar had not depreciated by 4 percent during those four months. It is also likely that these calculations underestimate storage losses, which may increase rapidly after a threshold period of several months.

Government Policy and the Foreign Exchange Rate

Although government policy for corn has not been so extensive as that for rice, various policies have had major impact on corn production and trade. Trade and price policies directly affect international trade, but macroeconomic policies, particularly foreign exchange rate, budget, interest rate, and wage rate policies, also have important indirect effects. All of these policies alter the competitiveness of Indonesia's corn exports, public and private investment in infrastructure, and decision making of private traders. The fertilizer subsidy, the intensification program for non-rice staples, and government seed policy have an impact on corn trade through their influence on domestic production. These policies have been discussed in the context of production issues, however, and are mentioned here only as a reminder that policies not directly involving trade or procurement do affect corn trade.

A major factor in determining the price competitiveness of Indonesia's corn on the world market is the foreign exchange rate, which converts the world price of corn, usually quoted in U.S. dollars, into a domestic price in rupiahs. When the rupiah is overvalued, Indonesia's domestically produced goods become less competitive relative to those in the world market. Rupiah prices of imported goods are made artificially low, which pressures domestic producers to lower prices of goods that compete with imports. Export goods must be sold at low rupiah prices to compete in the world export market. The exchange rate along with world corn prices determine the *level* of the f.o.b.-c.i.f. band, whereas transport and handling costs determine the *width* of the band.

The major trends and breaks in Indonesia's trade patterns are reflected in the changes in relative prices shown in Figure 9.1. The competitive-

FIGURE 9.1. *Corn price trends, 1974–1984*

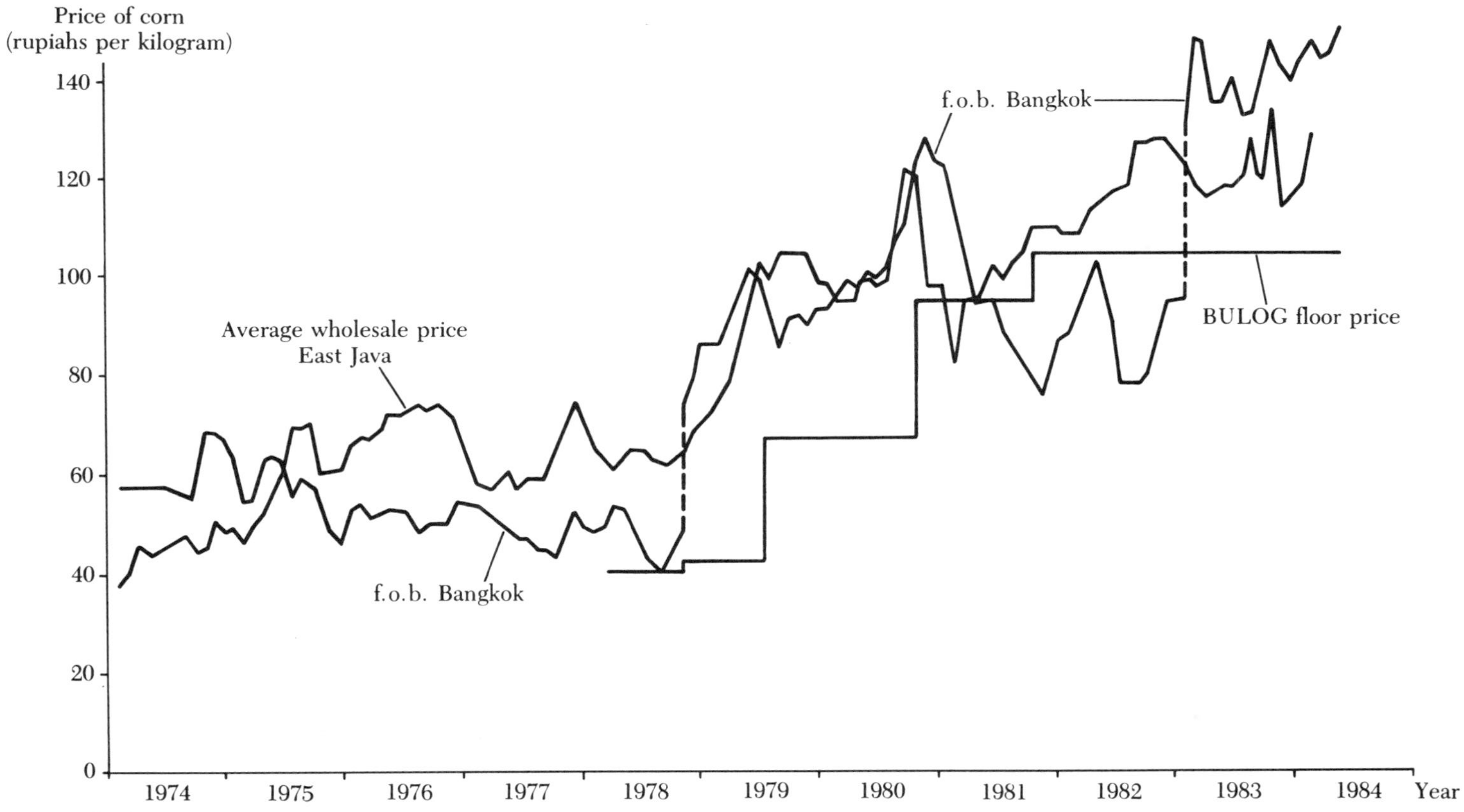

NOTE: Dashed lines indicate when the devaluation of the rupiah occurred.

ness of Indonesian corn on the world market during the early 1970s is seen in the low price of Surabaya corn relative to the Bangkok price.[2] The rapid rise in domestic price relative to the world price in the mid-1970s corresponds to Indonesia's shift from exporter to net importer of corn. From 1976 to 1981, net trade in corn was small, and throughout most of this period Indonesia's domestic price was inside the f.o.b.-c.i.f. band, which made both exports and imports unprofitable for private traders.

The devaluation of March 1983, which was a major factor in the dramatic shift in Indonesia's net corn trade position from 1982 to 1984, illustrates the importance of the exchange rate in determining trade. By 1982 the rupiah exchange rate (per U.S. dollar) was again overvalued because almost all the improvement in the real exchange rate resulting from the 1978 devaluation had been lost due to rates of inflation higher than those of Indonesia's trading partners. BULOG, which suffered substantial losses from storing domestically procured corn in 1981, turned to the world market for corn supplies for domestic feed mills in the months following the major corn harvests in Java. From August through December 1982, f.o.b. corn prices in Bangkok were over Rp 40 per kilogram lower than average wholesale prices in East Java. With transport costs to Jakarta only about US $25 per ton (Rp 17 per kilogram at the then prevailing exchange rate), the low rupiah price of imported corn provided a highly profitable alternative to domestic supplies in a low production year, and BULOG imported a record 190,000 tons of corn.

The 38 percent devaluation of the rupiah in March 1983 eliminated the profit margin for corn imports and made private market corn exports possible. Wholesale prices in East Java, which were more than Rp 30 per kilogram higher than f.o.b. Bangkok prices just before the devaluation, overnight became Rp 10 per kilogram lower than the Thai price, and corn exports from East Java were again competitive on the world market. The March 1983 devaluation was somewhat late to spur exports from the main corn crop in 1982–1983 harvested in December and January, but exports in 1983–1984 climbed to over 160,000 tons in response to the new exchange rate and higher world market prices for corn.

A second example of how the exchange rate influences trade is the case of Indonesia's overvalued exchange rate in the mid-1970s, which reduced Indonesia's competitiveness on the world market and contributed to a shift from net exports to net imports of corn. Indonesia maintained a fixed exchange rate (relative to the U.S. dollar) from August 1971 to November 1978. During this period, inflation in Indonesia outpaced that of the

[2]Transport and handling costs from the wholesale level to f.o.b. help account for the difference between the two prices during this period when Indonesia was exporting corn. Had estimates of the Surabaya f.o.b. price been used for Indonesia's price in Figure 9.2, the gap between the Indonesian and world price in the early 1970s would have been smaller.

TABLE 9.5. *Impact of the real exchange rate on the Indonesian corn system*

	1972	1974	1977
Wholesale East Java corn price (rupiahs per kilogram)	21.7	44.6	61.7
f.o.b. Bangkok corn price (rupiahs per kilogram)	23.6	59.1	48.7
Price index Jakarta	100.0	184.2	291.9
World price index[a]	100.0	140.1	194.6
Real East Java price of corn (1972 rupiahs per kilogram)	21.7	24.2	21.1
Real world price of corn (1972 rupiahs per kilogram)	23.6	42.2	21.1
Exchange rate	415	415	415
Real exchange rate	100	132	150
East Java price as percent of world price	92	75	127
Real price ratio index (1972=100)	100	62	109
Net Indonesian exports (000 tons)	79	197	1

SOURCES: Export share weights from Warr (1984); consumer price indexes and exchange rates are from International Monetary Fund, "International Financial Statistics," various issues.

[a]Weighted average of consumer price indexes of Indonesia's major trading partners converted to U.S. dollars.

United States and Indonesia's other major trading partners. Large oil revenues spent in the domestic economy helped fuel this inflation, but they also provided sufficient foreign exchange and access to credit to keep the country from experiencing balance of payments problems. The fixed nominal exchange rate, however, reduced the competitiveness of Indonesia's non-oil exports, including corn. Table 9.5 shows the change in the relative domestic to international price of corn, along with a breakdown of this change into real and nominal components. The first half of 1972 was chosen as a base period for corn price comparisons since it marked the end of Indonesian corn exports before the large increase in world corn prices in 1973 and 1974, yet it followed the devaluation of 1971.

Between 1972 and 1974, Indonesia's domestic inflation was 32 percent higher than that of its major trading partners, but the nominal exchange rate was held fixed at 415 rupiahs per U.S. dollar. High world prices in 1974 kept Indonesian corn competitive on the world market, but the real domestic price of corn rose only slightly, while the real world price of corn almost doubled. Thus Indonesian producers did not enjoy the large gain in real corn prices (and income) experienced by corn farmers in other countries. Had Indonesia maintained a constant real exchange rate by correcting for differential inflation in domestic prices relative to that of its major trading partners, 1974 domestic corn prices would have been about 30 percent higher. The overvalued exchange rate thus served in effect to tax producers and subsidize consumers of corn.

Table 9.6 shows the size of the gain in consumer surplus and loss of producer surplus because of the overvalued exchange rate. Lower rupiah prices of corn in 1974 due to the overvalued exchange rate increased corn consumption and led to lower corn production. Corn consumers enjoyed

TABLE 9.6. *Breakdown of gains and losses from exchange rate overvaluation, 1974*

	Actual	With devaluation	Change
Wholesale price of corn (rupiahs per kilogram)	44.6	58.7[a]	31.6[b]
Corn production (000 tons)	3,011	3,106[c]	95
Corn consumption (000 tons)	2,513	2,116[d]	−397
Corn exports (000 tons)	197	679[e]	482
Producers' surplus (billion rupiahs)	—	—	43
Consumers' surplus (billion rupiahs)	—	—	−33
Foreign exchange earnings (millions U.S. dollars)	20[f]	68	49

SOURCES: Note (c): 1974 data base from Indonesia, Central Bureau of Statistics, *Statistical Pocketbook of Indonesia*, 1975; note (f): Indonesia, Central Bureau of Statistics, "Exports," 1974.

[a]Assumes 31.6 percent devaluation increases corn price by full 31.6 percent.

[b]Percentage.

[c]Using supply elasticity of 0.1.

[d]Assumes that 10 percent of production is lost to waste and that the aggregate domestic consumption (including livestock) elasticity is −0.5.

[e]New export total calculated as production less losses and consumption.

[f]Based on actual 1974 average export price of US $100.7 per ton.

an increase of Rp 33 billion in consumer surplus, while corn producers suffered a Rp 43 billion loss of producer surplus. The exchange rate policy led not only to lower corn production and higher corn consumption but also to reduced exports of corn, which amounted to an estimated loss of US $49 million in foreign exchange in 1974.

The numbers presented in Table 9.6 are meant to be only a rough estimate of the size of the impact of the overvalued exchange rate on the corn system. Elasticities of consumption and production used in the calculation were deliberately chosen to provide a conservative estimate of the exchange rate's impact on trade. Alternative plausible assumptions of 0.7 and 0.4 for price elasticities of demand and supply, respectively, would give only slightly different magnitudes for changes in consumer and producer surpluses (Rp 30 billion and Rp 46 billion, respectively). These alternative elasticity assumptions, however, imply a much larger level of corn exports of 1.27 million tons, an increase of $128 million relative to the historical level.

The turning point for Indonesian corn trade came in mid-1975 when the wholesale price in East Java, which was Rp 11 per kilogram (25 percent) below the Bangkok price in 1974, climbed past the Thai price. Net imports in 1976 reached over 50,000 tons. Despite large production increases in 1977 and 1978, which helped reduce the real price of corn by over 20 percent by 1978, domestic inflation and the fixed exchange rate kept the dollar price of Indonesian corn slightly above the world price. By 1977 the world price of corn (in real terms) had returned to almost that of 1972, as had real prices in East Java (see Table 9.5). But nominal East Java prices were then 27 percent over the nominal world price, largely due to the overvalued exchange rate. Had Indonesia maintained the 1972 real exchange rate, the domestic corn price would have been only 84 percent of the world price, and Indonesia would probably still have been exporting corn.

The 51 percent devaluation in November 1978 failed to boost corn exports significantly because the inflation that followed the devaluation canceled some of the improvement in the real exchange rate. Corn exports from several provinces were prohibited in early 1979 as rising corn prices threatened to increase the price of eggs at a time when the government was trying to slow down inflation through price controls (Dick 1979).

The sharp rise of domestic prices to world levels in early 1979 illustrated the rapidly deteriorating impact of the November 1978 devaluation. When world corn prices dropped in 1981 and 1982, licensing controls over imports prevented private traders from importing enough corn to lower Indonesia's domestic price. The wide gap between the East Java price and the f.o.b. Bangkok price in 1982 clearly shows the potential returns over costs for BULOG imports in that year. The quantity of BULOG imports was not sufficient to bring down domestic corn prices to the c.i.f. level, however. The impact of the March 1983 devaluation in restoring Indonesia's competitiveness is seen in the sharp increase in rupiah prices on the world market, which reflects a corresponding drop in the dollar price of Indonesian corn.

The exchange rate has important consequences for commodities other than corn, of course, but these consequences depend on specific commodity policy. Corn is an intermediate case between that of rice, in which government intervention has largely insulated the domestic market from year-to-year world price fluctuations, and that of dried cassava (*gaplek*), which has been essentially a freely traded good whose domestic price therefore reflects the world price. Domestic corn prices have not directly followed world corn prices because the domestic corn market has often been insulated from the world market by high transport costs and a wide f.o.b.-c.i.f. band, which made international trade unprofitable. Even when domestic prices in Indonesia were high enough to make private market imports profitable, as in 1982, corn imports were banned, and thus the link between domestic and world corn prices was broken. Had imports been allowed, the domestic price would have fallen toward world price levels. Exchange rate policy, however, had a direct impact on corn prices and the profitability of trade, and in 1983 it contributed to shifts from imports to exports of corn.

Future Prospects for International Corn Trade

For a given foreign exchange rate and set of local supply and demand conditions, Indonesia's corn trade depends on world market prices. As

TABLE 9.7. *World corn production and trade, 1980/81–1982/83 average*

Country	Production: Total (million tons)	Production: Share of world (percent)	Trade: Exports (million tons)	Trade: Imports (million tons)	Trade: Share of world export (import) trade (percent)
United States	196.8	45.9	54.0		75.8
China	60.9	14.2		1.5	(2.1)
Eastern Europe	31.8	7.4		5.3	(7.4)
Brazil	22.9	5.3		0.2	(0.3)
Economic Community	18.5	4.3		8.6	(12.1)
Soviet Union	10.3	2.4		11.7	(16.4)
Mexico	10.0	2.3		2.9	(4.1)
Argentina	9.8	2.3	6.4		9.0
South Africa	9.1	2.1	3.8		5.3
Thailand	3.6	0.8	2.5		3.5
Indonesia	3.2[a]	0.7		0.1	(0.1)
Japan	0.0	—		13.8	(19.4)
Other	51.9	12.3	4.5	27.1	
World total	428.8	100.0	71.2	71.2	

SOURCES: U.S. Department of Agriculture (1983a, 1983b); Indonesia; Central Bureau of Statistics, *Statistical Pocketbook of Indonesia*, various years.
[a]1980–1982 calendar-year average.

these prices rise and fall, the entire f.o.b.-c.i.f. band of prices in Indonesia rises and falls as well. Even if local supply and demand conditions set domestic prices within the f.o.b.-c.i.f. band under normal circumstances, unusually high or low export prices from U.S. markets can induce corn exports or imports from or into Indonesia unless government policy intervenes. The level of world prices provides the standard against which Indonesia's corn competes. High world prices in 1974 and 1984 contributed to the large levels of corn exports in those years; the drop in world corn prices after 1974 reinforced the impact of a rising real exchange rate in reducing the competitiveness of Indonesia's corn on the world market.

Indonesia's share in world corn trade is very small, less than 0.1 percent of the 70 million tons traded annually (see Table 9.7). Over 40 percent of total world supply and over 70 percent of exports come from the United States, which makes U.S. price policies and weather dominant forces in the world corn market. In 1983 an acreage reduction plan, the Payment-in-Kind program, along with bad weather, reduced corn production in the United States by about 50 percent. Drawdown of U.S. corn stocks and substitution of other feed grains by corn users helped limit the increase in 1984 corn prices to only 28 percent.[3] The Payment-in-Kind program for corn was discontinued in 1984, and with normal weather, United States corn production returned to the high levels of earlier years.

[3]Computed from average July–to–June wholesale prices for 1982–1983 and 1983–1984 (International Monetary Fund 1983, 1984).

The other major exporters, Argentina, Thailand, and South Africa, account for a much smaller share of world production and trade, and thus production fluctuations and policy changes in these countries have less impact on world prices. Corn export prices from these countries are highly correlated with U.S. export prices, and this is consistent with the concept of an integrated world corn market, driven to a large extent by U.S. prices (see Mink 1984c). Thailand, which accounts for much of the trade in small shipments of corn to countries in Southeast Asia, has been a major supplier of corn to Indonesia, as well as a principal competitor for Indonesia's corn exports.

Continued increases in yields for Indonesia's corn farmers could lead to considerable export potential—approximately 250,000 to 500,000 tons at a world price of $120 per ton. Several caveats need to be mentioned in assessing export potential, however. First, supply variations from year to year caused by weather or pest damage could result in large fluctuations in export supply, and imports could occur during years of low production. Second, even if a surplus is produced, a high-fructose corn syrup industry could use this corn domestically. Third, fluctuations in world price due to bumper crops or bad weather in the United States could make Indonesia's corn uncompetitive or boost exports in any given year. Finally, exchange rate and trade policy could hamper corn exports through an overvalued exchange rate, costly licensing requirements, or sporadic changes in government policy, which increase uncertainty and hamper planning by traders.

The market infrastructure in the mid-1980s is adequate for exporting small amounts of corn, but further capital investment in port facilities and dryers might be necessary if exportable surpluses continue to grow. Mechanical dryers will probably be necessary for large lots of corn to meet quality standards for exports by reducing mold and aflatoxin growth. Warehouse space near ports is also a constraint on large lots of corn. No storage facilities with capacities over 10,000 tons were available in the mid-1980s. Moreover, there were no bulk-loading facilities at Indonesian ports, thus necessitating bagging the corn. Although Thailand exports some of its corn in bags (usually in lots of 500 to 2,000 tons), most large importers prefer bulk shipments of 40,000 to 50,000 tons. The market for bagged corn is more specialized and concentrated in countries that lack bulk-loading facilities, such as many Middle Eastern and African countries. A sizable increase in the supply of bagged corn (1 million tons would represent about half of Thailand's annual exports) could eliminate the premium on bagged corn paid by small importers. Sustained competition from Indonesia for bagged corn exports, however, would probably lead Thailand to modernize its port facilities to enable more efficient bulk shipments.

Investments in Indonesia's export facilities will not be undertaken by the private sector unless there is a good prospect of stable long-run supplies of corn competitive in the world market. Several years of sizable exports would be necessary to make these investments profitable for the private sector. In determining whether these exports are likely, private investors take into account not only their own informal projections of domestic supply and demand but also government policies likely to be in effect.

PART FIVE

Policy Perspective

10. Corn in Indonesia's Food Policy

C. Peter Timmer

This chapter sketches an overview of Indonesia's corn system and, within that context, identifies the key policies that directly or indirectly influence the evolution of the system. The overview provides a flavor of the complex system that was observed by the project team and documented in extensive detail in individual working papers and the previous chapters.[1] The intent here is to capture a sense of the actual and potential dynamics of the corn system to convey to policymakers the likely impact of alternative policy choices. Much of this description is necessarily impressionistic, but it represents the collective impressions and judgments of nearly two years of effort by a team of a half-dozen researchers.

This chapter begins by reviewing the activities of the major government agencies that influence the corn system and then examining corn-specific policies and their impact on the development of the system. Corn production policies as well as trade and price policies are discussed first. Agricultural sector policies and macroeconomic policies progressively widen the scope of the analysis. The chapter concludes by examining the task of coordinating all the policies that affect the corn system.

An Overview of the Corn System

A *system* implies a set of things or people connected in such a manner that the whole is more than the sum of the individual parts. Indonesia's corn system certainly fits this definition, for corn producers, consumers, traders, and government agencies that deal with corn issues are linked to one another through economic forces, technological relationships, and bureaucratic rules and decisions. Although no master planner coordinates the development of the corn system, it is surprisingly well coordinated and is developing rapidly. A major task of this chapter is to understand how this coordination takes place currently and how it might be improved to serve better the interests of Indonesia's food policy objectives.

Perhaps the most fascinating aspect of Indonesia's corn system, and surely what makes analysis of corn policy so complex, is not the "intra-corn" connections but the links between corn and other commodities. At all five levels of the system—input supplier, producer, trader-processor,

[1]See especially Dorosh (1984a, 1984b, 1984c), Mink (1984a, 1984b), and Perry (1984a).

consumer, and government agency—decisions about non-corn commodities must be made simultaneously with corn-related decisions. Fertilizer dealers serve primarily rice farmers, but demand from corn growers is quite substantial in some areas. A multitude of Indonesian farming systems include corn somewhere in the rotation, but nearly always in potential competition with some other crop such as upland rice, cassava, soybeans, or vegetables.

Most traders deal in multiple commodities, their balance of business determined by the season and the crops farmers decide to grow. Purchase patterns of corn consumers are highly price sensitive among alternative starchy staples, whether for livestock rations or human diets. And government agencies, from agricultural extension agents, who must be knowledgeable about the wide range of crop choices available to individual farmers, to BULOG procurement officers, who must anticipate alternative commodity demands by the feed mill industry, must also cope with cross-commodity linkages in which corn is often at the center of potential choices.

As a consequence, the Indonesian corn system encompasses a set of horizontal and vertical links. The vertical links are primarily to corn-specific activities, and the horizontal links connect corn decision making with other commodities and with other aspects of the agricultural and macro economy. Ultimately, of course, the corn system is but one of many agricultural, industrial, and financial systems in the Indonesian economy, all of which are connected through general equilibrium mechanisms. Even some of these are important to the corn system itself, most notably the equilibrium value of the foreign exchange rate.

Within this maze of connections, three levels of policy concern can be identified. At the commodity-specific level, policies are designed primarily for their direct impact on the corn system. At the sectoral level, policies affect the entire agricultural sector, and the impact on the corn system is determined by the variety of cross-commodity links in production and consumption. The overall economic environment determined by macro policies faces all decision makers, including those in the corn system. Each of these levels of potential policy initiative and impact are treated in later sections. What is needed first is a better sense of the corn system itself.

Corn is unique in its capacity to serve commercially as the raw material for all major commodity end uses: food, feed, fuel, fructose (sweeteners), fats and oils, and factory input for processing. The commodity substitution framework presented in the introduction to the chapters on end uses explains why a wide variety of customers compete in the same market for corn. In Indonesia the most direct competition is between corn for direct consumption by humans, primarily by those in the bottom quarter of the rural income distribution, and corn as a major ingredient in livestock feed, which ultimately is a component of the meat and eggs consumed primarily by the upper quarter of the urban income distribution. This competition between food and feed, low income and high income, provides much of the concern at the policy level over the dynamics of the Indonesian corn system. This concern is probably premature. Good policy can lead to rapid exploitation of new technology involving improved seed and farming practices, which will permit enough corn to be produced to meet both demands and also generate surpluses for exports. The economic, technological, and policy links between the livestock feed industry and corn consumption by humans, however, need to be understood for the design of such policy.

Corn production technology in Indonesia is in the midst of a dramatic shift in potential productivity, which has consequences not only for the corn system but also for other commodities. Notable, but largely unnoticed, improvements in the yield potential of locally bred, open-pollinated varieties such as Arjuna and Harapan-6 have offered farmers the opportunity to increase yields through more intensive cultivation, especially through higher applications of fertilizer. Corn yields have increased more than 4 percent per year since the mid-1970s, and although some of the easy gains in plant breeding and farmer adoption have already been achieved, future gains seem even more promising.[2]

The new factor in the corn productivity picture is the development of the C-1 hybrid seed. Hybrid corn seed has been the basis of the corn industry in the United States since the 1930s, but hybrid seeds have played only a limited role in tropical corn systems until recently. This limited use of hybrids is due partly to the necessity for a sophisticated seed reproduction and distribution system that can provide farmers with new (and relatively expensive) seed for each planting season. The widespread planting of short-duration corn in intercrops and multiple-cropping systems also slowed the adoption of the relatively long-duration

[2]In a letter to the author, Larry Harrington of CIMMYT had the following observations about the relationship between corn varieties and fertilizer use:

> It should be noted that in many areas fertilizer efficiency is very low and higher doses are of little help. Often research will have to focus on fertilizer management issues: nitrogen-phosphorus balance and phosphorus fixation; micronutrient availability; number and timing of applications; interactions with manure; etc. For example, in Malang, CIMMYT is increasing yields on trial plots by lowering the nitrogen dose, introducing phosphorus, applying fertilizer earlier—but only *after* having solved the shootfly problems that lead to overplanting practices. . . . Variety is only one of several interacting factors that need to be looked at on a "site-specific" basis. For example, in Malang, new varieties (or the hybrid) are not likely to have any large effect on corn productivity until overplanting practices can be modified. Farmers will continue to overplant until they adopt some method (e.g., Furadan seed treatment) that controls early season pests (shootfly, white grub).

hybrids. The much shorter growing season for modern rice varieties has expanded farmer options to include longer-duration secondary crops, especially corn, where irrigation facilities do not permit continuous rice cultivation.

The rapid growth in the demand for corn from the livestock feed industry has spurred development of improved corn production technology and the interest of farmers in adopting it. Steady demand from local markets encourages both traders and farmers to expand corn activities. Exports can provide some of the same stimulus, but they involve much higher risks. The world market for corn is very large relative to any conceivable export of Indonesian corn, but Chapter 9 details how fluctuations in both the dollar price in international markets and the rupiah price when converted at the prevailing exchange rate have sharply altered the competitiveness of Indonesian corn exports from year to year. Indonesian corn exports are often priced at a discount compared to U.S. and Thai corn and even at a discount to prices in domestic markets. This discounting is due partly to Indonesia's sporadic export supplies, and hence its unreliability as a regular supplier, and partly to quality problems, especially high levels of aflatoxin contamination, caused by poor export infrastructure and handling facilities. The rapid growth of domestic demand from feed mills, rather than export demand, has served as the primary spur to local corn production.

Despite early concerns that this demand for corn from feed mills might set Indonesia on the same path as Taiwan, Mexico, Malaysia, and other middle-income countries that have become significant importers of feed grains, the productivity response now seems capable of meeting all sources of domestic demand with regular supplies available for export (barring the construction of a large-scale high-fructose corn sweetener plant or the elimination of the fertilizer subsidy). But the problems with the export market will be transmitted back to domestic traders and farmers unless policy initiatives are undertaken to promote the profitability of export trade. The necessary measures are discussed at length in several later sections; they involve actions specific to corn, especially with respect to export licensing arrangements and domestic price policy; sectoral policies with respect to fertilizer pricing, credit facilities for traders, and development of marketing infrastructure, particularly at ports; and price policies for other commodities. At the macro level, a long-term commitment to maintain the rupiah at competitive levels relative to foreign currencies will be essential for the private sector to make the investments necessary to build a capacity for efficient and reliable export marketing.

Indonesian policymakers must deal with these major topics in their efforts to foster the development of a healthy corn system. A "corn policy" can be only a part of this effort, albeit an important part. Corn is woven into the whole fabric of the Indonesian food system. What happens to the corn system has major implications for human welfare, because of the importance of corn in the diets of the rural poor, for the growth of an efficient livestock industry and its potential to create income-earning opportunities for producers and processors, and for such variables of concern to macro policy as food price stability, especially for poultry and eggs, and foreign exchange earnings from non-oil exports.

While recognizing that the health of the entire corn system depends on more than policy initiatives that are specific to corn, what should a broader policy perspective try to accomplish? The goals can be framed in traditional food policy terms: efficient growth, improved income distribution through rapid creation of productive jobs, adequate food consumption for the poor, and food security for the country. The corn system has been a contributor to all of these since the early 1970s, and the potential is bright for a similar period in the future.

The critical issue is to determine the appropriate role for policy in coordinating the development of the corn system because policy dictates the environment in which participants make the decisions that lead to a dynamic and socially productive corn system. A perspective that takes in the entire corn system is the key. Each individual participant—the farmer, trader, feed mill operator, consumer, or government bureaucrat—tends to have a myopic view of what will improve the functioning of the system. Feed mills, for example, might want close government control of prices to stabilize costs of their raw materials, but if this stability comes at the expense of Indonesia's ability to participate in export markets, the short-run gains may be small relative to the long-run opportunities to expand exports. If the whole system can grow and develop in reasonable balance, all the food policy objectives can be served in the long run. The issue is how such growth can be stimulated.

Role of the Public Sector

What does it mean for the corn system to be "coordinated"? At one level, the system is coordinated when supply equals demand and when investments in the system generate profits equal to those from investments elsewhere in the economy. From this simple perspective, coordination of the corn system is performed almost entirely by competitive market forces, and the role of the public sector is to create a policy environment that maintains competitive pressures on all participants. Such a limited government role may prove inappropriate if private participants lack adequate knowledge about future production potential or consumption needs, if market forces are inadequate to link producers with consumers efficiently, or if the consequences of the market outcome for income distribution are unacceptable. A more active public role will then likely be contemplated, either through more vigorous policy initiatives on technology, pricing, and trade or through direct involvement by government agencies in the corn system.

Such active government efforts to stimulate and coordinate must deal with a corn system in which an awesome number of decisions must balance for the system to be perfectly coordinated. Each farmer must find a buyer for just the quantity desired to be sold. Each consumer must find a source of supply for the quantity to be purchased. Both quantities are subject to many intervening variables, of which the price of corn is only one. Corn produced must somehow be allocated among the entire array of competitive end uses so that both feed mills and food consumers are satisfied. Corn produced in East Java must find its way to Jakarta's feed mills. Corn produced in February must be available for consumption in June. Corn must be cracked for home consumption or ground and blended to make complete feeds for livestock.

Each of these decisions and processes involves generally short-run allocations of resources. But investments in the corn sector also need to be made. Seed companies, farmers, traders, feed mills, even government agencies that request agricultural research budgets or that build warehouses must plan for the future. To plan accurately, their anticipated needs or supplies must match those that are forthcoming. How can all the short-run and long-run decisions be matched and each participant's prior expectations be fulfilled?

The answer, of course, is that all commodity systems, including Indonesia's corn system, are much too complicated and dynamic for this matching and full coordination to be achieved. Many decisions turn out to be wrong, and consumers, producers, or traders may be disappointed—even bankrupted. The sources of failure involve unexpected weather, price movements, actions of competitors, or changes in government policies. Such failures, however, should not hide just how much coordination actually takes place, and the mechanisms that lead participants to adjust to these failures indicate how coordination is achieved. Most of the short-run coordination at the micro level is achieved through market links and price signals. Much of the *environment* for long-run coordination and integration of the corn system into the macro economy is provided by government policy and by the activities of specific agencies with day-to-day responsibilities in the corn system. Relatively little of the *actual coordination*, however, can be provided by these agencies.

Coordinating Role of Markets

The analysis of corn marketing in Chapter 8 explains how traders and market price formation connect producers with consumers. In such a large and heterogeneous country as Indonesia, spatial coordination is one of the most difficult tasks to achieve, and the private sector is quite efficient in linking areas of major surplus with areas of major deficit. Areas of smaller surplus tend not to be so efficiently linked to primary wholesale markets, and in these cases government coordination, especially through trading activities of the cooperatives, has played an important role.

Both consumers and producers seem to respond flexibly to corn prices signaled from local markets. Most of the flexibility is due to the relative ease of commodity substitutions in either production or end use. The multi-staple food system of Indonesia sharply lowers the welfare costs of adjusting to shortages or surpluses of any single commodity, and price movements can be relatively small and still accomplish significant shifts in resource allocations. At the ends of the adjustment process in both production and consumption, however, are households with few alternatives to corn. Chapter 3 notes how tightly constrained farmers are in several of the corn systems in Central Java. They have few opportunities to increase output in the face of favorable prices or new technology and few options to switch to more profitable crops if corn prices fall as a result of increased productivity elsewhere. Similarly, Chapter 5 emphasizes the role of corn in the diets of the very poor. They will benefit if corn prices gradually decline in relative terms. If corn prices should rise, cassava is an alternative source of cheap energy, but it provides little protein. Low-quality rice, of which there was an abundance in the surplus environment of the mid-1980s, may be the best alternative staple for these households.

Competitive markets and flexible adjustments by producers and consumers provide much of the coordination needed by the corn system in the short run, but several important aspects are not particularly well served by such coordination under present circumstances. Government agencies and policies are an element in this failure. At times government agencies complement market coordination when they provide public goods and services essential to long-run efficiency of markets, and sometimes they intervene in market coordination to foster different outcomes in terms of distribution from what the market would achieve. Some government activities improve the capacity of the private sector to carry out market coordination, especially when it facilitates development of mechanisms for long-term contracts between feed mills and corn traders or farmers, whereas others can be quite disruptive at times to the efficient functioning of markets.

Not all food policy objectives can be served by efficient market coordination—private traders competing so that price margins equal marketing costs. Many government interventions have goals not related to efficiency, especially those that affect income distribution, and these efforts and their spillover effects on market performance are noted in the following section. Good policy often seeks to minimize such spillovers in order to maximize the benefits from market coordination and then seeks to target carefully the distributional benefits.

Unlike market coordination of the multitude of small-scale participants in the corn system, government policy and program coordination require specific thought and individual action. Adam Smith's "invisible hand" of competition does not guide policymakers automatically toward actions that improve the functioning of the system. Since so many agencies have some small piece of the "policy pie," the concern for coordinating the government's impact on the corn system is entirely legitimate and even more apparent when the roles of individual agencies are considered in detail.

Government Agencies and Programs

The three main government agencies that directly affect the corn system are BULOG (along with the Department of Cooperatives), the Department of Trade, and the Department of Agriculture. Agencies with secondary, indirect impact include the foreign and domestic investment licensing boards, the Departments of Industries, Finance, and Public Works, the Central Bureau of Statistics, the National Planning Agency, Bank Indonesia and various other banks, universities, and research institutes.

Within BULOG's broad mandate to insure Indonesia's food security, the agency has two specific roles in the corn system: support of a floor price for farmers, with cooperatives as the local buying agents; and stabilization of corn prices for feed mills so that stable costs of production are maintained for poultry and eggs. Similar to the rice price stabilization program, where implementation of floor and ceiling prices is through separate programs connected by the rice supplies purchased to defend the floor price, the two aspects of BULOG's corn activities are connected by the price levels set and by the costs of storing corn. In the marketing analysis in Chapter 8, the importance of the width of the price band, the stability of price signals provided by BULOG, and the frequent recourse to corn imports to prevent large, seasonal increases in corn prices were emphasized.

The Department of Trade plays a key role in the corn system by issuing licenses to export or import corn (even for trade by BULOG). After BULOG has certified that corn supplies are in surplus relative to domestic needs, an export license can be granted to a trading firm for shipment of corn overseas. In East Java, where corn has been exported regularly during the main harvest, this licensing process is quite routine and is accessible to a wide array of trading companies. In other areas, especially South Sulawesi and North Sumatra, much tighter controls on who will be permitted to export seem to exist. When imports are needed, BULOG acts as the sole handling agent.

The Department of Trade and BULOG also regulate the imports of protein meals used as ingredients for livestock feed. In the feed industry the competitiveness of corn in feed rations depends to some extent on which protein meals are permitted entry. BULOG's control over importing and pricing of soybean meal has provided the main impetus to the feed mills' interest in other protein meals, such as rapeseed or sesame seed, and in the expanding role of the Department of Trade in regulating these commodities. This result points to an apparent failure of coordination, since the secondary protein meals are more costly and less efficient than soybean meal and little, if any, foreign exchange is thus being saved. The lack of coordination may be desirable, however, because the feed industry has not been able to locate suitable domestic substitutes for any of these imported protein meals. Freer entry of soybean meal would solve the problem.

The Department of Agriculture has primary responsibility for increasing corn production. The task is complicated, and coordination within the department itself is difficult. Research to increase corn yields involves varietal improvements as well as on-farm research to improve entire cropping systems. Work on new corn varieties must follow several paths: open-pollinated as well as hybrid, white as well as yellow, varieties of very-short duration for tightly constrained farming systems and longer-duration ones for maximum yields where longer rotations permit. Plant breeders often do not have a clear notion of constraints on the farming system. These constraints dictate the type of seed technology appropriate in the short run and point to opportunities for plant breeders to expand farmers' choices in the long run.

Coordination with the extension service could help plant breeders if extension agents could develop a sufficiently accurate picture of farmers' operations through extensive on-farm research. In return, somewhat better recommendations for cultivation practices might be developed, especially for such critical farmer decisions as fertilizer applications and intercropping versus side-by-side-monocultures. But the vast diversity of Indonesia's farming systems that include corn makes it likely that the role of extension agents will be limited. Most farmers will have to discover the most appropriate techniques, varieties, and input levels through individual experimentation.[3]

[3]CIMMYT work in East Java suggests a substantial payoff to well-designed on-farm research. In a letter to the author, Larry Harrington noted that "[m]uch of the relevant agronomic research agenda requires the training and expertise of scientists/researchers, at a level beyond that of extension workers (whose cooperation in the research is nonetheless needed). A well-focused on-farm research program built on a framework of reasonably large environmental domains could be *very* effective."

The Department of Agriculture also has nearly complete responsibility for licensing new corn varieties and arranging for their production and distribution. A small but dynamic private seed sector, led by Cargill and Pokphand, has the potential to develop and market highly productive hybrid seed corn, but a serious bottleneck has been production of the seed. Close cooperation between the public and private sectors will be essential for rapid development of this new technology. Present efforts at solving the land constraint for hybrid seed production are promising, although they point to the need for public-private cooperation.

The remaining institutions play roles that bear importantly, but usually less directly, on the corn system. The Department of Finance, for instance, takes the lead in determining the price of fertilizer because of the substantial subsidies needed at present prices. In conjunction with the Central Bank and, indeed, the entire Economic Cabinet, the department determines foreign exchange rate policy, which has an immediate influence on the profitability of corn exports. The Department of Public Works invests in roads, irrigation works, and port facilities, all of which affect the corn system. Even the knowledge base is important to the corn system; both the public and private sectors can make informed decisions only if an accurate picture of the corn system has been assembled, along with sound analytical insights into the forces that are continually changing it.

The Central Bureau of Statistics, the universities, and research institutes, some of which are in the important ministries themselves, play a behind-the-scenes but surprisingly important role because coordination of government policy requires data and analysis. At the moment, the appropriate role for public agencies in fostering coordination of the corn system is not clearly understood, nor are the analytical inputs themselves well synchronized. Mechanisms for more effective food policy analysis and coordination from a corn system perspective are needed but can be designed only with a more detailed understanding of the various policies that currently affect the performance and development of the corn system.

Corn Production Policy

Programs and policies that are specific for corn emanate from the three government agencies with direct responsibilities for developing the corn system: the Department of Agriculture, BULOG, and the Department of Trade. From a long-run perspective, the productivity base being developed by research, extension, and investments in the Department of Agriculture dictates the nature of policy concerns and initiative everywhere else. If corn were gradually declining in output as more profitable competing crops crowded it out of farming systems, the policy discussions of marketing, pricing, and trade would have an entirely different focus than they do now. In mid-1985 the productivity outlook for corn in Indonesia was quite bright. Among Indonesian corn system specialists, there is a pervasive sense that in the right policy environment corn production could grow 4 to 8 percent per year until the mid-1990s. The essential task is to determine the nature of the "right" policy environment for corn.

The Department of Agriculture has the most complicated task. For corn production to reach its potential, several efforts are essential: continued seed development; further research on agronomic practices with respect to fertilizer, lime applications, and disease control; better understanding through on-farm research of appropriate cultivation practices in intercropped systems; and development of an extension strategy that recognizes the vast heterogeneity of Indonesian farming systems. Each research effort needs its own first-class program, but coordination of research and extension programs is also essential. Such coordination has become more difficult with the dynamic presence of private seed companies, whose success in seed production depends on a new degree of public-private cooperation.

Seed Development

The present enthusiasm for hybrid seed should not overshadow the urgent need for continued development of high-yielding open-pollinated corn varieties. Since the agronomic and economic conditions in which corn is grown are so diverse, no hybrid seed company will find it profitable in the short or medium run to fill the niches that require special characteristics. Many farmers will find it difficult to replenish their seed every growing season, and open-pollinated varieties have an enormous advantage where marketing systems for inputs are not yet well developed. Production of open-pollinated seed is much simpler and does not require the large blocks of land needed for the development of inbred lines and the production of hybrid seeds. This is not a reason, of course, to discourage hybrid seeds. To the contrary, where they fit in the farming system, hybrid corn offers the producer an excellent rate of return on full investment costs, including seed, fertilizer, disease control, and labor for cultivation and harvesting. Efforts between Cargill and the Department of Agriculture to remove the bottleneck to production of the C-1 hybrid are crucial to widespread realization of this return. But while the hybrid is the answer for some farmers, many others are left in need of similar yield potential from open-pollinated varieties.

Several difficult problems face Indonesia's corn breeders. Although the production survey in Chapter 3 emphasizes that a variety's days to maturity (duration) is not so serious an issue as previously thought for several high-productivity corn systems in East Java and Sumatra, many lower-productivity systems are fairly tightly constrained. Little modern seed technology is available in corn varieties that require 75 to 90 days. Unfortunately, the prospects for development of high-yielding, short-duration varieties are not very promising on the basis of current research knowledge.

Similarly, relatively little research has been done on white varieties. Because most growth in demand has come from feed mills with a very strong preference for yellow corn, plant breeders around the world have concentrated most of their attention there. But important pockets of white corn production exist to supply consumers who prefer white corn as well as to supply a noodle industry that has exacting requirements for milling characteristics and color purity. A potential export market for white corn to East Africa and South Korea might also be developed if export traders could be ensured regular supplies. This trade would almost certainly require a uniform variety with significantly greater yield potential than is now available.

Small farmers view new seeds with understandable suspicion, especially when they are as expensive as the new hybrid seed. Since farmers responded very favorably to fertilizer subsidies, a natural suggestion would be to subsidize the hybrid seeds to encourage rapid adoption. If adoption rates were low and hybrid seeds in excess supply, such a subsidy policy might well make sense. In the mid-1980s, however, hybrid seed had to be rationed even at full-cost pricing; under such circumstances a subsidy would have no impact on adoption and would serve instead to transfer income to farmers who obtain access to the seeds. Although these farmers would certainly benefit from such an income transfer, the seed industry itself might suffer. Pricing and distribution decisions that must be made by bureaucracies rather than market forces are inevitably slow and sometimes counterproductive to the real goal of the policies, which is to speed the production and widespread use of hybrid corn seed.

Agronomic Research

Several important research questions remain with respect to agronomic practices. Most farmers experiment with alternative levels of fertilizer, but extension agents probably need better guidance in helping farmers who are less innovative. More important, little is known about the productivity of liming acid soils to improve corn yields, and lime is not always available in the outer islands for farmers to try their own experiments. Perry's (1984b) work on liming issues emphasizes how complex this research will be. The problem typically involves the interaction of acidity (pH level), aluminum toxicity, and micronutrient availability to the corn plant. Considerable differences among corn varieties seem to exist, with different tolerances to these conditions, and thus the liming research will need to be coordinated with the corn breeding effort.

Diseases and pests remain a serious problem for corn growers, particularly in intercropped systems where infestations build up on bean crops before spreading to corn. Downy mildew is no longer the threat to high-yielding corn varieties that it was in the mid-1970s. A dual strategy of breeding resistance into the seed and treating seeds with Ridomil before planting has built the potential to manage the disease. Neither element of the strategy is fully developed, however, because Ridomil is not widely sold in local markets, it is quite expensive where it is available and many farmers do not fully understand how to use it. The breeding strategy must incorporate much fuller resistance into a far wider range of varieties, and it will probably have to continue to find and incorporate new sources of resistance because the disease itself evolves new infectious potential against current varieties.

As new seeds, especially hybrids, become available to farmers to incorporate into current corn farming systems, traditional planting and cultivation techniques are likely to be less than optimal. Each farmer will no doubt experiment to find better ways of doing things, but government research efforts can speed this process along and avoid the necessity for each farmer to reinvent the wheel. The most difficult issue is whether higher-yielding corn varieties will produce more profits for farmers (not necessarily high corn yields) when grown as an intercrop with beans, rice, or cassava, or whether side-by-side stands of monoculture crops will permit more precise management of each crop's needs. Current evidence hints at a trend toward increased monoculture, and analysis of recent agricultural census data, in combination with field trials, could provide much better guidance to extension agents as they talk to farmers about this question.

Extension Strategy for Corn

Few extension agents are as knowledgeable about corn-growing practices as they are about rice cultivation. Rice is a much more important crop in Indonesia, and greater attention and funds have been devoted to spreading the word about good cultivation practices. Rice cultivation is also simpler in that a uniform set of practices holds over a wide geographic range of wet-rice culture. Moreover, only since the late 1970s have extension agents had much to extend to corn farmers. For all of these reasons, but especially because of the vast heterogeneity of corn systems even within a *kabupaten* and province, extension agents have a difficult time providing farmers with more than vague and general recommendations on corn cultivation techniques.

Within these constraints, extension agents have done a creditable job.

By helping farmers become aware of the wide range of potential techniques, they help in the experimentation process. With such diversity, only the individual farmer can decide which techniques best suit each field. The multitude of corn production techniques observed in Indonesia does not reflect the failure of extension agents to convince all farmers of the one "right" way to grow corn. Rather it reflects different profitable choices in different circumstances, and a package-type approach to corn intensification similar to the BIMAS rice intensification package is thus unlikely to be widely acceptable. Extension policy should focus instead on presenting an array of corn varieties, input choices, and cultivation practices so that the farmer can choose an appropriate technology.

Research and extension policy for corn builds the productivity base on which farmers make decisions about which crops to grow and how intensively to use inputs to grow them. These decisions depend on the balance between costs and returns, and this balance is determined at least as much by prices as by technology. The trends established in the past decade by the interaction of these two factors have been positive, but accelerating these positive trends will require careful attention to corn trade and price policies as well as to the research and extension programs.

Corn Trade and Price Policies

Indonesia's corn system has established a dynamic of its own, subject to government influence of course, but moving with considerable momentum as a result of basic forces influencing the private participants. Understanding where these underlying forces are steering the corn system is a precursor to any discussion of the nature of government interventions designed to speed its development and improve the distribution of benefits flowing from expanded corn production, consumption, and trade.

Several trends of the corn economy are well established. Corn production is growing in areas where new technology, cheap fertilizer, and active marketing agents combine to make it profitable relative to production of competing crops. The share of corn consumed at home from this growth in production has apparently been quite large and helps account for a paradox: rising corn consumption per capita, rising incomes per capita, and a sharply negative income elasticity. As corn production becomes a more purely commercial activity, especially in those areas where the new corn technology has its greatest comparative advantage, the share of home consumption from increased own production is likely to drop quickly. Consequently, the volume of marketings from a given increase in production will be higher than in the 1970s, and the marketing system must provide efficient routes to alternative end uses—either the domestic livestock feed industry or exports.

The domestic feed industry is growing rapidly but from a very small base. The slowdown in economic growth has moderated the rapid growth in demand for livestock products and has increased competition for both the feed mills and livestock producers, especially egg and poultry producers. This sector will continue to grow, but the analysis in Chapter 6 suggests that the booming rates of the 1970s will not continue in the future. In combination, the underlying trend for domestic consumption of corn is likely to be slower growth than in the past, while the potential exists for corn production to grow even more rapidly than in the 1970s.

If both these trends continue, a third trend of the 1970s, rising imports of corn, will be reversed. Preliminary indications of an emerging export potential were seen in 1984, and this trend must continue for the Indonesian corn system to reach its full potential. Continued exports depend not only on Indonesia's supplies but also on conditions in the world market for corn. This market is reasonably well integrated in terms of price formations, as Mink's (1984c) analysis of world price formation indicates, but Indonesia's prospects for corn exports will depend not only on the overall world market, which the United States dominates, but also on the "local" Asian, Middle Eastern, and East African markets, in which Indonesia has some advantages in transport, handling, and quality.

Trade and price policy are implemented by BULOG and the Department of Trade. The efficacy and impact of this policy depend directly on how well corn markets are working. In particular, if private traders actively coordinate corn supplies over space and time, BULOG needs to handle little corn physically and can instead just monitor the need for imports or exports to maintain prices within the policy-determined band. Consequently, implementing price policy requires even more understanding of and coordination with the private sector than is required for production efforts.

Marketing Margins and Price Formation

The private sector must make a reasonable profit on its corn trading activities or it will leave the tasks to government. Profitability depends on two key factors,—the gross price margin between locations or points in time, for example, and the total costs of transporting or storing corn. The analysis of corn marketing in Chapter 8 shows that when substantial volumes are involved, the private sector is quite efficient in short-run spatial arbitrage—at transporting corn from surplus areas to wholesale markets.

This generalization is subject to two caveats. Where local markets traditionally demand white corn but yellow corn is marketed by newly commercial farmers who use higher-yielding varieties, traders have often required substantial profit premiums, which are created by heavily discounting the price of yellow corn, to undertake the risks of purchase.

Since the risks are real and unit costs are high until larger marketed volumes are available, a vicious circle develops in such circumstances. Farmers in such areas will not grow more yellow corn for the market because the price is so low, but traders will not offer higher prices until the marketed volumes are large enough to produce multiple truckload lots and hence induce competition among traders.

The government's policy response has been to institute a floor price for corn which is implemented through purchases by the cooperatives on behalf of the local DOLOG (regional BULOG) office. The formal floor price is for yellow corn, although an informal floor price for white corn is implemented in South Sulawesi, where the cooperatives pay Rp 10 per kilogram less than for yellow corn. Neither floor price has been high enough to generate substantial purchases; market prices have been higher for corn that meets the fairly stringent quality standards enforced by the DOLOGs.

Because marketing costs of DOLOG and cooperatives are no lower than those of the private trade, and usually are higher, a subsidy is needed to run the floor price operation where it is needed. As a temporary measure to build market volumes to a size sufficient to attract a competitive private sector, such subsidies are a good investment. If a long-run flow of funds is used to cover inefficient operating procedures and to prevent the development of private trading activities, however, the subsidies are likely to inhibit the growth of a commercial corn sector in new areas with high potential.

These relatively isolated market failures are likely to be transitory because of two factors: the sensible restraint on the volume of subsidies to be committed in the long run to trading activities of cooperatives; and the continued rapid increases in the productivity potential of yellow corn varieties. Commodity trading is an intensely competitive activity in Indonesia, especially when government policy helps remove barriers to entry and creates equal access to credit and licenses for both new and established trading firms. Corn storage activities, however, are not very satisfactory, and the efficiency of seasonal price formation is in serious doubt.

Seasonal price movements for corn in rural markets on Java are quite substantial, and historically prices have risen more than 50 percent on average over a seven-month period. Chapter 8, which devotes considerable attention to this problem, traces it to several causes. Much corn has traditionally been consumed within a month or so of harvest, so the months of high prices reflect very low volumes. In addition, storage losses remain very high due to high moisture content, fungal infections, and pest infestations, and the capacity to store corn for extended periods has thus been limited. Perhaps most important, few investments have been made to improve drying and storage facilities because wholesalers and feed mills have had little incentive to make these investments.

The lack of such investments is a direct reflection of government price and stock release policy. A year-round stable price from BULOG for corn supplies to feed mills certainly helps keep feed prices, and hence poultry and egg prices, stable. But some uncertainty for feed mills on how much corn will be available at the official price, plus the stable price itself, have created an unintended effect, which is to raise the risks to wholesale traders and feed mill operators of investing in substantial drying and storage facilities. The economic return to be expected from such facilities depends on the seasonal price margin and the volumes to be stored, and these are directly determined by BULOG's price and stock policy. At the moment, these policies have almost totally discouraged private investments that would lead to lower losses and storage costs.

The answer to this problem will depend largely on how domestic corn prices are structured relative to world prices. Chapter 8 makes clear that, without government intervention, very high storage costs mean that Indonesia is likely to be both an exporter during harvest months and an importer during shortage months. Such a pattern would be "efficient" in the context of high storage costs, but the more effective government intervention is continuation of the joint BULOG-TDRI (Tropical Development Research Institute) research on lowering storage losses as well as efforts to design a price policy that rewards investments in storage.

These two topics are related. If market prices do not provide premiums for corn in condition to store well, farmers and traders have no incentives to incur any costs in the critical two weeks after harvest when proper drying and handling can most easily prevent aflatoxin and pest contamination. The storage research project has been trying to develop small-scale drying techniques and a powder pesticide usable by farmers and small traders. So far, however, quality differentials in wholesale markets have not been adequate to justify these expenses. It will be a difficult task to introduce these quality standards into cooperative and DOLOG purchases, not to mention into purchases by the private trade, without seriously jeopardizing the farm-level price of corn. At least for corn destined for export, much more rapid bulking into modern drying and storage facilities may be necessary, with some of these facilities needed "upcountry" and some needed at the ports.

Competitiveness in the Corn Export Trade

The potential, even the desirability, for intra-year exports and imports of corn raises the issue of costs and efficiency of such international trade. At the moment, official port and ocean freight charges are extremely high by international standards, which thus puts Indonesian farmers at a serious competitive disadvantage during harvest months and puts domestic feed mills at a disadvantage when importing. Licensing procedures for exports do not improve the efficiency of such activities because the delays and uncertainties are transmitted back to lower farm prices. Analysis of Thailand's corn marketing system and export trade confirms that its price formation has been more efficient, with improved incentives to farmers, since licensing restrictions were lifted (see Chutikamoltham 1985). Requirements that markets on Java be supplied before exports are permitted from Sumatra or Sulawesi likewise reduce incentives to increase corn output on the outer islands. A free-trade zone for corn for Sulawesi would permit much more efficient competition with Thailand, which now operates an entirely free-trade corn export business.

Thailand is a formidable competitor in regional markets. Thailand and Indonesia rise and fall on the same world tide generated mainly by United States corn export prices, but the two Asian corn exporters compete head on for local market niches and the extra profits that go with them. Fortunately, the seasonal availability of Thai corn complements that of Indonesian corn, as the seasonal price indexes illustrated in Figure 10.1 show strikingly. Low prices for corn in rural markets on Java occur from February to May, whereas low prices in rural (local) wholesale markets in Thailand occur from August to November. Both countries could become more reliable year-round suppliers and reduce storage costs if ways could

FIGURE 10.1. *Seasonal price index, 1972–1983*

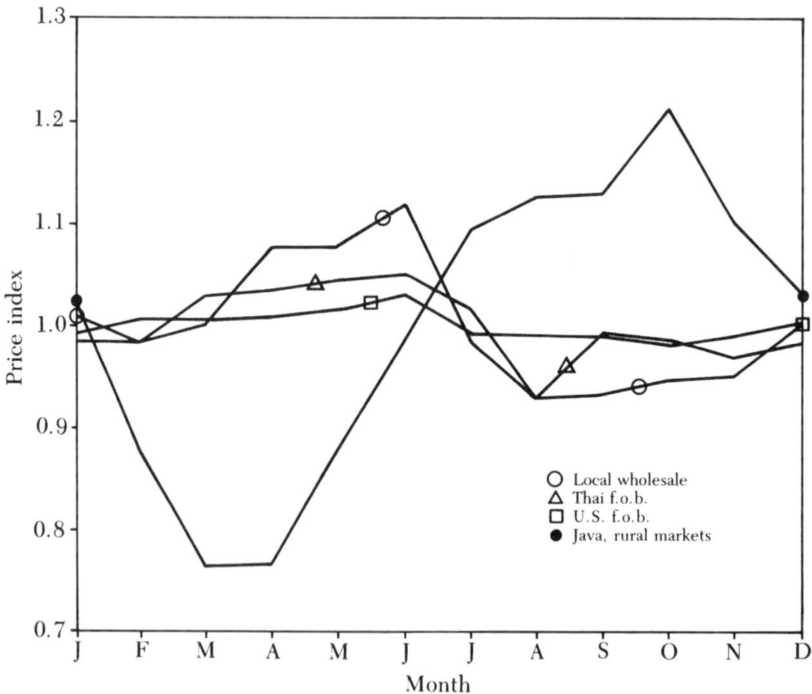

be found to cooperate in sharing export markets. Since Bangkok is no farther from Jakarta than is Menado in North Sulawesi, importing Thai corn is little different from shipping corn between provinces when viewed from a regional perspective. In the future, as Thailand uses more of its corn for domestic livestock feeding, reverse flows may eventually make sense as well.

Improving Indonesia's capacity to compete regularly with Thailand requires much lower port handling costs and shorter delays in scheduling and loading ships. The actions taken in April 1985 to expedite port procedures are certainly a positive step. In addition, competitive ocean freight rates from major and minor Indonesian ports are urgently needed to assist all non-oil exports, but corn will benefit as well. Clear signals to export trading companies that policy is pointed at making Indonesia a high-quality and reliable exporter of corn will encourage the necessary private investments in trucks, dryers, silos, and handling equipment. These signals are to a large extent the responsibility of the three agencies with direct input into commodity policy—BULOG and the Departments of Agriculture and Trade. These agencies might also find it necessary to provide guarantees or participate jointly with private firms in the development of modern commodity handling facilities at the major ports exporting corn.

Domestic and World Prices for Corn

The price of Indonesia's corn exports will depend primarily on the level of corn prices f.o.b. at United States ports. There is little reason to expect an upward trend in these prices in real terms from average levels in the early 1980s. Bad weather in the Corn Belt, sudden policy shifts in the United States such as the Payment-in-Kind program, or a sudden fall in the value of the dollar could put temporary upward pressure on world corn prices. Trends for the 1980s, however, are likely to reflect continued productivity growth on U.S. corn farms, slower growth in import demand from middle-income and Eastern European countries—the main sources of growth in demand for corn in the 1970s—and a relatively strong dollar, all of which point to continued low prices for corn in world markets. For Indonesia this means meeting a price of around $120 per ton f.o.b. Surabaya if exports are to be competitive on a regular basis through the mid-1990s.

World market prices for corn are considerably more stable than those for wheat or rice, primarily because corn sold in international trade is consumed mostly by livestock, for which elasticity of demand for a particular feedstuff is quite large. Especially when world stocks of wheat are burdensome, as they were in the mid-1980s, considerable stability is imparted to world corn and wheat markets via the feeding of wheat to livestock.

Such stability does not, of course, translate into stability in production and trade within Indonesia. Since much of Indonesia's corn production comes from rain-fed systems, weather variability is a significant factor in the domestic balance between supply and demand. More than 4 million tons of corn are produced, almost all of which is consumed domestically; thus small shifts in output due to good or bad weather can alter the balance from exports to imports, or vice versa, if domestic prices are determined by world prices. Because corn is a crop of low value relative to transportation costs, however, the shift from f.o.b. to c.i.f. price basis can be significant. A difference of $30 to $40 per ton can be expected, which means at least a 25 percent increase in domestic prices if bad weather causes Indonesia to switch from corn exporter to corn importer. The potential instability in domestic corn prices, which would be generated by weather variability and relatively free trade in corn, raises the obvious issue of appropriate price policy for corn. The issue has a seasonal component in addition to the structure of average domestic prices for corn relative to world prices. For the purposes of the following discussion, the level of the foreign exchange rate is assumed to be at an equilibrium value.

Alternative Price Policies

Any government's commodity policy is defined initially by its price policy, even if that policy is no policy. Price policy is defined relative to border prices: the issue is primarily the relationship of the domestic price to the border price *on average,* and, secondarily, the *stability* of the domestic price, both seasonally and year to year. Because world prices fluctuate, designing and implementing a relatively stable domestic price that still bears a reasonable long-run relationship to border prices are complicated analytical and managerial tasks.

Three basic price policy options are available: protection, discrimination, or free trade. It is possible to design price interventions that will produce these results consistently no matter what the world market does. An ad valorem import tax (or export subsidy) keeps domestic prices a given percentage above world prices, and thus corn farmers are protected. Similarly, an ad valorem import subsidy (or export tax) depresses domestic prices a certain percentage below world prices but follows world prices up and down; thus corn farmers are discriminated against at all times relative to world corn prices. Under a free-trade regime, domestic corn prices are set simply by the f.o.b. value when exporting and by the c.i.f. value when importing. Price formation is determined by local supply and demand factors if prices are within the f.o.b. to c.i.f. band determined by world prices.

Such simple price policies are usually implemented only for revenue purposes and not for developing commodity systems in the long run. When such broader objectives are incorporated into the design of price policy, the issues become much more complicated. Indonesia has had two important objectives for corn price policy: "reasonable" price stability (seasonal) throughout the year to protect feed mills, livestock producers, and poultry and egg consumers from highly variable costs; and stable and remunerative price incentives to corn farmers to stimulate greater output and higher incomes. An implicit constraint that determines the options available for implementing these conflicting objectives is that budget subsidies, on average, cannot be very large.

With these broader objectives and constraints understood, the three potential price policy options for corn can be discussed more concretely. Each has substantial merit individually, but also important trade-offs. Providing long-run price protection to corn consumers subsidizes the food intake of some of Indonesia's poorest population groups—those who consume substantial quantities of corn directly. Subsidizing corn as an input to the livestock industry provides indirect subsidies to much richer consumers, those who regularly buy poultry and eggs. Cheap corn speeds the growth of the livestock economy and has a beneficial impact on generation of employment and income of livestock producers. This price policy calls for maintaining corn prices below c.i.f. prices through regular import subsidies, and two obvious problems arise: continuing budget subsidies are required to implement such a price policy; and the lower prices are reflected in local markets for producers as well as consumers and thus significantly depress incentives to use modern inputs and increase output. Rural incomes almost certainly are reduced as a *net* effect, despite the positive impact on livestock producers.

The reverse policy is to maintain domestic corn prices well above world prices in order to protect corn farmers, stimulate production, and generate higher rural incomes. By limiting (or taxing) imports, or subsidizing exports if necessary, a wedge can be driven between local corn prices and world prices. The disadvantages of such a policy are its negative impact on low-income consumers, who still depend on corn for a significant share of their caloric intake, and the slowed momentum likely to be felt in the livestock sector. If Indonesia were a substantial importer of corn, this price policy would be attractive despite its impact on the poor because it would slow the growth in foreign exchange needed to import corn and would provide broadly based income subsidies in rural areas. Given the substantial overlap between corn producers and corn consumers, many poor consumers hurt by the higher price would be directly compensated as producers.

The problem with protecting corn producers is that limiting imports through direct controls or a revenue-generating tax will not work. Even at world prices that prevailed in the mid-1980s, Indonesia has the potential to be a corn exporter, and higher domestic prices would provide additional output incentives to producers and restrict consumption. Larger export supplies would thus be generated. To keep domestic prices high, these exports would have to be subsidized, and much of the economic rationale for developing an export potential is thus removed. It hardly makes sense to invest in an export industry that requires continuing subsidies on average.

For a potentially competitive sector such as corn, price policy attention turns rather naturally to the implications of determining domestic prices by world prices on average and to the attempt to maintain seasonal and year-to-year stability in price signals to producers and consumers. Domestic prices are then maintained by competitive trade forces within a band between the f.o.b. level for exports and the c.i.f. level for imports. With current transportation and handling costs to likely markets, the band is about $30 to $40 per ton. But this band could narrow if port costs were lowered and Indonesia's corn exports did not incur significant price discounts because of poor quality and the difficulties of finding new buyers on an irregular basis.

Without government intervention, the band between f.o.b. and c.i.f. levels would move up and down with world prices and thus transmit fluctuations in the border price directly into domestic markets—unless prices were determined by local supply and demand forces above the f.o.b. floor and below the c.i.f. ceiling. To reduce price risk for both producers and consumers, it may be desirable to stabilize domestic prices for a year or two at a time by announcing the f.o.b.-c.i.f. price band to be defended by government trade intervention. If the band floats year by year with world prices, no long-run subsidies are required, but domestic decision makers have the benefit of an annual planning horizon with a stable price band. This has roughly been the policy since the early 1980s, although recent emphasis has been on ensuring that no subsidies are needed for any floor price interventions.

The main issue is the width between the f.o.b. export price, which should be effective in local markets during the main harvest months of February to May, and the c.i.f. import price, which should be in force during the months of August to November when corn is in short supply. It must be determined whether a price rise from $30 to $40 from the harvest to the preharvest period is adequate to induce domestic storage and, likewise, whether exports are generated during the harvest and are then replaced by imports (from other provinces or Thailand) six to eight months later. A narrow seasonal price rise implies substantial trade at both ends of the price band—both exports and imports. A wide seasonal price rise induces more local storage but at the expense of seasonal price stability.

The marketing analysis in Chapter 8 shows that the seasonal price rise needed to induce adequate storage so that no imports are required depends directly on the monthly cost of storage. With storage costs of 3 percent per month, a seasonal price rise of 25 percent is adequate to induce the local storage needed to supply domestic requirements, but storage costs of 5 percent per month mean that costs would hit the seasonal price ceiling after only five months. Local supplies would be exhausted, and imports would then be used to cover requirements for the remaining two or three months before the next harvest.

Under current costs of corn storage and an expected f.o.b. export price that provides a domestic floor of $120 per ton, a $30 to $40 rise above the f.o.b. price to a c.i.f. price is probably inadequate to induce enough local storage to forestall imports late in the season. High storage losses and high costs of working capital from informal rural credit markets are equally the problem. If storage losses of 2 to 3 percent per month could be reduced to 1 percent through better drying and handling techniques and if effective interest rates could be reduced from the range of 3 to 4 percent to a range of 1.5 to 2 percent per month, price policy could probably be designed to eliminate seasonal imports in normal production years. Both tasks—lowering storage losses and integrating corn traders and feed mill operators into formal credit markets—should receive high priority in any set of policies aimed at improving the functioning of the corn system.

Agricultural Policies and the Corn System

Several sectoral policies and programs, designed for their impact outside the corn system, have important spillover effects on decision makers inside that system. This is as it should be. Irrigation facilities, fertilizer subsidies, and rice price policy are usually designed and implemented in terms of their impact on the rice economy. But where the spillover effects are significant, as they are in the examples just listed, those responsible for designing these policies should be aware of their impact on the corn system. Government agencies responsible for coordinating policies for corn must also know about these spillover effects because commodity policy pointed in one direction can easily be swamped by sectoral policy headed the other direction.

Fertilizer Subsidy Policy

The sectoral policy with the greatest potential to change fundamental relationships in the corn system is the fertilizer subsidy. Chapter 4 estimates that 10 to 15 percent of Indonesia's applications of fertilizer on food crops are for corn. No firm econometric estimates of the elasticity of farmer demand for fertilizer use on corn are available, but comparative estimates from other countries and from reasonably well-documented responsiveness of rice farmers in Indonesia suggest a range of −0.7 to −1.0 is plausible. This range and Mink's estimates in Chapter 4 of marginal physical product of corn from fertilizer application permit the loss in corn production, from a change in the fertilizer subsidy, to be calculated.

The fertilizer subsidy was quite large in 1985—over one-half billion dollars annually, even after the increase in the fertilizer price from Rp 90 to Rp 100 per kilogram in November 1984. If domestic marketing costs and the f.o.b. value of urea at domestic fertilizer factories are included, that price to farmers represented only about half the social opportunity cost of the fertilizer. The collapse in the world market price for rice and Indonesia's rice surplus of the 1980s (partly the cause of the low world price) mean that the social profitability of the fertilizer subsidy was negative at the margin. Continued budget pressures reinforce the economic analysis and suggest that fertilizer prices are likely to rise in real terms in the late 1980s, especially in relation to farm prices for rice and corn.

Rough calculations using reasonably conservative values for the key parameters—a fertilizer demand elasticity of −0.7 and a marginal output response of 2.5 kilograms of corn for each kilogram of urea use—indicate that each 10 percent increase in the relative price of fertilizer to corn will reduce corn production by about 70,000 metric tons from what it would have been otherwise. The potential export levels based on rapid growth in corn production are sensitive to significant efforts to reduce the fertilizer subsidy. A 50 percent increase in the real price for fertilizer would eliminate all but the internal marketing subsidies, for example, but would also eliminate 350,000 tons of corn production, or almost exactly the average export level expected in 1988–1989. Such a large price increase is not likely in the late 1980s, but an increase of 25 percent in real fertilizer prices was announced early in 1986 on the basis of the rice situation and the need to conserve budget resources (see Timmer 1986). With such fertilizer price increases and no compensation through higher corn prices, corn production might be 100,000 to 150,000 tons less than otherwise anticipated by the end of the 1980s.

Other sectoral policies might work in the opposite direction and offset some of the negative impact on corn caused by a reduction in the fertilizer subsidy. A major effort to improve soybean productivity by applying lime to acid soils on the outer islands could have a significant positive spillover for corn production. Although the marginal productivity of lime applications is uncertain, widespread availability of lime at very cheap prices (possibly even free) is likely to stimulate corn production whether corn is intercropped with soybeans or grown as a monoculture in rotation with soybeans. Farmers are likely to use some of the lime directly for corn production, despite the program's intent to target its use for soybeans.

Irrigation Policy

The development of irrigation facilities, especially on Java, has altered the profitability of corn production in surprising ways. The most direct and expected effect is seen where extension of controlled irrigation into traditional rain-fed lands has displaced corn in favor of the much more profitable multiple-cropped rice. Somewhat less expected has been the experience with local ground water irrigation, some of which was initially intended to counteract moisture stress in corn during the critical tasseling and grain formation stages of development. This availability of limited water in the dry season has instead often stimulated farmers to produce higher-value vegetable crops instead of corn. For these two reasons, irrigation has had some negative effects on expansion of corn production. This effect of irrigation on corn production is not uniform, however. Systems with technical irrigation are often "shut down" for a season so that channels can be maintained and continuous rice cultivation can be interrupted to control pests and diseases. If farmers know such plans in advance, they can take advantage of the nearly ideal conditions for high-yielding corn production; such fields are seen in East Java.

Perhaps an even more important effect of irrigation development on corn has come in combination with the shorter-duration rice varieties. In traditional rice-corn-corn or rice-rice-corn rotations, long-duration rice forced farmers to choose corn varieties of very short-duration, but none of these produced high yields. With the availability of short-duration rice varieties, however, some of the time pressure has been removed from the corn crop rotations. Many farmers find that varieties of 90 to 105 days fit their rotations comfortably, and several high-yielding varieties, including the Cargill hybrid C-1, fit this pattern.

Credit and Rural Infrastructure

The demise of the formal intensification program for rice (BIMAS) removed a major source of rural credit for farmers. Since credit is fungible and not all BIMAS credit was directly spent on inputs to grow rice, the loss of this program probably has had some negative impact on corn producers. Especially for farmers who use the hybrid seed, Ridomil treatment, and recommended fertilizer applications, the need for credit early in the planting season are substantial. The new rural credit program (KUPEDES) is not restricted to farmers or even targeted at former BIMAS participants, but its rapid expansion is likely to ease credit problems for the more intensive corn producers. More important, access of rural traders to the new program loans should stimulate healthy competition in the commodity marketing system, and traders are likely to offer farmers input credits to finance the crop.

The important role of rural infrastructure has been noted throughout this volume. The corn system receives no special priority for access to the roads, port facilities, rural electrical grid, or telephones which make transportation and communication cheaper and more efficient. But the state of these infrastructure investments significantly affects the profitability of producing for export a crop of relatively low value such as corn. Higher-value export crops, such as coffee, rubber, or spices, can survive high marketing costs and slow communications between markets. But corn must move on narrow margins and compete in a rapidly changing international market. The capacity for exporting Indonesia's corn depends on how rapidly these marketing costs can be brought down to levels that are internationally competitive.

Policy for the Livestock Sector

The stimulus to the corn system since the mid-1970s has come not from the commodity system itself but from its link to the dynamic feed-livestock sector. The poultry industry in particular has directly provided regular demand for yellow corn in several parts of the country, and the marketing sector has connected the booming Jakarta feed industry with the leading areas producing corn surpluses. As the analysis of the livestock feed sector in Chapter 6 emphasizes, continued growth of the poultry industry is expected to provide the major source of expansion in domestic demand for corn.

Government policy influences the poultry sector in important and controversial ways and has significant consequences for corn demand. The most pervasive effect has come from the government's attempt to reserve poultry production for small farmers by enforcing a limit on operations of 5,000 layers or 750 broilers per week. Evidence from other countries as well as Indonesia strongly suggests that significant economies of scale in poultry operations exist well beyond these limits—up to and probably beyond 50,000 birds.

These economies derive from three factors: greater technical efficiency of larger operations, especially through better disease control; lower input costs because of quantity discounts for feed, pharmaceuticals, and day-old chicks; and economies of scale for individual managers, who can easily handle operations of 50,000 to 100,000 birds. Compared with small operations, each of these competitive advantages to larger operations is real in the sense that fewer of society's scarce economic resources are required to produce a unit of output. Whether the consequences for income distribution are sufficiently better with the limit on size to warrant the higher costs is a legitimate social and political question, but the debate should recognize the trade-offs involved. It costs more to produce eggs and broilers in such small production units—perhaps 20 percent more according to calculations in Chapter 6.

The implications for the corn system are quite convoluted. Small-scale poultry producers use *more* corn per unit of output because of lower efficiencies of conversion (converting grain to eggs and meat). Small producers tend to use more "full-formula" feed from mills rather than mixing their own corn with mill-supplied supplements. But the correspondingly higher costs of production also translate into higher consumer prices. These prices reduce demand for poultry products and thus slow the expansion of the industry and slow the growth in demand for corn. If corn production is growing rapidly under the stimulus of new technology and export demand, the only adjustment required is a change from domestic to export market. But if the livestock feed industry provides direct stimulus to corn production, as it has since the mid-1970s, an evolving small-scale and high-cost poultry industry would also put a damper on the rapid growth in corn production.

Two additional policies for the livestock sector have implications for growth in demand for corn. The emphasis on price stability for eggs and broilers translates into a need for BULOG to stabilize the costs of primary ingredients for livestock feed. One implication of this stabilizing function has been an active government role in corn trade and pricing. The issues associated with this role have already been noted.

A second implication of price stabilization for inputs into livestock feed—BULOG's role in handling and pricing imported soymeal, the preferred protein supplement for most feed rations—also has ramifications for corn. Present policy limits the supplies and sets prices for soymeal, to domestic feed mills, well above world prices. The direct result is to raise the costs of feed and hence to slow the growth of the livestock industry. But the indirect result may well be more important for the corn system. High costs and uncertain availability of protein meal push optimal feed mixes to include more corn and less dried cassava (*gaplek*) than otherwise.

When corn was imported and dried cassava exported, such an effect was clearly undesirable since Indonesia received an f.o.b. price for dried cassava but paid a c.i.f. price for its corn, and thus more transportation costs were incurred than necessary. When both corn and dried cassava are exported, this consideration disappears. But should the European Community ever reduce imports of Indonesia's dried cassava, improving the technical capacity and profitability of including dried cassava in domestic feed rations will be important. Pricing of soymeal will be a key factor in this improvement in dried cassava's utilization potential. The impact on corn, of course, will be to free larger volumes for export at the expense of direct use in the domestic feed industry. This potential need to export corn again emphasizes the importance of developing efficient export channels as rapidly as possible.

Price Policy for Other Commodities

The last major sectoral influence on the corn system is perhaps in the long run the most powerful of all. Price policy for other commodities in Indonesia's food system conditions both the consumption and production of corn. Rice price policy is probably the most important simply because of the dominance of rice in food consumption and farming systems, but price policies for wheat and sugar can also have a major impact on the evolution of the corn system in the long run. In farming systems on rain-fed land, it is upland rice, rather than paddy rice, that directly competes with corn. Reduced area for upland rice has only limited impact on total rice production since upland rice provides less than 5 percent of Indonesia's production. But the impact on corn can be significant, since as much as one-third of corn production potentially competes with upland rice. Especially where *padi gogo rancah* is feasible, the corn-rice substitution in production is quite direct.

The competition on the consumption side is even more direct. Many corn consumers mix rice and corn (*beras jagung*) in proportions that vary with relative rice-to-corn prices. Monteverde (1987) estimated the cross-price elasticity of demand for corn with respect to rice prices to be about unity, which indicates substantial flexibility in consumption choices between the two commodities. Because of the large volumes of rice in storage in the mid-1980s, much low-quality rice was available in markets at prices that were increasingly competitive with market prices for cracked corn, and this cheap rice increased the potential substitutability with corn. Given the preference of most consumers for rice, downward pressure on rice prices, especially for qualities accessible to the very poor, will hasten the reduction in per capita consumption of corn that is already driven by the negative income elasticity. Lower prices for rice relative to corn will mean somewhat greater corn production, somewhat less corn consumption, and larger export supplies than otherwise projected.

Sugar prices have a less microeconomic connection to the corn system. Some production substitution between corn and sugar grown on rain-fed land appears to take place in East Java, but its impact is limited. More important, price policy for sugar makes a high-fructose corn sweetener plant attractive to private investors, although Chapter 7 shows that such an investment would not be socially profitable because of the low costs of sugar from world markets. The volume of corn used by such a plant is significant—about the potential level of corn exports in 1988–1989. Although the by-products from the plant would find a ready market in

Indonesia and would substitute for a small share of soymeal imports, a fructose sweetener plant would absorb much of the export surplus of corn projected for the late 1980s.

Wheat prices have no effect on corn production and only minor effects on direct corn consumption by humans since most wheat products are consumed in urban areas and most corn is consumed in rural areas. Wheat pollards, a milling by-product, however, do compete with corn in livestock feeds. Wheat prices thus have a double impact. Lower prices for wheat flour increase consumption and hence supplies of pollards to the livestock feed industry. Under competitive pricing arrangements, such lower prices for flour would come through lower prices for wheat grain, and so the price of pollards would be expected to fall as well and thus reinforce the quantity effect. In the Indonesian setting, however, domestic flour prices are set largely independent of imported wheat prices, and the net effect of changes in wheat flour prices is not at all clear. Since a share of the pollards is exported, the domestic price may well be mainly a function of world prices for livestock feeds, including corn. If domestic corn prices follow world prices, corn will probably remain competitive with pollards for livestock feed.

Indonesia's agricultural policies cannot be dictated by concerns for the development of the corn system, but neither should those concerns be ignored. The inevitable problem is one of balance and the need to judge total costs relative to total benefits rather than simply to calculate costs and benefits for the corn system alone. The problem needs to be addressed in an even larger context because macro policies also have a major impact on the agricultural sector and on the corn system. Just as commodity policies require coordination and integration with sectoral policies, so must these policies be consistent with macro policies.

Macro Policy and the Corn System

The speed of economic development and the distribution of its benefits are determined largely by macroeconomic policy. Within the context of a healthy economy, commodity systems can still fare badly, but few commodity systems are important enough for their performance, good or bad, to have significant consequences for the macro economy. The exceptions, however, indicate the nature of the links between commodity systems and the rest of the economy. In Indonesia the rice economy has powerful two-way connections to the rest of the economy. It is the largest employer, and rice is the greatest single item of expenditure in the average household budget. Changes in production, prices, and consumption of rice have macroeconomic consequences.

At the sectoral level, these consequences are even sharper since rice is the most important individual commodity in Indonesia's multi-commodity food and agricultural system. Corn is by no means trivial in this system. About 10 million farm households grow corn. Roughly 10 percent of average caloric intake comes from corn, and among the rural poor the figure rises to nearly 30 percent. The potential earnings of foreign exchange from corn could move it into the top ten non-oil export commodities. By the same token, it is important to keep the corn system in proper perspective. Its successful development will be a small but helpful contributor to overall development, but this success will depend critically *on* that overall development.

The primary issue is how the corn system is affected by Indonesia's macroeconomic policy. To say "what's good for corn is good for Indonesia" would be an exaggeration, but a macro policy that fosters the efficient growth of the food economy is also likely to be conducive to rapid growth in the rest of the economy. From this broader food policy perspective, identifying the components of a macro policy that helps the food system, and the corn system within that food system, will pay additional dividends in terms of the impact of the same macro policy on the productivity of the nonagricultural economy.

Three major aspects of macro policy condition the prospects for growth of the food economy and the corn system specifically: budget allocations; monetary and fiscal policy as it affects inflation; and efforts to influence macro prices. The commodity-specific aspects of trade policy have already been discussed, but the broader aspects of trade strategy raise further issues for the corn system.

The corn system makes numerous meritorious claims on the national budget. Subsidies for fertilizer, research funds for corn breeders, and investment allocations to modernize port facilities must compete with more schools, defense, and steel mills. The allocation process is inherently political, but well-documented analyses demonstrating the social profitability of a particular budget allocation can certainly influence that process. Being on the agenda counts. One of the main purposes of this study is to determine if corn should be on the national agenda of budget priorities. It should. No blank checks are requested or deserved, but it is clear that the potential gains in productivity in the corn system from a combination of good policy and well-designed investments will have high social payoff. The investments will be specific to commodity or sector and have been identified in earlier sections. Their legitimate claim on a share of the national budget is emphasized here.

Fiscal and monetary policy influences the corn system indirectly through its impact on the real exchange rate and directly through its effect on the rate and distribution of economic growth. Rising personal incomes influence corn demand in two counteracting ways. If the incomes of the rural poor increase, their demand for direct consumption of corn falls, which reflects the strong negative income elasticity. If the incomes of the top one-quarter of the income distribution—mostly urban residents—rise, demand for livestock products increases rapidly. Despite the small base, the income elasticity of 1.0 to 1.5 for these products drives a significant increase in demand for corn for livestock feed.

At least until the mid-1990s, direct demand for corn to be consumed by humans will be larger than indirect demand for livestock feed, and *equally distributed* growth in income will lead to a *reduction* in domestic demand for corn. Historical patterns suggest, however, that urban incomes will grow much more rapidly than the incomes of the rural poor, and without major changes in the structure of Indonesia's development, continued *increases* in domestic corn consumption due to economic growth are likely.

This structure of development is significantly influenced by a government's attempts to influence macro prices—wage rates, interest rates, and foreign exchange rates—and by basic trade and commodity pricing policy, especially for rural products and energy. The corn system has a heavy stake in these policies, for they influence the distribution of incomes, and hence growth in demand for corn from a given percentage of growth in aggregate income, and the structure of incentives to produce corn, and hence the rate at which new technology is adopted. Secondary influences via the choice of technique in corn production can also affect rural incomes, especially if capital costs for machinery are subsidized relative to wage costs, either directly through subsidized interest rates or indirectly through an overvalued exchange rate.

The exchange rate is clearly the key to the profitability of the corn sector in the short run and its continued capacity to develop and supply export markets. Chapter 9 demonstrates the role of devaluations in stimulating corn exports and the role of domestic inflation compared with that of trading partners in eroding the profitability of exports under a fixed exchange rate regime. The publicly announced policy in the mid-1980s was to maintain the competitiveness of the rupiah through a managed float, with the intent to stimulate exports of non-oil goods and services. As has been noted, continuation of such a policy is essential to continued exports of corn in the short run and to the investments needed to ensure a more competitive export position in the long run.

This policy of maintaining a competitive rupiah also has implications for broader trade strategy. Import-substituting industry will no longer require high tariff barriers to provide protection from an overvalued currency, and generalized trade liberalization thus might be increasingly feasible. Such liberalization runs head-on into the trend of banning imports to protect domestic markets for established manufacturers, a trend that has worrisome consequences for the rural-urban terms of trade. An urban industrial sector, heavily protected by quantitative restrictions, would not be a strong supporter of continued competitiveness for the rupiah, and rural interests alone represent a weak lobbying force.

The rapid development of Indonesia's promising potential for corn production depends on its competing for and holding export markets. Domestic demand is unlikely to provide adequate stimulus, even with the most optimistic of assumptions about the macroeconomic environment and the rate of growth in income. An export-oriented growth strategy contributes to such a healthy macroeconomic environment at the same time that it fosters competitiveness for Indonesia's corn exports.

Coordination of Policy

The main theme of this chapter is that market coordination of the corn system has been reasonably effective and could be even more effective with better government policies that have an impact on the corn system. But government policy is made in several agencies and ministries. Policy coordination—ensuring that policies are mutually reinforcing rather than conflicting—does not happen automatically, even when only one ministry is involved and certainly not when several important ministries and agencies each carry out significant interventions that directly or indirectly affect the corn system.

For a commodity as important as rice, a coordinating secretariat was established to focus efforts on behalf of rice intensification, but several topics, especially pricing and macroeconomic issues, did not come before this body. For corn, with its much smaller economic significance, no such special coordinating body is likely or desirable, but some coordination is needed. Because the necessary role of each agency depends to a large extent on the nature of the price policy that is implemented, the policy-coordinating role probably falls on the agencies that design and implement corn price policy. A working committee drawn from BULOG, the National Planning Agency (BAPPENAS), Department of Agriculture, Department of Trade, Department of Finance, and possibly representatives from the seed and feed industries would include all interested parties but leaves unanswered who would provide the ultimate direction. At one level, such direction comes from the Economic Cabinet and EKUIN, the coordinating ministry for economics, finance, and industry. The actual direction and coordination, however, will be provided by whichever agency develops the analytical capacity and perspective to formulate the agenda and deliver sensible policy analysis.

Knowledge is the ultimate coordinator of policy. Indonesia's corn system is highly dynamic, and no government official or academic adviser can know ahead of time just where internal and external forces will lead the system. Government policy can serve either to attempt bureaucratic control of the corn system in order to force it in directions perceived to be in society's interests or to provide adequate room for trial and error as millions of farmers, traders, and consumers try to participate effectively in the rapidly changing system. There are costs and benefits to both approaches, but a highly dynamic commodity system is difficult to control with regulation and administrative fiat. Relinquishing day-to-day control over the system, however, does not leave the government without significant influence over the corn system's development. The opportunity remains to develop effective government policies that will create a healthy environment for all participants to make responsible investments that provide long-run direction to Indonesia's corn system.

References

Afiff, Saleh, and C. Peter Timmer. 1971. "Rice Policy in Indonesia." *Food Research Institute Studies in Agricultural Economics, Trade, and Development*, vol. 10, no. 26: 131–159. Also in Randolph Barker, ed., *Viewpoints on Rice Policy in Asia*. Los Banos: International Rice Research Institute, 1971.

Afiff, Saleh, Walter P. Falcon, and C. Peter Timmer. 1980. "Elements of a Food and Nutrition Policy in Indonesia." In Gustav Papanek, ed., *The Economy of Indonesia*, pp. 406–428. New York: Praeger.

Alderman, Harold. 1985. "Is There 'Curvature' in the Slutsky Matrix?—A Rejoinder." Washington, D.C.: International Food Policy Research Institute, May. Typescript.

Argento, Gerrit, and Edward K. Wardrip. 1983. "High Fructose Syrup from Cassava in Indonesia: A Pre-Feasibility Report." Jakarta, March. Typescript.

Berger, Joseph. 1962. *Maize Production and the Manuring of Maize*. Geneva: Centre d'Etude de l'Azote.

Booth, Anne. 1977. "Irrigation in Indonesia." *Bulletin of Indonesian Economic Studies* (Canberra), vol. 13, nos. 1 and 2.

Chutikamoltham, Siriwan. 1985. "A Price Analysis of the Thai Corn Commodity System." D.B.A. diss., Harvard Business School, Boston, Mass.

Corn Refiners Association, Inc. 1979. *Nutritive Sweeteners from Corn*. Washington, D.C.: Corn Refiners Association.

Creswell, D. C., and Pius P. Ketaran. 1978. "Sorghum Grain in Broiler Diets." Report no. 8. Bogor: Centre for Animal Research and Development.

Cubenas, Gervasio J., Lee F. Schrader, and J. K. Deep Ford. 1979. "Cost of Producing High Fructose Corn Syrup: An Economic Engineering Analysis." Station Bulletin no. 239. West Lafayette, Ind.: Department of Agricultural Economics, Agricultural Experiment Station, Purdue University. September.

Dick, Howard. 1979. "Survey of Recent Developments." *Bulletin of Indonesian Economic Studies* (Canberra), vol. 15, no. 1.

Dixon, John A. 1982. "Food Consumption Patterns and Related Demand Parameters in Indonesia: A Review of Available Evidence." Working Paper no. 6. IFPRI/IRRI/IPDC Rice Policy Project for Southeast Asian Countries. Washington, D.C.: International Food Policy Research Institute. June.

____. 1984. "Consumption." In Walter P. Falcon, William O. Jones, Scott R. Pearson, et al., *The Cassava Economy of Java*. Stanford: Stanford University Press.

Dorosh, Paul A. 1984a. "The Economics of Corn Production in East Java: Survey

Results from Malang." BULOG-Stanford Corn Project Working Paper no. 1. Stanford, Calif.: Food Research Institute.

——. 1984b. "Corn Systems in Kediri, East Java." BULOG-Stanford Corn Project Working Paper no. 4. Stanford, Calif.: Food Research Institute.

——. 1984c. "Corn in Nusa Tenggara Timur—An Overview of Production and Marketing." BULOG-Stanford Corn Project Working Paper no. 7. Stanford, Calif.: Food Research Institute.

——. 1984d. "Indonesia's International Trade in Corn." BULOG-Stanford Corn Project Working Paper no. 11. Stanford, Calif.: Food Research Institute.

——. 1986. "Macroeconomic Policy and Agriculture in Indonesia." Ph.D. diss., Stanford University, Stanford, Calif.

Dorosh, Paul A., Stephen D. Mink, and Douglas H. Perry. 1984. *Corn Cropping Systems in Indonesia.* BULOG-Stanford Corn Project. Stanford, Calif.: Food Research Institute, July.

Falcon, Walter P., William O. Jones, Scott R. Pearson, et al. 1984. *The Cassava Economy of Java.* Stanford: Stanford University Press.

Food and Agriculture Organization of the United Nations and the World Bank Cooperative Program. 1978. "Report of the Indonesian Livestock Sector Survey." Jakarta.

Goldberg, Ray A., and Richard C. McGinity. 1979. *Agribusiness Management for Developing Countries: Southeast Asian Corn System and American and Japanese Trends Affecting It.* Cambridge, Mass.: Ballinger.

Hakim, Nurijadi. 1984. "Effects of Residual Organic Material, Lime, and Phosphate Fertilizer on Corn Production on Podzolic Soils of Sitiung" [Pengaruh sisa bahan organik, kapur dan pupuk P terhadap produksi jagung pada podzolic Sitiung II]. Padang: Research Station for Food Crops [Balai Penelitian Tanaman Pangan]. Typescript.

Harriss, Barbara. 1979. "There Is a Method to My Madness: or Is It Vice Versa? Measuring Agricultural Market Performance." *Food Research Institute Studies*, vol. 17, no. 2.

Harvard Institute for International Development. 1983. "Rice Intensification." Development Program Implementation Studies Report no. 2. Jakarta: Department of Finance. December. Typescript.

Indonesia, Central Bureau of Statistics [Biro Pusat Statistik]. 1977a. "Food Balance Sheet for Indonesia, 1968–74" [Neraca bahan makanan di Indonesia]. Jakarta, May.

——. 1977b. "Food Balance Sheet for Indonesia, 1975" [Neraca bahan makanan di Indonesia]. Jakarta, October.

——. 1980a. "Production of Annual Food Crops in Indonesia" [Produksi tanaman bahan makanan di Indonesia]. Jakarta.

——. 1980b. "Production of Annual Food Crops: Java and Madura" [Produksi tanaman bahan makanan di Jawa dan Madura]. Jakarta.

——. 1981a. "Area and Intensity of Pest and Disease Damage of Food Crops in Indonesia" [Luas dan intensitas serangan hama dan penyakit terhadap tanaman bahan makanan di Indonesia]. Jakarta.

——. 1981b. "Production of Annual Food Crops in Indonesia" [Produksi tanaman bahan makanan di Indonesia]. Jakarta.

———. 1981c. "Production of Annual Food Crops: Java and Madura" [Produksi tanaman bahan makanan di Jawa dan Madura]. Jakarta.

———. 1982a. "Food Balance Sheet for Indonesia, 1980" [Neraca bahan makanan di Indonesia]. Jakarta, August.

———. 1982b. "The National Socio-Economic Survey: Java, Madura, and Off Java" [Survei sosial-ekonomi nasional: Jawa, Madura, luar Jawa (SUSENAS)] for February 1979 Sub-round. Jakarta, March.

———. 1983. "Indonesian Population Projections: 1980–2000" [Proyeksi penduduk Indonesia, 1980–2000]. Jakarta.

———. Various years. "Agricultural Census" [Sensus pertanian]. Jakarta.

———. Various years. "Agricultural Survey" [Survei pertanian]. Jakarta.

———. Various years. "Exports" [Expor]. Jakarta.

———. Various years. "Imports" [Impor]. Jakarta.

———. Various years. "Inter-island Trade" [Lalu lintas angkutan antar pulau]. Jakarta.

———. Various years. "The National Socio-Economic Survey" [Survei sosial-ekonomi nasional (SUSENAS)]. Jakarta.

———. Various years. *Statistical Pocketbook of Indonesia* [Buku saku statistik Indonesia]. Jakarta.

Indonesia, Department of Agriculture. 1981. "Improved Varieties of Corn" [Varietas unggul jagung]. Information Bulletin [Informasi khusus] P3TP, no. 10. Bogor, February.

———. 1982. "Annual Report 1981–82" [Laporan tahunan, 1981–82]. Bogor: Central Research Institute for Agriculture [Puslitbangtan].

Indonesia, Department of Information. 1984. "Fourth Development Plan" [REPELITA IV]. Jakarta.

Indonesia, Department of Livestock Services (DGLS), various provinces. Various years. "Annual Report" [Laporan tahunan]. Jakarta.

Indonesia, Directorate General of Livestock (DGL). 1984. "Potential Domestic Needs for Animal Feed" [Prospek kebutuhan bahan makanan ternak dalam negeri]. Food Logistics Bureau (BULOG), Panel Discussion on the Animal Feed Situation [Panel diskusi pemantapan pengadaan bahan makanan ternak, BULOG]. Jakarta. January 30–31. Typescript.

International Monetary Fund. Various years. "International Financial Statistics." Washington, D.C.: International Monetary Fund.

Kingston, D. J., and D. C. Creswell. 1982. "Indigenous Chickens in Indonesia: Population and Production Characteristics in Five Villages in West Java." Report no. 2. Bogor: Research Institute for Animal Production.

Kingston, D. J., et al. 1977. "Dairy Farming in South Jakarta." Report no. 4. Bogor: Centre for Animal Research and Development.

Mears, Leon A. 1959. *Rice Marketing in the Republic of Indonesia*. Jakarta: Institute for Economic and Social Research, University of Indonesia, and P. T. Pembangunan.

———. 1981. *The New Rice Economy of Indonesia*. Yogyakarta: Gadjah Mada University Press.

Mink, Stephen D. 1984a. "The Rural Corn Economy of Grobogan Kabupaten,

Central Java." BULOG-Stanford Corn Project Working Paper no. 2. Stanford, Calif.: Food Research Institute.

——. 1984b. "Corn Production and Marketing in South Sulawesi." BULOG-Stanford Corn Project Working Paper no. 5. Stanford, Calif.: Food Research Institute.

——. 1984c. "International Trade in Corn: A Price Integration Analysis." BULOG-Stanford Corn Project Working Paper no. 8. Stanford, Calif.: Food Research Institute.

——. 1984d. "Corn Production in Indonesia: Systems and Economics." BULOG-Stanford Corn Project Working Paper no. 9. Stanford, Calif.: Food Research Institute.

——. 1984e. "Corn in the Indonesian Livestock Economy." BULOG-Stanford Corn Project Working Paper no. 10. Stanford, Calif.: Food Research Institute.

——. 1986. "Indonesia's Corn Economy." Ph.D. diss., Stanford University, Stanford, Calif.

Monteverde, Richard T. 1987. "Consumption of Food Staples in Indonesia: Comparison of Direct Estimates with Demand System Estimates." Ph.D. diss., Harvard University, Cambridge, Mass.

Monteverde, Richard T., and Stephen D. Mink. 1985. "Human Consumption of Corn in Indonesia." BULOG-Stanford Corn Project Working Paper no. 15. Stanford, Calif.: Food Research Institute.

Muller, Z. O. 1974. "Nutritive Value of Indonesian Feedstuffs." UNDP/FAO Project INS/72/009. Jakarta: Directorate General of Livestock.

Nell, Arend J., and D. H. L. Rollinson. 1974. "The Requirements and Availability of Livestock Feed in Indonesia." Working Paper no. 27. UNDP/FAO Project INs/72/009. Jakarta.

Nelson, Gerald C. 1983. "Time for Tapioca, 1970 to 1980: European Demand and World Supply of Dried Cassava." *Food Research Institute Studies*, vol. 19, no. 1.

——. 1984. "Starch." In Walter P. Falcon, William O. Jones, Scott R. Pearson, et al., *The Cassava Economy of Java*. Stanford; Stanford University Press.

Nyberg, Albert, and Dibyo Prabowo. 1979. "Status and Performance of Irrigation in Indonesia as of 1978 and the Prospects for 1990 and 2000." Report of the IFPRI/IRRI/IPDC Rice Policy Project for Southeast Asian Countries. Washington, D.C.: International Food Policy Research Institute.

Olman, L. P., and Darmiyati Sjarifuddin. 1977. "An Agriclimatic Map of Sulawesi," no. 33. Bogor: Central Research Institute for Agriculture [Puslitbangtan].

Pearson, Scott R. 1984. "Prospects for Corn Sweeteners in Indonesia." BULOG-Stanford Corn Project Working Paper no. 13. Stanford, Calif.: Food Research Institute.

Perry, Douglas H. 1984a. "Corn Production on Sumatra: Structure and Economics." BULOG-Stanford Corn Project Working Paper no. 3. Stanford, Calif.: Food Research Institute.

——. 1984b. "Lime Technologies for Tropical Corn Production." BULOG-Stanford Corn Project Working Paper no. 12. Stanford, Calif.: Food Research Institute.

Perry, Douglas H., with Marak Ali and Moehar Daniel. 1984. "Corn Production and Economics in Lampung Province, Sumatra." BULOG-Stanford Corn Project Working Paper no. 6. Stanford, Calif.: Food Research Institute.

Poultry Indonesia. 1984. No. 49 (February). Jakarta.

P. T. Indocorn. 1979. "Problems in the Procurement of Corn" [Problema pengadaan jagung]. In Faculty of Economics, Brawijaya University, *The Development of Corn as a Commodity in East Java* [Pengembangan komoditi jagung di Jawa Timur]. Malang.

Ravallion, Martin. 1986. "Testing Market Integration." *American Journal of Agricultural Economics*, vol. 68, no. 1 (February): 102–109.

Rix, Alan G. 1979. "The Mitsugoro Project: Japanese Aid Policy in Indonesia." *Public Affairs*, vol. 52, no. 1.

Roche, Frederick C. 1983. "Cassava Production Systems on Java and Madura." Ph.D. diss., Stanford University, Stanford, Calif.

Sajogyo et al. 1980. "Sectoral/Regional Projection Study on Household Income and Staple Intake Levels" [Proyeksi studi sektoral/regional penelitian atas tingkat pendapatan rumah tangga dan kecukupan pangan]. Bogor: Research Institute of Rural Sociology, Bogor Institute of Agriculture [Lembaga Penelitian Sociologi Pedesaan, Institut Pertanian], November.

Sayre, J. D. 1948. "Annual Report of Corn Production, Breeding, Diseases, and Quality Investigations." Ohio Agricultural Experiment Station, typescript. Quoted in George Sprague, ed., *Corn and Corn Improvement*. New York: Academic Press, 1955.

Schrader, Lee F., and Wallace E. Tyner. 1984. "A Review of Selected Technical and Economic Relationships for Sweeteners and Fuel Alcohol." Station Bulletin no. 440. West Lafayette, Ind.: Department of Agricultural Economics, Agricultural Experiment Station, Purdue University. January.

Soedomo, Reksohadiprodjo, and Lebdosukoyo Sukanto. 1982. "Least Cost Feed Rations: The Prospect for Substitution." Yogyakarta: Faculty of Animal Science [Fakultas Peternakan], Gadjah Mada University. Typescript.

Soeharto, Pr. D. K. K. 1983. "Research Report on Analysis of Income from Livestock Activities" [Laporan penelitian analisa pendapatan usaha-usaha peternakan]. Yogyakarta: Faculty of Animal Science, Gadjah Mada University.

Subandi et al. 1979. " Mean and Stability for Yield of Early and Late Varieties of Corn in Varying Environments." Contribution no. 51. Bogor: Central Research Institute for Agriculture [Puslitbangtan].

Sujudi. 1975. "The Corn Project of East Java as a Basic Idea of Promoting Corn Exports." Paper presented at the Indonesian Corn Commodity System First National Agribusiness Seminar Workshop, Bogor, Indonesia. Typescript.

Tate and Lyle Company. 1981. "Cassava and High Fructose Syrup in Indonesia." London. Typescript.

Tillman, Allan D. 1981. *Animal Agriculture in Indonesia*. Morrilton, Ark.: Winrock International.

Timmer, C. Peter. 1972. "A Perspective on Food Demand in Indonesia, 1965–1978." Harvard Advisory Group/BAPPENAS, Jakarta. Typescript.

——. 1974a. "A Model of Rice Marketing Margins in Indonesia." *Food Research Institute Studies*, vol. 13, no. 2:145–67.

———. 1974b. "A Review of *Food Grain Marketing in India* by Uma Lele." *Economic Development and Cultural Change*, vol. 22, no. 3:537–41.

———. 1975. "The Political Economy of Rice in Asia: Indonesia." *Food Research Institute Studies*, vol. 14, no. 3: 197–231.

———. 1978a. "The Impact of Indonesian Price Policy on the Distribution of Protein-Calorie Intake by Income Class and Commodity." Jakarta: Ford Foundation, February.

———. 1978b. "Factors Affecting Food Consumption in Indonesia: Some Preliminary Results." Jakarta: Ford Foundation, June.

———. 1981a. "China and the World Food System." In Ray A. Goldberg, ed., *Research in Domestic and International Agribusiness Management*, vol. 2: 75–118. Greenwich, Conn.: JAI Press.

———. 1981b. "Is There 'Curvature' in the Slutsky Matrix?" *Review of Economics and Statistics*, vol. 62, no. 3 (August): 395–402.

———. 1984a. "Corn Marketing and the Balance between Domestic Production and Consumption." BULOG-Stanford Corn Project Working Paper no. 14. Stanford, Calif.: Food Research Institute.

———. 1984b. "Energy and Structural Change in the Asia-Pacific Region: The Agricultural Sector." In Romeo M. Bautista and Seiji Naya, eds., *Energy and Structural Change in the Asia-Pacific Region: Papers and Proceedings of the Thirteenth Pacific Trade and Development Conference*. Manila: Philippine Institute for Development Studies and the Asian Development Bank.

———. 1985a. "The Role of Price Policy in Increasing Rice Production in Indonesia." HIID Development Discussion Paper no. 196. Cambridge, Mass.: Harvard Institute for International Development.

———. 1985b. "Corn in Indonesia's Food Policy." BULOG-Stanford Corn Project Working Paper no. 16. Stanford, Calif.: Food Research Institute.

———. 1986. "Food Price Policy in Indonesia." Harvard Business School, Boston, Mass., March. Typescript.

Timmer, C. Peter, and Harold Alderman. 1979. "Estimating Consumption Parameters for Food Policy Analysis." *American Journal of Agricultural Economics*, vol. 61 (December): 982–987.

Timmer, C. Peter, Walter P. Falcon, and Scott R. Pearson. 1983. *Food Policy Analysis*. Baltimore: Johns Hopkins University Press for the World Bank.

United States Department of Agriculture. 1981. *Agricultural Statistics, 1981*. Washington, D.C.: Government Printing Office.

———. 1983a. "Foreign Agriculture Circular: Grains." FG-16-83. Washington, D.C.: Foreign Agricultural Service, June 15.

———. 1983b. "Foreign Agriculture Circular: Grains." FG-19-83. Washington, D.C.: Foreign Agricultural Service, July.

———. 1984. "Sugar and Sweetener Outlook and Situation Report." SSRVON2. Washington, D.C.: Economic Research Service, June.

Unnevehr, Laurian S. 1984a. "Marketing and Price Formation." In Walter P. Falcon, William O. Jones, Scott R. Pearson, et al. *The Cassava Economy of Java*. Stanford: Stanford University Press.

———. 1984b. "Transport Costs, Tariffs and the Influence of World Markets on

Indonesian Domestic Cassava Prices." *Bulletin of Indonesian Economic Studies* (Canberra), vol. 20, no. 1.

Wallace, H. A., and E. N. Bressman. 1937. *Corn and Corn Growing*. New York: Wiley.

Warr, Peter G. 1984. "Exchange Rate Protection in Indonesia." *Bulletin of Indonesian Economic Studies* (Canberra), vol. 20, no. 2.

Wickizer, Vernon, and Merrill Bennett. 1941. *The Rice Economy of Monsoon Asia*. Stanford, Calif.: Food Research Institute.

World Bank. 1984. "Indonesian Demand for Secondary Food Crops as Livestock Feed." Jakarta: World Bank, May. Typescript.

Index

Library of Congress Cataloging-in-Publication Data

The Corn economy of Indonesia.

Includes index.
1. Corn—Indonesia. 2. Corn industry—Indonesia. 3. Corn—Indonesia—Utilization. I. Timmer, C. Peter.
SB191.M2C7827 1987 338.1'7315'09598 86-23939
ISBN 0-8014-1961-1 (alk. paper)